The Social Animal

A Series of Books in Psychology

EDITORS: Richard C. Atkinson
Gardner Lindzey
Richard F. Thompson

Fourth Edition

The Social Animal

Elliot Aronson
University of California, Santa Cruz

W. H. Freeman and Company
New York

Chapter-opening drawings by Saul Steinberg from *The Labyrinth, The New World,* and *The Catalogue.* Copyright © 1960, 1962, 1965 by Saul Steinberg. Permission granted by Julian Bach Literary Agency, Inc.

Cover drawing by Tom Durfee.

Library of Congress Cataloging in Publication Data

Aronson, Elliot.
The social animal.

Includes indexes.
1. Social psychology. I. Title.
HM251.A79 1984 302 84-1546
ISBN 0-7167-1605-4
ISBN 0-7167-1606-2 (pbk.)

Printed in the United States of America

4 5 6 7 8 9 MP 2 1 0 8 9 8 7 6 5

to Vera, of course

Acknowledgments

I am indicated on the title page as the sole author of this book, and it is certainly true that I wrote down all the words and did most of the thinking that produced them. Accordingly, if there are any stupidities in this book, they are mine, and if anything you read on these pages makes you angry, I'm the person you should yell at. At the same time, I want to confess that I never do anything entirely by myself: Many people contributed their knowledge and ideas to my word factory, and I would like to take this opportunity to thank them for their generous help.

Vera Aronson and Ellen Berscheid were particularly helpful. They painstakingly went over the original manuscript, page by page and line by line, making numerous suggestions and criticisms that had a significant impact on the final form of this book. Moreover, their enthusiasm for the project was infectious and helped me to climb out of frequent bouts of "writer's despair."

Several other people contributed valuable ideas and suggestions. I cannot possibly cite them all, but the most impactful contributors were Nancy Aston, Leonard Berkowitz, David Bradford, John Darley, Richard Easterlin, Jonathan Freedman, James Freel, Robert Helmreich, Michael Kahn, John Kaplan, Judson Mills, and Jev Sikes.

Thanks are also due to Judy Hilton and Faye Gibson, who typed and retyped various drafts of the manuscript as if they really enjoyed doing it; to Lyn Ellisor, who worked patiently on the bibliographical notes; and to William Ickes, who prepared the indexes. Most of this book was written while I was a Fellow at the Center for Advanced Study in the Behavioral Sciences at Stanford, California, and I am deeply grateful to the staff of that fine institution for providing me with the necessary leisure and facilities.

Finally, I am pleased to report that my friend and mentor, Leon Festinger, did not have anything to do with this manuscript—directly. He never read it, and, to my knowledge, he was not even aware that I was writing it. He is, however, responsible for its existence. I *could* say that he taught me all I know about social psychology, but that would be a gross understatement. He taught me something much more valuable than that: He taught me how to find out the things that neither I nor anybody else knew.

March 1972

• • •

For the second edition of this book, I am happy to acknowledge the important contributions made by Pilar Gottlieb and Grace Schmidt, who typed, edited, xeroxed, indexed, and cajoled me into meeting my deadlines. I would also like to mention my students. While working on this manuscript, I had occasion to reexamine a good deal of my own research and many of my own ideas; and, in so doing, I was struck again (as I have been many times in the past) with how fortunate I have been to have worked with so many talented students. These people have taught me a great deal—all of them—from my very first research assistants in 1960, Merrill Carlsmith and John Darley, to the people who are currently collaborating with me. Indeed, one of my current research assistants, Diane

Bridgeman, has made an important contribution to this revised edition, and I am pleased to acknowledge my gratitude to her.

September 1975

• • •

For the third edition, my secretary, Patti Fox, deserves special praise for the efficiency and good humor with which she worked on the manuscript. When I left things confused or ambiguous, she always managed to straighten them out. Darrin Lehman deserves special thanks for his tireless efforts indexing and proofreading.

I am also happy to acknowledge the many contributions made to this edition by Neal Osherow, a graduate student of rare ability and enthusiasm. He approached the task of helping me revise *The Social Animal* with a proper respect for the book's merits along with a critical eye toward its imperfections. In the process he learned to treat the manuscript with both the affection and the impatience that one usually reserves for a beloved but somewhat stodgy old friend.

January 1980

• • •

For the fourth edition I relied heavily on the considerable talents of my ace research and teaching assistant, Larry White, who worked hard and well to help me bring the present version up to date.

Valuable contributions were also made by Bill Talley, Lyn Sutherland, Joshua Aronson, Ellen Suckiel and Chalsa Loo. It is a pleasure to express my gratitude to all of these people as well as to countless undergraduates, who seemed to begin every conversation with "Why don't you ever . . . ."

October 1983 ELLIOT ARONSON

Contents

INK

Why I Wrote This Book

In 1970–71, I was invited to spend the year in Stanford, California, at the Center for Advanced Study in the Behavioral Sciences. During that year, I was given all the support, encouragement, and freedom to do whatever I wanted, and I was assured that I was not responsible to anyone for anything. There, on a beautiful hill, roughly 30 miles from San Francisco (my favorite city), with a whole year in which to do anything my heart desired, I chose to write this book. Surrounded as I was by the beauty of the countryside, and close as I was to the excitement of San Francisco, why did I lock myself in a cubicle and write a book? It's not that I'm crazy and it's not that I needed the money. If there's a single reason why I wrote this book, it's that I once heard myself tell a large class of sophomores that social psychology is a young science—and it made me feel like a coward.

Let me explain: We social psychologists are fond of saying

that social psychology is a young science—and it *is* a young science. Of course, astute observers have been making interesting pronouncements and proposing exciting hypotheses about social phenomena at least since the time of Aristotle, but these pronouncements and hypotheses were not seriously tested until well into the twentieth century. The first systematic social psychological experiment (to my knowledge) was conducted by Triplett in 1898 (he measured the effect of competition on performance), but it was not until the late 1930s that experimental social psychology really took off, primarily under the inspiration of Kurt Lewin and his talented students. By the same token it is interesting to note that, although Aristotle first asserted some of the basic principles of social influence and persuasion around 350 BC, it was not until the middle of the twentieth century that those principles were put to the experimental test by Carl Hovland and his associates.

In another sense, however, to claim that social psychology is a young science is to be guilty of a gigantic cop-out: It's a way of pleading with people not to expect too much from us. Specifically, it can be our way of dodging the responsibility for, and avoiding the risks inherent in, applying our findings to the problems of the world we live in. In this sense, protesting that social psychology is a young science is akin to claiming that we are not yet ready to say anything important, useful, or (if the reader will forgive an overused word) relevant.

The purpose of this volume is unashamedly (but with some trepidation) to spell out the relevance that sociopsychological research might have for some of the problems besetting contemporary society. Most of the data discussed in this volume are based on experiments; most of the illustrations and examples, however, are derived from current social problems—including prejudice, propaganda, war, alienation, aggression, unrest, and political upheaval. This duality reflects two of my own biases—biases that I cherish. The first is that the experimental method is the best way to understand a complex phenomenon. It is a truism of science that the only way to really know the world is to reconstruct it: That is, in order to truly understand what causes what, we must do more than simply observe—rather, we must be responsible for *producing* the first "what" so that we can be sure that it really *caused* the second "what." My second bias is that the only way to be *certain* that the causal relations uncovered in experiments are valid is to bring them out of the laboratory and into the real world. Thus, as a scientist, I like to work in a laboratory; as a citizen, however, I like to have windows through which I can look out upon the world. Windows, of course, work in both directions: we often derive hypotheses from everyday life. We can best test these hypotheses under the sterile conditions of the laboratory; and in order to try to keep our *ideas* from becoming sterile, we attempt to take our laboratory findings back out through the window to see if they hold up in the real world.

Implicit in all this is my belief that social psychology is extremely important—that social psychologists can play a vital role in making the world a better place. Indeed, in my more grandiose moments, I nurse the secret belief that social psychologists are in a unique position to have a profound and beneficial impact on our lives by providing an increased understanding of such important phenomena as conformity, persuasion, prejudice, love, and aggression. Now that my secret belief is no longer a secret, I can promise only to try not to force it down the reader's throat on the following pages. Rather, I'll leave it to the readers to decide, after they have finished this volume, whether social psychologists have discovered, or can *ever* discover, anything useful—much less anything uniquely important.

This is a slim volume, and purposely so. It is meant to be a brief introduction to the world of social psychology, not an encyclopedic catalogue of research and theory. Because I opted to make it brief, I had to be selective. This means both that there are some traditional topics that I chose not to cover and that I have not gone into exhaustive detail with those topics that I did choose to cover. Because of this, it was a difficult book to write. I have had to be more a "news analyst" than a "reporter." For example, there are many controversies that I did not fully describe. Rather, I exercised my own judgment; made an educated (and, I hope, honest) assessment of what is the most accurate description of the field, as of 1972; and stated it as clearly as I could.

This decision was made with the student in mind—this book

was written for students, not for my colleagues. If I have learned nothing else in fifteen years of teaching, I *have* learned that, although a detailed presentation of all positions is useful (and sometimes even fascinating) to one's colleagues, it tends to leave students cold. Students ask us what time it is, and we present them with a chart showing the various time zones around the world, a history of time-telling from the sun dial to the Bulova Accutron, and a detailed description of the anatomy of the wrist watch. By the time we've finished, they've lost interest in the question. Nothing is safer than to state all sides of all issues, but few things are more boring. Although I have discussed controversial issues, I have not hesitated to draw conclusions. In short, I have attempted to be brief without being unfair, and I have tried to present complex material simply and clearly without *over*simplifying. Only the reader can determine how successful I have been in accomplishing these goals.

1976

Early in 1975, I decided, with some reluctance, to revise this book. A lot has happened in three years. Not only have new things been discovered in the field of social psychology, but, even more important, the world has taken a few major turns since the winter of 1972, when I put the final scrawl on my yellow pad for the first edition. To name just a few of the major events: A brutal, draining, and divisive war came to an end; a vice-president and a president of the United States were forced to resign in humiliation; and the women's liberation movement was beginning to have a significant impact on the consciousness of the nation. These are sociopsychological events of the greatest significance. The indolent slob who lives inside me began to acknowledge (with a long sigh) that any book that purports to be about us and our lives must stay abreast of the times. So, here it is, an updated *Social Animal:* slightly longer, slightly more complex, but, I hope, not different in tone or approach from the original.

1980

The third edition, once again, is updated both to keep abreast of changing times and to catch up with recent research in social psychology. I think we have succeeded in staying current without sacrificing the tone or the flavor of the first and second editions.

1984

And so on . . . for the fourth edition.

The Social Animal

Man is by nature a social animal; an individual who is unsocial naturally and not accidentally is either beneath our notice or more than human. Society is something in nature that precedes the individual. Anyone who either cannot lead the common life or is so self-sufficient as not to need to, and therefore does not partake of society, is either a beast or a god.

Aristotle
Politics, c. 328 BC

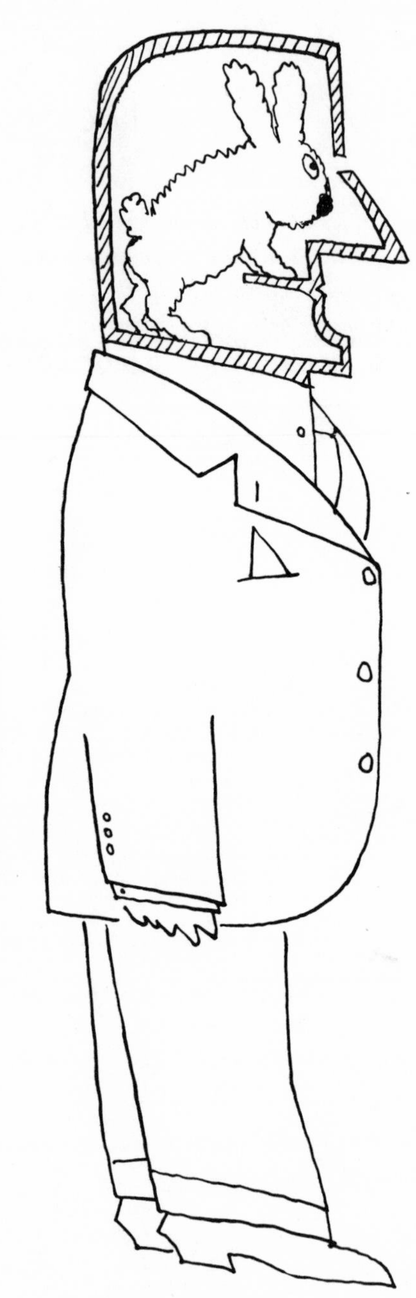

1

What Is Social Psychology?

As far as we know, Aristotle was the first person to formulate basic principles of social influence and persuasion; but, although he did say that man is a social animal, he was probably not the first person to make that observation. Moreover, chances are he was not the first person to marvel at the truth of that statement while simultaneously puzzling over its triteness and insubstantiality. Although it is certainly true that people are social animals, so are a host of other creatures, from ants and bees to monkeys and apes. What does it mean to say that humans are "social animals"? Let's look at some concrete examples:

> A college student named Sam and four of his acquaintances are watching a presidential candidate make a speech on television. Sam is favorably impressed; he likes him better than the opposing candidate because of his sincerity. After the speech, one of the other students asserts that she was turned off by the candi-

date—that she considered him to be a complete phony—and that she prefers the opposing candidate. All of the others are quick to agree with her. Sam looks puzzled and a trifle distressed. Finally, he mumbles to his acquaintances, "I guess he didn't come across as sincere as I would have hoped."

A second grade teacher stands before her class and asks, "What is the sum of six, nine, four, and eleven?" A girl in the third row puzzles over the question for several seconds, hesitates, raises her hand tentatively, and, when called on, haltingly answers, "Thirty?" The teacher nods, smiles at her, says, "Nice work, Peggy," and pastes a gold star on her forehead. She then asks the class, "What is the sum of seven, four, eight, three, and ten?" Without wasting a moment, Peggy leaps to her feet and shouts, "Thirty-two!"

A four-year-old girl is given a toy drum for her birthday. After pounding on it for a few minutes, she casts it aside and studiously ignores it for the next several weeks. One day, a friend comes to visit, picks up the drum, and is about to play with it. Suddenly the young "owner" tears the drum from her friend's grasp and proceeds to play with it as if it had always been her favorite toy.

A ten-year-old boy avidly consumes two bowls of Wheaties daily because an Olympic decathlon champion endorses the product and implies that he owes his athletic prowess, in part, to the consumption of that particular brand of cereal.

A shopkeeper who has lived his entire life in a small town in Montana has never had any contact with real, live black people, but he "knows" they are shiftless, lazy, and oversexed.

Charlie, a high school senior, has recently moved to a new city. He used to be quite popular, but not any more. Although the kids at school are civil to him, they have not been particularly friendly. He is feeling lonely, insecure, and unattractive. One day, during lunch period, he finds himself at a table with two of his female classmates. One of them is warm, attractive, brilliant, and vivacious; he has been admiring her and daydreaming about her. For several weeks he has been longing for an opportunity to talk to her. The other young woman is not nearly as appealing. Charlie ignores the vivacious woman of his dreams and begins an earnest conversation with her companion.

Following the 1970 tragedy at Kent State University, in which four students were shot and killed by Ohio National Guardsmen while demonstrating against the war in Southeast Asia, a high school teacher from Kent, Ohio, asserted that the slain students deserved to die. She made this statement even though she was well aware of the fact that at least two of the victims were not participating in the demonstration but were peacefully walking across campus at the time of the shooting. Indeed, she went on to say, "Anyone who appears on the streets of a city like Kent with long hair, dirty clothes, or barefooted deserves to be shot."[1]

When the Reverend Jim Jones sounded the alert, over 900 members of the People's Temple settlement in Guyana gathered before him. He knew that some of the members of a congressional investigation party had been murdered and that the sanctity and isolation of Jonestown would soon be violated. Jones proclaimed that it was time for them to die. Vats of poison were prepared, and amidst only scattered shouts of protest or acts of resistance, mothers and fathers administered the fatal mixture to their infants and children, drank it themselves, and lay down, arm in arm, waiting to die.

Mary has just turned nine. For her birthday, she received a Suzie Homemaker baking and cooking set—complete with "her own little oven." Her parents chose this present because she seems very interested in culinary things and is forever helping mommy set the table, prepare the meals, and clean the house. "Isn't it wonderful," says Mary's father, "how at age nine she is already interested in being a housewife? Little girls must have housewifery built into their genes. Those feminists don't know what they're talking about."

George Woods is black. When he and I were growing up together in Massachusetts in the 1940s, he considered himself a "colored boy" and felt inferior to his white friends. There were many reasons for this feeling. That George was treated like an inferior by the white community had a direct influence upon him, of course; and a number of other forces influenced him less directly. In those days, George could entertain himself by turning

> on the radio and listening to "Amos 'n Andy," a radio show in which black adults were portrayed as naive children, as stupid, lazy, and illiterate, but rather cute—not unlike friendly domesticated animals. The black characters were, of course, played by white actors. In films, George could see the stereotyped "colored man," usually a chauffeur or some other menial. A standard plot would have the "colored man" accompany the white hero into a haunted house, where they would hear a strange and ominous noise: The camera pans in on the "colored man's" face; his eyes grow large with fright; he screams, "Feets, do your stuff!" and dashes through the door, not taking time to open it first. We can only guess what George experienced while viewing these films in the company of his white friends.
>
> Most of George's acquaintances were blacks who "knew their place." They were obsequious to whites, used hair straightener in an attempt to look less black, and cared little about their African heritage. The idea was to be white, a goal which, of course, was unattainable. I would be amazed if this climate did not lower George's self-concept because such changes in self-concept are not atypical: A famous study of black children in the forties by Kenneth and Mamie Clark showed that, as early as age three, many of the children had learned to feel inferior to whites.[2]

Things change. Although discrimination and unfairness are still very much a part of our society, George Woods' children, growing up in the seventies and eighties, did not face quite the same prospect as George himself did. The mass media now depict blacks in roles that are not exclusively menial; a new pride in blackness is emerging, along with an interest in, and enthusiasm about, Afro-American history and culture; and sales of hair straightener are down. Society is influencing George's children in a much different way than it influenced George.

Although things do change, we should not complacently believe that all changes are in a linear, humanistic direction. On August 30, 1936, during the Spanish Civil War, a single plane bombed Madrid. There were several casualities, but no one was killed. The world was profoundly shocked by the idea of a congested city being attacked from the air. Newspaper editorials around the world expressed the general horror and indignation of the citizenry.[3] Only nine years later, American planes dropped nuclear bombs on Hiroshima and Nagasaki. More than one hundred thousand people were killed and countless thousands suffered severe injuries. Shortly thereafter, a poll indicated only 4.5 percent of the American population felt we should not have used those weapons, and an astonishing 22.7 percent felt we should have used many more of them before Japan had a chance to surrender. Clearly, something had happened during those nine years to influence opinion.

A Definition

What is social psychology? There are almost as many definitions of social psychology as there are social psychologists. Instead of listing some of these definitions, it might be more informative to let the subject matter define the field. The examples presented in the preceding pages are all illustrations of sociopsychological situations. As diverse as these situations may be, they do contain one common factor: social influence. The opinion of Sam's friends on the merits of the presidential candidate influenced Sam's judgment (or at least his public statement regarding that judgment). The rewards emanating from the teacher influenced the speed and vigor of Peggy's classroom responses. The four-year-old seemed to find her toy drum more attractive because of the inadvertent influence of her friends's interest. The Olympic athlete's influence on our Wheaties-eating youngster, on the other hand, was far from inadvertent; rather, it was intentionally designed to make him convince his mother to buy Wheaties. That Charlie ignored the woman of his dreams almost certainly has something to do with his fear of rejection, the way he was feeling about himself, and his implicit assumption about the relative likelihood of being rejected by either of the two women. The Montana shopkeeper was certainly not born with an unflattering stereotype of black people in his head—somebody, somehow, put it there. Exactly how the high-school teacher in Kent, Ohio, came to believe that innocent people deserved to die is a fascinating and frightening question; for now, let us simply say that this belief was probably influenced by her own indirect complicity in the tragic events on campus. A still more disturbing question arises from Jonestown: What forces could compel parents to help poison their children? Again, this is a complex question to which we hope to provide some partial answers and insights as this text unfolds. Turning to little Mary and her Suzie Homemaker set, it is conceivable, as Mary's father says, that "housewifery" is genetic, but it is far more likely that, from infancy onward, Mary was rewarded and encouraged every time she expressed an interest in such "feminine" things as cooking, sewing, and dolls—to a far greater extent than if she expressed an interest in football, boxing, and chemistry. It is also reasonable to assume that, if Mary's kid brother had shown an interest in "housewifery," he would *not* have received a Suzie Homemaker set for *his* birthday. Also, as with young George Woods, who felt inferior to his playmates, Mary's self-image could have been shaped by the mass media, which tend to depict women in roles that the culture encourages them to play: housewife, secretary, nurse, school teacher—the mass media rarely depict women as biochemists, college professors, or business executives. If we compare the young George Woods with his children, we will see that the self-images of minority-group members can change, and these changes can influence and be influenced by changes in the mass media and changes in the attitudes of the general population. This, of course, is graphically illustrated by the opinions of Americans about the use of nuclear weapons in 1945.

The key phrase in the preceding paragraph is "social influence." And this becomes our working definition of social psychology: the influences that people have upon the beliefs or behavior of others. Using this as our definition, we will attempt to understand many of the phenomena described in the preceding illustrations. How are people influenced? Why do they accept influence—or, put another way, what's in it for them? What are the variables that increase or decrease the effectiveness of social influence? Does such influence have a permanent effect, or is it merely transitory? What are the variables that increase or decrease the permanence of the effects of social influence? Can the same principles be applied equally to the attitudes of the high school teacher in Kent, Ohio, and to the toy preferences of young children? How does one person come to like another person? Is it through these same processes that we come to like our new sports car or a box of Wheaties? How does a person develop prejudices against an ethnic or racial group? Is it akin to liking—but in reverse—or does it involve an entirely different set of psychological processes?

Most people are interested in questions of this sort; in a sense, therefore, most people are social psychologists. Because most of us spend a good deal of our time interacting with other people—being influenced by them, influencing them, being delighted, amused, and angered by them—it is natural that most of us develop hypotheses about social behavior. Although most amateur social psychologists test these hypotheses to their own satisfaction, these "tests" lack the rigor and impartiality of careful scientific investigation. Often, the results of scientific research are identical with what most people "know" to be true. This is not surprising; conventional wisdom is usually based upon shrewd observation that has stood the test of time. But it is important that social psychologists conduct research to test hypotheses—even those hypotheses we all know are obviously true—because many things we "know" to be true turn out to be false when carefully investigated. Although it seems reasonable, for example, to assume that people who are threatened with severe punishment for engaging in a certain behavior might eventually learn to despise that behavior, it turns out that when this question is studied scientifically we find just the reverse is true: People who are threatened with mild punishment develop a dislike for the forbidden behavior; people who are severely threatened show, if anything, a slight *increase* in liking for the forbidden behavior. Likewise, most of us, from our own experience, would guess that if we overheard someone saying nice things about us (behind our backs), we would tend to like that person—all other things being equal. This turns out to be true. But what is equally true is that we tend to like that person even more if some of the remarks we overhear are anything *but* nice. More will be said about these phenomena in the following chapters.

In our attempt to understand human social behavior, we professional social psychologists have a great advantage over most amateur social psychologists. Although, like the amateur, we usually begin with careful observation, we can go far beyond that. We do not need to wait for things to happen so that we can observe how people respond; we can, in fact, make things happen. That is, we can conduct an experiment in which scores of people are subjected to particular conditions (for example, a severe threat or a mild threat; overhearing nice things or overhearing a combination of nice and nasty things). Moreover, we can do this in situations in which everything can be held constant except for the particular conditions being investigated. We can, therefore, draw conclusions based on data far more precise and numerous than those available to the amateur social psychologist, who must depend upon observations of events that occur randomly and under complex circumstances.

Virtually all the data presented in this book are based upon experimental evidence. It is important, for this reason, that the reader (1) understand what constitutes an experiment in social psychology and (2) understand the advantages, disadvantages, ethical problems, excitements, headaches, and heartaches associated with this kind of enterprise. Although an awareness of the experimental method is important, it is by no means essential for an understanding of the substantive material presented here. Therefore, the chapter "Social Psychology as a Science" is the final one in this book. As a reader, you may peruse this chapter before reading on (if you prefer to understand the technicalities before delving into the substantive material), or you can read it at any point on your journey through the book—whenever your interest is piqued.

People Who Do Crazy Things Are Not Necessarily Crazy

The social psychologist studies social situations that affect people's behavior. Occasionally, these natural situations become focused into pressures so great that they cause people to behave in ways easily classifiable as abnormal. (When I say "people" I mean very large numbers of people.) To my mind, it does not increase our understanding of human behavior to classify these people as psychotic. It is much more useful to try to understand the nature of the situation and the processes that were operating to produce the behavior. This leads us to Aronson's first law: "People who do crazy things are not necessarily crazy."

Let us take, as an illustration, the Ohio school teacher who asserted that the four Kent State students deserved to die. I don't think she was alone in this belief—and, although all the people who hold this belief *may* be psychotic, I seriously doubt it, and I doubt that so classifying them does much to extend our knowledge. Similarly, in the aftermath of the Kent slayings, the rumor spread that the slain girls were pregnant anyway—so that it was a blessing they died—and that all four of the students were filthy and so covered with lice that the mortuary attendants became nauseated while examining the bodies. These rumors, of course, were totally false. But, according to James Michener,[4] they spread like wild fire. Were all the people who believed and spread these rumors insane? Later in this book, we will examine the processes that produced this kind of behavior—processes to which most of us are susceptible, under the right sociopsychological conditions.

Ellen Berscheid[5] has observed that people have a tendency to explain unpleasant behavior by attaching a label to the perpetrator ("crazy," "sadistic," or whatever), thereby excluding that person from the rest of "us nice people." In that way, we no longer have to worry about the unpleasant behavior, because it has nothing to do with us nice folks. According to Berscheid, the danger in this kind of thinking is that it tends to make us smug about our own susceptibility to situational pressures producing unpleasant behavior, and it leads to a rather simple-minded approach to the solution of social problems. Specifically, such a simple-minded solution might include the development of a set of diagnostic tests to determine who is a liar, who is a sadist, who is corrupt, who is a maniac; social action might then consist of identifying these people and relegating them to the appropriate institutions. Of course, this is not to say that psychosis does not exist or that psychotics should never be institutionalized. Neither am I saying that all people are the same and respond exactly as crazily to the same intense social pressures. To repeat, what I *am* saying is that some situational variables can move a great proportion of us "normal" adults to behave in very unappetizing ways. It is of paramount importance that we attempt to understand these variables and the processes producing unpleasant behavior.

An illustration might be useful. Think of a prison. Consider the guards. What are they like? Chances are, most people would imagine prison guards to be tough, callous, unfeeling people. Some might even consider them to be cruel, tyrannical, and sadistic. People who take this kind of *dispositional* view of the world might suggest that the reason people become guards is to have an opportunity to exercise their cruelty with relative impunity. Picture the prisoners. What are they like? Rebellious? Docile? No matter what specific pictures exist inside our heads, the point is there *are* pictures there—and most of us believe that the prisoners and the guards are quite different from us in character and personality.

This *may* be true, but don't be too sure. In a dramatic piece of research, Philip Zimbardo and his students created a simulated prison in the basement of the Psychology Department at Stanford University. Into this "prison" he brought a group of normal, mature, stable, intelligent young men. By flipping a coin, Zimbardo designated one-half of them prisoners and one-half of them guards, and they lived as such for six days. What happened? Let's allow Zimbardo to tell us in his own words:

> At the end of only six days we had to close down our mock prison because what we saw was frightening. It was no longer apparent to us or most of the subjects where they ended and their roles began. The majority had indeed become "prisoners" or "guards," no longer able to clearly differentiate between role-playing and self. There were dramatic changes in virtually every aspect of their behavior, thinking and feeling. In less than a week, the experience of imprisonment undid (temporarily) a lifetime of learning; human values were suspended, self-concepts were challenged, and the ugliest, most base, pathological side of human nature surfaced. We were horrified because we saw some boys ("guards") treat other boys as if they were despicable animals, taking pleasure in cruelty, while other boys ("prisoners") became servile, dehumanized robots who thought only of escape, of their own individual survival, and of their mounting hatred of the guards.[6]

2

Conformity

One consequence of the fact that we are social animals is that we live in a state of tension between values associated with individuality and values associated with conformity. James Thurber has captured the flavor of one kind of conformity in the following description:

> Suddenly somebody began to run. It may be that he had simply remembered, all of a moment, an engagement to meet his wife, for which he was now frightfully late. Whatever it was, he ran east on Broad Street (probably toward the Maramor Restaurant, a favorite place for a man to meet his wife). Somebody else began to run, perhaps a newsboy in high spirits. Another man, a portly gentleman of affairs, broke into a trot. Inside of ten minutes, everybody on High Street, from the Union Depot to the Courthouse was running. A loud mumble gradually crystalized into the dread word "dam." "The dam has broke!" The fear was put into words by a little old lady in an electric, or by a traffic

> cop, or by a small boy: nobody knows who, nor does it now really matter. Two thousand people were abruptly in full flight. "Go east!" was the cry that arose—east away from the river, east to safety. "Go east! Go east!" . . .
>
> A tall spare woman with grim eyes and a determined chin ran past me down the middle of the street. I was still uncertain as to what was the matter, in spite of all the shouting. I drew up alongside the woman with some effort, for although she was in her late fifties, she had a beautiful easy running form and seemed to be in excellent condition. "What is it?" I puffed. She gave a quick glance and then looked ahead again, stepping up her pace a trifle. "Don't ask me, ask God!" she said.[1]

This passage from Thurber, although comical, is an apt illustration of people conforming. One or two individuals began running for their own reasons; before long, everyone was running. Why? Because others were running. According to Thurber's story, when the running people ralized that the dam hadn't given way after all, they felt pretty foolish. And yet, how much more foolish would they have felt if they hadn't conformed, and the dam had, in fact, burst? Is conformity good or bad? In its simplest sense, this is an absurd question. But words do carry evaluative meaning—thus, to be called an individualist or a nonconformist is to be designated, by connotation, as a "good" person. The label evokes an image of Daniel Boone standing on a mountain top with a rifle slung over his shoulder, the breeze blowing through his hair, as the sun sets in the background. To be called a conformist is somehow to be designated as an "inadequate" person. It evokes an image of a row of Madison Avenue admen with grey flannel suits, porkpie hats, and attache cases, looking as though they had been created by a cookie cutter, and all saying simultaneously, "Let's run it up the flagpole and see if anyone salutes."

But we can use synonymous words that convey very different images. For *individualist* or *nonconformist*, we can substitute *deviate;* for *conformist*, we can substitute *team player*. Somehow, *deviate* does not evoke Daniel Boone on the mountain top, and *team player* does not evoke the cookie-cutter-produced Madison Avenue adman.

When we look a little closer, we see an inconsistency in the way our society seems to feel about conformity (team playing) and nonconformity (deviance). For example, one of the best sellers of the 1950s was a book by John F. Kennedy called *Profiles in Courage*, wherein the author praised several politicians for their courage in resisting great pressure and refusing to conform. To put it another way, Kennedy was praising people who refused to be good team players, people who refused to vote or act as their parties or constituents expected them to. Although their actions earned Kennedy's praise long after the deeds were done, the immediate reactions of their colleagues were generally far from positive. Nonconformists may be praised by historians or idolized in films or literature long after the fact of their nonconformity, but they are usually not held in high esteem, at the time, by those people to whose demands they refuse to conform. This observation receives strong support from a number of experiments in social psychology, most notably from one by Stanley Schachter,[2] in which several groups of students participated. Each group met to read and discuss the case history of a juvenile delinquent named Johnny Rocco. After reading the case, each group was asked to discuss it and to suggest a treatment for Johnny on a scale that ranged from "very lenient treatment" on one end to "very hard treatment" on the other. A typical group consisted of approximately nine participants, six of whom were real subjects and three of whom were paid confederates of the experimenter. The confederates took turns playing one of three roles that they had carefully rehearsed in advance: the *modal* person, who took a position that conformed to the average position of the real subjects; the *deviate*, who took a position diametrically opposed to the general orientation of the group; and the *slider*, whose initial position was similar to the deviate's but who, in the course of the discussion, gradually "slid" into a modal, conforming position. The results clearly showed that the person who was liked most was the modal person who conformed to the group norm; the deviate was liked least.

Thus, the data indicate that the "establishment" or modal group tends to like conformists better than nonconformists. Clearly, there are situations in which conformity is highly desirable and nonconformity would constitute an unmitigated disaster. Suppose, for example, that I were suddenly to decide that I was fed up with being a conformist. So I hop in my car and start driving down the *left*-hand side of the road—not a very adaptive way of displaying my rugged individualism, and not very fair to you, if you happen to be driving toward me (conformist-style) on the same street. Similarly, consider the rebellious teenager who smokes cigarettes, stays out late, or dates a certain boy just because she knows that her parents disapprove. She is not manifesting independence so much as she is displaying *anticonformity*, not thinking for herself but automatically acting contrary to the desires or expectations of others. On the other hand, we do not intend to suggest that conformity is always adaptive and nonconformity always maladaptive. There are compelling situations in which conformity can be disastrous and tragic. One such example is illustrated in the memoirs of Albert Speer, one of Adolf Hitler's top advisors. Speer describes the circle around Hitler as one of total conformity—deviation was not permitted. In such an atmosphere, even the most barbarous activities seemed reasonable, because the absence of dissent, which conveyed the illusion of unanimity, prevented any individual from entertaining the possibility that other options might exist.

> In normal circumstances people who turn their backs on reality are soon set straight by the mockery and criticism of those around them. In the Third Reich there were not such correctives. On the contrary, every self-deception was multiplied as in a hall of distorting mirrors, becoming a repeatedly confirmed picture of a fantastical dream world which no longer bore any relationship to the grim outside world. In those mirrors I could see nothing but my own face reproduced many times over.[3]

A more familiar but perhaps less dramatic example concerns some of the men involved with Richard Nixon and his "palace guard" in the Watergate cover-up. Here, men in high government office—many of whom were attorneys—perjured themselves, destroyed evidence, and offered bribes without an apparent second thought. This was due, at least in part, to the closed circle of single-mindedness that surrounded the president in the early 1970s. This single-mindedness made deviation virtually unthinkable—until after the circle had been broken.

Once the circle was broken, several people (for example, Jeb Stuart Magruder, Richard Kleindienst, and Patrick Grey) seemed to view their illegal behavior with astonishment, as if it were performed during some sort of bad dream. John Dean put it this way:

> Anyway, when you picked up the newspaper in the morning and read the new cover story that had replaced yesterday's cover story, you began to believe that today's news was the *truth*. This process created an atmosphere of unreality in the White House that prevailed to the very end. . . . If you said it often enough, it would become true. When the press learned of the wire taps on newsmen and White House staffers, for example, and flat denials failed, it was claimed that this was a national-security matter. I'm sure many people believed that the taps *were* for national security; they weren't. That was concocted as a justification after the fact. But when they said it, you understand, they really *believed* it.[4]

What Is Conformity?

Conformity can be defined as a change in a person's behavior or opinions as a result of real or imagined pressure from a person or group of people. Most situations are not as extreme as the examples cited above. We will attempt to zero in on the phenomenon of conformity by beginning with a less extreme (and perhaps simpler) illustration. Let's return to our friend Sam, the hypothetical college student we first encountered in Chapter 1. Recall that Sam watched a presidential candidate on television and was favorably impressed with his sincerity. However, in the face of the unanimous opinion of his friends that the candidate was insincere, Sam acceded—verbally, at least—to their opinion.

Several questions can be asked about this kind of situation: (1) What causes people to conform to group pressure? Specifically, what was in it for Sam? (2) What was the nature of the group pressure? Specifically, what were Sam's acquaintances doing to induce conformity? (3) Did Sam revise his opinion of the candidate during that brief but horrifying period when he learned that *all* his fellow students disagreed with him? Or was it the case that Sam maintained his original opinion but only modified what he *said* about the candidate? If there was a change in opinion, was it permanent or merely transient?

Unfortunately, we cannot say precisely and definitely what was going on in Sam's mind at the time, because there are many factors in the situation that we don't know about. For example, we don't know how confident Sam was in his initial opinion; we don't know how much he liked the people with whom he watched the candidate; we don't know whether Sam considered himself to be a good judge of sincerity or whether he considered the others to be good judges of sincerity; we don't know whether Sam is generally a strong person or a wishy-washy person; and so on. What we can do is construct an experimental situation that is somewhat like the one in which Sam found himself, and we can control and vary the factors that we think might be important. Such a basic situation was devised by Solomon Asch[5] in a classic set of experiments. Put yourself in the following situation: You have volunteered to participate in an experiment on perceptual judgment. You enter a room with four other participants. The experimenter shows all of you a straight line (line *X*). Simultaneously, he shows you three other lines for comparison (lines *A*, *B*, and *C*). Your job is to judge which of the three lines is closest in length to line *X*. The judgment strikes you as being a very easy one. It is perfectly clear to you that line *B* is the correct answer, and when your turn comes, you will clearly say that *B* is the one. But it's *not* your turn to respond. The young man whose turn it is looks carefully at the lines and says "Line *A*." Your mouth drops open and you look

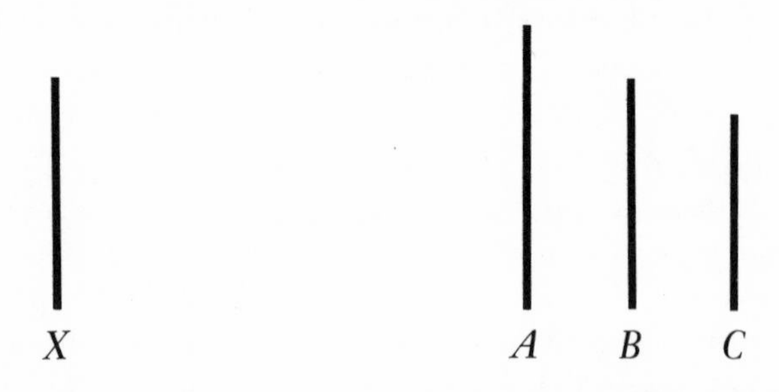

at him quizzically. "How can he believe it's *A* when any fool can see that it's *B?*" you ask yourself. "He must be either blind or crazy." Now it's the second person's turn to respond. He also chooses line *A*. You begin to feel like Alice in Wonderland. "How can it be?" you ask yourself. "Are *both* of these people blind or crazy?" But then the next person responds, and he also says, "Line *A*." You take another look at those lines. "Maybe *I'm* the only one who's crazy," you mutter inaudibly. Now it's the fourth person's turn, and he also judges the correct line to be *A*. Finally, it's your turn. "Why, it's line *A*, of course," you declare. "I knew it all the time."

This is the kind of conflict that the college students in Asch's experiment went through. As you might imagine, the individuals who answered first were in the employ of the experimenter and were instructed to agree on an incorrect answer. The perceptual judgment itself was an incredibly easy one. It was so easy that, when individuals were not subjected to group pressure, but were allowed to make a series of judgments of various sizes of lines while alone, there was almost a complete absence of errors. Indeed, the task was so easy, and physical reality was so clear-cut, that Asch himself firmly believed that there would be little, if any, yielding to group pressure. But his prediction was wrong. When faced with a majority of their fellow students agreeing on the same incorrect responses in a series of twelve judgments, approximately three quarters of the subjects conformed at least once by responding incorrectly. When we look at the entire spectrum of judgments, we find that an average of 35 percent of the overall responses conformed to the incorrect judgments rendered by Asch's accomplices.

The situation in the Asch experiment is especially intriguing because, unlike many situations in which we may tend to conform, there were no explicit constraints against individuality. In many situations, the sanctions against nonconformity are clear and unequivocal. For example, I hate to wear a tie, and under most circumstances I can get away with this minor idiosyncracy. On occasion, however, I can't. I often find myself stopped at the entrance to a restaurant and politely (but firmly) informed that if I refuse to don the tie offered me by the headwaiter, I cannot dine in the restaurant. I can either put on the tie and eat in the restaurant or leave, open-necked and comfortable, but hungry. The negative consequences of nonconformity are made very explicit.

But in Asch's experiment (and in the hypothetical example of Sam watching the candidate on television), the situations were much more subtle. In these situations, there were no explicit rewards for conformity and no explicit punishment for deviance. Why, then, did Asch's subjects and Sam conform? There seem to be two major possibilities; either they became convinced, in the face of the judgment of the unanimous majority, that their own opinions were wrong, or they "went along with the crowd" (while inwardly knowing that their judgments were right) in order to be accepted by the majority or to avoid being disliked by them for disagreeing.

In short, what we are suggesting is that these individuals had two important goals: the goal of being correct and the goal of staying in the good graces of other people by living up to their expectations. In many circumstances, both of these goals can be satisfied by a simple action. Driving on the right-hand side of the road is the correct thing to do, and it satisfies other people's expectations. So, too, is telephoning your mother on Mother's Day, giving proper directions to a visitor in town, and studying hard to perform well on an exam. Similarly, if others agreed with your judgment of the lengths of the lines, you could satisfy both goals by being true to your own estimate. But, in Asch's experiment, these two goals were placed in conflict. If you were a subject in that experiment, and you initially believed that the correct answer was line *B*, then saying so might satisfy your desire to be correct—but it might also violate the expectations of your peers, and they might think you a bit odd. On the other hand, choosing line *A* might win you the acceptance of the others, but, unless you became convinced that they were correct, it would violate your desire to be right.

Apparently, most people believe that *they* are motivated primarily by a desire to be correct, but that *others* are motivated primarily by a desire to stay in the good graces of other people. For example, when people unobtrusively observe an Asch-like conformity experiment, they typically predict the experimental subjects will conform more than they actually do.[6] Interestingly enough, these same surreptitious observers predict that *they* will conform *less* than people like themselves actually do. That is, we know *other* people conform, but we underestimate the extent to which *we* can be induced to follow the group.

Was Sam convinced by his fellow college students that his preferred presidential candidate was a phony, or did he simply go along with their judgment in order to be accepted, while continuing to believe in the sincerity of the candidate? Because Sam is a hypothetical person, we cannot answer that question definitively. Were the yielders in Asch's experiment convinced that their initial judgment was incorrect and the unanimous judgment of the others was right? We could ask them; indeed, in Asch's experiment, the yielders *were* asked afterward whether they really saw the lines differently or whether they merely said so. A few of the subjects insisted that they really saw it that way. But how can we be certain that the subjects were being truthful? Put yourself in a subject's place. Suppose you bowed to group pressure, even though you remained certain that your initial judgment was correct. This might be embarrassing for you to admit, because it would make you appear weak and wishy-washy. Moreover, you would be admitting that you were not following the experimenter's instruction to present *your own* judgment. Thus, it is quiet possible that subjects who said they actually saw it the way the group saw it might have been deceiving the experimenter in order to save face.

How, then, can we determine whether or not group pressure actually affects one's judgment? Let's speculate for a moment. If we could follow Sam into the voting booth and witness which candidate he chooses, we could discover whether he actually was convinced by his acquaintances that his original preference was a phony or if he merely mumbled his agreement with them while still privately trusting the candidate. But we can't follow Sam into the voting booth. Fortunately, we *can* determine whether the public behavior exhibited by subjects in the Asch experiment corresponds with their private acceptance of those judgments. Suppose we were to repeat the experiment, but, although we would allow the real subjects to see the responses of the accomplices as before, we would *not* require them to make their judgments in the presence of the others. If the subjects' private choices were identical with the accomplices' public ones, then we would see that those responses in the original experiment actually did convince the subjects that their initial judgments were wrong. If, on the other hand, the subjects were going against their own best judgment only in order to mollify the group, then there would be significantly less yielding to the judgments of others in decisions made in private. This proposition has been tested experimentally on several occasions. The results are consistent: Although assurance of total privacy has not been achieved in any of these studies, the greater the privacy, the less the conformity. This finding has held up consistently, whether the subjects were judging lengths of line,[7] the numbers of metronome clicks,[8] or the aesthetic value of a piece of modern art.[9] Thus, it appears that pressure to conform to the judgments of others has little (if any) effect on the *private* judgments of experimental subjects.

Variables That Increase or Decrease Conformity

In situations like the one investigated by Asch, one crucial factor that determines the likelihood that the subject will conform to the majority is whether or not the majority opinion is unanimous. If a participant is joined by even one ally who gives the correct response, the subject's tendency to conform to the erroneous judgment of the majority drops sharply.[10] In fact, *however* unanimity is broken, the power of the group is seriously diminished.[11] That is, if one of the other group members gives an incorrect response that is *different* from the error of the majority (answering that the correct line is *C*, as the rest of the group responds *A*), the presence of this fellow dissenter dramatically reduces the pressure to conform, and the subject is likely to give the correct response: line *B*. A fellow dissenter exerts a powerful freeing effect from the influence of the majority. If there *is* unanimity, however, the actual size of the majority need not be very great in order for it to elicit maximum conformity from a person. In fact, the tendency for someone to conform to group pressure is about as great when the unanimous majority consists of only three other people as it is when the unanimous majority is sixteen.

One way conformity to group pressure can be decreased is by inducing the individual to make some sort of commitment to his or her initial judgment. Picture yourself as an umpire at a major-league baseball game. There is a close play at first base and you call the runner out—in the presence of 50,000 fans. After the game, the three other umpires approach you and each says that he thought the runner was safe. How likely are you to alter your judgment? Compare this with a situation (like the Asch situation) in which each of the three umpires calls the runner safe and *then* it is your turn to make a judgment. Such a comparison was made in an experiment by Morton Deutsch and Harold Gerard,[12] who used the Asch paradigm and found that, where there was no prior commitment (as in the Asch experiment), 24.7 percent of the responses conformed to the erroneous judgment of the majority. But, when the individuals had publicly committed themselves *before* hearing the judgment of the other "umpires," only 5.7 percent of their new responses were conformist.

Two other important factors are what kind of person the individual is and who constitutes the group. Individuals who have a generally low opinion of themselves are far more likely to yield to group pressure than those with high self-esteem. Furthermore, task-specific self-esteem can be influenced within a given situation. Thus, individuals who are allowed to have prior successes with a task like judging the lengths of lines are far less likely to conform than those who walk into the situation cold. By the same token, if individuals believe they have little or no ability for the task at hand, their tendency to conform increases.[13] There are also cultural differences. For example, it has been shown that Norwegians conform to a greater extent than Frenchmen, and Japanese students are more willing to take a minority position than American students.[14] In addition, early studies seemed to show sex differences, with women conforming more than men when confronted face-to-face with the unanimous judgment of a group.[15] However, these differences were generally small. In recent, more careful studies, women conformed more than men only when the researcher was male or when the group task was male-oriented.[16]

The other side of that issue, of course, has to do with the makeup of the group exerting the pressure. A group is more effective at inducing conformity if (1) it consists of experts, (2) the members (individually or collectively) are important to the individual, or (3) the members (individually or collectively) are comparable to the individual in some way. Thus, to go back to Sam, our hypothetical college student, I would speculate that it is more likely that Sam would conform to the pressure exerted by his acquaintances if he thought they were expert in politics and in making judgments about human relations. Similarly, he would be more likely to yield to those people if they were important potential friends than if they were of no consequence to him. And finally, their being fellow students gives the judgments of Sam's acquaintances more impact on his behavior than, say, the judgment of a group of ten-year-old children, a group of hard-hats, or a group of Portuguese biochemists. There is at least one exception to the comparability phenomenon. Research has shown that, if the unanimous majority consists of white children, more conformity is induced in other children—both white *and* black.[17] Apparently, among children, whites are seen as having more power than blacks.[18] Thus, the power granted to whites by our culture is sufficient to overcome the tendency for people to be more influenced by comparable others, though this may be changing as blacks continue to gain power in our society.

The results for the black children may be due in part to feelings of insecurity. For example, to return to our previous illustration, if Sam had felt sure that he was liked and accepted by his acquaintances, he would be more likely to voice disagreement than if he felt insecure in his relationship with them. This assertion receives strong support from an experiment by James Dittes and Harold Kelley[19] in which college students were invited to join an attractive and prestigious group and subsequently were given information about how secure their position was in that group. Specifically, all members of the group were informed that, at any point during the lifetime of the group, the members could remove any member in the interest of efficiency. The group then engaged in a discussion of juvenile delinquency. Periodically, the discussion was interrupted and each member was asked to rate every other member's value to the group. After the discussion, each member was shown how the others rated him; in actuality, the members were given prearranged false feedback. Some members were led to believe they were well accepted, and others were led to believe they were not terribly popular. Each member's conformity was measured by the opinions he subsequently expressed in the discussion of juvenile delinquency and by his vulnerability to group pressure during the performance of a simple perceptual task. The results showed that, for the individuals who valued their membership in the group, those who were led to feel only moderately accepted were more likely to conform to the norms and standards set by the group than were those who were led to feel totally accepted. In other words, it's easier for an individual who is securely ensconced in a group to deviate from that group.

Rewards and Punishments Versus Information

As I suggested earlier, there are two possible reasons why people like us might conform. One is that the behavior of others might convince us that our initial judgment was erroneous. The other is that we may wish to avoid punishment (such as rejection or ridicule) or to gain a reward (such as love or acceptance) from the group. The behavior of the individuals in Asch's experiment and in similar other experiments seemed to be largely a matter of attempting to obtain a reward or to avoid punishment. This can be inferred from the fact that there was very little conformity when subjects were allowed to respond privately.

At the same time, there are many situations in which we conform to the behavior of others because their behavior is our only guide to appropriate action. In short, we often rely on other people as a means of determining reality. The quotation from Thurber at the beginning of this chapter gives an example of this type of conformity. According to Leon Festinger,[20] when physical reality becomes increasingly uncertain, people rely more and more on "social reality"—that is, they are more likely to conform to what other people are doing, not because they fear punishment from the group but because the group's behavior supplies them with valuable information about what is expected of them. An example should help clarify this distinction: Suppose that you need to use the toilet in an unfamiliar classroom building. Under the sign "Rest Rooms" there are two doors, but, unfortunately, a vandal has removed the specific designations from the doors—that is, you cannot be certain which is the Men's room and which is the Women's room. Quite a dilemma—you are afraid to open either door for fear of being embarrassed or embarrassing others. As you stand there in dismay and discomfort, hopping from one foot to the other, the door on your left opens and out strolls a distinguished-looking gentleman. With a sigh of relief, you are now willing to forge ahead, reasonably secure in the knowledge that left is for men and right is for women. Why are you so confident? As we have seen, research has shown that the more faith an individual has in the expertise and trustworthiness of the other person, the greater the tendency to follow his lead and conform to his behavior. Thus, the distinguished-looking gentleman would almost certainly be followed, to a greater extent than, say, a seedy-looking fellow with wildly darting eyes.

Let us take this one step further. Institutions frequently request us to perform certain behaviors without making an outright demand. For example, in the men's shower room at my university's field house, there is a sign asking us to practice conservation by turning off the water while soaping up. Since this behavior is slightly inconvenient, I was not surprised when our systematic observation revealed only six percent of the students conformed to this request. Subsequently, Michael O'Leary and I conducted a simple experiment aimed at inducing a greater number of people to conserve water and the energy needed to heat it.[21] We reasoned that people would be more likely to turn off the shower while soaping up if they believed other students took the request seriously. Accordingly, we enlisted the aid of a few male students who simply acted as models for the desired behavior. But we didn't want people to conform out of a fear of disapproval or punishment, so we set up the experiment in the following way: Our model entered the shower room (an open shower room consisting of eight shower nozzles spaced at regular intervals) when it was empty, went to the far end, turned his back to the entrance, and turned on the shower. As soon as he heard someone enter, he turned off the shower, soaped up, turned it back on, briefly rinsed off, and left the room without so much as glancing at the student who had entered. As he left, another student (our observer) entered and surreptitiously noted whether the "subject" turned off the shower while soaping up. We found that 49 percent of the students followed suit! Moreover, when two students simultaneously modeled the appropriate behavior, the percentage of people obeying the sign zoomed to 67. Thus, in an ambiguous situation, other people can induce conformity by simply providing us with information suggestive of what people generally do in a given situation.

It is often easy to distinguish between behavior induced by fear of punishment and behavior induced by information. Imagine that, in the mythical nation of Freedonia, it is considered gracious for guests to belch after eating, as a way of showing the host they enjoyed the meal. Suppose you didn't know this, and you were visiting the home of a Freedonian dignitary in the company of some diplomats from the U.S. State Department. If, after the meal, these gentlemen began to belch, chances are you would belch also. They are providing you with valuable information. On the other hand, if you were in the same home in the company of a crew of behemoths from the Freedonian Olympic wrestling team and these stalwarts belched after their meal, my guess is that you would avoid belching. That is, you would likely consider this an act of bad manners. However, if they glared at you for your failure to follow suit, you might indeed belch too—not because of the information they supplied, but because you feared rejection or reprisals for refusing to be a good sport by going along with their boorish behavior.

I would suggest that conformity resulting from the observation of others for the purpose of gaining information about proper behavior tends to have more powerful ramifications than conformity in the interest of being accepted or of avoiding punishment. I would argue that, if we were to find ourselves in an ambiguous situation wherein we must use the behavior of other people as a template for our own behavior, it is likely we will repeat our newly learned behavior, without cue, on subsequent similar occasions. This would be the case unless, of course, we later received clear evidence that our actions were inappropriate or incorrect. Thus, to go back to our example, suppose you are reinvited to the home of the Freedonian dignitary for dinner. But this time you are the only guest. The question is: Do you or don't you belch after the meal? A moment's reflection should make the answer perfectly clear: If you had belched after the first meal at his home because you realized it was the proper thing to do (as would have been the case had you dined in the company of the diplomats), you would be quite likely to belch when dining alone with the dignitary. However, if you had belched the first time out of fear of rejection or punishment (as would have been the case had you dined in the company of the wrestlers), you would almost certainly *not* belch when you were the lone guest. To go back to Sam and the political candidate on television, you can now readily understand one of the many reasons why it would be so difficult for us to predict how Sam would actually vote in the election. If he had been merely going along with the group to avoid punishment or to gain acceptance, he would be likely, in the privacy of the polling booth, to vote in opposition to the view expressed by his acquaintances. If, on the other hand, Sam had been using the group as a source of information, he would almost certainly vote against the candidate that he had initially preferred.

Social Influence and Emotion. To repeat: When reality is unclear, other people become a major source of information. The generality of this phenomenon is nicely illustrated by some research performed by Stanley Schachter and Jerome Singer, who demonstrated that people conform to others even in assessing something as personal and idiosyncratic as the quality of their own emotions.[22] Before describing this research, we must first clarify what we mean by "emotions." According to William James,[23] an emotion has both a "feeling" content and a cognitive content. His two-part conception of emotions can be likened to the process of playing a song on a juke box: First you need to activate the machine by inserting the coin; then you select the song you want to hear by pushing the right buttons. An emotion also requires both physiological arousal and a label. Specifically, if we are walking in the forest and bump into a hungry and ferocious bear, we undergo a physiological change. This change produces excitement—physiologically, this is a response of the sympathetic nervous system similar to one that might be produced by coming across a person with whom we are angry. We interpret this response as fear (rather than anger, say, or euphoria) only when we cognitively become aware that we are in the presence of a fear-producing stimulus (a ferocious bear). But what if we experienced physiological arousal in the absence of an appropriate stimulus? For example, what if someone surreptitiously slipped into our drink a chemical that produced the same physiological response? Would we experience fear? William James would probably say that we wouldn't—not unless there was an appropriate stimulus around.

Here is where Schachter and Singer enter the picture. In one experiment, subjects were injected either with epinephrine—a synthetic form of adrenalin, which causes physiological excitation—or with a harmless placebo. All the subjects were told that this chemical was a vitamin supplement called "suproxin." Some of the subjects who received epinephrine were informed there would be side effects, including palpitations of the heart and hand tremors. These, indeed, are some of the effects of epinephrine. Accordingly, when these subjects experienced the epinephrine symptoms, they had an appropriate explanation. In effect, when the symptoms appeared, they would say to themselves, "My heart is pounding and my hands are shaking because of this injection I received and for no other reason." But other subjects were not forewarned about these symptoms. Thus, when their hearts started pounding and their hands started trembling, what were they to make of it? The answer is they made of it whatever the people around them made of it. Specifically, a stooge was introduced into the situation and the subjects were informed that he had also received an injection of "suproxin." In one situation, the stooge was programmed to behave in a euphoric manner; in another, he was programmed to express a great deal of anger. Picture yourself in this situation: You are alone in this room with a person who supposedly has just been injected with the same drug you received. He bounces around energetically, and happily wads up paper into balls and begins sinking hook shots into the waste basket. His euphoria is obvious. Gradually, the chemical you were given begins to take effect, and you begin to feel your heart pounding, your hands trembling, and so on. What emotion do you feel? Most subjects in this situation reported a feeling of euphoria—and behaved happily. On the other hand, imagine that instead of being placed in a room with a euphoric stooge you were placed in a room with a stooge programmed to behave in an angry manner. He complains about a questionnaire you both are filling out and eventually, in a fit of extreme annoyance, he rips the questionnaire up and angrily hurls it into the waste basket. Meanwhile, the symptoms of epinephrine are becoming apparent; you feel your own heart pounding, and your hands begin to tremble. How do you feel? In this situation, the vast majority of the subjects felt angry and behaved in an angry fashion.

It should be noted that, if subjects were given a placebo (that is, an injection of a benign solution that produces no symptoms), or if they were forewarned about the symptoms of the drug that they *had* been given, they were relatively unaffected by the antics of the stooge. To sum up this experiment: When physical reality was clear and explainable, the subjects' emotions were not greatly influenced by the behavior of other people—but when they were experiencing a strong physiological response, the origins of which were not clear, they interpreted their own feelings as either anger or euphoria, depending on the behavior of other people who supposedly were in the same chemical boat.

Social Influence: Life and Death. As we have seen, the influence of other people, whether intentional or not, can have an important effect on a person's behavior. Unless we understand how this process works, these effects can have major unwanted consequences for society as well. A recent investigation by Craig Haney into the *death qualification procedure* provides an interesting and instructive example.[24] Basically, the death qualification procedure refers to the process whereby, in selecting a jury for a murder trial in a state where capital punishment is an option, prospective jurors who are opposed to the death penalty are systematically excluded from sitting on the jury. This procedure takes place in the presence of those people who are eventually selected to serve on the jury. Haney, who is both an attorney and a social psychologist, reasoned it is possible that when a juror who believes in capital punishment witnesses others being dismissed because they oppose the death penalty, this may subtlely suggest to him or her that the law disapproves of people who oppose the death penalty. This may increase their tendency to impose the death penalty. To test this notion, Haney performed an experiment in which a random sample of adults were shown a videotape of a convincing jury selection procedure filmed in the moot courtroom of a law school—a highly realistic setting complete with legal accouterments. Experienced trial lawyers served as prosecutor, defense attorney, and judge on the videotape. In one condition the procedure included a segment on death qualification; in the other condition (control), this segment did not appear. Compared to subjects in the control condition, subjects who viewed the death qualification segment were more convinced of the defendant's guilt, they believed it was more likely that he would receive the death penalty, and they also believed that the judge thought he was guilty. They themselves were also more likely to impose the death penalty if the defendant were convicted. Thus, the factors that influence our opinions and behavior can be subtle—and they might be a matter of life and death.

Responses to Social Influence

Thus far, we have been describing two kinds of conformity in more or less commonsensical terms. This distinction was based upon (1) whether the individual was being motivated by rewards and punishments or by a need to know, and (2) the relative permanence of the conforming behavior. Let us move beyond this simple distinction to a more complex and useful classification that applies not only to conformity but to the entire spectrum of social influence. Instead of using the simple term *conformity*, I would like to distinguish among three kinds of responses to social influence: *compliance*, *identification*, and *internalization*.[25]

Compliance. This term best describes the mode of behavior of a person who is motivated by a desire to gain reward or avoid punishment. Typically, the person's behavior is only as long-lived as is the promise of reward or the threat of punishment. Thus, one can induce a rat to run a maze efficiently by making it hungry and placing food at the end of the maze. One can also get most peasants from an underdeveloped country to recite the pledge of allegiance to the American flag by threatening them with pain if they don't comply or by promising to feed and enrich them if they do. On the level of compliance, many experimenters see little difference between animals and humans, because all organisms respond to rewards and punishments. Thus, remove the food from the goal box and the rat will eventually stop running; remove the food or the threat of punishment and the peasant will refuse to recite the pledge of allegiance.

Identification. This is a response to social influence brought about by an individual's desire to be like the influencer. In identification, as in compliance, the individual does not behave in a particular way because such behavior is intrinsically satisfying; rather, he adopts a particular behavior because it puts him in a satisfying relationship to the person or persons with whom he is identifying. Identification differs from compliance in that the individual does come to believe in the opinions and values he adopts, although he does not believe in them very strongly. Thus, if an individual finds a person or a group attractive or appealing in some way, he will be inclined to accept influence from that person or group and adopt similar values and attitudes—not in order to obtain a reward or avoid a punishment (as in compliance), but simply to be like that person. I refer to this as the good-old-Uncle-Charlie phenomenon. Suppose you have an uncle named Charlie who happens to be a warm, dynamic, exciting person; and ever since you were a young child you loved him a lot and wanted to grow up to be like him. Uncle Charlie is a corporation executive who has a number of strong opinions, including a deep antipathy to social-welfare legislation—that is, he is convinced that anyone who really tries can earn a decent wage, and that, by handing money to people, the government only succeeds in eliminating their desire to work. As a young child, you heard Uncle Charlie announce this position on several occasions, and it has become part of your system of beliefs—neither because you thought it through and it seemed right to you, nor because Uncle Charlie rewarded you for adopting (or threatened to punish you for *not* adopting) this position. Rather, it has become part of your system because of your liking for Uncle Charlie, which has produced in you a tendency to incorporate into your life that which is his.

Internalization. The internalization of a value or belief is the most permanent, most deeply rooted response to social influence. The motivation to internalize a particular belief is the desire to be right. Thus, the reward for the belief is intrinsic. If the person who provides the influence is perceived to be trustworthy and of good judgment, we accept the belief he or she advocates and we integrate it into our system of values. Once it is part of our own system, it becomes independent of its source and is extremely resistant to change.

Let us discuss some of the important distinguishing characteristics of these three responses to social influence. Compliance is the least enduring and has the least effect on the individual, because people comply merely to gain reward or to avoid punishment. The complier understands the force of the circumstance and can easily change his or her behavior when the circumstance no longer prevails. At gunpoint, I could be made to say most anything; but with the threat of death removed, I could quickly shrug off those statements and their implications. If a child is kind and generous to his younger brother in order to obtain a cookie from his mother, he will not necessarily become a generous person because of it. He has not learned that generosity is a good thing in and of itself—what he *has* learned is that generosity is a good way to get cookies. When the cookie supply is exhausted, his generous behavior will eventually cease, unless that behavior is bolstered by some other reward (or punishment). Rewards and punishments are very important means, then, to get people to learn and to perform specific activities but are very limited as techniques of social influence because they must be ever present to be effective—unless the individual discovers some additional reason for continuing the behavior. This last point will be discussed shortly.

Continuous reward or punishment is not necessary for the response to social influence we call identification. The person with whom the individual identifies need not be present at all; what is needed is only the individual's desire to be like that person. For example, if Uncle Charlie moves to a different city, and months (or even years) go by without your seeing him, you will continue to hold beliefs similar to his as long as (1) he remains important to you, (2) he still holds the same beliefs, and (3) these beliefs are not challenged by counteropinions that are more convincing. But, by the same token, these beliefs *can* be changed if Uncle Charlie has a change of heart, or if your love for Uncle Charlie begins to fade. They can also change if a person or group of people who are more important to you than Uncle Charlie professes a different set of beliefs. For example, suppose you are away at college and you find yourself a group of new, exciting friends who, unlike Uncle Charlie, are strongly in favor of social welfare. If you admire them as much as (or more than) your uncle, you may change your beliefs in order to be more like them. Thus, a more important identification may supersede a previous identification.

The effect of social influence through identification can also be dissipated by a person's desire to be right. If you have taken on a belief through identification and you are subsequently presented with a counterargument by an expert and trustworthy person, you will probably change your belief. Internalization is the most permanent response to social influence precisely because a person's motivation to be right is a powerful and self-sustaining force that does not depend upon constant surveillance in the form of agents of reward or punishment, as does compliance, or on your continued esteem for another person or group, as does identification.

It is important to realize that any specific action may be due to either compliance, identification, or internalization. For example, let us look at a simple piece of behavior: obedience of the laws pertaining to fast driving. Society employs highway patrol officers to enforce these laws, and, as we all know, people tend to drive within the speed limit if they are forewarned that a certain stretch of highway is being carefully scrutinized by these officers. This is compliance. It is a clear case of people obeying the law in order to avoid paying a penalty. Suppose you were to remove the highway patrol. As soon as people found out about it, many would increase their speed. But some people might continue to obey the speed limit; a person might continue to obey because Dad (or Uncle Charlie) always obeyed speed limits or always stressed the importance of obeying traffic laws. This, of course, is identification. Finally, people might conform to the speed limit because they are convinced that speed laws are good, that obeying such laws helps to prevent accidents, and that driving at moderate speed is a sane and reasonable form of behavior. This is internalization. And with internalization you would observe more flexibility in the behavior. For example, under certain conditions—at 6:00 A.M., say, on a clear day with perfect visibility and with no traffic for miles around—the individual might exceed the speed limit. The compliant individual, however, might fear a radar trap, and the identifying individual might be identifying with a very rigid model—thus, both would be less responsive to important changes in the environment.

Let us look at the major component in each response to social influence. In compliance, the important component is *power*—the power of the influencer to dole out the reward for compliance and punishment for noncompliance. Parents have the power to praise, give love, provide cookies, scream, give spankings, withhold allowances, and so on; teachers have the power to paste gold stars on our foreheads or flunk us out of college; and employers have the power to praise, promote, humiliate, or discharge us. The United States government has the power to increase or withhold economic and military aid to or from a dependent nation. Thus, our government can use this technique to influence, say, some country in Latin America to hold a more or less democratic election. Rewards and punishments are effective means for producing this kind of compliance, but we might ask whether or not mere compliance is desirable: To induce a nation to hold a democratic election is easier than to induce the rulers of that nation to think and rule democratically.

In identification, the crucial component is *attractiveness*—the attractiveness of the person with whom we identify. Because we identify with the model, we want to hold the same opinions that the model holds. Suppose a person you admire takes a particular stand on an issue. Unless you have strong feelings or solid information to the contrary, there will be a tendency for you to adopt this position. Incidentally, it is interesting to note that the reverse is also true: If a person or group that you dislike announces a position, there will be a tendency for you to reject that position or adopt its opposite. Suppose, for example, that you dislike some particular group (say, the American Nazi party), and that group comes out against draft registration. If you know nothing about the issue, your tendency will be to favor draft registration—all other things being equal.

In internalization, the important component is *credibility*—the credibility of the person who supplies the information. For example, if you read a statement by a person who is highly credible—that is, someone who is both expert and trustworthy—you would tend to be influenced by it, because of your desire to be correct. Recall our earlier example of the diplomats at the Freedonian dinner party. Your acceptance of their expertise made their behavior (belching after the meal) seem like the right thing to do. Accordingly, my guess is that this behavior (your tendency to belch after a meal at the home of a Freedonian dignitary) would become internalized—you would do it, thereafter, because you believed it to be right.

Recall the experiment on conformity performed by Solomon Asch, in which social pressure induced many subjects to conform to the erroneous statements of a group. Recall further that, when the subjects were allowed to respond in private, the incidence of conformity dropped considerably. Clearly, then, internalization or identification was not involved. It seems obvious that the subjects were *complying* to the unanimous opinion of the group in order to avoid the punishment of ridicule or rejection. If either identification or internalization had been involved, the conforming behavior would have persisted in private.

The trichotomy of compliance, identification, and internalization is a useful one. At the same time, it should be made clear that, like most ways of classifying the world, it is not perfect; there are some places where the categories overlap. Specifically, although it is true that compliance and identification are generally more temporary than internalization, there are circumstances that can increase their permanence. For example, permanence can be increased if an individual makes a firm commitment to continue to interact with the person or group of people that induced the original act of compliance. Thus, in an experiment by Charles Kiesler and his associates,[26] when subjects believed that they were going to continue to interact with an unattractive discussion group, they not only complied publicly but also seemed to internalize their conformity—that is, they changed their private opinions as well as their public behavior. This kind of situation will be discussed in greater detail in Chapter 4.

Permanence can also result if, while complying, we discover something about our actions, or about the consequences of our actions, that makes it worthwhile to continue the behavior even after the original reason for compliance (the reward or punishment) is no longer forthcoming. For example, when the speed limit was reduced nationally from 70 to 55 miles per hour, the law was strictly enforced and most drivers reduced their speed. Some people found they enjoyed the less hectic pace and the increased safety and gas mileage, so that, even when the enforcement effort decreased and highway speeds picked up, they continued to drive within the speed limit. The generalizability of this phenomenon, called a *secondary gain*, is borne out by some of the research done on that aspect of social learning known as *behavior modification*. Typically, in behavior modification, an attempt is made to eliminate unwanted or maladaptive behavior by systematically punishing that behavior, by rewarding alternative behaviors, or both. For example, various attempts have been made to use this technique as a way of getting people to stop excessive drinking or smoking cigarettes.[27] Individuals might be given a series of painful electric shocks while performing the usual rituals of smoking—that is, while lighting a cigarette, bringing it up to their lips, inhaling, and so on. After several trials, the individual will refuse to smoke. Unfortunately, it is fairly easy for people to notice a difference between the experimental situation and the world outside: They realize they will not be shocked when smoking outside of the experimental situation. Consequently, though a person may later experience a little residual anxiety when lighting a cigarette, because electric shocks are clearly not forthcoming, the anxiety eventually fades. Thus, many people who temporarily cease smoking after this form of behavior modification eventually return to cigarettes after electric shock is no longer a threat. How about those who stay off cigarettes after behavior modification? Here is the point: Once we have been induced to comply, and therefore do not smoke for several days, it is possible for us to make a discovery. Over the years, we may have come to believe it was inevitable that we awaken every morning with a hacking cough and a hot, dry mouth, but, after refraining from cigarettes for a few days, we may discover how delightful it feels to have a clear throat and a fresh, unparched mouth. This discovery may be enough to keep us from smoking again. Thus, although compliance alone usually does not produce long-lasting behavior, it might set the stage for events that will lead to more permanent effects.

Obedience as a Form of Compliance

I indicated that acts of compliance are, in general, ephemeral. This does not mean they are trivial. Impermanent behavior can be extremely important. This fact has been demonstrated dramatically by Stanley Milgram in his studies of obedience.[28] Picture the scene: Subjects volunteer for an experiment advertised as a study of learning and memory. But this is just the cover story; actually, it is a study of the extent to which people will obey authority. When the volunteer appears at the lab for his appointment, he is paired with another participant, and a somewhat stern experimenter in a technician's coat explains that they will be testing the effects of punishment on learning. The exercise requires one participant, the learner, to memorize a list of word pairs on which the other participant, the teacher, will test him. The subject and his partner draw slips to determine roles; the subject draws the role of teacher. He is led to a "Shock Generator," which has an instrument panel with a row of 30 toggle switches, calibrated from a low point of 15 volts (labeled "Slight Shock") and extending through levels of moderate and severe shocks to a high of 450 volts (labeled "XXX"). By throwing the successive switches, the teacher is to deliver an increasingly intense shock each time the learner fails to answer correctly. Then the teacher follows the experimenter and the other participant into the next room, where the learner is strapped into an electric chair apparatus and is attached by electrodes to the "Shock Generator." In response to the learner's inquiry about his mild heart condition, the experimenter reassures him, "Although the shocks can be extremely painful, they cause no permanent tissue damage."

In actuality, the learner knows that he needn't worry. He is an accomplice of the experimenter, and the drawing to assign roles has been rigged so that he would play the role of the learner and the subject would be the teacher. The learner is not really wired to the electricity. But the teacher, who *is* the real subject, firmly believes that the victim in the next room *is* wired to the "Shock Generator" that he operates. He has himself experienced a sample shock (from a 45-volt battery inside the machine), he hears the learner react as if he is really being hurt, and he is convinced the shocks are extremely painful. The subject does not realize that what he is actually hearing is a tape recording, or that the learner is answering according to a prepared script.

As the exercise begins, the learner responds correctly several times but makes mistakes on a few trials. With each error, the subject throws the next switch, supposedly administering a shock of increasing intensity. With the fifth shock, at 75 volts, the victim begins to grunt and moan. At 150 volts, he asks to be let out of the experiment. At 180 volts, he cries out that he can't stand the pain. As the shock levels approach the point labeled "Danger: Extreme Shock," the subject hears the victim pound the wall and beg to be let out of the room. But this, of course, does not constitute a correct response, so the experimenter instructs the teacher to increase the voltage and deliver the next shock by throwing the next switch.

The participants in this experiment were a random sample of businessmen, professional men, white-collar workers, and blue-collar workers. What percentage of these people continued to administer shocks to the very end of the experiment? How long would you have continued? Every year in my social psychology class, I pose these questions, and every year some 99 percent of the 240 students in the class indicate they would not continue to administer shocks after the learner began to pound on the wall. The guesses made by my students are consistent with the results of Milgram's survey of forty psychiatrists at a leading medical school. The psychiatrists predicted most subjects would quit at 150 volts, when the victim first asks to be freed. These psychiatrists also predicted that only about 4 percent of the subjects would continue to shock the victim after he refused to respond (at 300 volts), and that less than 1 percent would administer the highest shock on the generator.

How do subjects respond when they are actually in the situation? Milgram found that, in the typical study as described above the great majority of his subjects—more than 62 percent—continued to administer shocks to the very end of the experiment, although some of them required a degree of prodding from the experimenter. The obedient subjects did not continue administering shocks because they were sadistic or cruel; nor were they insensitive to the apparent plight of the victim. Some protested; many subjects were observed to sweat, tremble, stutter, or show other signs of tension; and, strangely enough, they occasionally had fits of nervous laughter. But they obeyed.

This behavior is not limited to American men living in Connecticut. Wherever the Milgram procedure has been tried it has produced a significant degree of obedience. For example, replications of the experiment[29] have demonstrated that people in Australia, Jordan, Spain, and West Germany react in much the same way Milgram's subjects did. Similarly, women have been found to be at least as obedient as men.[30]

Milgram's results are provocative and somewhat dismaying in their implications: An astonishingly large proportion of people will cause pain to other people in obedience to authority. The research may have important counterparts in the world outside of the experimental laboratory. For example, it is difficult to read these studies without noticing a loose kind of similarity between the behavior of Milgram's subjects and the blind obedience expressed by Adolf Eichmann, who attributed his responsibility for the murder of thousands of innocent civilians to the fact that he was a good bureaucrat merely obeying orders issued by his superiors in the Nazi regime. Similarly, in our own recent history, Lieutenant William Calley, who was convicted of the deliberate and unprovoked murder of Vietnamese women and children at My Lai, freely admitted to these acts, but said he felt this was justifiable obedience to the authority of his superior officers. Interestingly, one of Milgram's subjects, obedient throughout the experiment, reported when questioned after the session, "*I* stopped, but he [the experimenter] made me go on."

As provocative as these comparisons are, we should be cautious lest we overinterpret Milgram's results. Given that 62 percent of the subjects in Milgram's experiment complied with the experimenter's command, some commentators have been tempted to suggest that perhaps most people would have behaved as Adolf Eichmann or Lieutenant Calley did if they found themselves in a similar situation. This *may* be true; but it should be emphasized that there are, in fact, some important factors in the situation encountered by Milgram's subjects that tend to maximize obedience. The subject has consented to participate, and he assumes the victim has also volunteered; he may perceive an obligation on their part to avoid disrupting the experiment. He faces the demands of the experimenter alone; a variation of the study demonstrated that the proportion of fully obedient subjects drops to just 10 percent when they are joined by two fellow teachers who defy the experimenter.[31] Also, in most of Milgram's studies, the authority figure issuing the orders was a scientist in a prestigious laboratory at Yale University, and his cover story credits the experiment as being an investigation of an important scientific question. In our society, we have been conditioned to believe that scientists tend to be responsible, benevolent people of high integrity. This is especially true if the scientist is affiliated with a well-known and highly respected institution like Yale. The subjects might reasonably assume, then, that no scientist would issue orders that would result in the death or injury of a human as a part of his experiment. This was clearly not true in either the Eichmann or the Calley example.

Some evidence in support of this conjecture comes from further research by Milgram. He conducted a separate study[32] comparing the obedience of subjects to the commands of a scientist at Yale University with the obedience of subjects to the commands of a scientist working in a suite of offices in a rather rundown commercial building in the downtown shopping area of the industrial city of Bridgeport, Connecticut. In this study, the Yale scientist achieved an obedience rate of 65 percent, while only 48 percent of the subjects in Bridgeport were obedient. Thus, removing the prestige of Yale University did seem to reduce the degree of obedience somewhat. Of course, 48 percent is still a high figure. My guess is that, if the person conducting the study were not a scientist, even fewer people would have been obedient.

Another factor that reduces the extent of obedience is the physical absence of the authority figure. Milgram found that, when the experimenter was out of the room and issued his orders by telephone, the number of *fully* obedient subjects dropped to below 25 percent. Moreover, several of the subjects who did continue with the experiment "cheated"; specifically, they administered shocks of lower intensity than they were supposed to—and never bothered to tell the experimenter they deviated from the proper procedure. This last datum, I feel, respresents a touching attempt by some individuals to be responsive to the demands of legitimate authority while, at the same time, minimizing the pain they inflict on others. It is reminiscent of the behavior of Dunbar, a character in Joseph Heller's novel *Catch 22;* unwilling either to rebel openly or to harm innocent civilians, he drops his bombs over empty fields close to the Italian villages designated as his targets.

Some subjects in the Milgram experiments chose to defy the experimenter, and human history is replete with inspiring examples of courage. For example, there are "freedom museums" in Norway, Denmark, and other European countries that celebrate the efforts of a heroic few to resist the occupation of the Nazis. But these acts of mercy and bravery, however encouraging, should not blind us to the pervasiveness of our tendency to obey authority. Many of us tour such museums and admire the displays, certain that we, too, would exhibit such courage. We harbor a myth of our personal invulnerability. When subjects were asked to predict their own performance in the Milgram study, their values and self-conceptions caused all of them to predict they would discontinue the shocks at the moderate level.[33] But we have seen how the forces of the actual situation override those values and self-conceptions. One year, when I asked my social psychology students whether they might continue delivering shocks until the end of the scale, only one hand slowly rose—everyone else in the class was confident that he or she would defy the experimenter's instructions. But the student who raised his hand was a Vietnam veteran who was in a position to know; he had experienced the impact of similar pressures, and he painfully and tragically came to recognize his own vulnerability in certain situations. Indeed, not only do we find it difficult to resist pressures to hurt people, we often avoid taking action when presented with opportunities to help other humans.

The "Uninvolved" Bystander as Conformist

Several years ago, a young woman named Kitty Genovese was stabbed to death in New York City. This was a tragic event, but not, in itself, a particularly novel occurrence. After all, in a major population center, brutal murders are not uncommon. What is interesting about this event is that no fewer than 38 of her neighbors came to their windows at 3:00 AM in response to her screams of terror—and remained at their windows watching in fascination for the 30 minutes it took her assailant to complete his grisly deed, during which time he returned for three separate attacks. No one came to her assistance; no one so much as lifted the phone to call the police, until too late.[34] Why?

Well, perhaps the onlookers were sleepy or dazed. After all, people are hardly in full control of their mental faculties at three o'clock in the morning. Perhaps. But it was in broad daylight that Eleanor Bradley, while shopping on Fifth Avenue in New York, tripped, fell, and broke her leg. She lay there for 40 minutes in a state of shock, while literally hundreds of passersby paused momentarily to gawk at her and then kept on walking.

Why did these bystanders fail to help? Are people impervious to the distress of others? Have they become so accustomed to disaster that they can be nonchalant in the face of pain and violence? Were the bystanders in these situations different from you and me in some way? The answer to all of these questions appears to be no. Interviews conducted with the bystanders in the Genovese murder revealed that they were anything but nonchalant—they were horrified. Why, then, didn't they intervene? This is a difficult question to answer.

One possible explanation concerns the existence of different norms for helping in large cities, as opposed to smaller towns. Several experiments[35] have found that the likelihood of receiving help is greater in nonurban than in urban locales. However, these studies examined small requests for help—change for a quarter, the time, and so forth. Whether or not these rural-urban differences occur in serious emergency situations, like those faced by Kitty Genovese and Eleanor Bradley, is unclear.

More convincing explanations have been suggested by a series of ingenious experiments conducted by John Darley, Bibb Latane, and their colleagues.[36] These investigators hypothesized that the very number of people witnessing the tragedies mitigated against anyone's helping—that is, a victim is less likely to get help if there is a large number of people watching his or her distress. Thus, nonintervention can be viewed as an act of conformity. In this case, it appears that, for each individual, the other people were defining the reasonableness and appropriateness of helping or not helping. As we have seen, it is often reasonable to take one's cue from others. Occasionally, however, it can be misleading; and it tends to be particularly misleading in critical situations. In our society, it is considered "uncool" to reveal strong emotions in public. When we are with others, most of us try to appear less fearful, less worried, less anxious, or less sexually aroused then we really are. For example, from the blasé looks on the faces of the patrons of topless night clubs, one would never guess they were turned on, or even interested. Similarly, the proverbial visitor from Mars would never suspect the anxiety of the patients in a dentist's waiting room by observing the impassive looks on their faces.

With these things in mind, let us consider the case of the woman who fell and broke her leg on Fifth Avenue. Suppose you arrived at the scene 10 minutes after she fell. You see a woman lying on the ground in apparent discomfort. What else do you see? You see scores of people walking past the woman, glancing at her, and continuing on their way. How will you define the situation? You may conclude that it's inappropriate for you to intervene. Perhaps it's not serious; perhaps she's intoxicated; perhaps she is playacting; perhaps the whole thing is staged for "Candid Camera," and you will make a fool of yourself on national television if you intervene. "After all," you ask yourself, "if it's so damn important, why are none of these other people doing anything about it?" Thus, the fact that there are a lot of other people around, rather than increasing the likelihood that *someone* will help, actually *decreases* the likelihood that any *one* of them will help.[37]

This is an interesting conjecture, but is it true? To find out, Bibb Latane and Judith Rodin[38] conducted an experiment constructed around a "lady in distress." In this experiment, a female experimenter asked college students to fill out a questionnaire. The experimenter than retired to the next room through an unlocked collapsible curtain saying she would return when they finished the questionnaire. A few minutes later, she staged an "accident." What the students actually heard was the sound (from a hidden tape recording) of the young woman climbing a chair, followed by a loud scream and a crash, as if the chair had collapsed and she had fallen to the floor. They then heard moaning and crying and the anguished statement, "Oh, my God, my foot . . . I . . . I . . . can't move it. Oh . . . my ankle . . . I can't get this thing off me." The cries continued for about a minute and gradually subsided.

The experimenters were interested in determining whether or not the subjects would come to the young woman's aid. The important variable in the experiment was whether or not the subjects were alone in the room. Of those who were alone, 70 percent offered to help the young woman; of those who were participating in pairs with strangers, only 20 percent offered help. Thus, it is clear that the presence of another bystander tends to inhibit action. When interviewed subsequently, the unhelpful subjects who had been in the room with another subject said they had concluded the accident probably wasn't serious, at least in part because of the inactivity of their partner.

In the Genovese murder, there was probably an additional reason the bystanders did not help. In such a situation, it may be that, if people are aware an event is being witnessed by others, the responsibility felt by any individual is diffused. Each witness to the Genovese slaying who noticed lights flick on and faces watching in several other windows might have felt no personal responsibility to act. Since others were watching, each bystander could have concluded that someone else was calling the police or that it was someone else's duty to do so. To test this idea, Darley and Latane[39] arranged an experimental situation in which subjects were placed in separate rooms but were able to communicate with each other by microphones and earphones. Thus, the subjects could hear one another but couldn't see one another. The investigators then staged a simulated epileptic attack: They played a tape recording that imitated an epileptic seizure on the part of one of the participants. In one experimental condition, each subject was led to believe that he or she was the only one whose intercom was tuned in during the seizure; in other conditions, each subject was led to believe that one or more people were tuned in also. Subjects who thought they were the only listener were far more likely to leave their room and try to help than those who thought others were listening, too. As the number of people listening increased, the likelihood of assistance decreased.

The behavior of the onlookers in the Genovese murder case and the subjects in the Darley-Latane experiments projects a rather grim picture of the human condition. Is it true that people avoid helping each other if at all possible—that is, if someone provides a bad example by not intervening, or if the responsibility for action seems the least bit diffuse? Perhaps not.

Perhaps there are situations in which people are inspired to come to the aid of their fellows. An incident in my own experience may shed some light on this issue. I was camping in Yosemite National Park several years ago. It was late at night, and I was just dropping off to sleep when I heard a man's voice cry out. I couldn't be certain whether it was a cry of pain, surprise, or joy. I had no idea whether some people were just horsing around or whether one of my fellow campers was being attacked by a bear. I crawled out of my sleeping bag and looked around, trying to shake the cobwebs out of my head and trying to ascertain the place from which the scream had come, when I noticed a strange phenomenon. From all over the area, a myriad of flickering lights were converging on a single point. These were lanterns and flashlights being carried by dozens of campers running to the aid of the individual who had screamed. It turned out his scream had been one of surprise caused by a relatively harmless flare-up in his gasoline stove. The other campers seemed almost disappointed when they learned no help was needed. They trudged back to their tents and, I assume, dropped off to sleep immediately. Not so with me, however: I tossed and turned, unable to get back to sleep. As a social psychologist with a great deal of faith in scientific data, I spent the night puzzling over the fact that my fellow campers had behaved in a totally different manner from the subjects in the Darley-Latane experiments.

Why had the campers behaved so differently? In what way were the situations different? There were at least two factors operating in the campground that were either not present or were present only to a very small degree in the situations previously discussed. One of these factors is reflected in my use, in the preceding paragraph, of the term "my fellow campers." Specifically, a feeling of "common fate" or mutuality may be engendered among people sharing the same interests, pleasures, hardships, and environmental conditions of a closed environment like a campground, a feeling of mutuality that is stronger than among people who are merely residents of the same country, county, or city. A second, somewhat related factor is that there was no escape from the face-to-face aspect of the situation: The onlookers in the Genovese case could walk away from their windows into the relative protection and isolation of their own homes; the people on Fifth Avenue could walk past the woman lying on the sidewalk and keep on going, right out of her environment; the subjects in the Darley-Latane experiments were not in a face-to-face relationship with the victim, and they knew they could escape from the environment in a very short time. In the campground, the events were occurring in a relatively restricted environment; whatever the campers allowed to happen that night they were going to have to face squarely the next morning. It seems that, under these circumstances, individuals are more willing to take responsibility for each other.

Of course, this is mere speculation. The behavior of the campers at Yosemite—while provocative—is not conclusive, because it was not part of a controlled experiment. One of the major problems with observational data like these is that the observer has no control over who the people in the situation are. Thus, differences between people always loom as a possible explanation for the differences in their behavior. For example, one might argue that individuals who go camping are—by nature or experience—kinder, gentler, more thoughtful, and more humane than New Yorkers. Perhaps they were Boy Scouts and Girl Scouts as children—hence the interest in camping—and, in scouting, they were taught to be helpful to other people. One of the reasons for doing experiments is to control this kind of uncertainty. Indeed, a subsequent experiment lends support to my speculation about my campground experience. This was an experiment performed by Irving Piliavin and his associates[40] in one of the cars of a train in the New York subway system. In this experiment, an accomplice of the experimenters staggered and collapsed in the presence of several individuals riding the subway. The "victim" remained stretched out on the floor of the train, staring at the ceiling. This scene was repeated one hundred and three times under a variety of conditions. The most striking result was that, a large part of the time, people spontaneously rushed to the aid of the "stricken" individual. This was especially true when the victim was made to seem obviously ill; in more than 95 percent of the trials, someone offered help immediately. Even when the "victim" had been given a liquor bottle to carry and was made to reek of alcohol, he received immediate help from someone on 50 percent of the trials.

Unlike the behavior of the subjects that Darley and Latane dealt with, the helping behavior of the people on the subway train was not affected by the number of bystanders. People helped just as often and just as speedily on crowded trains (where there could be a diffusion of responsibility) as they did on virtually empty trains. Although the people doing the helping were New Yorkers (as in the Genovese case, the Fifth Avenue case, and the Darley-Latane experiments), they were also in an environment that, although very much unlike Yosemite National Park, did have two things in common with the campground: (1) people riding on the same subway car do have the feeling of sharing a common fate, and (2) they were in a face-to-face situation with the victim from which there was no immediate escape.

How can the tendency to help be increased? Consider the questions that would run through your mind should you confront a possible emergency: "Is the situation really serious? Does it require my personal intervention? Will helping be difficult or costly for me? Will my help benefit the victim? Can I easily leave?" Your response will depend on your answers to each of these questions.

The first prerequisite for helping is to define the situation as an emergency. We have seen that the cues provided by the presence of unresponsive bystanders can discourage other onlookers from concluding that an emergency exists. But the interpretations of bystanders can also influence perceptions in the opposite direction. In an experiment conducted by Leonard Bickman,[41] female students sitting in cubicles and listening over intercoms heard a crash and a victim's scream, followed by the reaction of a witness to the apparent accident. When the subjects heard the witness interpret the event as a certain emergency, they helped more frequently and more quickly than when the interpretation was uncertain or when the event was labeled a nonemergency. The less ambiguous the emergency, the greater the likelihood of helping.

Defining the situation as an emergency is the first step; assuming personal responsibility for intervening is the next. Onlookers are more likely to help when they cannot reduce their sense of responsibility by assuming others will act. We have described an experiment by Darley and Latane demonstrating that people help more when they think they are the only ones aware of an emergency; in Bickman's experiments, though the subjects thought others were *aware* of the situation, some were led to believe that the other participants were unable to respond. Specifically, some of the female students were informed that the other participants they would hear over the intercom were located in nearby cubicles, while others were told that one voice (turning out to be the victim's) was originating from a nearby cubicle but that the other participant was speaking from a different building. Subjects responded significantly more speedily to the emergency in the latter condition, when perceiving that the other bystander was unable to help. In fact, those subjects who could not diffuse their responsibility intervened as quickly as those who thought nobody else heard the accident.

Although an event might be a clear emergency that demands their aid, people help less when the costs of their assistance are high. In a variation of the Piliavins' subway experiments,[42] the victim sometimes bit a capsule of red dye as he collapsed, so he appeared to be bleeding from the mouth. Though the "blood" made the emergency appear more serious, bystanders helped the victims who bled less frequently than those who collapsed without bleeding. Apparently, potential helpers were scared or repulsed by the blood, reducing their inclination to help. Other kinds of costs also can enter the calculation, including seemingly trivial ones, as John Darley and Daniel Batson[43] cleverly illustrated. They enlisted divinity students at Princeton Theological Seminary, ostensibly for the purpose of recording a speech. Each subject practiced his talk in one room; then he was instructed to walk to another building, where his presentation would be taped. At this point, some of the students were told they were late for their appointments and were hurried out. Others were told they were on time, and the rest that they had time to spare. On his way to the recording session in the other building, the subject encountered a victim slumped in a doorway, with head down and eyes closed, who coughed as the subject went by. Students in a hurry were more likely to pass by the victim. While over half of the subjects who were early or on time stopped to assist the victim, only 10 percent of the students who thought they were late for their appointment offered help, even when the speech they were to deliver involved the parable of the Good Samaritan!

In addition to assessing the costs of helping, people consider the benefits their assistance will provide. There is a good deal of evidence that people will help one another if they are certain they can do something helpful.[44] For example, in one experiment, Robert Baron[45] showed that, when an individual was in obvious pain—and when the bystander knew his or her response could alleviate the suffering—then, the greater the apparent pain, the more quickly the bystander responded. In the same experiment, it was shown that, when the bystander did not believe he or she could reduce the victim's pain, there was an inverse relationship between pain and speed of responding—that is, the greater the apparent pain, the more slowly the bystander responded. To make sense out of these results, we need to make use of the concept of *empathy:* in this case, our tendency to experience unpleasant physiological responses at the sight of another person in pain. The more the victim's pain, the greater our unpleasant feeling. We can reduce this unpleasant feeling either by helping the victim or by psychologically removing ourselves from the situation. If there is clearly something we can do about it, we act quickly—especially when the victim is in great pain. If we believe there is nothing we can do about it, the greater will be our tendency to turn away from it (in order to reduce our own feelings of unpleasantness), especially if the victim is in *great* pain.

Up to this point, we have been focusing on the considerations surrounding a decision to help a victim. As this discussion of empathy exemplifies, it is clear the bystander also considers the personal benefits and costs of not helping. The discomfort aroused by seeing a victim's plight can be allayed if the witness can redefine the incident as a nonemergency or relinquish the responsibility for intervening. When it is easy to remove oneself from the situation, helping is reduced. Several factors, however, strengthen the connection the bystander feels with the victim and thereby discourage leaving. We have all heard anecdotes of people going to extraordinary lengths—entering burning buildings or stepping in front of moving cars—to save members of their family. We tend to feel more empathy and assume more responsibility when the victim is someone close to us. The connection can be more superficial; for instance, potential helpers render more assistance to those who exhibit attitudes similar to their own. In 1971, as protesters demonstrated in Washington against President Nixon's Vietnam policy, Peter Suedfeld and his colleagues[46] staged an experiment to test the relationship between similarity of attitudes and willingness to help. They trained a young woman to approach individual demonstrators with a request to help her male friend, who was ill. Her ailing friend carried a sign reading either "Dump Nixon" or "Support Nixon." Demonstrators offered more assistance to a fellow protester carrying the anti-Nixon placard than to a seeming supporter of Nixon. Finally, as I mentioned when discussing the Yosemite camping incident and the subway experiments, helping is more likely when people share a sense of common fate. This sense of interdependence is easily disregarded in our society; the predominant explanation given by the 38 onlookers to the Genovese murder was, "I didn't want to get involved."

A Note on Ethics

In their quest for knowledge, experimental social psychologists occasionally subject people to some fairly intense experiences. In this chapter alone we have discussed experiments in which people have been led into conflict between the evidence of their own eyes and the unanimous judgments of other people, in which they have been ordered to deliver intense electric shock to an apparently suffering victim, and in which scores of innocent people riding a subway have been forced to witness the apparent agony of a person in distress.

These procedures raise serious ethical problems. A more complete treatment of ethics is presented in Chapter 9; here, let it suffice to make two general points: First, it is the responsibility of all experimenters in this field to protect the experimental subject from all harm. The experimenter must take steps to ensure that subjects leave the experimental situation in a frame of mind that is at least as sound as it was when they entered the experimental situation. This frequently requires postexperimental "debriefing" procedures that require more time and effort than the main body of the experiment.

Given the ethical thin ice that experimenters must skate upon, why bother with these kinds of experiments at all? This brings me to the second point of ethics I want to emphasize at this time: For social psychologists, the ethical issue is not a one-sided affair. In a real sense, they are obligated to use their research skills to advance our knowledge and understanding of human behavior for the ultimate aim of human betterment. In short, social psychologists have an ethical responsibility to society as a whole; they would be remiss if they failed to conduct research to the best of their ability. Social psychologists face a dilemma when their general ethical responsibility to society conflicts with their more specific ethical responsibility to each individual experimental subject; and to compound the situation, the conflict is greatest when investigating such important issues as conformity, obedience, helping, and the like, because, in general, the more important the issue, (1) the greater the potential benefit for society and (2) the more likely it is that an individual subject will experience discomfort, anxiety, or upset. Again, for a more complete treatment of this topic, the reader is directed to Chapter 9.

3

Mass Communication, Propaganda, and Persuasion

In 1977, over 130 million viewers tuned in to watch at least one of the segments of "Roots," the ABC television network's production of Alex Haley's history of several generations of a black family in America. The shows received widespread acclaim for promoting awareness of black history and for inspiring blacks' pride in their heritage. A year later, NBC broadcast "Holocaust," a miniseries that documented and dramatized the Nazis' destruction of the European Jews. Its impact extended beyond the interest and controversy aroused in the United States—the miniseries attracted a huge audience when telecast in West Germany and is credited with providing the impetus for the passage of a law preventing Nazi war criminals from escaping prosecution. In 1983, ABC presented an 18-hour miniseries based on Herman Wouk's novel, *The Winds of War*, which attracted an audience in excess of 140 million—the largest audience ever to watch a drama at the same time. The major theme of this sprawling melodrama (if there *was* a theme) was our nation's lack of preparedness for World War II. A few days later, President Ronald Reagan speculated that the program would probably help muster public support for the massive military budget which was being debated in Congress at that time. In 1974, CBS aired a film called "Cry Rape." Essentially, the story made it clear that a rape victim who chooses to press charges against her attacker runs the risk of undergoing an ordeal that may be as harrowing as the rape itself. In this case, the rapist, exuding boyish innocence, presented a convincing argument to the effect that he had been seduced by the woman. During the next few weeks, there was a sharp decrease in the number of rapes reported by victims to police—apparently because victims, taking their cue from the television movie, feared the police would not believe them.[1]

It is a truism to say we live in an age of mass communication; indeed, it can even be said that we live in an age characterized by attempts at mass persuasion. Every time we turn on the radio or television set, every time we open a book, magazine, or newspaper, someone is trying to educate us, to convince us to buy a product, to persuade us to vote for a candidate, or to subscribe to some version of what is right, true, or beautiful. This aim is most obvious in advertising: Manufacturers of nearly identical products (aspirins, for example, or toothpastes, or detergents) spend vast amounts of money to persuade us to buy the product in *their* package. Influence through the mass media need not be so blatant—the impact of "Roots" and "Holocaust," for instance, extended far beyond their most obvious effects as documentaries or dramatizations. This influence can be very subtle indeed, even unintentional. As the example of the movie about rape aptly illustrates, even when communicators are not making a direct attempt to sell us something, they can succeed in influencing the way we look at the world and the way we respond to important events in our lives.

Let's look at something supposedly objective—like the news. Are the newscasters *trying* to sell us anything? Probably not. But television is such a powerful medium that it can exert a strong influence on our behavior. For example, in a recent study, Kenneth Bollen and David Phillips[2] found a sharp increase in suicides in the United States immediately after the report of a suicide on the television evening news. Apparently, people imitate what they see on television. Moreover, those who produce television news shows can exert a more subtle influence on our opinions simply by determining which events are given exposure. And what factors determine which news items are selected for television newscasts? It has been said by no less an expert than the director of the British Broadcasting Corporation that television news is a form of *entertainment*. A study of why people watch the news agrees, concluding most viewers want to be amused and diverted, and being informed is only a secondary motive for watching.[3] Accordingly, when those in charge of news programming make decisions about which news event to cover and which fraction of the miles of daily video tape to present to the public, they make their decisions, at least in part, on the basis of the entertainment value of their material. Film footage of a flooded metropolis has much more entertainment value than footage devoted to a dam built to prevent such a flooding: It is simply not very exciting to see a dam holding back a flood. And yet, the dam may be more important news. Just as such action events as football games are more entertaining on television than such quiet events as chess matches, so it is more likely that riots, bombings, earthquakes, massacres, and other violent acts will get more air time than stories about people helping each other or people working to prevent violence. Thus, news telecasts tend to focus on the violent behavior of individuals—terrorists, protesters, strikers, or police—because action makes for more exciting viewing than does a portrayal of people behaving in a peaceful, orderly manner. Such coverage does not present a balanced picture of what is happening in the nation, not because the people who run the news media are evil and trying to manipulate us but simply because they are trying to entertain us. And, in trying to entertain us, they may unwittingly influence us to believe people behave far more violently now than ever before. This may cause us to be unhappy and even depressed about the temper of the times or the state of the nation. Ultimately, it might affect our vote, our desire to visit major urban centers, our attitudes about other nations, and so on. As we shall see, it may actually *cause* people to behave violently.

Such biased coverage was dramatically illustrated by the manner in which the media handled the nonriot that occurred in Austin, Texas during the first week in May, 1970. The background of the story was a familiar one on college campuses during the war in Southeast Asia. Tensions were running high between University of Texas students and local police following a confrontation at an impromptu student demonstration against the invasion of Cambodia by U.S. troops. During the demonstration, some 6000 students marched on the state capitol, broke a few windows, and skirmished with police; the students were teargassed and several police officers and students were injured. But this was a mere preface—a minor event compared to what seemed to be coming. A few days later, students at the University of Texas were outraged at the wanton slaying of four students at Kent State University by members of the Ohio National Guard. To protest this event, the Texas students planned a gigantic march into downtown Austin—20,000 students were expected to turn out. The Austin City Council, fearing trouble, refused to issue a parade permit. In frustration and anger, the students decided to march anyway; their leaders opted to confine the march to the sidewalks, where, technically, it would not be illegal. Rumors spread that hundreds of armed rednecks and hooligans were descending on Austin from all over the state with the intention of assaulting the students. Other rumors abounded to the effect that state troopers and Texas Rangers (not known for their friendliness to students) had been called in and were determined to take strong and violent action against anyone disobeying the law by straying or falling off the sidewalk. In retrospect, it appears these rumors were almost certainly untrue, but the important point is they were widely believed. Because the probability of keeping a crowd of 20,000 people from pushing itself off the sidewalk was remote, the situation seemed certain to be a prelude to extreme violence. Sniffing an exciting story, news teams affiliated with the major television networks were alerted. As it turned out, however, the explosive situation was defused at the eleventh hour: A team of university psychologists, law professors, and law students succeeded, at the last moment, in convincing a federal judge to issue a temporary restraining order to prevent the city from enforcing the antiparade ordinance. Moreover, it quickly became known that the testimony of several members of the police force, *in favor of allowing the students to march*, was instrumental in the judge's decision. This event—especially because of the role played by the police—resulted not only in the total absence of violence but in a genuine explosion of good will and solidarity among various diverse elements of the community. Twenty thousand students did march, but they marched in a spirit of harmony. Some of them offered cold drinks to the police officers who were diverting traffic away from the parade route; students and police exchanged friendly greetings, shook hands warmly, and so on. Interestingly enough, the national television networks completely ignored this encouraging turn of events. Because most of us were aware that teams of nationally prominent newsmen from a variety of news media had descended on the city during the week, the lack of coverage seemed puzzling indeed. An unsettling explanation was provided by Phillip Mann and Ira Iscoe, who stated: "Since there was no violence, news media teams left town and there was no national publicity, a commentary whose implications are by now sadly self-evident."[4]

It is interesting to note that, in the same city thirteen years later, a great deal of coverage was given to an event of higher drama but of far less importance. On February 19, 1983, some fifty members of the Ku Klux Klan staged a march to the Capitol building in Austin. They were greeted by about 1000 hecklers. Some rocks and bottles were thrown and a few people received minor cuts and bruises. The skirmish was featured in network television news reports and major stories as well as photographs appeared in newspapers from coast to coast.

Similarly, in October 1982, when seven people in the Chicago area died after taking Tylenol headache capsules laced with cyanide, the tragedy was widely publicized by the national news media. Indeed, for several days it was difficult to turn on the TV, the radio, or pick up a newspaper without learning about the Tylenol poisonings. Of course, it was both tragic and bizarre—and therefore *very good* copy. The effects of this prominent coverage were immediate: Similar poisonings were reported in cities across the country, involving contaminations of mouthwash, eyedrops, nasal spray, soda pop, even hot dogs.

Dramatically billed as "copycat poisonings," these poisonings, in turn, received widespread media attention. The public reaction took on all the properties of a spiral: Many people panicked, seeking medical aid for burns and poisonings when they suffered from no more than common sore throats and stomach aches. False alarms outnumbered actual cases of product-tampering by seven to one.[5] Because these events occurred just prior to Halloween, worried officials in scores of communities banned trick-or-treating, fearing that many individuals might mimic the murders by contaminating children's candy.

The initial Chicago poisonings were almost certainly the work of one person. Subsequent events were caused by the publicity given to the Chicago poisonings. But the belief was spread that the wave of poisoning constituted "an epidemic without a cure" in the words of one news service,[6] and was itself the symptom of a "sick" society, a country going "crazy." Many newspapers found themselves in the ironic position of first sensationalizing the poisoning incidents and then sensationalizing the subsequent critical comments of media experts discussing the disastrous consequences of such publicity.

The Tylenol poisonings were newsworthy. I am not suggesting that the media created the event or that it should not have been reported. Rather, I am underlining the obvious fact that selective emphasis puts the media in the position of determining subsequent events—not simply reporting them.

As I stated earlier, this form of influence is probably unintentional; the news media are not *trying* to foster violence or create the illusion that most people are cruel. Let us look at a more conscious, more direct attempt to persuade people by the judicious selection of material to be presented in the media. Imagine the following hypothetical situation: Two men are running for the Senate. One of the candidates has far less money to spend on his campaign than the other. Accordingly, in order to get maximum free exposure, he consents to numerous interviews and appears frequently at news conferences and on panel-type programs on television. The interviewers on these occasions are seasoned reporters who are not always sympathetic to the candidate. Frequently, they ask him difficult questions—occasionally, they ask him questions that are downright hostile. The candidate finds himself forever on the defensive. Sometimes, the camera catches him at an unflattering angle or in the act of scratching his nose, yawning, or fidgeting. While viewing at home, his mother is surprised at the bags under his eyes and at how tired and old he looks. Sometimes, when faced with a tough or unexpected question, he has difficulty finding the right response; he hems and haws and sounds inarticulate.

His opponent with the well-stocked campaign chest does not need to appear in these kinds of forums. Instead, he spends vast amounts of money videotaping spot commercials. Because he pays the camera crew and the director, his countenance is captured only from the most flattering angles. His personal makeup person works extra hard to cover the bags under his eyes and to make him appear young and dynamic. His mother, watching him at home, never saw him looking so well. The interviewer asks him questions prepared and rehearsed in advance, so that his answers are reasonable, concise, and articulate. If the candidate does happen to stumble over a word or to draw a blank, the cameras are stopped and the scene is shot over and over again until it is letter-perfect.

The situation outlined above is no nightmarish projection into the future. As a matter of fact, it closely approximates what occurred, on a much more important and dramatic scale, during the 1968 *presidential* election. In the extraordinary behind-the-scenes account of Richard Nixon's campaign, journalist Joe McGinness reported on the adeptness with which Nixon's advisors controlled the image of the candidate that was projected to the American people. In reporting these events, McGinness suggests television may be a powerful means of seducing voters to vote for *images* of candidates rather than the candidates themselves. Or, as one Nixon staffer put it: "This is the beginning of a whole new concept. . . . This is the way they'll be elected forevermore. The next guys up will have to be performers."[7] This proved to be prescient indeed—for in 1980, a seasoned movie and television personality was swept into office. Moreover, he managed to retain his *personal* popularity, in spite of the fact public opinion polls indicated most Americans felt he was not doing a good job.

Back to Nixon. His staffer was referring specifically to a

television program that was arranged to look as though candidate Nixon was spontaneously answering questions phoned in by voters. In reality, he was answering questions prepared by his staff and carefully rehearsed. When a voter asked a question on the telephone, Nixon's staff simply reworded it in the form of the prepared question, attributed the question to the voter, and allowed candidate Nixon to recite his prepared answer.

When McGinness' book made its appearance, many people were shocked and appalled at what they considered to be unethical and dishonest behavior. On the other hand, the overwhelming majority of voters either did not care or thought Nixon's deceptiveness was merely an indication that he was a clever, shrewd politician. Richard Nixon's popularity remained high throughout his first term in office, and in 1972 he was reelected in one of the most lopsided landslides in our nation's history, despite the fact that, at the time, it was known that a group of individuals financed by the Committee to Reelect the President had been caught breaking into the offices of the Democratic National Committee in a building called Watergate.

Nixon's large margin of victory in 1972 could be interpreted as indicating that such deceptive programming was effective in spite of its blatant manipulativeness. On the other hand, one astute observer, John Kenneth Galbraith, has commented that Nixon may have won in 1968 *in spite of* these devices. Unfortunately, there is no way to assess how well this strategy actually worked in these campaigns. No one studied its effectiveness at the time of the elections. What we *can* do is look at this and other issues in a more general way. First, let us look at the broad issue of persuasion through the mass media. Subsequently, we will look at specific techniques of persuasion.

Effectiveness of Media Appeals

The broad question is this: How credible and effective are obvious attempts to package and sell products (toothpaste, aspirin, presidential candidates) through the mass media? The prima-facie evidence suggests they are extremely effective: Why else would corporations spend hundreds of millions of dollars a year trumpeting their products? Moreover, as parents, most of us have seen our children being seduced by toy commercials that artfully depict even the most drab toys in an irresistible way. Similarly, a child watching cartoons on any Saturday morning is deluged by fast-paced ads for cereal, carry-out food, and candy. The aim is to get kids to demand that their parents buy them the products they have seen in the commercials, and it seems to work. Over 90 percent of preschool-age children asked for toys or food they saw advertised on televisicn, according to a survey of their mothers.[8] In fact, almost two-thirds of the mothers reported hearing their children sing commercial jingles they learned from television, most by the age of *three*.

Most children do catch on after a time; I've seen my own children, after several disappointments, develop a healthy skepticism (alas, even a certain degree of cynicism) about the truthfulness of these commercials. Indeed, a survey[9] found that only 12 percent of sixth graders believed television commercials told the truth all or most of the time; by tenth grade, only 4 percent felt they were truthful even most of the time. This kind of skepticism is common among adults as well. A public opinion poll showed that the overwhelming majority of adult respondents believed television commercials contain untruthful arguments. Moreover, the results indicate the more educated the person, the more skeptical, and that people who are skeptical believe their skepticism makes them immune to persuasion. This might lead us to conclude that merely knowing a communicator is biased serves to protect us from being influenced by the message. This is probably not true, however. Simply because we *think* we are immune to persuasion does not necessarily mean we *are* immune to persuasion. In the case of many consumer products, the public will tend to buy a specific brand for no other reason then the fact that it is heavily advertised.

Let's look at the headache remedy business. Daryl Bem,[10] a social psychologist, provides us with an interesting analysis of our susceptibility to television commercials even when we know they are biased. According to Bem, a well-known brand of aspirin (which we will call "Brand A") advertises itself as 100 percent pure aspirin; the commercial goes on to say that government tests have shown that no other pain remedy is stronger or more effective than Brand A. What the maker didn't bother to mention is that the government test actually showed that no brand was any weaker or less effective than any of the others. In other words, all tested brands were equal—except in price, that is. For the privilege of gulping down Brand A, consumers must pay approximately three times the price of an equally effective but unadvertised brand. Or perhaps you prefer an aspirin proclaiming it is "unsurpassed in speed—no other brand works faster," buffered so "none is gentler to your stomach." The same government test showed this buffered brand works no faster than regular aspirin, nor is there any difference between the two in the frequency of stomach upset. This well-known brand sells briskly at five times the price of equally effective products with less familiar brand names.

Another product proclaims it uses the ingredient "that doctors recommend." By reading the label, we discover the "magic" ingredient to be good old, inexpensive aspirin. Several pharmaceutical companies also market "extra strength" varieties of "arthritic pain" formulations. You will pay a premium price for these products, but are they worth it? Actually, their extra strength comes from extra aspirin (or acetaminophen, an aspirin substitute), along with a dose of caffeine. Taking additional aspirin would be less expensive, but it sounds great in the ads: "Not one, but a combination of medically proven ingredients in an extra-strength formula."

Such blatant attempts at mass persuasion seem pitifully obvious. Yet the cash registers ring, and tremendous numbers of consumers apparently set aside their skepticism even though they know the message is an obvious attempt to sell a product. Of course, there may be a basic difference between susceptibility to aspirin commercials and susceptibility to commercials for presidential candidates. When we are dealing with identical or very similar products, mere familiarity may make a huge difference. Robert Zajonc[11] has shown that, all other things being equal, the more familiar an item is, the more attractive it is. Suppose I walk into a grocery store looking for a laundry detergent. I go to the detergent section and I am staggered by the wide array of brand names. Because it doesn't matter too much to me which I buy, I may simply reach for the most familiar one—and chances are it is familiar because I've heard and seen the name on television commercials over and over again. If this is the case, then sudden increases in television exposure should produce dramatic changes in familiarity and, perhaps, in sales. Let's look at the data. Several years ago, the Northwest Mutual Life Insurance Company conducted a nationwide poll to find out how well the public recognized its name. It came out thirty-fourth among insurance companies. Two weeks later the company repeated the poll. This time it came out third in name familiarity. Wht caused this amazing leap from obscurity to fame? Two weeks and one million dollars worth of advertising on television. Of course familiarity does not necessarily mean sales, but the two are frequently linked. Thus, A & W root beer boosted its share of the market from 15 percent to 50 percent after six months of television advertising. Grapenuts was a venerable but nearly forgotten cereal. Suddenly, a well-known natural-foods enthusiast began plugging it in a series of commercials which increased the sales of this rather bland cereal by 30 percent in just a few months. By switching the channel on a Saturday morning, a child can watch "Ronald McDonald" in up to a dozen colorful, fast-paced commercials *each hour;* perhaps this is one reason why the chain sells so many billions of hamburgers.

But is voting for a presidential candidate the same kind of decision as choosing a soft drink or a breakfast cereal? Surprisingly, the answer may be yes. After the 1972 U.S. Congressional primary elections, a group of researchers[12] estimated the amount of media coverage devoted to individual candidates. Basing their decisions solely on which candidates received the most media coverage, these researchers were able to predict 83% of the winners. This figure may be misleading. Perhaps it is rather that more media coverage is accorded to front-runners than that the media creates front-runners. My guess is that, on important issues like elections, massive media "blitzes" primarily influence those voters who are least interested and least informed. However, this may represent a sizable enough minority to swing some elections.

Education or Propaganda?

Aspirin commercials are obvious attempts to sell something at a high price by intentionally misleading the audience. They can be considered propaganda. "Selling" a presidential candidate, however, is much more complicated. Thus, the devices used by Nixon's staff to display him in a favorable manner could conceivably be considered as education—an attempt to educate the public on the policies and virtues of the candidate by allowing him to present his views as clearly, efficiently, and articulately as possible. What is the difference between propaganda and education? *The American Heritage Dictionary of the English Language* defines *propaganda* as "the systematic propagation of a given doctrine" and *education* as "the act of imparting knowledge or skill." Again, we might all agree that aspirin ads are progaganda designed to promote the sale of a certain brand. But what about American television, which still tends to depict women, old people, and minorities in stereotyped roles? Or, more subtly, what about the vast majority of high school textbooks in American history that virtually ignore the contributions of blacks and other minorities to the American scene? Is this merely imparting knowledge?

The problem of distinguishing between education and propaganda can be more subtle still. Let us look at arithmetic as taught in the public schools. What could be more educational? By that I mean, what could be more pure, objective, factual, untainted by doctrine? Watch out. Do you remember the examples used in your elementary school arithmetic text? Most of the examples dealt with buying, selling, renting, working for wages, and computing interest. As Zimbardo, Ebbesen, and Maslach[13] point out, these examples do more than simply reflect the capitalistic system in which the education is occurring: They systematically endorse the system, legitimize it, and, by implication, suggest it is the natural and normal way. As a way of illustrating multiplication and percentages, the textbook might have Mr. Jones borrowing $8000 at 14 percent interest from a bank in order to purchase a new car. Would this example be used in a society that felt it was sinful to charge interest, as early society that believed people shouldn't seek possessions they can't afford? I am not suggesting it is wrong or evil to use these kinds of illustrations in arithmetic books; I am merely pointing out they can be viewed as a form of subtle progaganda and that it might be useful to recognize them as such.

In practice, whether a person regards a particular course of instruction as educational or propagandistic depends to a large extent on his or her values. Reflect, for a moment, on a film about drug abuse my children were required to see in their high school. At one point, the film mentioned that many hardcore narcotics addicts began by sampling marijuana. I'm certain that most school officials probably regard the presentation of this piece of factual knowledge as "imparting knowledge" and that most marijuana users would think of it as "the systematic propagation of a given doctrine"—that is, the implication that marijuana leads to the use of addictive drugs. By the same token, as an exercise, reflect on the topic of sex education in the schools—as viewed by a member of the Moral Majority on the one hand or by the editors of *Playboy* magazine on the other. Similarly, what the Reverend Sun Myung Moon calls reeducation is "brainwashing" to many parents of young "Moonies." This is not to say that all communications are drastically slanted and one-sided. Rather, when we are dealing with an emotionally charged issue about which people's opinions differ greatly, it is probably impossible to construct a communication that people on both sides of the issue would agree was fair and impartial.

Whether we label it propaganda or education, persuasion is a reality. It won't go away if we ignore it. As we have pointed out, each one of us is the frequent, and often unwitting, target of persuasive messages, so we should be aware of some of the techniques involved in their communication. Before outlining factors that determine the effectiveness of a message, we should mention a basic issue: the ethics of persuasion. For not only are we the recipients of persuasive communication, we are also the sources of such messages. Sometimes we play the role innocently, recommending a particular restaurant or a certain brand of stereo equipment to a friend. Sometimes it's not quite that innocuous. Many jobs—retail sales is a good example—demand a high degree of persuasive skill. Likewise, people who work for political candidates or in support of other social causes depend on their persuasive abilities to attract votes, to garner signatures for petitions, or to spread information. In fact, we can be said to be engaging in attempts at persuasion any time we praise or criticize an item, defend or attack an idea, and advocate or oppose a position. Before discussing how *best* to deliver these messages, it would be worthwhile to consider explicitly how to decide *whether or not* to do so.

The ethical question is a complex one with many grey areas. As with the distinction between propaganda and education, one's beliefs and values will affect the calculation. While it would be inappropriate to launch into a detailed and sophisticated discussion of moral philosophy in an introductory social psychology textbook, I feel obliged to point out the existence and importance of ethical issues and to suggest a few ways to consider them. One approach is to judge the ethics of a persuasive attempt by assessing its goals; the extreme statement of this viewpoint would be that the ends justify the means. Suppose you were living in Poland in 1942. The Nazis are rounding up Jews and sending them to the death camps; you are safeguarding a Jewish family, hiding them in your cellar. When the Nazis knock at your door asking if there are any Jews inside, you answer that there are not. Few people would argue that to lie in this instance was immoral or unethical; lying was necessary to save the people's lives.

When the goals of a persuasive attempt aren't so easily defensible, the ethical issues become more problematical. Imagine you are employed as a salesperson at a clothing store selling blue jeans. Your boss suggests you tell your customers "no jeans have been shown to wear longer than ours." This is technically correct, though it is also true that *your* jeans also have not been shown to wear longer than any *other* jeans. Furthermore, suppose you are paid a sizable commission for every pair of jeans you sell. Would you feel any hesitation in using the sales pitch? Would this change if you really *believe* the jeans were extraordinarily durable and inexpensive? What if you believed they *weren't?* Finally, if you are reluctant to use this sales pitch, what message *would* you feel comfortable with? With this last question, we have broadened our focus from the goals of the communication to include explicitly a consideration of the content of the message.

Another perspective on ethics is to judge actions according to the means employed by the source of the communication. Generally, it can be agreed that one should avoid knowingly dispensing false information, hiding facts, or using specious reasoning. But problems arise from this approach, too: What about a white lie, for example, where a person might use deception in order to avoid hurting someone's feelings unnecessarily?

Evaluating the ethics of a persuasive attempt requires the consideration of both the goals and the content of the message. Let's say you are a staunch opponent of nuclear power, convinced that all nuclear power plants should be shut down immediately. You are on your way home to visit your father, and you feel it is important to convince him to join you in your opposition. In past conversations, you have told him that the waste generated by nuclear plants, which is highly radioactive and currently impossible to dispose of safely, creates a serious and ever-increasing threat; he responded that "good old American know-how" will solve the problem in time. You have argued that it is wrong for energy to be controlled and distributed for profit by the centralized, big business interests necessary to finance nuclear power plants; your father merely scoffed, chuckling about "the Marxist stuff they're teaching in school these days." So, when thinking about your upcoming visit, you admit to yourself that he will probably remain unpersuaded by your two major reasons for opposing nuclear power. Since you believe the threat is such that convincing him of the danger of nuclear power is crucial, you begin to search for additional arguments to present. Recalling that your father is quite afraid of cancer, you consider emphasizing the potential effects of the radiation emanating from the plants, though you are aware the risks are undocumented. Knowing his business relies on a dependable energy supply and that he is concerned about the costs, you plan to avoid mentioning the reduction in electricity and increase in costs a nuclear shutdown would entail. Just before arriving, you think about whether your attempt to convince him is ethical.

You tell yourself your cause is a vital one, you aren't telling any direct falsehoods, and you are merely presenting your arguments in their best possible light. On the other hand, you feel uneasy that you are not sharing all the information as you know it.

The judgment is not an easy one. You may believe strongly enough in an issue to have no qualms about presenting the information in the best way to further your cause, or you might feel uncomfortable giving anything but as complete and neutral an account as you can. Your decision will depend in part on the situation. For example, a trial lawyer, who is expected (and compelled) to advocate a given position, might be less constrained by ethical considerations than a speaker who is thought to be nonpartisan. Someone whose message is preceded or followed by counterarguments might feel free to take more liberties than someone who will speak uncontested. Some people would assert that important causes justify the use of strong persuasive tactics; others would argue the converse, that the more important the topic, the greater the necessity for objectivity. As mentioned previously, the ethical issues are complex and cannot possibly be answered here. At the same time, because of the pervasiveness of influence attempts and the multitude of ethically grey areas, it is essential that they be raised.

Let us now turn to the factors that determine the effectiveness of a persuasive communication. It is possible to increase the persuasiveness of a message without resorting to distortions or untruths. Basically, there are three classes of variables that are important: (1) the source of the communication, (2) the nature of the communication, and (3) the characteristics of the audience. Put most simply: *Who* says *what* to *whom?*

The Source of the Communication

Credibility. Picture the following scene: Your doorbell rings, and, when you answer it, you find a middle-aged man in a rather loud, checkered sports jacket. His tie is loose, his collar is frayed, his pants need ironing, he needs a shave, and his eyes keep looking off to the side and over your head as he talks to you.

He is carrying a small can in his hand with a slot on the top and he's trying to convince you to contribute a few dollars to a charitable organization you've never heard of. Although his actual pitch sounds fairly reasonable, what are the possibilities of his succeeding in prying you loose from your money? Now let's turn back the clock a few minutes: You open your door in response to the ringing of the doorbell, and standing there is a middle-aged man in a conservative business suit, well-tailored and well-pressed. He looks you squarely in the eye, introduces himself as a vice-president of the City National Bank, and asks you if you would contribute a few dollars to a charitable organization (that you've never heard of), using exactly the same words as the fellow in the loud, checkered jacket. Would you be more likely to contribute some money?

I was struck by this phenomenon several years ago when I saw the poet Allen Ginsberg on one of the late-night talk shows. Ginsberg was one of the most popular poets of the so-called beat generation; his poem "Howl" had shocked and stimulated the literary establishment in the fifties. On the talk show, Ginsberg was at it again: Having just finished boasting about his homosexuality, he was talking about the generation gap. The camera panned in. He was fat, bearded, and looked a trifle wild-eyed (was he stoned?); long hair grew in unruly patches from the sides of his otherwise bald head; he was wearing a tie-dyed T-shirt with a hole in it, and a few strands of beads. Although he was talking earnestly—and, in my opinion, very sensibly—about the problems of the young, the studio audience was laughing. They seemed to be treating him like a clown. It dawned on me that, in all probability, the vast majority of the people at home, lying in bed watching the poet from between their feet, could not possibly take him seriously—no matter how sensible his message, and no matter how earnestly he delivered it. His appearance and his reputation were, in all probability, overdetermining the audience's reaction. The scientist in me longed to substitute the conservative-looking banker in the neatly pressed business suit for the wild-eyed poet and have him move his lips while Ginsberg said the same words off camera. My guess is that, under these circumstances, Ginsberg's message would have been well received.

No need. Similar experiments have already been done. Indeed, speculations about the effects of prestige on persuasion are ancient. More than 300 years before Christ, Aristotle, the world's first published social psychologist, wrote:

> We believe good men more fully and more readily than others: this is true generally whatever the question is, and absolutely true where exact certainty is impossible and opinions are divided. . . . It is not true, as some writers assume in their treatises on rhetoric, that the personal goodness revealed by the speaker contributes nothing to his power of persuasion; on the contrary, his character may almost be called the most effective means of persuasion he possesses.[14]

It required some 2300 years for Aristotle's observation to be put to a rigorous scientific test. This was accomplished by Carl Hovland and Walter Weiss.[15] What these investigators did was very simple: They presented large numbers of people with a communication that argued a particular point of view—for example, that building atomic-powered submarines was a feasible undertaking (this experiment was performed in 1951, when harnessing atomic energy for such purposes was merely a dream). Some of the people were informed that the argument was made by a person possessing a great deal of credibility; for others, the same argument was attributed to a source with low credibility. Specifically, the argument that atomic-powered submarines could be built in the near future was attributed to J. Robert Oppenheimer, a nationally known and highly respected atomic physicist, or to *Pravda*, the official newspaper of the Communist Party in the Soviet Union—a publication not famous in the United States for its objectivity and truthfulness. Before reading the arguments, the members of the audience were asked to fill out some rating scales that revealed their opinions on the topic. They then read the communication. A large percentage of those people who believed the communication came from J. Robert Oppenheimer changed their opinions—they then believed more strongly in the feasibility of atomic submarines. Very few of those who read the identical communication attributed to *Pravda* shifted their opinions in the direction of the communication.

This same phenomenon has received repeated confirmations

by several different investigators using a wide variety of topics and attributing the communications to a wide variety of communicators. Careful experiments have shown that a judge of the juvenile court is better than most people at swaying opinion about juvenile delinquency, that a famous poet and critic can sway opinion about the merits of a poem, and that a medical journal can sway opinion about whether or not antihistamines should be dispensed without a prescription. What do the physicist, the judge, the poet, and the medical journal have that *Pravda* doesn't have? That is, what is the difference that makes the difference in their effectiveness? Aristotle said we believe "good men," by which he meant people of high moral caliber. Hovland and Weiss use the term *credible*, which removes the moral connotations present in the Aristotelian definition. Oppenheimer, a juvenile court judge, and the poet are all credible—that is, they are not necessarily "good," but they are both *expert* and *trustworthy*. It makes sense to allow yourself to be influenced by communicators who are trustworthy and who know what they are talking about. It makes sense for people to be influenced by J. Robert Oppenheimer when he is voicing an opinion about atomic power, and it makes sense for people to be influenced by someone like T. S. Eliot when he is talking about poetry. These are expert, trustworthy people. But not all people are equally influenced by the same communicator. Indeed, the same communicator may be regarded by some as possessing high credibility and by others as possessing low credibility. Moreover, certain peripheral attributes of the communicator may loom large for some members of the audience; such attributes can serve to make a given communicator either remarkably effective or remarkably ineffective.

This phenomenon was forcefully demonstrated in an experiment I performed in collaboration with Burton Golden,[16] in which we presented sixth graders with a speech extolling the usefulness and importance of arithmetic. The communicator was introduced either as a prize-winning engineer from a prestigious university or as someone who washed dishes for a living. As one might expect, the engineer was far more effective at influencing the youngsters' opinions than the dishwasher. This finding is consistent with previous research; in and of itself, it is obvious and not very interesting. But, in addition, we varied the race of the communicator: In some of the trials the communicator was white, and in others, black. Several weeks prior to the experiment, the children had filled out a questionnaire designed to measure the degree of their prejudice against black people. The results were striking: Among those children who were most prejudiced against blacks, the black engineer was *less* influential than the white engineer, although both delivered the same speech. Moreover, among those children who were the least prejudiced against blacks, the black engineer was *more* influential than the white engineer. It seems unreasonable that such a peripheral attribute as skin color would affect a person's credibility. It might be argued that, in a purely rational world, a prestigious engineer should be able to influence sixth graders about the importance of arithmetic regardless of the color of his or her skin, but apparently this is not a purely rational world. Depending upon listeners' attitudes toward blacks, they were either *more* influenced or *less* influenced by a black communicator than an otherwise identical white communicator.

This kind of behavior is not very adaptive. If the quality of your life depended on the extent to which you were to allow a communication about arithmetic to influence your opinion, the expertise and trustworthiness of the communicator would seem to be the most reasonable factors to heed. To the extent other factors (such as skin color) decrease or increase your susceptibility to persuasion on an issue irrelevant to such factors, you are behaving in a maladaptive manner. But, although such behavior is maladaptive, it should not be very astonishing to anyone who has ever watched commercials on television. For example, Robert Young has starred in a series of commercials in which he encounters a friend who is distraught, nervously pacing around, slamming the door, or yelling at the children. He asks why his friend is so upset. When it is suggested that the problem might be due to too much caffeine, Young shakes his head sympathetically, agrees that he has heard this can be a problem, and recommends a particular brand of decaffeinated coffee. What makes Robert Young an expert on health? For several seasons on television, he played Marcus Welby, an extremely competent and compassionate doctor. Similarly, Karl Malden has starred in a series of commercials in which Americans traveling in a foreign country either lose all their money or have it stolen. The tourists are distraught, humiliated, traumatized, panicky. At the end of the commercial Karl Malden appears and, in an authoritative voice, warns us not to carry money while traveling—and recommends "American Express Travelers Cheques—don't leave home without 'em." What makes Karl Malden an expert on vacation financing? Nothing, but he is perceived as somewhat of an expert on *crime*. For several television seasons, Malden portrayed Lieutenant Mike Stone in *The Streets of San Francisco*, a popular detective show. Though Mr. Young and Mr. Malden probably know no more about medicine, crime, travelers cheques, or even coffee than the viewers, they almost certainly gain credibility and trust from being identified with their particular roles.

Not only are such peripheral aspects of the communicator often emphasized in commercials, frequently they are the *only* aspects of the communicator the viewer is able to perceive. Who is an expert on the topic of razor blades or shaving cream? Well, perhaps a barber; maybe a dermatologist or a cosmetologist. Who is it that tells us what blades or lather we should use? Most often, it is some mountainous professional football player who must squint hard at the cue card in order to make out the name of the sponsor's product. Throughout the 1950s and 1960s, one of the most persistent peddlers of breakfast food was former Olympic decathlon champion Bob Richards, who was probably far more effective at selling Wheaties than some learned professor of nutrition, no matter *how* expert he would be. How attractive *are* these people? Well, when Bob Richards was finally replaced in the 1970s, the Wheaties people again decided not to use a nutritionist and hired Bruce Jenner, the new Olympic decathlon gold medalist. This would suggest that whoever handles advertising for Wheaties is convinced of the effectiveness of famous athletes. Is this conviction justified? Ask yourself: Would you buy a certain brand of motor oil because golfer Arnold Palmer exhorted you to do so? Can tennis star Chris Evert Lloyd sell you her brand of instant tea? Do you think you would patronize a specific car rental service because you have seen O. J. Simpson dashing and leaping through airports? Would you buy light beer because half the athletes in America told you it was less filling yet tastes great?

It is certainly true that people recognize athletes. D. E. Hutchins, director of advertising of AT&T, said: "We have discovered through various surveys that the sports star enjoys a tremendous recognition factor—superior to that of Hollywood movie stars and nameless models picked on looks."[17] But believability is something else. Will people be influenced by an ad just because a prominent sports personality is involved? Several years ago, a survey was conducted in which 2500 heads of households were asked whether they could be influenced by such sports personalities as Joe Namath and Muhammad Ali. The overwhelming majority said they didn't think they could—that they didn't trust these athletes. Can people predict their own behavior? Before answering, let's take a closer look at the factor of "trust."

Increasing Trustworthiness. Clearly, trust is an important factor in determining whether or not a communicator will be effective. It may be that the crucial reason why the relatively more prejudiced sixth graders in the Aronson-Golden experiment were less influenced by the black engineer than by the white engineer was that they simply did not trust blacks. If this is true, then if we could offer the audience clear independent evidence that a person is trustworthy, that person should be a very effective communicator.

How might communicators make themselves seem clearly trustworthy to us? One way is to argue against their own self-interest. If a person has nothing to gain (and perhaps something to lose) by convincing us, we will trust him and he will be more effective. An illustration may be helpful. Suppose a habitual criminal recently convicted as a smuggler and peddler of heroin was delivering a communication on the abuses of the American judicial system. Would he influence you? Probably not. Most people would probably regard him as unattractive and untrustworthy: He seems clearly outside of the Aristotelian definition of a "good man." But suppose he was arguing that criminal justice was too *lenient*—that criminals almost always beat the rap if they have a smart lawyer and even if they *are* convicted, the sentences normally meted out are too soft. Would he influence you? I'm certain he would; in fact, a few years ago I performed this very experiment in collaboration with Elaine Walster and Darcy Abrahams,[18] and it confirmed our hypothesis. In the actual experiment, we presented our subjects with a newspaper clipping of an interview between a news reporter and Joe "The Shoulder" Napolitano, who was identified in the manner described above. In one experimental condition, Joe "The Shoulder" argued for stricter courts and more severe sentences. In another condition, he argued that courts should be more lenient and sentences less severe. We also ran a parallel set of conditions in which the same statements were attributed to a respected public official. When Joe "The Shoulder" argued for more lenient courts, he was totally ineffective; indeed, he actually caused the subjects' opinions to change slightly in the opposite direction. But when he was arguing for stricter, more powerful courts, he was extremely effective—as effective as the respected public official delivering the same argument. This study demonstrates that Aristotle was not completely correct—a communicator can be an unattractive, immoral person and still be effective, as long as it is clear the person has nothing to gain (and perhaps something to lose) by persuading us.

Why was Joe "The Shoulder" so effective in our experiment? Let's take a closer look. Most people would not be surprised to hear a known convict arguing in favor of a more lenient criminal justice system. Their knowledge of the criminal's background and self-interest would lead them to expect such a message. When they receive the opposite communication, however, these expectations are shaken. To make sense of this contradiction, the members of the audience might conclude either that the convict had reformed or that he was under some kind of pressure to make the anticrime statements. In the absence of any substantiating evidence however, another explanation becomes more reasonable: Maybe the truth of the issue is so compelling that, even though it apparently contradicts his background and self-interest, the spokesman sincerely believes in the position he espouses. Think back to the incident of the "non-riot" in Austin, and recall the controversy surrounding the enforcement of the antiparade ordinance. When the police, who were assumed to dislike protests and were expected to oppose the demonstration, testified in favor of permitting the parade, their testimony was very influential.

Further evidence for this phenomenon comes from a more recent experiment. Alice Eagly and her colleagues[19] presented students with a description of a dispute between business interests and environmental groups over a company polluting a river. The students then read a statement about the issue. In some conditions the spokesman was described as having a business background and was said to be speaking to a group of businessmen. In others, his background and audience was varied, thereby altering the subjects' expectations for his message. The results supported the reasoning above; where the message conflicts with their expectations, the audience perceived the communicator as being more sincere and they were more persuaded by his statement. Similarly, among the most effective spokespersons for the anti-nuclear arms movement in recent years have been several professionals who have taken stands which seemingly contradict their backgrounds. These communicators—for example, a respected nuclear physicist who cautions against the further development of nuclear technology, and a former naval commander who campaigns for a halt to military growth—have been perceived as highly credible precisely because of the discontinuity between their messages and the apparent interests of their professions. First of all, they are experts. Secondly, since they have nothing to gain (and perhaps collegial esteem to lose) it seems that only the compelling need for disarmament has led them to speak out. Not only do we tend to take more notice of unexpected events, we also attribute more credibility to speakers who appear to resist the pressures of their colleagues and who take stands in opposition to their backgrounds.

The trustworthiness of a person can also be increased if the audience is absolutely certain the person is not *trying* to influence them. Suppose a stockbroker calls you up and gives you a hot tip on a particular stock. Will you buy? It's hard to be sure. On the one hand, the broker is probably an expert, and this might influence you to buy. On the other hand, the stockbroker has something to gain by giving you this tip (a commission), and this could lower her effectiveness. But suppose you happened to overhear her telling a friend a particular stock was about to rise. Because she was obviously not *trying* to influence you, you might be more readily influenced. Indeed, a non-hypothetical brokerage firm, E. F. Hutton, has incorporated this very scenario into its advertising. A typical commercial opens with a shot of two people engaged in private conversation in a noisy and crowded restaurant. When one person begins to pass on some stock advice from E. F. Hutton, a sudden hush falls over the room and everyone—waiters, customers, even busboys—strains toward the speaker to better "overhear" the tip. "When E. F. Hutton talks," says the announcer, "people listen." The implication is clear: Everyone in the restaurant is getting in on advice that wasn't intended for them, and the information is all the more valuable as a result. When communicators are not *trying* to influence us, their potential to do so is increased. This is exactly what was discovered in an experiment by Elaine Walster and Leon Festinger.[20] In this study, a conversation was staged between two graduate students in which one of them expressed his opinion on an issue. The situation was arranged so that an undergraduate subject was allowed to overhear this conversation. In one experimental condition, it was clear to the subject that the graduate students were aware of his presence in the next room; therefore, the subject knew anything being said could conceivably be directed at him with the intention of influencing his opinion. In the other condition, the situation was arranged so that the subject believed the graduate students were unaware of his presence in the next room. In this condition, the subject's opinion changed significantly more in the direction of the opinion expressed by the graduate students. This phenomenon may explain the preponderance of "hidden camera" advertisements on television; if we are convinced a person has been caught unaware, we don't attribute a persuasive intent to the message. Believing the person is acting spontaneously, we are more persuaded by his or her testimony.

Attractiveness

Where do these findings leave our friend the football player holding up his can of shaving cream? Clearly he is *trying* to influence us—the shaving cream company is not paying him all that money *not* to sell shaving cream. Moreover, he seems to be operating in his own self-interest; if we were to take a good look at the situation, it would be clear to us the only reason he's up there with the shaving cream is to make a buck. We expect him to recommend a certain brand, and we know he expects us to see the commercial. These factors should make him less trustworthy. And apparently they do—as indicated by the results of the research I have just described. But does that make him less effective? Not necessarily. Although the majority of the heads of household said they did not trust Joe Namath, that does not necessarily mean they wouldn't buy the products he was endorsing. Another crucial factor determining the effectiveness of communicators is how attractive or likeable they are—regardless of their overall expertise or trustworthiness. Several years ago, Judson Mills and I did a simple laboratory experiment demonstrating that a beautiful woman—simply because she was beautiful—could have a major impact on the opinions of an audience on a topic wholly irrelevant to her beauty, and, furthermore, that her impact was greatest when she openly expressed a desire to influence the audience.[21] More recently Alice Eagly and Shelly Chaiken carried out an experiment that not only replicated the finding that more likable communicators are more persuasive but went on to show that attractive sources are expected to support desirable positions.[22] It appears we associate the attractiveness of the communicator with the desirability of the message. We seem to be influenced by people we like. Where our liking for a communicator is involved (rather than his or her expertise), we behave as though we were trying to please that source. Accordingly, the more that communicator wants to change our opinions, the more we change them—but *only about trivial issues*. That is, it is true that football players can get us to use a particular shaving cream and that beautiful women can get us to agree with them on an abstract topic whether or not we are willing to admit it. At the same time, it is unlikely they could influence us to vote for their presidential candidate or to adopt their position on the morality of abortion.

To summarize this section, we might list these phenomena:

1. Our opinions are influenced by individuals who are both expert and trustworthy.
2. A communicator's trustworthiness (and effectiveness) can be increased if he or she argues a position apparently opposed to his or her self-interest.
3. A communicator's trustworthiness (and effectiveness) can be increased if he or she does not seem to be trying to influence our opinion.
4. At least where trivial opinions and behaviors are concerned, if we like and can identify with a person, his or her opinions and behaviors will influence our own more than their content would ordinarily warrant.
5. Again, where trivial opinions and behaviors are concerned, if we like a person, we will tend to be influenced even if it is clear he or she is trying to influence us and stands to profit by doing so.

The Nature of the Communication

The manner in which a communication is stated plays an important role in determining its effectiveness. There are several ways in which communications can differ from one another. I have selected five I consider to be among the most important: (1) Is a communication more persuasive if it is designed to appeal to the audience's reasoning ability, or is it more persuasive if it is aimed at arousing the audience's emotions? (2) Are people more swayed by a communication if it is tied to a vivid personal experience or if it is bolstered by a great deal of clear and unimpeachable statistical evidence? (3) Should the communication present only one side of the argument, or should it also attempt to refute the opposing view? (4) If two sides are presented, as in a debate, does the order in which they are presented affect the relative impact of either side? (5) What is the relationship between the effectiveness of the communication and the discrepancy between the audience's original opinion and the opinion advocated by the communication?

Logical versus Emotional Appeals. Several years ago, I was living in a community that was about to vote on whether or not to fluoridate the water supply as a means of combating tooth decay. An information campaign that seemed quite logical and reasonable was launched by the proponents of fluoridation. It consisted largely of statements by noted dentists describing the benefits of fluorides and discussing the evidence on the reduction of tooth decay in areas with fluoridated water, as well as statements by physicians and other health authorities to the effect that fluoridation has no harmful effects. The opponents used an appeal much more emotional in flavor. For example, one leaflet consisted of a picture of a rather ugly rat, along with the inscription "Don't let them put rat poison in your drinking water." The referendum to fluoridate the water supply was soundly defeated. Of course, this incident doesn't prove conclusively that emotional appeals are superior, mainly because the incident was not a scientifically controlled study. We have no idea how the people would have voted on fluoridation if *no* publicity were circulated, nor do we know whether the antifluoridation circular reached more people, whether it was easier to read than the proponents's literature, and so forth. Although the actual research in this area is far from conclusive, there is some evidence favoring an appeal that is primarily emotional. In one early study, for example, George W. Hartmann[23] tried to measure the extent to which he could induce people to vote for a particular political candidate as a function of what kind of appeal he used. He demonstrated that individuals who received a *primarily* emotional message voted for the candidate endorsed by the message more often than did people who received a *primarily* logical message.

The word *primarily* is italicized for good reason—it defines the major problem with research in this area. Namely, there are no foolproof, mutually exclusive definitions of "emotional" and "rational." In the fluoridation illustration, for example, most people would probably agree the antifluoridation pamphlet was designed to arouse fear; yet, it is not entirely illogical, because it is indeed true that the fluoride used in minute concentrations to prevent tooth decay is used in massive concentrations as a rat poison. On the other side, to present the views of professional people is not entirely free from emotional appeal; it may be comforting (on an emotional level) to know physicians and dentists endorse the use of fluorides.

Because, in practice, operational distinctions between "logical" and "emotional" are difficult to draw, some researchers have turned to an equally interesting and far more researchable problem: the problem of the effect of various levels of a specific emotion on opinion change. Suppose you wish to arouse fear in the hearts of your audience as a way of inducing opinion change. Would it be more effective to arouse just a little fear, or should you try to scare the hell out of them? For example, if your goal is to convince people to drive more carefully, would you be more effective if you showed them gory technicolor films of the broken and bloody bodies of the victims of highway accidents, or would you be more effective if you soft-pedaled your communication—showing crumpled fenders, discussing increased insurance rates due to careless driving, and pointing out the possibility that people who drive carelessly may have their driver's licenses suspended? Common sense argues on both sides of this street. On the one hand, it suggests that a good scare will motivate people to action; on the other hand, it argues that too much fear can be debilitating—that is, it might interfere with a person's ability to pay attention to the message, to comprehend it, and to act upon it. We've all believed, at one time or another, "it only happens to the other guy—it can't happen to me." Thus, people continue to drive at very high speeds, and to insist on driving after they've had a few drinks, even though they should know better. Perhaps this is because the possible negative consequences of these actions are so great we try not to think about them. Thus, it has been argued that, if a communication arouses a great deal of fear, we tend *not* to pay close attention to it.

What does the evidence tell us? The overwhelming weight of experimental data suggests that, all other things being equal, the more frightened a person is by a communication the more likely he or she is to take positive preventive action. The most prolific researchers in this area have been Howard Leventhal and his associates.[24] In one experiment, they tried to induce people to stop smoking and to take chest x-rays. Some subjects were exposed to a low-fear treatment: They were simply presented with a recommendation to stop smoking and get their chests x-rayed. Others were subjected to moderate fear: They were shown a film depicting a young man whose chest x-rays revealed he had lung cancer. The people subjected to the high-fear condition saw the same film the "moderate-fear" people saw—and, in addition, they were treated to a rather gory color film of a lung-cancer operation. The results showed that those people who were most frightened were also most eager to stop smoking and most likely to have chest x-rays taken.

Is this true for all people? It is not. There is a reason why common sense suggests that a great deal of fear leads to inaction: It does—for certain people, under certain conditions. What Leventhal and his colleagues discovered is that people who have a reasonably good opinion of themselves (high self-esteem) are the ones who are most likely to be moved by high degrees of fear arousal. People with low opinions of themselves were the least likely to take immediate action when confronted with a communication arousing a great deal of fear—but (and here is the interesting part) after a delay, they behaved very much like the subjects with high self-esteem. That is, if immediate action was not required but action could be taken later, people with low self-esteem were more likely to take that action if they were exposed to a communication arousing a great deal of fear. People who have a low opinion of themselves may have a great deal of difficulty coping with threats to themselves. A high-fear communication overwhelms them and makes them feel like crawling into bed and pulling the covers up over their heads. Low or moderate fear is something they can more easily and immediately deal with. But, if given time—that is, if it's not essential that they act immediately—they will be more likely to act if the message truly scared the hell out of them.

Subsequent research by Leventhal and his co-workers lends support to this analysis. In one study, subjects were shown films of serious automobile accidents. Some subjects watched the films on a large screen from up close; others watched them from far away on a much smaller screen. Among those subjects with high or moderate self-esteem, those who saw the films on the large screen were much more likely to take protective action, subsequently, then were those who saw the films on the small screen.

Subjects with low self-esteem were more likely to take action when they saw the films on a small screen; those who saw the films on a large screen reported a great deal of fatigue and stated they had great difficulty even thinking of themselves as victims of automobile accidents. Thus, people with low self-esteem are apparently overwhelmed by fear, if an immediate response is necessary.

It should be relatively easy to make people with high self-esteem behave like people with low self-esteem. We can overwhelm them by making them feel there is nothing they can do to prevent or discover a threatening situation. This will lead most people to bury their heads in the sand—even those who have high self-esteem. Conversely, suppose you wanted to reduce the automobile accident rate or to help people give up smoking, and you were faced with low self-esteem people. How would you proceed? If you construct a message containing clear, specific, and optimistic instructions, it might increase the feeling among the members of your audience that they can confront their fear and cope with the danger. These speculations have been confirmed; experiments by Howard Leventhal and his associates show that fear-arousing messages containing specific instructions about how, when, and where to take action are much more effective than recommendations not including such instructions. For example, a campaign conducted on a college campus urging students to take tetanus shots included specific instructions about where and when they were available. The campaign materials included a map showing the location of the student health service and a suggestion that each student set aside a convenient time to stop by. The results showed high-fear appeals to be more effective than low-fear appeals in producing favorable *attitudes* toward tetanus shots among the students, and they also increased the students' stated intentions to take the shots. The highly specific instructions about how to get the shots did not in any way effect these opinions and intentions, but the instructions did have a big effect on the *actual behavior:* Of those subjects who were instructed about how to proceed, 28 percent actually got the tetanus shots, but of those who received no specific instructions, only 3 percent went down to get them. In a control group exposed only to the action instructions—no fear-arousing message—there was no shot-taking. Thus, specific instructions alone are not enough to produce action—fear is a necessary component for action in such situations.

Very similar results were uncovered in Leventhal's cigarette experiment. Leventhal found that a high-fear communication produced a much greater *intention* to stop smoking. Unless it was accompanied by recommendations for specific behavior, however, it produced little results. Similarly, specific instructions ("buy a magazine instead of a pack of cigarettes; drink plenty of water when you have the urge to smoke," and so on) without a fear-arousing communication were relatively ineffective. The combination of fear arousal and specific instructions produced the best results; the students in this condition were still smoking less four months after they were subjected to the experimental procedure.

Let us look at people's reactions to the threat of nuclear war. Several years ago, studies revealed that many people were worried about nuclear war but felt that it was beyond their power to do anything about the problem.[25] But since 1980 several million Americans have seen films, heard lectures, or witnessed dramatizations designed to convey the horrifying consequences of nuclear war. One widely-viewed film *(The Last Epidemic)* describes in chilling detail exactly what would happen to the city of San Francisco in a nuclear attack. According to pollster Lou Harris,[26] Americans have now become "genuinely frightened—[but] frightened in an activated as opposed to a passive way." What might have intervened to alter this state of affairs? As we have seen, fear-provoking communications are most effective when they are accompanied by specific recommendations for action. The Nuclear Freeze proposal, developed in 1980, provided just such clear-cut, immediate goals. It recast a bewildering set of issues in concrete and understandable terms and provided the focus for millions of individual efforts to circulate petitions, write political representatives, and educate co-workers, friends, and relatives. Instead of feeling frightened and powerless, people began to feel there was something they could do.

Consensual Statistical Evidence versus A Single Personal Example. Suppose you are in the market for a new car and the most important things you are looking for are reliability and longevity. That is, you don't care about looks, style, or mileage—what you *do* care about is the frequency of repair. As a reasonable and sensible person, you consult *Consumer Reports* and learn that the car with the best repair record is clearly the Volvo. No other model even comes close. Naturally, you decide to buy a Volvo. But suppose the night before you are to make the purchase, you attend a dinner party and announce your intention to one of your friends. He is incredulous: "You can't be serious," he says, "my cousin bought a Volvo last year and has had nothing but trouble ever since. First the fuel injection system broke down; then the transmission fell out; then strange undiagnosable noises started to come from the engine; finally, oil started to drip from some unknown place. My poor cousin is literally afraid to drive the car for fear of what will happen next."

Let's suppose the ranking made by *Consumer Reports* was based on a sample of 1000 Volvo owners. Your friend's cousin's unfortunate experience has increased the size of the sample to 1001. It has added one negative case to your statistical bank. Logically, this should not affect your decision. But a plethora of research by Richard Nisbett and his associates[27] (from whose work this example was "borrowed") indicates that such occurrences, because of their vividness, assume far more importance than their logical, statistical status would imply. Indeed, such occurrences are frequently decisive. Thus, it would be very difficult for you to rush out and purchase a Volvo with the plight of your friend's cousin firmly fixed in your mind. All other things equal, most people are more deeply influenced by one clear, vivid, personal example than by an abundance of statistical data. We have a strong tendency to attribute typicality to a single isolated incident. Thus, your friend's communication was an extraordinarily powerful one.

One-Sided versus Two-Sided Arguments. Suppose you are about to make a speech attempting to persuade your audience that capital punishment is necessary. Would you persuade more people if you simply stated your view and ignored the arguments against capital punishment, or would you be more persuasive if you discussed the opposing arguments and attempted to refute them? Before trying to answer this question, let us try to understand what is involved. If a communicator mentions the opposition's arguments, it might indicate he or she is an objective, fair-minded person; this could enhance the speaker's trustworthiness and thus increase his or her effectiveness. On the other hand, if a communicator so much as mentions the arguments on the other side of the issue, it might suggest to the audience that the issue is a controversial one; this could confuse the audience, make them equivocate, and ultimately reduce the persuasiveness of the communication. With these possibilities in mind, it should not come as a surprise to the reader that there is no simple relation between one-sided arguments and the effectiveness of the communication. It depends to some extent upon the intelligence of the audience: The more intelligent the members of the audience are, the less likely they are to be persuaded by a one-sided argument and the more likely they are to be persuaded by an argument that brings out the important opposing arguments and then proceeds to refute them. This makes sense: An intelligent person is more likely to know some of the counterarguments—when the communicator avoids mentioning these, the intelligent members of the audience are likely to conclude the communicator is either unfair or is unable to refute such arguments. On the other hand, an unintelligent person is less apt to know of the existence of opposing arguments. If the counterargument is ignored, the less intelligent members of the audience are persuaded; if the counterargument is presented, they may get confused.

Another factor playing a vital role is the initial position of the audience. As we might expect, if a member of the audience is already predisposed to believe the communicator's argument, a one-sided presentation has a greater impact on his or her opinion than a two-sided presentation. If, however, a member of the audience is leaning in the opposite direction, then a two-sided refutational argument is more persuasive.[28] Most politicians seem to be well aware of this phenomenon; they tend to present vastly different kinds of speeches, depending upon who constitutes the audience. When talking to the party faithful, they almost invariably deliver a hell-raising set of arguments favoring their own party platform and candidacy. If they do mention the opposition, it is in a derisive, mocking tone. On the other hand, when appearing on network television or when speaking to any audience of mixed loyalties, they tend to take a more diplomatic position, giving the opposing view a reasonably accurate airing before proceeding to demolish it.

The Order of Presentation. Imagine you are running for the city council. You and your opponent are invited to address a large audience in the civic auditorium. It is a close election—many members of the audience are as yet undecided—and the outcome may hinge on your speech. You have worked hard on writing and rehearsing it. As you take your seat on the stage, the master of ceremonies asks you whether you would prefer to lead off or speak last. You ponder this for a moment. You think, *Speaking first may have an advantage, because first impressions are crucial; if I can get the audience on my side early, then my opponent will not only have to sell himself, he'll also have to unsell the audience on me—he'll be bucking a trend. On the other hand, if I speak last, I may have an advantage, because when the people leave the auditorium, they may remember the last thing they heard. The early statements made by my opponent, no matter how powerful, will be buried by my rhetoric simply because my speech will be more memorable.* You stammer: "I'd like to speak first . . . no, last . . . no, first . . . no, wait a minute." In confusion, you race off the stage, find a phone booth, and phone your friend the social psychologist. Surely, she must know which order has the advantage.

I'm afraid that if you expect a one-word answer, you are in for a disappointment. Moreover, if you wait to hear all of the social psychologist's elaborations and qualifying remarks, you might miss the opportunity of ever delivering your speech at all. Indeed, you might miss the election itself.

Needless to say, the issue is a complex one involving both learning and retention. I'll try to state it as simply as possible. The issues are similar to the common-sense issues that you, as our hypothetical politician, pondered alone. It is true that, all other things being equal, the audience's memory should be better for the speech made last, simply because it is closer in time to the election. On the other hand, the actual learning of the second material will not be as thorough as the learning of the first material, simply because the very existence of the first material disrupts and inhibits the learning process. Thus, from our knowledge of the phenomena of learning, it would appear that, all other things being equal, the first argument will be more effective; we'll call this the *primacy effect*. But from our knowledge of the phenomena of retention, on the other hand, it would appear that, all other things being equal, the last argument will be more effective; we'll call this the *recency effect*.

The fact that these two approaches seemingly make for opposite predictions does not mean it doesn't matter which argument comes first; nor does it mean that it is hopeless to attempt to make a definitive prediction. What it does mean is that, by knowing something about the way both inhibition and retention work, we can predict the conditions under which either the primacy effect or the recency effect will prevail. The crucial variable is *time*—that is, the amount of time separating the events in the situation: (1) the amount of time between the first communication and the second communication, and (2) the amount of time between the end of the second communication and the moment when the members of the audience must finally make up their minds. Here are the crucial points: (1) Inhibition (interference) is greatest if very little time elapses between the two communications; here, the first communication produces maximum interference with the learning of the second communication, and a primacy effect will occur—the first speaker will have the advantage. (2) Retention is greatest, and recency effects will therefore prevail, when the audience must make up its mind immediately after hearing the second communication.

Okay. Is the candidate for city council still on the phone? Here's the plan: If the two speakers are to present their arguments back to back, and if the election is still several days away, you should speak first. The primacy of your speech will interfere with the audience's ability to learn your opponent's arguments; with the election several days away, differential effects due to memory are negligible. But if the election is going to be held immediately after the second speech, and there is to be a prolonged coffee break between the two speeches, you would do well to speak last. Because of the coffee break between speeches, the interference of the first speech with the learning of the second speech will be minimal; because the audience must make up its mind right after the second speech, as the second speaker, you would have retention working for you. Therefore the recency effect would be dominant: All other things being equal, the last speech will be the more persuasive.

These speculations were confirmed in a clever experiment by Norman Miller and Donald Campbell.[29] In this experiment, a simulated jury trial was arranged, in which subjects were presented with a condensed version of the transcript of an actual jury trial of a suit for damages brought against the manufacturers of an allegedly defective vaporizer. The *pro* side of the argument consisted of the testimony of witnesses for the plaintiff, cross-examination of defense witnesses by the plaintiff's lawyer, and the opening and closing speeches of the plaintiff's lawyer. The *con* side of the argument consisted of the testimony of witnesses for the defense, the defense lawyer's cross-examinations, and his opening and closing speeches. The condensed version of this transcript was arranged so that all of the *pro* arguments were placed in one block and all of the *con* arguments were placed in another block. The investigators varied the interval between the reading of the two arguments and between the reading of the last argument and the announcement of the verdict. A recency effect was obtained when there was a large interval between the first and second arguments and a small interval between the second argument and the verdict. A primacy effect was obtained when there was a small interval between the first and second arguments and a large interval between the second argument and the verdict. The topic of this experiment (a jury trial) serves to underscore the immense practical significance these two phenomena may have. Most jurisdictions allow the prosecution to go first (opening statement and presentation of evidence) *and* last (closing arguments), thus giving the state the advantage of both primacy and recency effects. Because the order of presentation may influence a jury's verdict of guilt or innocence, I would recommend that our trial procedures be modified to prevent any possible miscarriages of justice due to primacy or recency effects.

The Size of the Discrepancy. Suppose you are talking to an audience that strongly disagrees with your point of view. Will you be more effective if you present your position in its most extreme form or if you modulate your position by presenting it in such a way that it does not seem terribly different from the audience's position? For example, suppose you believe people should exercise vigorously every day to stay healthy; any physical activity would be helpful, but at least an hour's worth would be preferable. Your audience consists of college professors who seem to believe that turning the pages of a book is sufficient exercise for the average person. Would you change their opinion to a greater extent by arguing people should begin a rigorous daily program of running, swimming, and calisthenics or by suggesting a briefer, less taxing regimen? In short, what is the most effective level of discrepancy between the opinion of the audience and the recommendation of the communicator? This is a vital issue for any propagandist or educator.

Let us look at this situation from the audience's point of view. As I mentioned in Chapter 2, most of us have a strong desire to be correct—to have "the right" opinions and to perform reasonable actions. When someone comes along and disagrees with us, it makes us feel uncomfortable because it suggests our opinions or actions may be wrong or based on misinformation. The greater the disagreement, the greater our discomfort. How can we reduce this discomfort? Simply by changing our opinions or actions. The greater the disagreement, the greater our opinion change will be. This line of reasoning, then, would suggest the communicator should argue for the daily program of rigorous exercise; the greater the discrepancy, the more opinion changes: Indeed, several investigators have found that this "linear" relation holds true. A good example of this relation was provided by an experiment by Philip Zimbardo.[30] Each of the college women recruited as subjects for the experiment was asked to bring a close friend with her to the laboratory. Each pair of friends was presented with a case study of juvenile delinquency, and then each of the subjects was asked, separately and in private, to indicate her recommendations on the matter. Each subject was led to believe her close friend disagreed with her—either by a small margin or by an extremely large margin. Zimbardo found that the greater the apparent discrepancy, the more often the subjects changed their opinions toward what they supposed were the opinions of their friends.

However, a careful look at the research literature also turns up several experiments that belie the line of reasoning presented above. For example, Carl Hovland, O. J. Harvey, and Muzafer Sherif[31] argued that, if a particular communication differs considerably from a person's own position, it is, in effect, outside of one's "latitude of acceptance," and the individual will *not* be much influenced by it. They conducted an experiment and found a *curvilinear* relation between discrepancy and opinion change. By "curvilinear," I mean that, as a small discrepancy increased somewhat, so did the degree of opinion change; but as the discrepancy continued to increase, opinion change began to slacken; and finally, as the discrepancy became large, the amount of opinion change became very small. When the discrepancy was very large, almost no opinion change was observed.

Let's take a closer look at this experiment. The communication was based on a red-hot issue—one the subjects felt strongly about: whether their state should remain "dry" or "go wet"—that is, whether or not to change the law prohibiting the distribution and sale of alcoholic beverages. The voters of the state were virtually equally divided on this issue, and the subjects were a representative sample: Some of them felt strongly that the state should remain dry, others felt strongly it should go wet, and the rest took a moderate position. The subjects were divided into groups of people reflecting all three positions. The members of each group were presented with communications supporting one of the three opinions, so that, in each group, there were subjects who found the communication close to their own position, some who found it moderately discrepant from their own position, and some who found it extremely discrepant from their own position. Specifically, some groups were presented with a "wet" message, which argued for the unlimited and unrestricted sale of liquor; some groups were presented with a "dry" message, which argued for complete prohibition; and some groups with a moderately "wet" message, which argued to allow some drinking but with certain controls and restrictions. The greatest opinion changes occurred when there was a *moderate* discrepancy between the actual message and the opinions of individual members of the groups.

What an exciting state of affairs! When there exists a substantial number of research findings pointing in one direction and a similarly substantial number of research findings pointing in a different direction, it doesn't necessarily mean someone has to be wrong; rather, it suggests that there is a significant factor that hasn't been accounted for—and this is indeed exciting, for it gives the scientist an opportunity to play detective. I beg the reader's indulgence here, for I would like to dwell on this issue—not only for its substantive value, but also because it provides us with an opportunity to analyze one of the more adventurous aspects of social psychology as a science. Basically, there are two ways of proceeding with this game of detective. We can begin by assembling all the experiments that show one result and all those that show the other result and (imaginary magnifying glass in hand) painstakingly scrutinize them, looking for the one factor common to the experiments in group A and lacking in group B; then we can try to determine, *conceptually*, why this factor should make a difference. Or, conversely, we can begin by speculating conceptually about what factor or factors might make a difference and then glance through the existing literature, with this conceptual lantern in hand, to see if the experiments in group A differ from the experiments in group B on this dimension.

As a scientist, my personal preference is for the second mode. Accordingly, with two of my students—Judith Turner and J. Merrill Carlsmith—I began to speculate about what factor or factors might make such a difference. We began by accepting the notion discussed above: The greater the discrepancy, the greater the discomfort for the members of the audience. But we reasoned that this does not necessarily mean the members of an audience will change their opinion. There are at least four ways in which the members of an audience can reduce their discomfort: (1) they can change their opinion; (2) they can induce *the communicator* to change his or her opinion; (3) they can seek support for their original opinion by finding other people who share their views, in spite of what the communicator says; or (4) they can derogate the communicator—convince themselves the communicator is stupid or immoral—and thereby invalidate that person's opinion.

In a great many communication situations, including those in these experiments, the message is delivered either as a written statement (as a newspaper or magazine article, for example) or by a communicator who is not approachable by the audience (as on television, on the lecture platform, and so on). Also, the subject is often alone or part of an audience whose members have no opportunity to interact with each other. Thus, under these circumstances, it is virtually impossible for the recipients of the communication either to have immediate impact on the communicator's opinion or to seek immediate social support. This leaves the recipients with two major ways of reducing their discomfort—they can change their opinion, or they can derogate the communicator.

Under what circumstances would an individual find it easy or difficult to derogate the communicator? It would be very difficult to derogate a liked and respected personal friend; it would also be difficult to derogate someone who is a highly trustworthy expert on the issue under discussion. But if the communicator's credibility were questionable, it would be difficult *not* to derogate him. Following this line of reasoning, we suggested that, if a communicator's credibility were high, the greater the discrepancy between the communicator's opinions and the audience' opinions, the greater the influence exerted on the opinions of the audience. However, if the communicator's credibility were not very high, he would be, by definition, subject to derogation. This is not to say he couldn't influence the opinions of the audience. He would probably be able to influence people to change their opinions, if his opinions were not too different from theirs. But the more discrepant such a communicator's position is from those of his audience, the more the audience might begin to question his wisdom, intelligence, and sanity. And the more they question his wisdom, intelligence, and sanity, the less likely they are to be influenced.

Let's return to our example involving physical exercise: Imagine a 73-year-old man, with the body of a man half his age, who had just won the Boston Marathon. If he told me that a good way to stay in condition and live a long healthy life was to exercise vigorously for at least two hours every day, I would believe him. Boy, would I believe him! He would get much more exercise out of me than if he suggested I should exercise for only ten minutes a day. But suppose a person somewhat less credible, such as a high school track coach, were delivering the communication. If he suggested I exercise ten minutes a day, his suggestion would be within my own latitude of acceptance, and he might influence my opinion and behavior. But if he advised me to embark on a program of vigorous exercise requiring two hours every day, I would be inclined to write him off as a quack, a health freak, a monomaniac—and I could comfortably continue being indolent. Thus, I would agree with Hovland, Harvey, and Sherif: People will consider an extremely discrepant communication to be outside their latitude of acceptance—but only if the communicator is not highly credible.

Armed with these speculations, my students and I scrutinized the existing experiments on this issue, paying special attention to the ways in which the communicator was described. Lo and behold, we discovered that each of the experiments showing a direct linear relation between discrepancy and opinion change happened to describe the source of the communication as more credible than did those whose results showed a curvilinear relation. This confirmed our speculations about the role of credibility. But we didn't stop there: We constructed an experiment in which we systematically investigated the size of the discrepancy and the credibility of the communicator in one research design.[32] In this experiment, college women were asked to read several stanzas from obscure modern poetry and to rank them in terms of how good they were. Then each woman was given an essay to read purporting to be a criticism of modern poetry that specifically mentioned a stanza she had rated poorly. For some subjects, the essayist described this particular stanza in glowing terms—this created a large discrepancy between the opinion of the communicator and the opinion voiced by the students in this experimental condition. For some subjects, the essayist was only mildly favorable in the way he described the stanza—this set up a moderate discrepancy between the essayist and the students in this condition. In a third condition, the essayist was mildly scornful in his treatment of the stanza—which placed the recipients of this communication in a "mild-discrepancy" situation. Finally, to one-half of the women in the experiment, the writer of the essay was identified as the poet T. S. Eliot, a highly credible poetry critic; to the rest of the subjects, the essay writer was identified as a college student. The subjects were subsequently allowed to rank the stanzas once again. When T. S. Eliot was ostensibly the communicator, the essay had the most influence on the students when its evaluation of the stanza was most discrepant from theirs; when a fellow student of medium credibility was identified as the essayist, the essay produced a little opinion change when it was slightly discrepant from the opinion of the students, a great deal of change when it was moderately discrepant, and only a little opinion change when it was extremely discrepant.

To sum up this section, the conflicting results are accounted for: When a communicator has high credibility, the greater the discrepancy between the view he or she advocates and the view of the audience, the more the audience will be persuaded; on the other hand, when a communicator's credibility is doubtful or slim, he or she will produce maximum opinion change at moderate discrepancies.

Characteristics of the Audience

All listeners, readers, or viewers are not alike. Some people are more difficult to persuade. In addition, as we have seen, the kind of communication that appeals to one person may not appeal to another. For example, recall that the intelligence of the audience and their prior opinions will play major roles in determining whether a two-sided communication will be more effective than a one-sided communication.

Self-Esteem. What effect does an individual's personality have on his or her persuasibility? The one personality variable most consistently related to persuasibility is self-esteem. Individuals who feel inadequate are more easily influenced by a persuasive communication than individuals who think highly of themselves.[33] This seems reasonable enough; after all, if people don't like themselves, then it follows they don't place a very high premium on their own ideas. Consequently, if their ideas are challenged, they may be willing to give them up. Recall that people want to be right. If Sam, who has high self-esteem, listens to a communication at variance with his own opinion, he must make up his mind whether he stands a better chance of being right if he changes his opinion or if he stands pat. A person with high self-esteem may experience some conflict when he finds himself in disagreement with a highly credible communicator. He might resolve this conflict by changing his opinion, or he might remain firm. But if Sam had low self-esteem, there would be little or no conflict—because he doesn't think very highly of himself, he probably believes that he stands a better chance of being right if he goes along with the communicator.

Prior Experience of the Audience. Another audience-related factor of considerable importance is the frame of mind the audience is in just prior to the communication. An audience can be made receptive to a communication if it has been well fed and is relaxed and happy. Indeed, as Irving Janis and his associates have discovered, people who have been allowed to eat desirable food while reading a persuasive communication are more influenced by what they read than are people in a control (noneating) group.[34]

Conversely, members of an audience can be made less receptive and less persuadable. As we noted, people *predict* they will be able to resist persuasive communications such as TV commercials. One way of decreasing their persuasibility is by forewarning the individuals that an attempt is going to be made to persuade them.[35] This is especially true if the content of the message differs from their own beliefs. I would argue that the phrase, "And now, a message from our sponsor" renders that message less persuasive than it would have been if the communicator had simply glided into it without prologue. The forewarning seems to say "Watch out, I'm going to try to persuade you" and people tend to respond by marshalling defenses against the message. This phenomenon was demonstrated in an experiment by Jonathan Freedman and David Sears.[36] Teenagers were told they would be hearing a talk entitled "Why Teenagers Should Not Be Allowed To Drive." Ten minutes later, the speaker presented them with a prepared communication. In a control condition, the same talk was given without the ten-minute forewarning. The subjects in the control condition were more thoroughly convinced by the communication than were those who had been forewarned.

People tend to protect their sense of freedom. According to Jack Brehm's theory of *reactance*,[37] when our sense of freedom is threatened, we attempt to restore it. For example, I like to receive birthday presents. But if a borderline student (in danger of flunking my course) presented me with an expensive birthday present just as I was about to read term papers, I would feel uncomfortable. My sense of freedom or autonomy had been challenged. Similarly, persuasive communications, if blatant or coercive, can be perceived as intruding upon one's freedom of choice, activiating a person's defenses to resist the messages. For example, if an aggressive salesperson tells me I *must* buy something, my first reaction is to reassert my independence by leaving the store. Suppose that, as I walk down the street, I am asked (in a much gentler manner) to sign a petition. I don't know much about the issue, and, as it is being explained to me, another person accosts us and begins to pressure me not to sign. Reactance theory predicts that, to counteract this pressure and reassert my freedom of choice, I would be more likely to sign. This scenario was actually staged by Madeline Heilman,[38] and the results confirmed her production that, under most circumstances, the more intense the attempts to prevent subjects from signing, the more likely they were to sign the petitions. Of course, as we have seen in this chapter and the preceding one, people *can be* and *are* influenced and do comply to implicit social pressures, as in the Asch experiment. But when that pressure is so blatant that it threatens one's feelings of freedom, people not only resist it, but they tend to react in the opposite direction.

There is still another aspect of this need for freedom and autonomy that should be mentioned. All other things being equal, when faced with information that runs counter to important beliefs, people have a tendency, whenever feasible, to invent counterarguments on the spot.[39] In this way, they are able to prevent their opinions from being unduly influenced and protect their sense of autonomy. But it is possible to overcome some of this resistance. Leon Festinger and Nathan Maccoby[40] conducted an experiment in which they attempted to prevent members of their audience from inventing arguments in refutation of the message being presented to them. This was accomplished by simply distracting the audience somewhat while the communication was being presented. Two groups of students who belonged to a college fraternity were required to listen to a tape-recorded argument about the evils of college fraternities. The argument was erudite, powerful, and, as you might imagine, widely discrepant from the beliefs of the audience. During the presentation of the communication, one of the groups was distracted. Specifically, they were shown a highly entertaining silent film. Festinger and Maccoby reasoned that, because this group was engaged in two tasks simultaneously—listening to the tape-recorded argument against fraternities and watching an entertaining film—their minds would be so occupied they would have little or no opportunity to think up arguments in refutation of the tape-recorded message. The members of the control group, on the other hand, were not distracted by a film; therefore, they would be better able to devote some of their thoughts to resisting the communication by thinking up counterarguments. The results of the experiment confirmed this reasoning. The students who were distracted by watching the film underwent substantially more opinion change against fraternities than did the students who were not distracted.

How many of us have been distracted by a movie during an important persuasive appeal? Not many, I bet. But most of us are familiar with another form of distraction—political heckling. Lloyd Sloan, Robert Love, and Thomas Ostrom[41] examined the effect of heckling on the attitudes of an audience toward a political speaker. Specifically, they measured subjects' attitudes toward Senator Edmund Muskie before having the subjects view a videotaped presentation of Muskie's 1970 election eve broadcast. During the presentation, confederates vocally attacked Muskie and his views. After the broadcast, the subjects' opinions of Muskie were measured again. For those subjects who were initially neutral in their feelings toward Muskie, the presence of hecklers produced opposition to the speaker; for those subjects with initially extreme opinions (either positive or negative), heckling produced a change toward neutrality. Thus, the effects of distraction seem to depend on a person's initial opinion and, contrary to popular belief, heckling may actually cause those who are most persuasible (that is, the undecideds) to evaluate a speaker's message more negatively.

Let us take a closer look at the other side of the issue. How can we help people to resist attempts to influence them? An elaborate method for inducing such resistance has been developed by William McGuire and his associates. This method has been appropriately dubbed the *inoculation effect*. We have already seen that a two-sided (refutational) presentation is more effective for convincing most audiences than a one-sided presentation. Expanding on this phenomenon, McGuire suggested that, if people receive prior exposure to a brief communication they are then able to refute, they tend to be "immunized" against a subsequent full-blown presentation of the same argument, in much the same way a small amount of an attenuated virus immunizes people against a full-blown attack by that virus. In an experiment by William McGuire and Dimitri Papageorgis,[42] a group of people stated their opinions; these opinions were then subjected to a mild attack—and the attack was refuted. These people were subsequently subjected to a *powerful* argument against their initial opinions. Members of this group showed a much smaller tendency to change their opinions than did the members of a control group whose opinions had not been previously subjected to the mild attack. In effect, they had been inoculated against opinion change and made relatively immune. Thus, not only is it often more effective as a propaganda technique to use a two-sided refutational presentation, but, if it is used skillfully, such a presentation tends to increase the audience's resistance to subsequent counterpropaganda.

In an exciting field experiment, Alfred McAlister[43] inoculated seventh-grade students against existing peer pressures to smoke cigarettes. For example, the students were shown advertisements inplying that truly liberated women are smokers—"You've come a long way, baby!" They were then inoculated by being taught that a woman couldn't possibly be liberated if she was hooked on tobacco. Similarly, since teenagers tend to smoke because it seems virile (like the Marlboro man), McAlister felt that peer pressure might take the form of being called "chicken" if one didn't smoke. Accordingly, the seventh-graders role-played a situation in which they practiced countering that argument by saying something like "I'd be a real chicken if I smoked just to impress you." This inoculation against peer pressure proved to be very effective. By the time the students were in the ninth grade, they were half as likely to smoke as those in a control group from a similar junior high school.

Recent research[44] has found that, in producing resistance, inoculation is most effective when the belief under attack is a cultural truism. A cultural truism is a belief accepted as unquestionably true by most members of a society, like "The United States is the best country in the world to live in" or "If people are willing to work hard, they can succeed." Cultural truisms are rarely called into question; when they are not, it is relatively easy for us to lose sight of why we hold them. Thus, if subjected to a severe attack, such beliefs may crumble. To motivate us to bolster our beliefs, we must be made aware of their vulnerability, and the best way to do this is to attack those beliefs mildly. Prior exposure, in the form of a watered-down attack on people's beliefs, produces resistance to later persuasion because (1) we become motivated to defend our beliefs and (2) we gain some practice in doing so. We are then better equipped to resist a more serious attack.

This is an important point frequently ignored or misunderstood by policymakers. For example, in the aftermath of the Korean War, when several of our prisoners of war were supposedly brainwashed by the Chinese Communists, a Senate committee recommended that, in order to build resistance among the people to brainwashing and other forms of Communist propaganda, courses on "patriotism and Americanism" should be instituted in our public school system. But William McGuire's results suggest that the best way to help our soldiers resist anti-American propaganda would be to challenge their belief in the American way of life, and the best way to build resistance to pro-Communist propaganda would be to teach courses on Communism, presenting both sides of the argument. If such an idea had been proposed in the 1950s, when the cold war was in full swing and Senator Joseph McCarthy was conducting his witch hunt, this idea would probably have been considered to be part of the Communist conspiracy. It is hoped the day of the ostrich is over; we cannot resist propaganda by burying our heads in the sand. The easiest person to brainwash is the person whose beliefs are based on slogans that have never been seriously challenged.

How Well Do the Principles Work?

Suppose you inherited controlling interest in a television network. Here is a golden opportunity to influence people's opinions on important issues. Let's say you are an enthusiastic proponent of national health insurance, and you would like to persuade others to agree with you. Having just finished reading this chapter, you know how to do it, and you are in control of a very powerful medium of communication. How do you set about doing it? That's simple: You choose a time slot following a highly intellectual program (in order to be certain that intelligent people are watching) and, accordingly, you present a two-sided argument (because two-sided arguments work best on intelligent people). You arrange your arguments in such a manner that the argument in favor of national health insurance is stronger and appears first (in order to take advantage of the primacy effect). You describe the plight of the poor, how they get sick and die for lack of affordable medical care. You use vivid personal examples of people you know. You discuss these events in a manner that inspires a great deal of fear; at the same time, you offer a specific plan of action, because this combination produces the most opinion change and the most action in the most people. You present some of the arguments against your position and offer strong refutation of these arguments. You arrange for the speaker to be expert, trustworthy, and extremely likable. You make your argument as strongly as you can, in order to maximize the discrepancy between the argument presented and the initial attitude of the audience. And then you sit back, relax, and wait for those opinions to start changing.

It's not that simple. Imagine a typical viewer: Let's say she is a 45-year-old middle-class real estate broker who believes that the government interferes too much in the private lives of individuals. She feels any form of social legislation undermines the spirit of individuality which is the essence of democracy. She comes across your program while looking for an evening's entertainment. She begins to hear your arguments in favor of free health care. As she listens, she becomes slightly less confident in her original convictions. She is not quite as certain as she had been that the government shouldn't intervene in matters of health. What does she do? If she is anything like the subjects in Lance Canon's[45] experiment, she would reach over, turn the dial on her television set, and begin to watch "LaVerne and Shirley." Canon found that, as one's confidence is weakened, a person becomes less prone to listen to arguments against his or her beliefs. Thus, the very people you most want to convince and whose opinions might be the most susceptible to being changed are the ones *least* likely to continue to expose themselves to a communication designed for that purpose.

Must you resign yourself to broadcasting your message to an audience composed of viewers who already support national health insurance? That may be so—if you insist on airing a serious documentary devoted to the issue. After considering your alternatives, however, you might decide to take another approach. You call a meeting of your network executives. The programming director is instructed to commission a couple of scripts dramatizing the plight of families facing financial ruin due to costs associated with serious illness. You order the news department to investigate the success of national health insurance in other countries. Finally, you provide the late-night talk show host with a couple of jokes he might tell about his inept but affluent doctor. While none of these communications would match the documentary in terms of the information provided, their cumulative impact could be more significant. Embedded in dramas or news segments, they would not necessarily come labeled as arguments supporting national health insurance; they seem innocuous, but their message is clear. Not appearing to be explicit attempts at persuasion, they should arouse little resistance, avoiding an inoculation effect and inhibiting the formation of counterarguments by distracting the audience. Most importantly, people will probably *see* them without switching channels.

I do not mean to imply that television executives conspire to disguise persuasive communications within other contexts, but, as I stated near the beginning of this chapter, television plays a major role in shaping how we perceive the world. The sheer volume of television children see is staggering. The average child under 12 watches upward of 26 hours per week,[46] and the average high school graduate has spent much less time in the classroom than in front of the TV.[47] Children come to *care* about television to an extent that seems bizarre. Three examples will suffice to illustrate our point. A University of Nebraska survey asked 15,000 children which they would want more—a father or a television set. Half of the children said they preferred to have the television. A 15-year-old boy recently committed suicide, leaving behind a note that blamed the cancellation of his favorite television series for his death. Another youngster killed himself after his father took his TV set away. The 13-year-old's suicide note said "I can't stand another day . . . without television . . . In my heart I will take my TV with me."[48]

The medium has impact, and the view of reality it transmits seldom remains value-free. As an illustration of the implicit values propagated by the television medium, consider the manner in which men and women are portrayed. An analysis of almost 200 television commercials[49] found that not only were more men shown, but their roles differed from those of women. Men were depicted as authority figures and experts who sought advancement; women were seen as willing users of products and as individuals seeking approval. This stereotyping extends to our earliest educational materials. For example, Lenore Weitzman and her colleagues[50] examined picture books for preschool children and discovered females were greatly underrepresented in the titles, main roles, and illustrations; where they did appear, they were passive and servile. Boys could aspire to a number of occupations, but adult women were pictured only as wives and mothers.

George Gerbner and his associates[51] have conducted the most extensive analysis of television yet. Between 1967 and 1981, these researchers videotaped and analyzed more than 1600 prime-time television programs and 19,000 characters. Their findings, taken as a whole, suggest that television's representation of reality is grossly inaccurate and misleading. In prime-time programming, males outnumber females by three to one; women are rarely shown working outside of the home, even though over 50 percent do in real life. Nonwhites (especially Hispanics), young children, and the elderly are underrepresented; blacks are often cast in subservient, supporting roles. Although 60 percent of the work force in the United States is employed in a blue-collar or service job, only six to ten percent of TV characters hold such jobs. Finally over half of TV's prime-time characters are involved in a violent confrontation each week; in real life, the actual figure is less than one percent. David Rintels, a television writer and former president of the Writers Guild of America, summed it up best when he said, "From 8 to 11 o'clock each night, television is one long lie."[52]

Gerbner and his associates have also compared the attitudes and beliefs of heavy viewers (those who watch more than four hours a day) and light viewers (those who watch less than two hours a day). They found that heavy viewers (1) express more racially prejudiced attitudes; (2) overestimate the number of people employed as physicians, lawyers, and athletes; (3) eat more, drink more, and exercise less; (4) are more fearful of being victimized by crime; and (5) believe old people are less healthy today than they were 20 years ago (the opposite is true). Gerbner concludes that these attitudes and beliefs stem from the inaccurate portrayals of American life provided to us by television.*

Of course, each of us has had extensive personal contact with many people in a myriad of social contexts; the media are just one source of our knowledge about the sexes and different ethnic or occupational groups. The information and impressions we receive through the media are probably less influential when we also can rely on firsthand experience. Thus, those of us who have been in close contact with several women in jobs outside of the home are probably less susceptible to the stereotype of

*It should be noted that Gerbner's research is *correlational*, not experimental. It is conceivable that prejudiced attitudes and inaccurate beliefs stem from being poor and undereducated, and that these people tend to watch more television—not the other way around, as Gerbner suggests. In defense of Gerbner, though, he sampled viewers from all age, education, income, and ethnic groups. The relationship between heavy viewing and inaccurate beliefs occurred in *every* category.

women portrayed on television. On the other hand, while each of us has formed conceptions about crime and violence, it is unlikely that many of those opinions developed from our personal experience. Television is virtually our only vivid source of information about crime. Crime shows comprise a major portion of television programming—the average 15-year-old has viewed over 13,000 TV killings. In a penetrating analysis of "television criminology," Craig Haney and John Manzolati[53] point out that crime shows dispense remarkably consistent images of both the police and criminals. For example, they found that television policemen are amazingly effective, solving almost every crime, and are infallible in one regard: The wrong person was *never* in jail at the end of a show. Television fosters an illusion of certainty in crimefighting. Television criminals generally turn to crime because of psychopathology or insatiable (and unnecessary) greed. Television emphasizes criminals' personal responsibility for their actions, and largely ignores situational pressures correlated with crime, such as poverty and unemployment. Haney and Manzolati go on to demonstrate that this portrayal has important social consequences. People who watch a lot of television come to adopt this belief system, which affects their expectations and can cause them to take a hardline stance when serving on juries. Heavy viewers are likely to reverse the presumption of innocence, believing "defendants must be guilty of *something*, otherwise they wouldn't be brought to trial."

It has also been shown that the incidence of larceny (theft) increases when television is introduced into an area.[54] Why should this be the case? The most reasonable explanation is that television promotes the consumption of goods through advertisements; it also depicts upper-class and middle-class lifestyles as the norm. This illusion of widespread wealth and consumption may frustrate and anger deprived viewers who compare their lifestyles with those portrayed on television, thereby motivating them to "share in the American dream" any way they can.

It is nearly impossible to specify the precise extent to which exposure to the media influences public opinion and behavior. Too many other factors are involved. Because the research described above is not *experimental*, it is difficult to separate the effects of mass communications from the impact of personal experiences and contact with family and friends. But experiments can be done. For example, let's suppose that, as the network executive, you went ahead with your original plan to televise the documentary on national health care. In this instance, it would be relatively easy for you to determine whether your message was persuasive. At the most basic level, both before and after the telecast you could poll cross-sections of viewers about their opinions concerning national health insurance. If they changed in a favorable direction, you might conclude your program was effective. If you were interested in maximizing its effectiveness, you might tape several versions of the documentary to test different speakers, arguments, and styles of presentation. If you presented these versions to various test audiences, you could compare the effects of different combinations of factors. Indeed, this scenario approximates the way most of the research described earlier in this chapter was carried out. Communications about a variety of topics were prepared. Certain aspects were manipulated—the credibility of the speakers, for example, or the order of the arguments—and the resulting versions of the message were presented to audiences. By polling audience opinion, the effects of the variables can be measured. This procedure allows great control over the message and is well-suited for testing large numbers of subjects. This method is so efficient, in fact, that it has been adapted to a computer-controlled procedure for varying certain factors surrounding the messages and presenting them to people seated at computer consoles.[55] With the advent of cable television networks with the technological capability for home viewers to communicate back to the station, such as the QUBE-TV system, it is now possible to instantaneously sample the responses of thousands of viewers to actual presentations.

Suppose that, instead of deciding to televise the documentary, you opted to broadcast the series of more subtle messages disguised within the regular programs and presented repeatedly. It would be much more difficult to measure and assess the impact of this approach, but it probably is more common. Rarely are we presented with explicit persuasive messages in favor of a given position immediately prior to deciding on an issue, except perhaps during political campaigns. Most of our beliefs develop more gradually, through repeated contacts with people and information over an extended period of time. In general, beliefs people hold important are difficult to change through direct communication. There appears to be a basic difference between an issue like national health insurance, on the one hand, and issues like the feasibility of atomic-powered submarines, whether antihistamines should be sold without a prescription, and the practical importance of arithmetic, on the other. What is the difference? One difference is that the medical-care issue is more important. Who cares about the feasibility of atomic-powered submarines, anyway? It is a trivial issue. But what is the criterion for judging whether an issue is important or trivial?

To provide an answer to this question, we must first examine what we mean by the term *opinion*, which we have been using throughout this chapter. On the simplest level, an opinion is what a person believes to be factually true. Thus, it is my opinion that there are fewer than 9000 students enrolled at the University of California at Santa Cruz, that wearing seat belts reduces traffic fatalities, and that New York City is hot in the summer. Such opinions are primarily cognitive—that is, they take place in the head rather than in the gut. They are also transient—that is, they can be changed by good, clear evidence to the contrary. Thus, if consumer advocate Ralph Nader (whom I regard as a highly credible source on the traffic issue) presented me with data indicating that seat belts, as they are currently constructed, do not reduce fatalities significantly, I would change my opinion on that issue.

On the other hand, suppose a person holds the opinion that Jews engage in "sharp" business practices, or that Asians are sneaky, or that people under twenty-five have a special wisdom, or that the United States of America is the greatest (or most awful) country in the history of the world, or that New York City is a jungle. How do these opinions differ from the ones stated in the preceding paragraph? They tend to be both emotional and evaluative—that is, they imply likes or dislikes. Believing Asians are sneaky implies that the person doesn't like Asians. The opinion that New York City is a jungle is different from the opinion that New York City is hot in the summer. The opinion that New York City is a jungle is not simply cognitive—it carries with it a negative evaluation and some degree of fear or anxiety. An opinion that includes an evaluative and an emotional component is called an *attitude*. Compared to opinions, attitudes are extremely difficult to change.

Suppose Sam is an ardent liberal and humanist who swears by Ralph Nader. Accordingly, Sam is influenced by everything Nader uncovers about cars, safety, government abuse, the military-industrial complex, and so on. But suppose, for example, Nader conducted an exhaustive study indicating that, in terms of intelligence, blacks were genetically inferior to whites. Would this be likely to affect Sam's opinion? Because the issue is rooted in an emotional complex, it is likely that such a statement by Nader would not influence Sam as easily or as thoroughly as a statement by Nader about cars, sealing wax, cabbages, or kings. We tend to resist having our attitudes changed; thus, direct communications that challenge existing attitudes tend to be less influential. To change attitudes, it is essential first to understand what motivates this resistance. Why do we distort messages that differ from our deeply felt attitudes? Why do we invent counterarguments? Why is it important for us to avoid changing our attitudes? These are important and complex questions, and I will attempt to answer them in the next chapter.

4

Self-Justification

Picture the following scene: A young man named Sam is being hypnotized. The hypnotist places him under a posthypnotic suggestion and tells him that, when the clock strikes four, he will (1) go to the closet, get his raincoat and galoshes, and put them on; (2) grab an umbrella; (3) walk eight blocks to the supermarket and purchase six bottles of bourbon; and (4) return home. Sam is told that, as soon as he reenters his apartment, he will "snap out of it" and be himself again.

When the clock strikes four, Sam immediately heads for the closet, dons his raincoat and galoshes, grabs his umbrella, and trudges out the door on his quest for bourbon. There are a few strange things about this errand: (1) it is a clear, sunshiny day—there isn't a cloud in the sky; (2) there is a liquor store half a block away that sells bourbon for the same price as the supermarket eight blocks away; and (3) Sam doesn't drink.

Sam arrives home, opens the door, reenters his apartment,

snaps out of his "trance," and discovers himself standing there in his raincoat and galoshes, with his umbrella in one hand and a huge sack of liquor bottles in the other. He looks momentarily confused. His friend, the hypnotist, says,

"Hey, Sam, where have you been?"

"Oh, just down to the store."

"What did you buy?"

"Um . . . um . . . it seems I bought this bourbon."

"But you don't drink, do you?"

"No, but . . . um . . . um . . . I'm going to do a lot of entertaining during the next few weeks, and some of my friends do."

"How come you're wearing all that rain gear on such a sunny day?"

"Well . . . actually, the weather is quite changeable this time of year, and I didn't want to take any chances."

"But there isn't a cloud in the sky."

"Well, you never can tell."

"By the way, where did you buy the liquor?"

"Oh, heh,heh. Well, um . . . down at the supermarket."

"How come you went that far?"

"Well, um . . . um . . . it was such a nice day, I thought it might be fun to take a long walk."

Most people are motivated to justify their own actions, beliefs, and feelings. When a person does something, he or she will try, if at all possible, to convince himself or herself (and others) that it was a logical, reasonable thing to do. There *was* a good reason why Sam performed those silly actions—he was hypnotized. But, because Sam didn't know he had been hypnotized, and because it was apparently difficult for him to accept the fact that he was capable of behaving in a totally nonsensical manner, he went to great lengths to convince himself (and his friend) that there was a method to his madness and that his actions were actually quite sensible.

The experiment by Stanley Schachter and Jerry Singer discussed in Chapter 2 (pp. 29–30) can also be understood in these terms. Recall that these investigators injected people with epinephrine. Those who were forewarned about the symptoms caused by this drug (palpitations of the heart, sweaty palms, and hand tremors) had a sensible explanation for the symptoms when they appeared. "Oh, yeah, that's just the drug affecting me." Those who were misled about the aftereffects of the drug, however, had no such handy, logical explanation for their symptoms. But they couldn't leave the symptoms unjustified—they tried to account for them by convincing themselves they were either deliriously happy or angry, depending on the social stimuli in the environment.

The concept of self-justification can be applied more broadly still. Suppose you are in the midst of a great natural disaster, such as an earthquake. All around you buildings are toppling and people are getting killed and injured. Needless to say, you are frightened. Is there any need to seek justification for this fear? Certainly not, the evidence is all around you; the injured people and the devastated buildings are ample justifications for your fear. But suppose, instead, the earthquake occurred in a neighboring town. You can feel the tremors, and you hear stories of the damage done to the other town. You are terribly frightened, but you are not in the midst of the devastated area; neither you nor the people around you have been hurt, and no buildings in your town have been damaged. Would you need to justify this fear? Yes. Much like the people in the Schachter-Singer experiment experiencing strong physical reactions to epinephrine but not knowing why, and much like our hypnotized friend in the raincoat and galoshes, you would be inclined to justify your own actions or feelings. In this situation, you see nothing to be afraid of in the immediate vicinity, so you would be inclined to seek justifications for the fact that you are scared out of your wits. These disaster situations are not hypothetical examples—they actually occurred several years ago in India. In the aftermath of an earthquake, investigators collected and analyzed the rumors being spread. What they discovered was rather startling: Jamuna Prasad,[1] an Indian psychologist, found that, when the disaster occurred in a neighboring town such that the residents of the village in question could feel the tremors but were not in impending danger, there was an abundance of rumors forecasting impending doom. Specifically, the residents of this village believed and helped spread rumors to the effect that (1) a flood was rushing toward them; (2) February 26 would be a day of deluge and destruction; (3) there would be another severe earthquake on the day of the lunar eclipse; (4) there would be a cyclone within a few days; and (5) unforeseeable calamities were on the horizon.

Why in the world would people invent, believe, and communicate such stories? Were these people masochists? Were they paranoid? Certainly, these rumors would not encourage the people to feel calm and secure. One rather compelling explanation is that the people were terribly frightened and, because there was not ample justification for this fear, they invented their own justification. Thus, they were not compelled to feel foolish. After all, if a cyclone is on the way, isn't it perfectly reasonable that I should be wild-eyed with fear? This explanation is bolstered by Durganand Sinha's study of rumors.[2] Sinha investigated the rumors being spread in an Indian village following a disaster of similar magnitude. The major difference between the situation in Prasad's study and the one in Sinha's study was that the people being investigated by Sinha had actually suffered the destruction and witnessed the damage. They were scared, but they had good reasons to be frightened—they had no need to seek additional justification for their fears. Thus, their rumors contained no prediction of impending disaster and no serious exaggeration. Indeed, if anything, the rumors were comforting. For example, one rumor predicted (falsely) that the water supply would be restored in a very short time.

The kind of process we have been discussing here has been encapsulated into a theory of human cognition and motivation by Leon Festinger.[3] Called the theory of *cognitive dissonance,* it is, as theories go, remarkably simple; but—as we shall see—the range of its application is enormous. First, we will discuss the formal aspects of the theory, and then we will discuss its ramifications. Basically, cognitive dissonance is a state of tension that occurs whenever an individual simultaneously holds two cognitions (ideas, attitudes, beliefs, opinions) that are psychologically inconsistent. Stated differently, two cognitions are dissonant if, considering these two cognitions alone, the opposite of one follows from the other. Because the occurrence of cognitive dissonance is unpleasant, people are motivated to reduce it; this is roughly analogous to the processes involved in the induction and reduction of such drives as hunger or thirst—except that, here, the driving force arises from cognitive discomfort rather than physiological needs. To hold two ideas that contradict each other is to flirt with absurdity, and—as Albert Camus, the existentialist philosopher, has observed—humans are creatures who spend their lives trying to convince themselves that their existence is not absurd.

How do we convince ourselves that our lives are not absurd—that is, how do we reduce cognitive dissonance? By changing one or both cognitions in such a way so as to render them more compatible (more consonant) with each other, or by adding more cognitions that help bridge the gap between the original cognitions. Let me cite an example, that is, alas, all too familiar to many people. Suppose a person smokes cigarettes and then reads a report of the medical evidence linking cigarette smoking to lung cancer and other respiratory diseases. The smoker experiences dissonance. The cognition "I smoke cigarettes" is dissonant with the cognition "cigarette smoking produces cancer." Clearly, the most efficient way for a person to reduce dissonance in such a situation is to give up smoking. The cognition "cigarette smoking produces cancer" is *consonant* with the cognition "I do not smoke." But, for most people, it is not easy to give up smoking. Imagine Sally, a young woman who tried to stop smoking but failed. What does she do to reduce dissonance? In all probability, she will try to work on the other cognition: "Cigarette smoking produces cancer." Sally might attempt to make light of evidence linking cigarette smoking to cancer. For example, she might try to convince herself that the experimental evidence is inconclusive. In addition, she might seek out intelligent people who smoke and, by so doing, reason that if Debbie, Nicole, and Larry smoke, it can't be all that dangerous. Sally might switch to a filter-tipped brand and delude herself into believing that the filter traps the cancer-producing materials. Finally, she might add cognitions that are consonant with smoking in an attempt to make the behavior less absurd in spite of its danger. Thus, Sally might enhance the value placed on smoking; that is, she might come to believe smoking is an important and highly enjoyable activity that is essential for relaxation: "I may lead a shorter life, but it will be a more enjoyable one." Similarly, she might actually try to make a virtue out of smoking by developing a romantic devil-may-care self-image, flouting danger by smoking cigarettes. All such behavior reduces dissonance by reducing the absurdity of the notion of going out of one's way to contract cancer. Sally has justified her behavior by cognitively minimizing the danger or by exaggerating the importance of the action. In effect, she has succeeded either in constructing a new attitude or in changing an existing attitude.

Indeed, shortly after the publicity surrounding the original Surgeon General's report in 1964, a survey was conducted[4] to assess people's reactions to the new evidence that smoking helps cause cancer. Nonsmokers overwhelmingly believed the health report, only 10 percent of those queried saying the link between smoking and cancer had not been proven to exist; these respondents had no motivation to disbelieve the report. The smokers faced a more difficult quandary. Smoking *is* a difficult habit to break; only 9 percent of the smokers had been able to quit. To justify continuing the activity, smokers tended to debunk the report. They were more likely to deny the evidence: 40 percent of the heavy smokers said a link had not been proven to exist. They were also more apt to employ rationalizations: Over twice as many smokers as nonsmokers agreed that there were many hazards in life and that both smokers and nonsmokers get cancer.

Smokers who are painfully aware of the health hazards associated with smoking may reduce dissonance in yet another way—by minimizing the extent of their habit. A recent study[5] found that, of 155 smokers who smoked between one and two packs of cigarettes a day, 60 percent considered themselves moderate smokers; the remaining 40 percent considered themselves heavy smokers. How can we explain these different self-perceptions? Not surprisingly, those who labeled themselves as "moderates" were more aware of the pathological, long-term effects of smoking than were those who labeled themselves as heavy smokers. That is, these particular smokers apparently reduced dissonance by convincing themselves that smoking one or two packs a day isn't really all that much. "Moderate" and "heavy" are, after all, subjectives terms.

Imagine a teenage girl who has not yet begun to smoke. After reading the Surgeon General's report, is she apt to believe it? Like most of the nonsmokers in the survey, she should. The evidence is objectively sound, the source is expert and trustworthy, and there is no reason not to believe the report. And this is the crux of the matter. Earlier in this book I made the point that people strive to be right and that values and beliefs become internalized when they appear to be correct. It is this striving to be right that motivates people to pay close attention to what other people are doing and to heed the advice of expert, trustworthy communicators. This is extremely rational behavior. There are forces, however, that can work against this rational behavior. The theory of cognitive dissonance does not picture people as rational beings; rather, it pictures them as rationa*lizing* beings. According to the underlying assumptions of the theory, we humans are motivated not so much to *be* right; rather, we are motivated to *believe* we are right (and wise, and decent, and good). Sometimes, our motivation to be right and our motivation to *believe* we are right are working in the same direction. This is what is happening with the young woman who doesn't smoke and therefore finds it easy to accept the notion that smoking causes lung cancer. This would also be true for a smoker who encounters the evidence linking cigarette smoking to lung cancer and *does* succeed in giving up cigarettes. Occasionally, however, the need to reduce dissonance (the need to convince oneself that one *is* right) leads to behavior that is maladaptive and therefore irrational. For example, psychologists who have helped people give up smoking have reported that people who try to give up smoking and *fail* will come, in time, to develop a less intense attitude toward the dangers of smoking than those who have not yet made a concerted effort to give it up. The key to this apparent paradox is a person's degree of commitment to a particular action. The more a person is committed to an action or belief, the more resistant that person will be to information that threatens the belief, and the more he or she will attempt to bolster the action or belief. If a smoker has tried to quit and has failed, he or she is committed to smoking. Thus, the person becomes less intense in believing smoking is dangerous. By the same token, I would argue that a person who had recently built a magnificent new house smack on the San Andreas fault near San Francisco would be less receptive to arguments predicting an imminent earthquake than would a person who was only renting the house for a few months. The new homeowner is committed and doesn't want to believe that he or she has done an absurd thing.

Let us stay with cigarette smoking for a moment and present an extreme example: Suppose you were the vice-president of a major cigarette company—you are in a situation of maximum commitment to the idea of cigarette smoking. Your job consists of producing, advertising, and selling cigarettes to millions of people. If it is true that cigarette smoking causes cancer, then, in a sense, you are partially responsible for the illness and death of a great many people. This would produce a painful degree of dissonance: Your cognition "I am a decent, kind human being" would be dissonant with your cognition "I am contributing to the early death of a great many people." In order to reduce this dissonance, you must refute the evidence that suggests a causal link between cigarettes and cancer. Moreover, in order to further convince yourelf you are a good, moral person, you might go so far as to demonstrate how much you disbelieve the evidence by smoking a great deal yourself. If your need is great enough, you might even succeed in convincing yourself that cigarettes are good for people. This, in order to convince yourself that you are wise, good, and right, you take action that is stupid and detrimental to your health. This analysis is so fantastic that it's almost beyond belief—*almost*. The following is a verbatim account of the first part of a news item released several years ago by the *Washington Post* News Service:

> Jack Landry pulls what must be his 30th Marlboro of the day out of one of the two packs on his desk, lights a match to it and tells how he doesn't believe all those reports about smoking and cancer and emphysema.
>
> He has just begun to market yet another cigarette for Philip Morris U.S.A. and is brimming with satisfaction over its prospects.
>
> But how does he square with his conscience the spending of $10 million in these United States over the next year to lure people into smoking his new brand?

"It's not a matter of that," says Landry, Philip Morris' vice president for marketing. "Nearly half the adults in this country smoke. It's a basic commodity for them. I'm serving a need."

"There are studies by pretty eminent medical and scientific authorities, one on a theory of stress, on how a heck of a lot of people, if they didn't have cigarette smoking to relieve stress, would be one hell of a lot worse off. And there are plenty of valid studies that indicate cigarette smoking and all those diseases are not related."

His satisfaction, says Landry, comes from being very good at his job in a very competitive business, and he will point out that Philip Morris and its big-selling Marlboro has just passed American Tobacco as the No. 2 cigarette seller in America (R. J. Reynolds is still No. 1).

Why a new cigarette now?

Because it is there to be sold, says Landry.

And therein lies the inspiration of the marketing of a new American cigarette, which Landry confidently predicts will have a 1 percent share of the American market within 12 months. That 1 percent will equal about five billion cigarettes and a healthy profit for Philip Morris U.S.A.[6]

Do you think any amount of rational evidence or argument could induce Mr. Landry to believe cigarette smoking causes cancer? Near the close of the preceding chapter, we discussed the fact that information campaigns are relatively ineffective when they attempt to change deep-seated attitudes. We can now see precisely why information campaigns are of limited effectiveness. If people are committed to an attitude, the information the communicator presents arouses dissonance; frequently, the best way to reduce the dissonance is to reject or to distort the evidence. The deeper a person's commitment to an attitude, the greater his or her tendency to reject dissonant evidence.

The reader may or may not be convinced by the case of Mr. Landry. It is always possible that Landry believed cigarettes were good for people even before he began to peddle them. Obviously, if this were true, his excitement about the benefits of cigarette smoking could hardly be attributed to dissonance. Much more convincing would be a demonstration of a clear case of attitudinal distortion in a unique event. Such a demonstration was provided several years ago by (of all things) a football game in the Ivy League. An important game between Princeton and Dartmouth, the contest was billed as a grudge match, and this soon became evident on the field: The game is remembered as the roughest and dirtiest in the history of either school. On the Princeton team was an All-American named Dick Kazmaier; as the game progressed, it became increasingly clear that the Dartmouth players were out to get him. Whenever he carried the ball, he was gang-tackled, piled on, and mauled. He was finally forced to leave the game with a broken nose. Meanwhile, the Princeton team was not exactly inactive: Soon after Kazmaier's injury, a Dartmouth player was carried off the field with a broken leg. Several fistfights broke out on the field in the course of the game, and many injuries were suffered on both sides.

Sometime after the game, a couple of psychologists—Albert Hastorf of Dartmouth and Hadley Cantril of Princeton[7]—visited both campuses and showed films of the game to a number of students on each campus. The students were instructed to be completely objective and, while watching the film, to take notes of each infraction of the rules, how it started, and who was responsible. As you might imagine, there was a huge difference in the way this game was viewed by the students at each university. There was a strong tendency for the students to see their own fellow students as victims of illegal infractions rather than as perpetrators of such acts of aggression. Moreover, this was no minor distortion: It was found that Princeton students saw fully twice as many violations on the part of the Dartmouth players as the Dartmouth students saw. Again, people are not passive receptacles for the deposition of information. The manner in which they view and interpret information depends on how deeply they are committed to a particular belief or course of action. Individuals will distort the objective world in order to reduce their dissonance. The manner in which they will distort and the intensity of their distortion are highly predictable.

Lenny Bruce, a perceptive comedian and social commentator (who almost certainly never read about cognitive dissonance theory), had the following insight into the 1960 presidential election campaign between Richard Nixon and John Kennedy:

> I would be with a bunch of Kennedy fans watching the debate and their comment would be, "He's really slaughtering Nixon."

> Then we would all go to another apartment, and the Nixon fans would say, "How do you like the shellacking he gave Kennedy?" And then I realized that each group loved their candidate so that a guy would have to be this blatant—he would have to look into the camera and say: "I am a thief, a crook, do you hear me, I am the worst choice you could ever make for the Presidency!" And even then his following would say, "Now there's an honest man for you. It takes a big guy to admit that. There's the kind of guy we need for President."[8]

People don't like to see or hear things that conflict with their deeply held beliefs or wishes. An ancient response to such bad news was to kill the messenger—literally. A modern-day figurative version of "killing the messenger" is to blame the media for the presentation of material that produces the pain of dissonance. For example, in the summer of 1973, Richard Nixon's deep involvement in the illegal events surrounding the Watergate cover-up was coming into sharp focus; a Senate committee was holding hearings, and talk of impeachment was beginning to be heard among members of Congress. When the news magazines reported these events, readers who were committed to Richard Nixon found it difficult to take without lashing out—sometimes violently. The following letter, written to *Newsweek*, provides a vivid example:

> Sir:
>
> You infamous bastards will live to regret your continued scurrilous attacks upon the person and integrity of the President of the United States. I hope to live long enough to see that NEWSWEEK (together with *The Washington Post*, *Time*, and *The New York Times*) is reduced to ashes and rubble by an incensed public.
>
> In the event of any civil disorder, which will certainly develop if any formal action is taken to remove President Nixon, I will be in the forefront, lending a hand to destroy all who would be responsible for that dreadful event. And, NEWSWEEK, you will be at the top of the list. Revolution and civil war may bring down our country, but in that atmosphere we can cleanse our nation of you vermin with swift drumhead justice—on the spot! I further enlighten you to the fact that our armed forces, our police and all related agencies will be with us to bring you down.[9]

Dissonance Reduction and Rational Behavior

I have referred to dissonance-reducing behavior as "irrational." By this I mean it is often maladaptive, in that it can prevent people from learning important facts or from finding real solutions to their problems. On the other hand, it does serve a purpose: Dissonance-reducing behavior is ego-defensive behavior; by reducing dissonance, we maintain a positive image of ourselves—an image that depicts us as good, or smart, or worthwhile. Again, although this ego-defensive behavior can be considered useful, it can have disastrous consequences. In the laboratory, the irrationality of dissonance-reducing behavior has been amply demonstrated by Edward Jones and Rika Kohler.[10] These investigators selected individuals who were deeply committed to a position on the issue of racial segregation—some of the subjects were in favor of segregation, and others were opposed to it. These individuals were then allowed to read a series of arguments on both sides of the issue. Some of these arguments were extremely sensible and plausible, and others were so implausible they bordered on the ridiculous. Jones and Kohler were interested in determining which of the arguments people would remember best. If people were purely rational, we would expect them to remember the plausible arguments best and the implausible arguments the least; why in the world would people want to keep implausible arguments in their heads? Accordingly, the rational person would rehearse and remember all the arguments that made sense and would slough off all ridiculous arguments. What does the theory of cognitive dissonance predict? It is comforting to have all the wise people on your side and all the fools on the other side: A silly argument in favor of one's own position arouses some dissonance, because it raises some doubts about the wisdom of that position or the intelligence of the people who agree with it. Likewise, a plausible argument on the other side of the issue also arouses some dissonance, because it raises the possibility that the other side is right. Because these arguments arouse dissonance, one tries not to think about them—that is, one might not learn them very well, or one might simply forget about them. This is exactly what Jones and Kohler found. Their subjects did not remember in a rational-functional manner. They tended to remember the plausible arguments agreeing with their own position and the *implausible* arguments agreeing with the opposing position.

In a conceptually similar experiment, Charles Ford, Lee Ross and Mark Lepper[11] showed that we do not process information in an unbiased manner. Rather, we distort it in a way that fits our preconceived notions. These investigators selected several Stanford University students who opposed capital punishment and several who favored capital punishment. They showed the students two research articles that discussed whether or not the death penalty tends to deter violent crimes. One of the studies confirmed and the other study refuted the existing beliefs of the students. If these students were perfectly rational, they might conclude that the issue is a complex one and, accordingly, the two groups of students might move closer to each other in their beliefs about capital punishment. On the other hand, dissonance theory would predict that individuals will distort the articles such that they will clasp the confirming article to their bosom and hail it as clearly supportive of their belief—while finding methodological or conceptual flaws in the refuting article, and thus refusing to be influenced by it. This is precisely what happened. Indeed, rather than coming closer in their beliefs, after being exposed to this two-sided presentation, the two groups of students were in greater disagreement with one another than they were beforehand. This process probably accounts for the fact that, on issues like politics and religion, people who are deeply committed will almost never come to see things *our* way, no matter how powerful and balanced our arguments are.

Those of us who have worked extensively with the theory of cognitive dissonance do not deny that humans are capable of rational behavior. The theory merely suggests a good deal of our behavior is not rational—although, from inside, it may seem very sensible indeed. If you ask the hypnotized young man why he wore a raincoat on a sunny day, he'll come up with an answer he feels is sensible; if you ask the vice-president of Philip Morris why he smokes, he'll give you a reason that makes sense to him—he'll tell you how good it is for everyone's health; if you ask Jones and Kohler's subjects why they remembered a particular set of arguments rather than others, they'll insist that the arguments they remembered were a fair and representative sample of those they read. Similarly, the students in the experiment on capital punishment will insist that the evidence against their position is flawed. It is important to note that the world is not divided into rational people on the one side and dissonance-reducers on the other. People are not all the same, and some people are able to tolerate dissonance better than others, but we are all capable of rational behavior and we are all capable of dissonance-reducing behavior, depending on the circumstances. Occasionally, the same person can manifest both behaviors in rapid succession.

The rationality and irrationality of human behavior will be illustrated over and over again during the next several pages as we list and discuss some of the wide ramifications of our need for self-justification. These ramifications run virtually the entire gamut of human behavior, but, for the sake of conserving time and space, we will sample only a few of these. Let us begin with the decision-making process, a process that shows humans at their most rational and their most irrational in quick succession.

Dissonance as a Consequence of Making a Decision

Suppose you are about to make a decision—about the purchase of a new car, for example. This involves a significant amount of money, so it is, by definition, an important decision. You want a car because you like to go traveling and camping, but what kind should you choose? After looking around, you are torn between getting a van or purchasing a foreign compact model. There are various advantages and disadvantages to each: The van would be convenient for camping, and has plenty of room and power, but it gets atrocious mileage and is difficult to park. The foreign model is less roomy, and you are concerned about its safety, but it is less expensive to buy and operate and you've heard it has an excellent repair record. My guess is that, *before* you make the decision, you will seek as much information as you can. Chances are you will read *Consumer Reports* to find out what this expert, unbiased source has to say. Perhaps you'll confer with friends who own a van or a compact car. You'll probably visit the automobile dealers to test-drive the vehicles to see how each one feels. All of this predecision behavior is perfectly rational. Let us assume you make a decision—you buy the small import. What happens next? Your behavior will begin to change: No longer will you seek objective information about all makes of cars. Chances are you may begin to spend more time talking with the owners of foreign makes. You will begin to talk about the number of miles to the gallon as though it were the most important thing in the world. My guess is you will not be prone to spend much time thinking about the fact that you can't sleep in your compact, which is barely large enough for your camping equipment. Similarly, your mind will skim lightly over the fact that your new car may be particularly vulnerable in a collision and that the brakes are not very responsive, although your failure to attend to these shortcomings could conceivably cost you your life.

How does this sort of thing come about? Following a decision—especially a difficult one, or one that involves a significant amount of time, effort, or money—people almost always experience dissonance. This is so because the chosen alternative is seldom entirely positive and the rejected alternatives are seldom entirely negative. In this example, your cognition that you bought a compact is dissonant with your cognition about any deficiencies the car may have. Similarly, all the positive aspects of the other cars that you considered buying but did not purchase are dissonant with your cognition that you did not buy one of them. A good way to reduce such dissonance is to seek out exclusively positive information about the car you chose and avoid negative information about it. One source of safe information is advertisements; it is a safe bet an ad will not run down its own product. Accordingly, one might predict that a person who had recently purchased a new car will begin to read advertisements selectively, reading more ads about his or her car *after the purchase* than people who have *not* recently purchased the same model. Moreover, owners of new cars will tend to steer clear of ads for other makes of cars. This is exactly what Danuta Ehrlich and her colleagues[12] found in a well-known survey of advertising readership. In short, Ehrlich's data suggest that, *after* decisions, people try to gain reassurance that their decisions were wise by seeking information that is certain to be reassuring.

People do not always need help from Madison Avenue to gain reassurance; they can do a pretty good job of reassuring themselves. An experiment by Jack Brehm[13] demonstrates how this can come about. Posing as a marketing researcher, Brehm showed each of several women eight different appliances (a toaster, an electric coffee maker, a sandwich grill, and the like) and asked that she rate them in terms of how attractive each appliance was to her. As a reward, each woman was told she could have one of the appliances as a gift—and she was given a choice between two of the products she had rated as being equally attractive. After she chose one, it was wrapped up and given to her. Several minutes later, she was asked to rate the products again. It was found that after receiving the appliance of her choice, each woman rated the attractiveness of that appliance somewhat higher and decreased the rating of the appliance she had a chance to own but decided against. Again, making a decision produces dissonance: Cognitions about any negative aspects of the preferred object are dissonant with having chosen it, and cognitions about the positive aspects of the unchosen object are dissonant with *not* having chosen it. To reduce dissonance, people cognitively spread apart the alternatives. That is, *after the decision*, the women in Brehm's study emphasized the positive attributes of the appliance they decided to own while de-emphasizing its negative attributes; for the appliance they decided *not* to own, they emphasized its negative attributes and de-emphasized its positive attributes. This basic phenomenon has been extended and further clarified by a number of different investigators.[14]

Some Historical Examples of the Consequences of Decisions. It is impossible to overstate the potential dangers of this phenomenon. When I mentioned that ignoring potential danger in order to reduce dissonance could conceivably lead to a person's death, I meant that literally. Suppose a madman has taken over your country and has decided to eradicate all members of your religious group. But you don't know that for sure. What you *do* know is that your country is being occupied, that the leader of the occupation forces does not like your religious group very much, and that, occasionally, members of your faith are forced to move from their homes and are kept in detention camps. What do you do? You could try to flee from your country; you could try to pass as a member of a different religious group; or you could sit tight and hope for the best. Each of these options is extremely dangerous: It is difficult to escape or to pass and go undetected; and if you are caught trying to flee or disguising your identity, the penalty is immediate execution. On the other hand, deciding to sit tight could be a disastrous decision if it turns out your religious group *is* being systematically annihilated. Let us suppose you decide not to take action. That is, you commit yourself to sit tight—turning your back on opportunities either to try to escape or try to pass. Such an important decision naturally produces a great deal of dissonance. In order to reduce dissonance, you convince yourself you made a wise decision—that is, you convince yourself that, although people of your religious sect are made to move and are being treated unfairly, they are *not* being killed unless they break the law. This is not difficult to maintain because there is no unambiguous evidence to the contrary.

Suppose that, months later, a respected man from your town tells you he has witnessed all the men, women, and children who had recently been deported from the town being butchered mercilessly. I would predict you would try to dismiss this information as untrue—that you would attempt to convince yourself the reporter was lying or hallucinating. Accordingly—although, if you had listened to the man who tried to warn you, it is conceivable you might have escaped—you end up being slaughtered.

Fantastic? Impossible? How could anyone not take the "respected man" seriously? The events described above are an accurate accounting of exactly what happened, in 1944, to the Jews in Sighet, a small town in Hungary.[15]

The processes of cognitive distortion and selective exposure to information may have comprised an important factor in the escalation of the war in Vietnam. In a thought-provoking analysis of the Pentagon Papers, Ralph White suggested that dissonance blinded our leaders to information incompatible with the decisions they had already made. As White put it, "There was a tendency, when actions were out of line with ideas, for decision-makers to align their ideas with their actions." To take just one of many examples, the decision to continue to escalate the bombing of North Vietnam was made at the price of ignoring crucial evidence from the CIA and other sources that made it clear that bombing would not break the will of the North Vietnamese people, but, quite the contrary, would only strengthen their resolve:

> It is instructive, for instance, to compare McNamara's highly factual evidence-oriented summary of the case against bombing in 1966 (pages 555–563 of the Pentagon Papers) with the Joint Chief's memorandum that disputed his conclusion and called the bombing one of our two trump cards, while it apparently ignored all of the facts that showed the opposite. Yet it was the Joint Chiefs who prevailed.[16]

White surmises the reason they prevailed was that their advice was consonant with decisions already made and with certain key assumptions then operating that later proved to be erroneous.[17]

Escalation is self-perpetuating. Once a small commitment is made, it sets the stage for ever-increasing commitments. The behavior needs to be justified, so attitudes are changed; this change in attitudes influences future decisions and behavior. The flavor of this kind of cognitive escalation is nicely captured in an analysis of the Pentagon Papers by the news magazine *Time:*

> Yet the bureaucracy, the Pentagon Papers indicate, always demanded new options; each option was to apply more force. Each tightening of the screw created a position that must be defended; once committed, the military pressure must be maintained.[18]

The process underlying escalation has been explored, on a more individual level, under controlled experimental conditions. Suppose you would like to enlist someone's aid in a massive undertaking, but you know the job you have in mind for the person is so difficult, and will require so much time and effort, that the person surely will decline. What should you do? One possibility is to get the person involved in a much smaller aspect of the job, one so easy that he or she wouldn't dream of turning it down. This action serves to commit the individual to "the cause." Once people are thus committed, the likelihood of their complying with the larger request increases. This phenomenon was demonstrated by Jonathan Freedman and Scott Fraser.[19] They attempted to induce several homeowners to put up a huge sign in their front yard reading "Drive Carefully." Because of the ugliness and obtrusiveness of this sign, most residents refused to put it up; only 17 percent complied. A different group of residents, however, were first "softened up" by an experimenter who "put his foot in the door" by getting them to sign a petition favoring safe driving. Because signing a petition is an easy thing to do, virtually all who were asked agreed to sign. A few weeks later, a different experimenter went to each resident with the obtrusive ugly sign reading "Drive Carefully." More than 55 percent of these residents allowed the sign to be put up on their property. Thus, when individuals commit themselves in a small way, the likelihood that they will commit themselves further in that direction is increased. This process of using small favors to encourage people to accede to larger requests has been dubbed the foot-in-the-door technique. It is effective because having done the smaller favor sets up pressures toward agreeing to do the larger favor; in effect it provides justification in advance for complying with the large request.

Similar results were obtained by Patricia Pliner[20] and her associates. These investigators found that 46 percent of their sample was willing to make a small donation to the Cancer Society when they were approached directly. A similar group of people were asked one day earlier to wear a lapel pin publicizing the fund raising drive. When approached the next day, approximately twice as many of these people were willing to make a contribution.

The Importance of Irrevocability. One of the important characteristics of the examples presented above is the relative irrevocability of the decision. This needs some explaining: Occasionally, we make tentative decisions. For example, if you had indicated you might buy an expensive house near San Francisco, but the decision was not finalized, chances are you would not expend any effort trying to convince yourself of the wisdom of the decision. Once you had put your money down, however, and you knew you couldn't easily get it back, you would probably start minimizing the importance of the dampness in the basement, the cracks in the foundation, or the fact that it happened to be built on the San Andreas fault. Similarly, once a European Jew has decided *not* to pass and has allowed himself to be identified as a Jew, it is irrevocable—he can't very easily pretend to be a Gentile. By the same token, once Pentagon officials intensified the bombing, they could not undo it. And once a homeowner has signed the petition, commitment to safe driving is established.

Some direct evidence for the importance of irrevocability comes from a clever study of the cognitive gyrations of gamblers at a race track. The race track is an ideal place to scrutinize irrevocability because once you've placed your bet, you can't go back and tell the nice man behind the window you've changed your mind! Robert Knox and James Inkster[21] simply intercepted people who were on their way to place $2 bets. They had already decided on their horses and were about to place their bets when the investigators asked them how certain they were their horses would win. Because they were on their way to the $2 window, their decisions were not irrevocable. The investigators collared other bettors just as they were leaving the $2 window, *after* having placed their bets, and asked them how certain they were their horses would win. Typically, people who had just placed their bets gave their horse a much better chance of winning than did those who were about to place their bets. But, of course, nothing had changed except the finality of the decision. Similar results were obtained in a survey of Canadian voters.[22] Those voters interviewed immediately *after* voting were more certain their candidate would win and liked their candidate more than those voters interviewed immediately *before* they had cast their vote. In short, when a decision is irrevocable, more dissonance gets reduced; people are more certain they are right *after* there is nothing they can do about it.

While the irrevocability of a decision always increases the

tendency to reduce dissonance, there are circumstances in which irrevocability is unnecessary. Let me explain with an example. Suppose you enter an automobile showroom intent on buying a new car. You've already priced the car you want at several dealers—you know you can purchase it for about $9300. Lo and behold, the salesman tells you he can sell you one for $8942. Excited by the bargain, you agree to the deal and write out a check for the down payment. While the salesman takes your check to the manager to consummate the deal, you rub your hands in glee as you imagine yourself driving home in your shiny new car. But alas, ten minutes later, the salesman returns with a forlorn look in his face—it seems he made a calculation error and the sales manager caught it. The price of the car is actually $9384. You can get it cheaper elsewhere; moreover, the decision to buy is not irrevocable. And yet, far more people in this situation will go ahead with the deal than if the original asking price had been $9384—even though the reason for purchasing the car from *this* dealer (the bargain price) no longer exists. Indeed, Robert Cialdini,[23] a social psychologist who temporarily joined the sales force of an automobile dealer, discovered that the strategy described above is a common and successful sales ploy called *lowballing* or "throwing the customer a lowball."

What is going on in this situation? There are at least three important things to notice. First, while the customer's decision to buy is certainly reversible, there *is* a commitment emphasized by the act of signing a check. Second, this commitment triggered the anticipation of a pleasant or interesting experience: driving out with a new car. To have the anticipated event thwarted (by not going ahead with the deal) would have produced dissonance and disappointment. Third, although the final price is substantially higher than the customer thought it would be, it is only slightly higher than the price somewhere else. Under these circumstances, the customer in effect says, "Oh, what the hell. I'm already here, I've already filled out the forms—why wait?"[24] Clearly, such a ploy would not be effective if the consequences were somewhat higher—as in the case of the house on the San Andreas fault described above.

The Decision to Behave Immorally. How can an honest person become corrupt? Conversely, how can we get a person to be *more* honest? One way is through the dissonance that results from making a difficult decision. Suppose you are a college student enrolled in a biology course. Your grade will hinge on the final exam you are now taking. The key question on the exam involves some material you know fairly well—but, because of anxiety, you draw a blank. You are sitting there in a nervous sweat. You look up and, lo and behold, you happen to be sitting behind a woman who is the smartest person in the class (who also happens, fortunately, to be the person with the most legible handwriting in the class). You glance down and notice that she is just completing her answer to the crucial question. You know you could easily read her answer if you chose to. What do you do? Your conscience tells you it's wrong to cheat—and yet, if you don't cheat, you are certain to get a poor grade. You wrestle with your conscience. Regardless of whether or not you decide to cheat, you are doomed to experience dissonance. If you cheat, your congnition "I am a decent moral person" is dissonant with your cognition "I have just committed an immoral act." If you decide to resist temptation, your cognition "I want to get a good grade" is dissonant with your cognition "I could have acted in a way that would have ensured a good grade, but I chose not to."

Suppose that, after a difficult struggle, you decide to cheat. How do you reduce the dissonance? Before you read on, think about it for a moment. One way to reduce dissonance is to minimize the negative aspects of the action you have chosen (and to maximize the positive aspects)—much the same way the women did after choosing an appliance in Jack Brehm's experiment. In this instance, an efficacious path of dissonance reduction would entail a change in your attitude about cheating. In short, you will adopt a more lenient attitude. Your reasoning might go something like this: "Cheating isn't so bad, under some circumstances. As long as nobody gets hurt, it's really not very immoral—anybody would do it—therefore, it's a part of human nature . . . so how could it be bad? Since it *is* only human, those who get caught cheating should not be severely punished but should be treated with understanding."

Suppose that after a difficult struggle, you decide *not* to cheat. How would you reduce dissonance? Once again, you could change your attitude about the morality of the act—but in the opposite direction. That is, in order to justify the fact that you gave up a good grade, you must convince yourself that cheating is a heinous sin, that it's one of the lowest things a person can do, and that cheaters should be found out and severely punished.

The interesting and important thing to remember here is that two people acting in the two different ways described above could have started out with almost identical attitudes. Their decisions may have been a hair's breadth apart—one came within an ace of resisting but decided to cheat, while the other came within an ace of cheating but decided to resist. Once they have made their decisions, however, their attitudes toward cheating will diverge sharply as a consequence of their decisions.

These speculations were put to the test by Judson Mills[25] in an experiment with sixth graders. Mills first measured their attitudes toward cheating. He then had them participate in a competitive exam with prizes being offered to the winners. The situation was arranged so it was almost impossible to win without cheating; also it was easy for the children to cheat, thinking they would not be detected. As one might expect, some of the students cheated and others did not. The next day, the sixth graders were again asked to indicate how they felt about cheating. In general, those children who had cheated became more lenient toward cheating, and those who resisted the temptation to cheat adopted a harsher attitude toward cheating.

The data from Mills' experiment are provocative indeed. One thing they suggest is that the most zealous opponents of a given position are not those who have always been distant from that position. For example, one might hazard a guess that the people who are most angry at the apparent sexual promiscuity associated with the current generation of young people may *not* be those who have never been tempted to be sexually promiscuous themselves. Indeed, Mills' data suggest the possibility that the people who have the strongest need to crack down hard on this sort of behavior are those who have been sorely tempted, who came dangerously close to giving in to this temptation, but who finally resisted. People who *almost* decide to live in glass houses are frequently the ones who are most prone to throw stones.

Early in this chapter, I mentioned that the desire for self-justification is an important reason why people who are strongly committed to an attitude on an issue tend to resist any direct attempts to change that attitude. In effect, such people are invulnerable to the propaganda or education in question. We can now see that the same mechanism that enables a person to cling to an attitude can induce that individual to *change* an attitude. It depends on which course of action will serve most to reduce dissonance under the circumstances. A person who understands the theory can set up the proper conditions to induce attitude change in other people by making them vulnerable to certain kinds of beliefs. For example, if a modern Machiavelli were advising a contemporary ruler, he might suggest the following strategies based on the theory and data on the consequences of decisions:

1. If you want people to form more positive attitudes about an object, get them to commit themselves to that object.
2. If you want people to soften their moral attitudes about some misdeed, tempt them so that they perform that deed; conversely, if you want people to harden their moral attitudes about a misdeed, tempt them—but not enough to induce them to commit the deed.

The Psychology of Inadequate Justification

Attitude change as a means of reducing dissonance is not, of course, limited to postdecision situations. It can occur in countless other contexts, including every time a person says something he or she doesn't believe or does something stupid or immoral. The effects can be extremely powerful. Let us look at some of them.

In a complex society, we occasionally find ourselves saying or doing things we don't completely believe. To illustrate we will choose a frankly stereotypical, cartoonlike example. Joe Businessman enters the office and sees Mabel, his secretary, wearing a perfectly atrocious outfit with pink stripes and orange polka dots. "How do you like my new dress?" she asks. "Very pretty, Mabel," he answers. Theoretically, Joe's cognition "I am a truthful person" is dissonant with his cognition "I said that dress was very pretty, although I believe it to be a disaster." Whatever dissonance might be aroused by this inconsistency can easily and quickly be reduced by Joe's cognition that it is important not to hurt other people: "I lied so as not to hurt Mabel; why should I tell her it's an ugly dress? It serves no useful purpose." This is an effective way of reducing dissonance, because it completely justifies the action Joe took. In effect, the justification is situation-determined. We will call this *external justification*.

But what happens if there is not ample justification in the situation itself? For example, imagine that Joe Businessman, who is politically conservative, finds himself at a cocktail party with many people he doesn't know very well. The conversation turns to politics. The people are talking with horror about the fact that the United States seems to be drastically escalating its friendly overtures toward Castro's regime in Cuba. Joe's belief is a complicated one; he has mixed feelings about the topic, but generally he is opposed to our forming an alliance with the Cuban dictatorship because he feels it is an evil regime and we should not compromise with evil. Partly because Joe's companions are sounding so pious, and partly as a lark, he gradually finds himself taking a much more radical position than the one he really holds. As a matter of fact, Joe even goes so far as to assert that Fidel Castro is an extraordinarily gifted leader and that the Cuban people are better off with communism than they've been in hundreds of years. Somebody counters Joe's argument by talking about the many thousands of people that Castro is alleged to have murdered or imprisoned in order to achieve a unified government. In the heat of the situation, Joe replies that those figures are grossly exaggerated. Quite a performance for a man who does, in fact, believe that Castro killed thousands of innocent people during his rise to power.

When Joe awakes the next morning and thinks back on the previous evening's events, he gasps in horror. "Oh, my God, what have I done?" he says. He is intensely uncomfortable. Put another way, he is experiencing a great deal of dissonance. His cognition "I misled a bunch of people; I told them a lot of things about Cuba that I don't really believe" is dissonant with his cognition "I am a reasonable, decent, and truthful person." What does he do to reduce dissonance? He searches around for *external justifications.* First, it occurs to Joe that he might have been drunk and therefore not responsible for what he said. But he remembers he had only one or two beers—no external justification there. Because Joe cannot find sufficient external justification for his behavior, it is necessary for him to attempt to justify his behavior *internally*, by changing his attitude in the direction of his statements. That is, if Joe can succeed in convincing himself that his statements were not so very far from the truth, then he will have reduced dissonance; his behavior of the preceding night will no longer be absurd in his own view. I do not mean to imply that Joe would suddenly become an avowed communist revolutionary. What I do mean is that he might begin to soften his attitude about the Cuban regime than he had felt before he made those statements. Most events and issues in our world are neither completely black nor completely white; there are many grey areas. Thus, Joe might begin to take a different look at some of the events that have taken place in Cuba during the past 50 years. He might start looking into Castro's politics and decisions and become more disposed toward seeing wisdom that he hadn't seen before. He might also begin to be more receptive to information that indicates the extent of the corruption, brutality, and ineptitude of the previous government. To repeat: If an individual makes a statement of belief that is difficult to justify *externally*, that person will attempt to justify it *internally* by making his or her attitudes more consistent with the statement.

We have mentioned a couple of forms of external justification. One is the idea that it's all right to tell a harmless lie in order to avoid hurting a person's feelings—as in the case of Joe Businessman and his secretary. Another is drunkenness as an excuse for one's actions. Still another form of external justification is reward. Put yourself in Joe's shoes for a moment, and suppose you and I both were at that cocktail party, and that I am an eccentric millionare. As the conversation turns to Cuba, I pull you aside and say, "Hey, I would like you to come out strongly in favor of Fidel Castro and Cuban communism." What's more, suppose I hand you $5000 for doing it. After counting the money, you gasp, put the $5000 in your pocket, return to the discussion, and defend Fidel Castro to the hilt. The next morning when you wake up, would you experience any dissonance? I don't think so. Your cognition "I said some things about Fidel Castro and Cuban communism that I don't believe" is dissonant with the cognition "I am a truthful and decent person." But, at the same time, you have adequate external justification for having made that statement: "I said those favorable things about Cuban communism in order to earn $5000—and it was worth it." You don't have to soften your attitude toward Castro in order to justify that statement, because you know why you made those statements: You made them *not* because you think they are true, but in order to get the $5000. You're left with the knowledge you sold your soul for $5000—not a bad price!

Saying is believing. That is, dissonance theory predicts we begin to believe our own lies—but only if there is not an abundance of external justification for making the statements that run counter to our original attitude. We can now begin to elaborate on our earlier discussion of conformity. Recall that in Chapter 2 we found that the greater the reward for compliance, the greater the probability a person will comply. Now we can go one step further: When it comes to producing a *lasting* change in attitude, the greater the reward, the *less* likely any attitude change will occur. If all I want you to do is recite a speech favoring Fidel Castro, the Marx brothers, socialized medicine, or anything else, the most efficient thing for me to do would be to give you the largest possible reward. This would increase the probability of your complying by making that speech. But suppose I have a more ambitious goal: Suppose I want to effect a lasting change in your attitudes and beliefs. In that case, just the reverse is true. The smaller the external reward I give to induce you to recite the speech, the more likely it is you will be forced to seek additional justification for delivering it, in the form of convincing yourself that the things you said were actually true. This would result in an actual change in attitude, rather than mere compliance. The importance of this technique cannot be overstated. If we change our attitudes because we have made a public statement for minimal external justification, our attitude change will be relatively permanent; we are not changing our attitudes because of a reward (compliance) or because of the influence of an attractive person (identification). We are changing our attitudes because we have succeeded in *convincing ourselves* that our previous attitudes were incorrect. This is a very powerful form of attitude change.

Thus far, we have been dealing with highly speculative material. These speculations have been investigated scientifically in several experiments. Among these is a classic study by Leon Festinger and J. Merrill Carlsmith.[26] Festinger and Carlsmith asked college students to perform a very boring and repetitive series of tasks—packing spools in a tray, dumping them out, and then refilling the tray over and over, or turning rows and rows of screws a quarter turn and then going back and turning them another quarter turn. The students engaged in these activities for a full hour. The experimenter then induced them to lie about the task; specifically, he employed them to tell a young woman (who was waiting to participate in the experiment) that the task she would be performing was interesting and enjoyable. Some of the students were offered twenty dollars for telling the lie, others were offered only one dollar for telling the lie. After the experiment was over, an interviewer asked the "lie-tellers" how much they had enjoyed the tasks they had performed earlier in the experiment. The results were clear-cut: Those students who had been paid twenty dollars for lying—that is, for saying the spool-packing and screw-turning had been enjoyable—actually rated the activity as dull. This is not surprising—it *was* dull. But what about the students who had been paid only one dollar for telling their fellow student that the experiment was enjoyable? They did, indeed, rate the task as an enjoyable one. In other words, people who received an abundance of external justification for lying told the lie but didn't believe it, whereas those who told the lie *in the absence* of a great deal of external justification did, indeed, move in the direction of believing that what they said was true.

Research support for the "saying is believing" phenomenon has extended beyond relatively unimportant attitudes like the dullness of a monotonous task. Attitude change has been shown on such important issues as police brutality and the legalization of marijuana. In one experiment, Arthur R. Cohen[27] induced Yale men to engage in a particularly difficult form of counter-attitudinal behavior. Cohen conducted his experiment immediately after a student riot in which the New Haven police had behaved in a rather brutal manner toward the students. The students (who strongly believed that the police had behaved badly) were asked to write an essay in support of the actions taken by the police. Students were urged to write the strongest, most forceful defense of the police actions they could muster. Before writing the essay, students were paid for their efforts. There were four conditions: Some students were paid ten dollars; others, five dollars; still others, one dollar; and a fourth group, the paltry sum of fifty cents. After writing his essay, each young man was asked to indicate his own private attitudes about the police actions. The results were perfectly linear: the smaller the reward, the greater the attitude change. Thus, students who wrote in support of the New Haven police for the meager sum of fifty cents developed a more favorable attitude than did those who wrote the essay for one dollar; the students who wrote the essay for one dollar developed a more favorable attitude toward the actions of the police than did those who wrote the essay for ten dollars; and so on. The less the external justification in terms of money, the greater the attitude change.[28]

What Is Inadequate Justification? Throughout this section, we have made reference to situations where there is "inadequate" external justification and to those with "an abundance" of external justification. These terms require some additional clarification. In the Festinger-Carlsmith experiment, all of the subjects did, in fact, agree to tell the lie—including all of those paid only one dollar. In a sense, then, one dollar was *adequate*—that is, adequate to induce the subjects to tell the lie; but, as it turns out, it wasn't sufficient to keep them from feeling foolish. In order to reduce their feelings of foolishness, they had to reduce the dissonance that resulted from telling a lie for so paltry a sum. This entailed additional bolstering in the form of convincing themselves that it wasn't completely a lie and that the task wasn't quite as dull as it seemed at first—as a matter of fact, when looked at in a certain way, it was actually quite interesting.

It would be fruitful to compare these results with Judson Mills' data on the effects of cheating among sixth graders.[29] Recall that, in Mills' experiment, the decision about whether or not to cheat was almost certainly a difficult one for most of the children. This is why they experienced dissonance regardless of whether they cheated or resisted temptation. One could speculate about what would happen if the rewards to be gained by cheating were very large. For one thing, it would be more tempting to cheat—therefore, more children would actually cheat. But, more important, if the gains for cheating were astronomical, those who cheated would undergo very little attitude change. Much like the college students who lied in Festinger and Carlsmith's twenty-dollar condition, those children who cheated for a great reward would have less need to reduce dissonance, having been provided with "an abundance" of external justification for their behavior. In fact, Mills did include this refinement in his experiment, and his results are consistent with this reasoning: Those who cheated in order to obtain a small reward tended to soften their attitudes about cheating more than those who cheated in order to obtain a large reward. Moreover, those who refrained from cheating in spite of the temptation of a large reward—a choice that would create a great deal of dissonance—*hardened* their attitudes about cheating to a greater extent than those who refrained in the face of a small reward—just as one might expect.

Dissonance and the Self-Concept. The analysis of the dissonance phenomenon presented in this section requires a departure from Festinger's original theory. In the experiment by Festinger and Carlsmith, for example, the original statement of dissonance went like this: The cognition "I believe the task is dull" is dissonant with the cognition "I said the task was interesting." Several years ago, I reformulated the theory in a way that focuses more attention on the way people conceive of themselves.[30] Basically, this reformulation suggests that dissonance is most powerful in situations in which the self-concept is threatened. Thus, for me, the important aspect of dissonance in the situation described above is not that the cognition "I said 'X' " is dissonant with the cognition "I believe 'not X.' " Rather, the crucial fact is that I have misled people: The cognition "I have said something I don't believe and it could have bad consequences for people" is dissonant with my self-concept; that is, it is dissonant with my cognition that "I am a decent, reasonable, truthful person."

This formulation is based on the assumption that most individuals like to think of themselves as decent people who wouldn't ordinarily mislead someone unless there was good reason for it, especially if, in misleading that person, the consequences for the target of the lie could be disastrous. For example, consider Kathy, who believes marijuana is dangerous and should definitely not be legalized. Suppose she is induced to make a speech advocating the use of marijuana. Let us assume she makes the speech to an audience consisting of individuals whom she knows to be irrevocably opposed to the use of marijuana (for example, the members of a vice squad, the Daughters of the American Revolution, or prohibitionists). In this case, there are no dangerous consequences for the audience, because they are unlikely to be changed by Kathy's communication. That is, the communicator is in little danger of doing anyone any harm. According to my view of dissonance theory, Kathy would not change her attitude, because she is not doing anyone any harm. Similarly, if Kathy were asked to make the same statement to a group of individuals whom she knows to be irrevocably committed to the use of marijuana, there would be no possibility of a negative behavioral change in the audience. Again, she stands little chance of doing harm, because the members of her audience already believe what she is telling them. On the other hand, if Kathy were induced to make the identical speech to a group of individuals who have no prior information about marijuana, we would expect her to experience much more dissonance than in the other situations. Her cognition that she is a good and decent person is dissonant with her cognition that she has said something she doesn't believe; moreover, her statement is likely to have serious *belief* or *behavioral consequences* for her audience. To reduce dissonance, she should convince herself the position she advocated is correct. This would allow her to believe she has not harmed anyone. Moreover, in this situation, the smaller the incentive she receives for advocating the position, the greater the attitude change. I tested and confirmed this hypothesis in collaboration with Elizabeth Nel and Robert Helmreich.[31] We found an enormous change in attitudes toward marijuana when subjects were offered a small reward for making a video tape recording of a speech favoring the use of marijuana—but only when they were led to believe that the tape would be shown to an audience that was *uncommitted on the issue.* On the other hand, when subjects were told the tape would be played to people who were irrevocably committed on the subject of marijuana (one way or the other), there was relatively little attitude change on the part of the speaker. Thus, lying produces greater attitude change when the liar is undercompensated for lying, especially when the lie is apt to cause another person some harm.*

The findings of recent research[32] support this reasoning and allow us to state a general principle about dissonance and the self-concept: Dissonance effects are greatest when (1) people feel personally responsible for their actions and (2) their actions have serious negative consequences. That is, the greater the harm and the greater our responsibility for it, the greater the dissonance; the greater the dissonance, the greater our attitude change.

My notion that dissonance is aroused whenever the self-concept is challenged has many interesting ramifications. Let us look at one in some detail. Suppose you are at home and someone knocks at your door, asking you to contribute to a worthy charity. If you didn't contribute, you probably wouldn't find it too difficult to come up with reasons for declining—you don't have much money, your contribution probably wouldn't help much anyway, and so on. But suppose that, after delivering a standard plea for a donation, the fundraiser adds that "even a penny will help." Refusing to donate after hearing this statement would undoubtedly stir up some dissonance by challenging your self-concept. After all, what kind of person is it who is too mean or stingy to come up with a penny? No longer would your pre-

*It should be mentioned that, in this as well as in the other experiments discussed here, each subject was completely debriefed as soon as he or she had finished participating in the experiment. Every attempt was made to avoid causing a permanent change in the attitudes of the subjects. It is always important to debrief subjects after an experiment; it is especially important when the experiment induces a change in an important attitude or has important behavioral consequences.

vious rationalizations apply. Such a scenario was tested experimentally by Robert Cialdini and David Schroeder.[33] Students acting as fundraisers went door to door, sometimes just asking for donations and sometimes adding that "even a penny will help." As conjectured, the residents who were approached with the "even-a-penny" request gave contributions more often, donating almost twice as frequently as those getting just the standard plea. Furthermore, on the average, the "even-a-penny" contributors were likely to give as much money as the others; that is, the statement legitimizing the small donation did not reduce the size of the contributions. Why? Apparently, not only does the lack of external justification for refusing to donate encourage people to give money, but, after they have decided *whether* to contribute, the desire to avoid appearing stingy affects their decision of *how much* to give. Once people reach into their pockets, emerging with a mere penny is self-demeaning; a larger donation is consistent with their self-perception of being reasonably kind and generous.

Inadequate Rewards as Applied to Education. A great deal of research has shown that the insufficient-reward phenomenon applies to all forms of behavior—not simply the making of counterattitudinal statements. For example, it has been shown that, if people actually *perform* a dull task for very little external justification, they rate the task as more enjoyable than if they had a great deal of external justification for performing it.[34] This does not mean people would rather receive low pay than high pay for doing a job. People prefer to receive high pay—and they often work harder for high pay. But if they are offered low pay for doing a job and still agree to do it, there is dissonance between the dullness of the task and the low pay. To reduce the dissonance, they attribute good qualities to the job and, hence, come to enjoy the mechanics of the job more if the salary is low than if it is high. This phenomenon may have far-reaching consequences. For example, let's look at the elementary school classroom. If you want Johnny to recite a table of multiplication problems, then you should reward him; gold stars, praise, high grades, presents, and the like are good external justifications. Will Johnny recite the equations just for the fun of it, long after the rewards are no longer forthcoming? In other words, will the high rewards make him enjoy the task? I doubt it. But if the external rewards are not too high, Johnny will add his own justification for performing the math drill; he may even make a game of it. In short, he is more likely to continue to memorize the multiplication tables long after school is out and the rewards have been withdrawn.

For certain rote tasks, we, as educators, probably do not care whether Johnny enjoys them or not, as long as he masters them. On the other hand, if Johnny can learn to enjoy them, he will perform them outside of the educational situation. Consequently, with such increased practice, he may come to gain greater mastery over the procedure—and he may retain it indefinitely. Thus, at least under some conditions, it may be a mistake to dole out extensive rewards as an educational device. If students are provided with just barely enough incentive to perform the task, we may succeed in allowing them to maximize their enjoyment of the task. This may serve to improve long-range retention and performance. I am not suggesting that inadequate rewards are the only way people can be taught to enjoy material that lacks inherent attractiveness. What I *am* saying is that piling on excessive external justification inhibits one of the processes that can help set the stage for increased enjoyment.

Several experiments by Edward Deci[35] and his colleagues make this point very nicely. Indeed, Deci carries our analysis one step further by demonstrating that offering rewards to individuals for performing a pleasant activity actually *decreases* the intrinsic attractiveness of that activity. In one experiment, for example, college students worked individually on an interesting puzzle for an hour. The next day, the students in the experimental condition were paid one dollar for each piece of the puzzle they completed. The students in the control group worked on the puzzle as before, without pay. During a third session, neither group was paid. The question is: How much liking did each group have for the puzzles? Deci measured this during the third session by noting whether or not each student worked on the puzzle during a free break during which they could do whatever they pleased. The results show a strong tendency for the *unrewarded* group to spend more free time on the task than the rewarded group. The rewarded group did work harder on the task during the rewarded session, but their interest waned in the final session. The unrewarded group showed an increase in interest during the third session.

In a similar vein, Mark Lepper and David Greene found the same kind of relationship with preschool children.[36] Half of the children were induced to work on a set of plastic jigsaw puzzles by the promise of a more rewarding activity later. Others were not promised the more rewarding activity. After playing with the puzzles, *all* of the children were allowed to engage in the "more rewarding activity" (but recall that only half of them were led to believe this was a reward for having worked on the puzzles). A few weeks later, all the youngsters were turned loose on the puzzles. Those who had worked on the puzzles in order to earn the chance to engage in the more rewarding activity spent less of their free time playing with the puzzles. In short, by offering the children a reward for playing, the experimenters succeeded in turning play into work.

Insufficient Punishment. Thus far, we have been discussing what happens when a person's *rewards* for saying or doing something are meager. The same process works for punishment. In our everyday lives, we are continually faced with situations wherein those who are charged with the duty of maintaining law and order are threatening to punish us if we do not comply with the demands of society. As adults we know that if we exceed the speed limit and get caught, we will end up paying a substantial fine. If it happens too often, we will lose our license. So we learn to obey the speed limit when there are patrol cars in the vicinity. Youngsters in school know that, if they cheat on an exam and get caught, they could be humiliated by the teacher and severely punished. So they learn not to cheat while the teacher is in the room watching them. But does harsh punishment teach them not to cheat? I don't think so. I think it teaches them to try to avoid getting caught. In short, the use of threats of harsh punishment as a means of getting someone to refrain from doing something he or she enjoys doing necessitates constant harassment and vigilance. It would be much more efficient and would require much less noxious restraint if, somehow, people could enjoy doing those things that contribute to their own health and welfare—and to the health and welfare of others. If children would enjoy *not* beating up smaller kids or enjoy *not* cheating or *not* stealing from others, then society could relax its vigilance and curtail its punitiveness. It is extremely difficult to persuade people (especially young children) that it's not enjoyable to beat up smaller people. But it is conceivable that, under certain conditions, they will *persuade themselves* such behavior is unenjoyable.

Let's take a closer look. Picture the scene: You are the parent of a five-year-old boy who enjoys beating up on his three-year-old sister. You've tried to reason with him, but to no avail. So, in order to protect the welfare of your daughter, and in order to make a "nicer" person out of your son, you begin to punish him for his aggressiveness. As a parent, you have at your disposal a number of punishments that range from the extremely mild (a stern look) to the extremely severe (a hard spanking, forcing the child to stand in the corner for two hours, and depriving him of TV privileges for a month). The more severe the threat, the greater the likelihood the youngster will mend his ways *while you are watching him*. But he may very well hit his sister again as soon as you turn your back.

Suppose instead you threaten him with a very mild punishment. In either case (under threat of severe punishment or of mild punishment), the child experiences dissonance. He is aware he is not beating up his little sister—and also aware he would very much *like* to beat her up. When the child has the urge to hit his sister and doesn't, he asks himself, in effect, "How come I'm not beating up my little sister?" Under severe threat, he has a ready-made answer in the form of sufficient external justification: "I'm not beating her up because, if I do, that giant over there (my father) is going to spank me, stand me in the corner, and keep me from watching television for a month." The severe threat has provided the child ample external justification for not hitting his sister while he's being watched.

The child in the mild-threat situation experiences dissonance, too. But when he asks himself, "How come I'm not beating up my little sister?" he doesn't have a good answer, because the threat is so mild it does not provide a superabundance of justification. The child is *not* doing something he wants to do—and while he does have *some* justification for not doing it, he lacks complete justification. In this situation, he continues to experience dissonance. He is unable to reduce the dissonance by simply blaming his inaction on a severe threat. The child must find a way to justify the fact he is not aggressing against his little sister. The best way is to try to convince himself that he really doesn't like to beat his sister up, that he didn't want to do it in the first place, that beating up little kids is not fun. The less severe the threat, the less external justification; the less external justification, the greater the need for internal justification. Allowing people the opportunity to construct their own internal justification can be a large step toward helping them develop a permanent set of values.

To test this idea, I performed an experiment at the Harvard University nursery school in collaboration with J. Merrill Carlsmith.[37] For ethical reasons, we did not try to change basic values like aggression—parents, understandably, might not approve of our changing important values. Instead, we chose a trivial aspect of behavior—toy preference.

We first asked five-year-old children to rate the attractiveness of several toys; then in each instance, we chose one toy that the child considered quite attractive and told him he couldn't play with it. We threatened half the children with mild punishment for transgression—"I would be a little angry"; we threatened the other half with more severe punishment—"I would be very angry; I would have to take all of the toys and go home and never come back again; I would think you were just a baby." After that, we left the room and allowed the child to play with the other toys—and to resist the temptation of playing with the forbidden one. Each of the children resisted the temptation—none played with the forbidden toy.

On returning to the room, we again asked the child to rate the attractiveness of all the toys. Our results were both striking and exciting. Those children who underwent a mild threat now found the forbidden toy less attractive than before. In short, lacking adequate external justification for refraining from playing with the toy, they succeeded in convincing themselves that they hadn't played with it because they didn't really like it. On the other hand, the toy did not become less attractive for those who were severely threatened. These children continued to rate the forbidden toy as highly desirable—indeed, some even found it more desirable than they had before the threat. The children in the severe-threat condition had good external reasons for not playing with the toy—they therefore had no need to find additional reasons—and, consequently, they continued to like the toy.

Jonathan Freedman[38] extended our findings and dramatically illustrated the permanence of the phenomenon. He used as his "crucial toy" an extremely attractive battery-powered robot that scurries around hurling objects at a child's enemies. The other toys were sickly by comparison. Naturally, all of the children preferred the robot. He then asked them not to play with that toy, threatening some children with mild punishment and others with severe punishment. He then left school and never returned. Several weeks later, a young woman came to the school to administer some paper-and-pencil tests to the children. The children were unaware of the fact she was working for Freedman or that her presence was in any way related to the toys or the threats that had occurred earlier. But it just so happened she was administering her test in the same room Freedman had used for his experiment—the room where the same toys were casually scattered about. After she administered the test to each child, she asked him to hang around while she scored it—and suggested, offhandedly, that he might want to amuse himself with those toys someone had left in the room.

Freedman's results are highly consistent with our own. The overwhelming majority of the children who had been mildly threatened weeks earlier rufused to play with the robot; they played with the other toys instead. On the other hand, the great majority of the children who had been severely threatened did, in fact, play with the robot. In sum, a severe threat was not effective in inhibiting subsequent behavior—but the effect of one *mild* threat inhibited behavior as much as nine weeks later. Again the power of this phenomenon rests on the fact the child did not come to devalue this behavior (playing with the toy) because some adult told him it was undesirable, he *convinced himself* that it was undesirable.

My guess is that this process may well apply beyond mere toy preference to more basic and important areas, such as the control of aggression. Partial support for this guess can be derived from some correlational studies performed in the area of child development indicating that parents who use severe punishment to stop a child's aggression tend to have children, who, while not very aggressive at home, display a great deal of aggression at school and at play away from home.[39] This is precisely what we would expect from the compliance model discussed in Chapter 2.

The Justification of Effort

Dissonance theory leads to the prediction that, if a person works hard to attain a goal, that goal will be more attractive to the individual than it will be to someone who achieves the same goal with little or no effort. An illustration might be useful: Suppose you are a college student who decides to join a fraternity. In order to be admiteed, you must pass an initiation; let us assume it is a rather severe one that involves a great deal of effort, pain, or embarrassment. After successfully completing the ordeal, you are admitted to the fraternity. When you move into the fraternity house, you find your new roommate has some peculiar habits: For example, he plays his stereo loudly after midnight, borrows money without returning it, and occasionally leaves his dirty laundry on your bed. In short, an objective person might consider him to be an inconsiderate slob. But you are not an objective person any longer: Your cognition that you went through hell and high water to get into the fraternity is dissonant with any cognitions about your life in the fraternity that are negative, unpleasant, or undesirable. In order to reduce dissonance, you will try to see your roommate in the most favorable light possible. Again, there are constraints imposed by reality—no matter how much pain and effort you went through, there is no way an inconsiderate slob can be made to look much like Prince Charming—but, with a little ingenuity, you can convince yourself he isn't so bad. What some people might call sloppy, for example, you might consider casual. This, his playing the stereo loudly at night and his leaving his dirty laundry around only serves to demonstrate what an easy-going fellow he is—and because he's so nice and casual about material things, it's certainly understandable he would forget about the money he owes you.

A Prince Charming he isn't, but he's certainly tolerable. Contrast this viewpoint with your attitude had you made no investment of effort: Suppose you had moved into a regular campus dormitory and encountered the same roommate. Because there was no investment of effort in obtaining this room, there is no dissonance; because there is no dissonance, there is no need for you to see your roommate in the best possible light. My guess is you would quickly write him off as an inconsiderate slob and try to make arrangements to move to a different location.

These speculations were tested in an experiment I performed several years ago in collaboration with my friend Judson Mills.[40] In this study, college women volunteered to join a group that would be meeting regularly to discuss various aspects of the psychology of sex. The women were told that, if they wanted to join, they would first have to go through a screening test designed to insure that all people admitted to the group could discuss sex freely and openly. This instruction served to set the stage for the initiation procedure. One-third of the women were assigned to a severe initiation procedure, which required them to recite aloud (in the presence of the male experimenter) a list of obscene words and a few rather lurid sexual passages from contemporary novels. (This experiment was performed in the late fifties, when this kind of procedure was far more embarrassing for most women than it would be today.) One-third of the students underwent a mild procedure, in which they recited a list of words that were sexual but not obscene. The final one-third of the subjects were admitted to the group without undergoing an initiation. Each subject was then allowed to listen in on a discussion being conducted by the members of the group she had just joined. Although the women were led to believe that the discussion was a "live," ongoing one, what they actually heard was a prerecorded tape. The taped discussion was arranged so that it was as dull and as bombastic as possible. After it was over, each subject was asked to rate the discussion in terms of how much she liked it, how interesting it was, how intelligent the participants were, and so forth.

The results supported the predictions: Those subjects who underwent little or no effort to get into the group did not enjoy the discussion very much. They were able to see it as it was—a dull and boring waste of time. Those subjects who went through a severe initiation, however, succeeded in convincing themselves that the same discussion was interesting and worthwhile.

The same pattern has been shown by other investigators using different unpleasant initiations. For example, Harold Gerard and Grover Mathewson[41] conducted an experiment similar in concept to the Aronson-Mills study, except that the subjects in the severe-initiation condition were given painful electric shocks instead of a list of obscene words to read aloud. The results paralleled those of the Aronson and Mills: Subjects who underwent a series of severe electric shocks in order to become members of a group liked that group better than subjects who underwent a series of mild electric shocks.

It should be clear we are *not* asserting that people enjoy painful experiences—they do not; nor are we asserting that people enjoy things because they are associated with painful experiences. What we *are* stating is that, if a person goes through a difficult or a painful experience *in order to attain* some goal or object, that goal or object becomes more attractive. This, if on your way to a discussion group you got hit on the head by a brick, you would not like that group any better; but, if you volunteered to get hit on the head by a brick *in order to join* the discussion group, you would definitely like the group better. The importance of *volunteering* to go through the unpleasant experience was nicely demonstrated in a recent experiment by Joel Cooper.[42] The subjects in this experiment were people who had serious snake phobias. The extent of their fear of snakes was first measured unobtrusively by seeing how closely they would approach a six-foot boa constrictor which was housed in a glass tank. Subjects were then put through either a highly stressful or a highly effortful set of experiences which they were informed might have some therapeutic value in helping reduce their fear of snakes. But—and this is the crucial part—half of the subjects were simply told about the procedure and then put through it. The others were induced to volunteer; they were told that they were not obliged to go through the procedure and were free to leave whenever they wished. After going through the "therapeutic" procedure, each subject was then brought back into the presence of the boa constrictor and asked to approach it as closely as they could. Only those who had been induced to volunteer for the unpleasant therapeutic procedured showed improvement—they were able to come much closer to the boa constrictor than they had before. Those who were simply put through the unpleasant therapeutic procedures (without actually volunteering) showed very little improvement.

In most dissonant situations, there is more than one way to reduce dissonance. In the initiation experiment, for example, we found that people who go through a great deal of effort to get into a dull group convince themselves that the group is more interesting. Is this the only way they could have reduced dissonance? No. They could have convinced themselves that their effort wasn't so great. Indeed, they could have used both strategies simultaneously. This presents a practical problem: To the extent that all of a subject's energies are not aimed in one direction, the potency of any one particular effect is diminished. Thus, suppose you are a basketball coach and you want your team to have a great deal of team spirit, cohesiveness, and camaraderie. You might put each player through a rugged initiation in order to join the team. Naturally, you would want all of the dissonance produced by the initiation to be reduced by each player's deciding he likes his teammates more. If a player chooses, instead, to convince himself that, "Ah, it wasn't such a tough initiation," he reduces dissonance without increasing his esteem for his teammates. As a coach, you might succeed in channeling the dissonance-reducing energy in the direction of intragroup cohesiveness by making the initiation so severe that a person would be unable to consider it a lark. You might bolster this "channeling" by orally emphasizing how severe the initiation is, in order to make it even more difficult for a player to think of it as easy.

The Justification of Cruelty

Over and over again I have made the point that we have a need to convince ourselves that we are decent, reasonable people. We have seen how this can cause us to change our attitudes on issues important to us. We have seen, for example, that if a person makes a counterattitudinal speech favoring the use and legalization of marijuana, for little external justification, and learns that the video tape of that speech will be shown to a group of persuadable youngsters, the individual tends to convince him or herself that marijuana isn't so bad—as a means of feeling less like an evil person. In this section, we will discuss a variation of this theme: Suppose you performed an action that caused a great deal of harm to an innocent young man. Let us further suppose the harm was real and unambiguous. Your cognition "I am a decent, fair, and reasonable person" would be dissonant with your cognition "I have hurt another person." If the harm is clear, then you cannot reduce the dissonance by changing your opinion on the issue, thus convincing yourself you've done no harm, as the people in the marijuana experiment did. In this situation, the most effective way to reduce dissonance would be to maximize the culpability of the victim of your action—to convince yourself the victim deserved what he got, either because he did something to bring it on himself or because he was a bad, evil, dirty, reprehensible person.

This mechanism might even operate if you did not directly cause the harm that befell the victim, if you only disliked him (prior to his victimization) and were hoping that harm would befall him. For example, after four students at Kent State University were shot and killed by members of the Ohio National Guard, several rumors quickly spread to the effect that (1) both of the women who were slain were pregnant (and therefore, by implication, were oversexed and wanton); (2) the bodies of all four students were crawling with lice; and (3) the victims were so ridden with syphilis they would have been dead in two weeks anyway.[43]

These rumors were totally untrue. It *was* true the slain students were all clean, decent, bright people. Indeed, two of them were not even involved in the demonstrations that resulted in the tragedy but were peacefully walking across campus when they were gunned down. Why were the townspeople so eager to believe and spread these rumors? It is impossible to know for sure, but my guess is that it was for reasons similar to the reasons rumors were spread among the people in India studied by Prasad and Sinha (see pp. 115–116)—that is, because the rumors were comforting. Picture the situation: Kent is a conservative small town in Ohio. Many of the townspeople were infuriated at the radical behavior of some of the students. Some were probably hoping the students would get their comeuppance; but death was more than they deserved. In such circumstances, any information putting the victims in a bad light helped to reduce dissonance by implying that it was, in fact, a good thing they died. In addition, this eagerness to believe that the victims were sinful and deserved their fate was expressed in ways that were more direct: Several members of the Ohio National Guard stoutly maintained that the victims deserved to die, and a Kent high school teacher, whom James Michener interviewed, even went so far as to state "anyone who appears on the streets of a city like Kent with long hair, dirty clothes or barefooted deserves to be shot." She went on to say this dictum applied even to her own children.[44]

It is tempting simply to write such people off as crazy—but we should not make such judgments lightly. Although it's certainly true all people are not as extreme as the high-school teacher, it is also true that just about everyone can be influenced in this direction. To illustrate this point, let's look at the behavior of Nikita Khrushchev, just before he became Premier of the Soviet Union. In his memoirs, Khrushchev described himself as a tough and skeptical person who certainly wasn't in the habit of believing everything he was told. He cited several examples of his own skepticism and reluctance to believe scandalous stories about people and compared himself favorably, in this regard, with Stalin. But let's look at Khrushchev's credulity when it suited his own needs. Soon after Stalin's death, the head of the secret police, Lavrenty Beria, was on the verge of assuming leadership. Khrushchev convinced the other members of the Presidium that Beria was a dangerous man. Beria was then arrested, imprisoned, and eventually executed. Dissonance theory would lead to the prediction that, because of his central role in Beria's downfall, Khrushchev might be willing to believe negative things about him—no matter how absurd. But let's allow Khrushchev to tell it in his own words:

> After it was all over [Beria's arrest], Malenkov took me aside and said, "Listen to what my chief bodyguard has to say." The man came over to me and said, "I have only just heard that Beria has been arrested. I want to inform you that he raped my step-daughter, a seventh-grader. A year or so ago her grandmother died and my wife had to go the hospital, leaving the girl at home alone. One evening she went out to buy some bread near the building where Beria lives. There she came across an old man who watched her intently. She was frightened. Someone came and took her to Beria's home. Beria had her sit down with him for supper. She drank something, fell asleep, and he raped her.". . . Later we were given a list of more than a hundred girls and women who had been raped by Beria. He had used the same routine on all of them. He gave them some dinner and offered them wine with a sleeping potion in it.[45]

It seems fantastic that anyone would believe Beria had actually perpetrated this deed on more than one hundred women. And yet, Khrushchev apparently believed it—perhaps because he had a strong need to believe it.

These examples fit our analysis based on dissonance theory, but they do not offer definitive proof. For example, it might be that the National Guardsmen at Kent State believed the students deserved to die even *before* they fired at them. Perhaps Khrushchev would have believed those fantastic stories about Beria even *before* he had caused Beria's demise; it might even be true Khrushchev *didn't* believe those stories but merely presented them in order to discredit Beria.

To be more certain the justification of cruelty can occur in such situations, it is essential for the social psychologist to step back from the helter-skelter of the real world (temporarily) and test predictions in the more controlled world of the experimental laboratory. Ideally, if we want to measure attitude change as a result of dissonant cognitions, we should know what the attitudes were *before* the dissonance-arousing event occurred. Such a situation was produced in an experiment performed by Keith Davis and Edward Jones.[46] They persuaded students to volunteer to help with an experiment: Each student's participation consisted of watching another student being interviewed and then, on the basis of this observation, telling the other student that he believed him to be a shallow, untrustworthy, and dull person. The major finding in this experiment was that subjects who volunteered for this assignment succeeded in *convincing themselves* that they didn't like the victim of their cruelty. In short, *after* saying things certain to hurt the other student, they convinced themselves he deserved it—that is, they found him less attractive than they did *before* they hurt him. This shift occurred *in spite of* the fact the subjects were aware that the other student had done nothing to merit their criticism and that their victimizing him was merely in response to the experimenter's instructions.

An experiment by David Glass[47] had a similar result. In this study, when induced to deliver a series of electric shocks to other people, individuals who considered themselves good and decent people derogated their victims as a result of having caused them this pain. This result is clearest among people with high self-esteem. If I consider myself to be a scoundrel, then causing others to suffer does not introduce as much dissonance; therefore, I have less of a need to convince myself they deserved their fate. Consider the irony: It is precisely because I think I am such a nice person that, if I do something that causes you pain, I must convince myself that you are a rat. In other words, because nice guys like me don't go around hurting innocent people, you must have deserved every nasty thing I did to you.

There are circumstances that limit the generality of this phenomenon. One of those was mentioned above: Namely, people with low self-esteem have less need to derogate their victims. Another factor limiting the derogation phenomenon is the capacity of the victim to retaliate. If the victim is able and willing to retaliate at some future time, then a harm-doer feels equity will be restored and thus has no need to justify the action by derogating the victim. In an ingenious experiment by Ellen Berscheid and her associates,[48] college students volunteered for an experiment in which each of them delivered a painful electric shock to a fellow student; as expected, each subject derogated the victim as a result of having delivered the shock. But half of the students were told there would be a turnabout—that is, the other students would be given the opportunity to shock *them*. Those who were led to believe their victims would be able to retaliate did *not* derogate them. In short, because the victims were able to retaliate, dissonance was reduced. The harm-doers had no need to belittle their victims in order to convince themselves that the victims deserved it.

These results suggest that, during a war, soldiers might have a greater need to derogate civilian victims (because they can't retaliate) than military victims. During the court-martial of Lt. William Calley for his role in the slaughter of innocent civilians at My Lai, his psychiatrist reported that the Lieutenant came to regard the Vietnamese people as less than human. Perhaps the research reported in this section helps to shed some light on this phenomenon. Social psychologists have learned that people do not perform acts of cruelty and come out unscathed. I do not know for sure how Lt. Calley (and thousands of others) came to regard the Vietnamese as subhuman, but it seems reasonable to assume that, when we are engaged in a war in which, through our actions, a great number of innocent people are being killed, we might try to derogate the victims in order to justify our complicity in the outcome. We might poke fun at them, refer to them as "gooks," dehumanize them; but, once we have succeeded in doing that, watch out—because it becomes easier to hurt and kill "subhumans" than to hurt and kill fellow human beings. Thus, reducing dissonance in this way has terrible future consequences—it increases the likelihood that the atrocities we are willing to commit will become greater and greater. We will elaborate on this theme in the next chapter. For now, I would like to enlarge on a point I made in Chapters 1 and 2: In the final analysis, people are accountable for their own actions. Not everyone behaved as Lt. Calley behaved. At the same time, it should be noted that Lt. Calley was not alone in his behavior; he stands as a striking example of a rather common phenomenon. With this in mind, it is important to acknowledge that certain situational factors can exert a very powerful impact upon human actions. Accordingly, before we can write off such behavior as merely bizarre, or merely crazy, or merely villainous, it would be wise to examine the situation that sets up the mechanism for this kind of behavior. We can then begin to understand the terrible price we are paying for allowing certain conditions to exist. Perhaps, eventually, we can do something to avoid these conditions. Dissonance theory helps to shed some light on this mechanism.

Of course, this kind of situation is not limited to wars. A great number of violent acts can be perpetrated on innocent victims that can lead to justifications, which in turn, can lead to more violence. Imagine you live in a society that is unfair to minority groups like blacks and Chicanos. Just to take a wild example, let us pretend that for several decades the white majority was not allowing the blacks and Chicanos to attend first-rate public schools but instead was providing them with a second-rate and stultifying education. As a consequence of this "benign neglect," the average black child and the average Chicano child are less well educated and less motivated than the average white child at the same grade level. They demonstrate this by doing poorly on achievement tests. Such a situation provides a golden opportunity for civic leaders to justify their discriminatory behavior, and hence, to reduce dissonance. "You see," they might say, "colored people are stupid (because they perform poorly on the achievement test); see how clever we were when we decided against wasting our resources by trying to provide them with a high-quality education. These people are unteachable." We call this phenomenon a *self-fulfilling prophecy*. It provides a perfect justification for cruelty and neglect. So, too, is the attribution of moral inferiority to blacks and Chicanos. We imprison racial minorities in overcrowded ghettos; and we set up a situation in which skin color almost inevitably unleashes forces preventing people from participating in the opportunities for growth and success existing for most white Americans. Through the magic of television, they see people succeeding and living in the luxury of middle-class respectability. They become painfully aware of the opportunities, comforts, and luxuries unavailable to them. If their frustration leads them to violence or if their despair leads them to drugs, it is fairly easy for their white brothers and sisters to sit back complacently, shake their heads knowingly, and attribute this behavior to some kind of moral inferiority. As Edward Jones and Richard Nisbett[49] point out, when some misfortune befalls *us*, we tend to attribute the cause to something in the environment; but when we see the same misfortune befalling *another person*, we tend to attribute the cause to some weakness inherent in that person's personality.

The Psychology of Inevitability

George Bernard Shaw was hard hit by his father's alcoholism, but he tried to make light of it. He once wrote: "If you cannot get rid of the family skeleton, you may as well make it dance."[50] In a sense, dissonance theory describes the ways people have of making their skeletons dance—of trying to live with unpleasant outcomes. This is particularly true when a situation arises that is both negative and inevitable. Here people attempt to make the best of things by cognitively minimizing the unpleasantness of the situation. In one experiment, Jack Brehm[51] got children to volunteer to eat a vegetable they had previously said they disliked a lot. After they had eaten the vegetable, the experimenter led half of the children to believe they could expect to eat much more of that vegetable in the future; the remaining children were not so informed. The children who were led to believe it was inevitable that they would be eating the vegetable in the future succeeded in convincing themselves that the particular vegetable was not so very bad. In short, the cognition "I dislike that vegetable" is dissonant with the cognition "I will be eating that vegetable in the future." In order to reduce the dissonance, the children came to believe the vegetable was really not as noxious as they had previously thought. John Darley and Ellen Berscheid[52] showed that the same phenomenon works with people as well as vegetables. In their experiment, college women volunteered to participate in a series of meetings in which each student would be discussing her sexual behavior and sexual standards with another woman whom she didn't know. Before beginning these discussion sessions, each subject was given two folders. Each of the folders contained a personality description of a young woman who had supposedly volunteered for the same experience; the descriptions contained a mixture of pleasant and unpleasant characteristics. Half of the subjects were led to believe they were going to interact with the young woman described in folder A, and the remaining subjects were led to believe they were going to interact with the one described in folder B. Before actually meeting these women, the subjects were asked to evaluate each of them on the basis of the personality descriptions they had read. Those subjects who felt it was inevitable they were going to share their intimate secrets with the young woman described in folder A found her much more appealing as a person than the one described in folder B, whereas those who believed they had to interact with the young woman described in folder B found *her* much more appealing. Just as with vegetables, inevitability makes the heart grow fonder. The knowledge that one is inevitably going to be spending time with another person enhances the positive aspects of that person—or at least deemphasizes his or her negative aspects. In short, people tend to make the best of something they know is bound to occur.

The Importance of Self-Esteem

Throughout this chapter, we have seen how our commitment to a particular course of action can freeze or change our attitudes, distort our perception, and determine the kind of information we seek out. In addition, we have seen that a person can become committed to a situation in a number of different ways—by making a decision, by working hard in order to attain a goal, by believing something is inevitable, by engaging in any action having serious consequences (such as hurting someone), and so on. As we have mentioned before, the deepest form of commitment takes place in those situations in which a person's self-esteem is at stake. Thus, if I perform a cruel or a stupid action, this threatens my self-esteem, because it turns my mind to the possibility I am a cruel or stupid person. In the hundreds of experiments inspired by the theory of cognitive dissonance, the clearest results were obtained in those situations in which a person's self-esteem was involved. Moreover, as one might expect, we have seen that those individuals with the highest self-esteem experience the most dissonance when they behave in a stupid or cruel manner.

What happens when an individual has low self-esteem? Theoretically, if such a person were to commit a stupid or immoral action, he or she would not experience much dissonance. The cognition "I have done an immoral thing" is *consonant* with the cognition "I am a schlunk." In short, people who believe themselves to be schlunks expect to do schlunky things. In other words, people with low self-esteem will not find it terribly difficult to commit immoral acts—because committing immoral acts is not dissonant with their self-concept. On the other hand, people with high self-esteem are more likely to resist the temptation to commit immoral acts, because to behave immorally would produce a great deal of dissonance.

I tested this proposition in collaboration with David Mettee.[53] We predicted that individuals who had a low opinion of themselves would be more likely to cheat (if given the opportunity) than individuals who had a high opinion of themselves. It should be made clear we were not making the simple prediction that people who believe themselves to be dishonest will cheat more than people who believe themselves to be honest. Our prediction was a little more daring; it was based on the assumption that, if normal people receive a temporary blow to their self-esteem (for example, if they are jilted by their lover or flunk an exam) and thus feel low and worthless, they are more likely to cheat at cards, kick their dog, wear mismatched pajamas, or do any number of things consistent with a low opinion of themselves. As a function of feeling they are low people, individuals will commit low acts.

In our experiment, we temporarily modified the self-esteem of female college students by giving them a false information about their personalities. After taking a personality test, one-third of the students were given positive feedback; specifically, they were told the test indicated they were mature, interesting, deep, and so forth. Another one-third of the students were given negative feedback; they were told the test indicated they were relatively immature, uninteresting, rather shallow, and the like. The remaining one-third of the students were not given any information about the results of the test.

Immediately afterwards, the students were scheduled to participate in an experiment, conducted by a different psychologist, that had no apparent relation to the personality inventory. As a part of this second experiment, the subjects participated in a game of cards against some of their fellow students. This was a gambling game in which the students were allowed to bet money and were told they could keep whatever money they won. In the course of the game, the subjects were presented with a few opportunities to cheat in a situation where it seemed impossible to be detected. The situation was arranged so that, if a student decided *not* to cheat, she would certainly lose, whereas, if she decided to cheat, she would be certain to win a sizable sum of money.

The results clearly showed that those students who had previously received information designed to lower their self-esteem cheated to a far greater extent than those who had received the high self-esteem information. The control group—those receiving no information—fell exactly in between. These findings suggest it would be well worth the effort of parents and teachers to alert themselves to the potentially far-reaching consequences of their own behavior as it affects the self-esteem of their children and students. Specifically, if low self-esteem is an important antecedent of criminal or cruel behavior, then we might want to do everything possible to help individuals learn to respect and love themselves.

Physiological and Motivational Effects of Dissonance

How far can the effects of dissonance extend? In the past several years, researchers have shown it can go beyond attitudes; it can modify the way we experience basic physiological drives. Under certain well-specified conditions, dissonance reduction can lead hungry people to experience less hunger, thirsty people to experience less thirst, and people undergoing intensive electric shock to experience less pain. Here's how it works: Imagine Vic Volunteer is induced to *commit himself* to a situation in which he will be deprived of food or water for a long time, or in which he will experience electric shock. If Vic has *low external justification* for doing this, he will experience dissonance. His cognitions concerning his hunger pangs, his parched throat, or the pain of electrical shock are each dissonant with his cognition that he volunteered to go through these experiences and is not getting very much in return. In order to reduce this dissonance, Vic convinces himself the hunger isn't so intense, or the thirst isn't so bad, or the pain isn't so great. This should not be astonishing. Although hunger, thirst, and pain all have physiological bases, they also have a strong psychological component. For example, through suggestion, meditation, hypnosis, placebo pills, the bedside manner of a skillful physician, or some combination of these, perceived pain can be reduced. Experimental social psychologists have shown that, under conditions of high dissonance arousal, ordinary people, without any special skills in hypnosis or meditation, can accomplish the same ends for themselves.

Thus, Philip Zimbardo and his colleagues[54] have subjected many people to intense electric shocks. Half of these people were in a high-dissonance condition—that is, they were induced to *commit themselves* to volunteer for the experience and were given very little external justification—and the other half were in a low-dissonance condition—that is, they had no choice in the matter and had a great deal of external justification. The results showed that the people in the high-dissonance condition reported experiencing less pain than the people in the low-dissonance condition. Moreover, this phenomenon extended beyond their subjective reports: There is clear evidence that the physiological response to pain (as measured by the galvanic skin response) was somewhat less intense in the high-dissonance condition. In addition, the pain of subjects in the high-dissonance condition interfered less with the tasks they were performing. Thus, not only was their pain *reported* as less intense, but it also affected their behavior less intensely.

Similar results have been shown for hunger and thirst. Jack Brehm[55] reported a series of experiments in which people were deprived of either food or water for long periods of time. In addition to experiencing hunger or thirst, these individuals were experiencing either high or low dissonance for much the same reasons Zimbardo's subjects were experiencing high or low dissonance. Specifically, some of the subjects had low external justification for undergoing the hunger or thirst, while others had high external justification. For the subjects experiencing great dissonance, the best available way to reduce it was to minimize the experience of hunger or thirst. In separate experiments on hunger and thirst, Brehm reported that the subjects in the high-dissonance condition said they were less hungry (or thirsty) than low-dissonance subjects who were deprived of food (or water) for the same length of time. Again, this was no mere verbal report—after the experiment, when all of the subjects were allowed to eat (or drink) freely, the high-dissonance subjects actually consumed less food (or water) than the low-dissonance subjects.

A Critical Look at Cognitive Dissonance as a Theory

I'd like to invite the reader backstage again. Recall that, in the preceding chapter (pp. 94–97), we went backstage to look at how scientists worked to make sense out of conflicting data about how the size of a discrepancy affects opinion change. This time we will go behind the scenes to look at the evolution and development of a theory. Why do scientists invent theories? A theory is proposed in order to make sense out of an occurrence or a number of apparently unrelated occurrences. In addition, by providing us with a new way of looking at the world, a theory can generate new hypotheses, new research, and new facts. Theories are neither right nor wrong. Rather, theories are judged according to how useful they are; they are more or less useful depending on how well they account for the existing facts and how fruitful they are at generating new information. But no theory provides us with a perfect accounting of the way the world is. Thus, theories are frequently challenged and criticized. These challenges inevitably result in the reformulation of an existing theory or in the invention of an entirely new theory that seems to provide a better fit. When theories are reformulated, they are altered either to increase or decrease their scope. For example, if a theory is too vague or imprecise, an attempt may be made to simplify it, to limit its domain, or to restructure its language in order to increase our certainty about the nature of the prediction being made. With this in mind, let us examine the theory of cognitive dissonance.

The Refinement of Dissonance Theory. As we have seen, dissonance theory has proved to be a useful way of looking at human interaction. But there were some serious conceptual problems with the theory as originally stated. Perhaps the major difficulty stems from the fact the original statement was conceptually vague. Recall the original theoretical statement: "Cognitive dissonance is a state of tension that occurs whenever an individual simultaneously holds two cognitions that are psychologically inconsistent. Because the occurrence of cognitive dissonance is unpleasant, people are motivated to reduce it." But precisely in what way are cognitions inconsistent? The vagueness stems from the fact that the scope of the theory was not limited to situations inconsistent on logical grounds alone. Rather, the inconsistencies that produce dissonance are *psychological* inconsistencies. Indeed, this makes the theory exciting and increases its scope. Unfortunately, it also renders the theory less than perfectly precise. It would be relatively easy to make a precise statement about the domain of the theory if its predictions were limited to instances of logical inconsistency because there are strict rules for determining whether conclusions do or do not follow from premises on the basis of formal logic. For example, take the famous syllogism:

> All men are mortal.
> Socrates is a man.
> Therefore, Socrates is mortal.

If someone believed Socrates was not mortal, while accepting the first two premises, this would be a clear case of dissonance. By contrast, let us take the typical dissonance situation:

I believe that smoking cigarettes causes cancer.
I smoke cigarettes.

The cognition "I smoke cigarettes" is not inconsistent with the cognition "cigarette smoking causes cancer" *on formal logical grounds.* It is inconsistent on psychological grounds; that is, the implications of the two statements are dissonant because we know most people do not want to die. But it is sometimes difficult to be certain what will be psychologically inconsistent for any one person. For example, suppose you have great admiration for Franklin Delano Roosevelt; then you learn that, throughout his marriage, he was carrying on a clandestine love affair. Will that cause dissonance? It is difficult to know. If you place a high value on marital fidelity *and* you also believe great historical figures should not violate this sanction, then you will experience some dissonance. To reduce it you will either change your attitudes about Roosevelt or soften your attitudes about marital infidelity. Because a large number of people probably do not hold these values simultaneously, however, they will not experience dissonance. Moreover, even if a person *does* hold these two values simultaneously, the cognitions may not be particularly salient—so how do we know whether or not they cause dissonance? This leads us to a major point: Even when the cognitions are undeniably salient, the degree of dissonance is certain to be small compared to what it would be if *you* had violated your own values—as was true, for example, in Judson Mills' experiment with the youngsters who cheated on their tests.

In recent years, a great deal of the initial vagueness of the conceptual statement has been reduced by several theorists.[56] For example, as discussed earlier in this chapter, my own research[57] has led me to conclude that dissonance effects may be limited to situations in which our behavior violates our own self-concept. This can happen in one of two ways: (1) if we consciously and knowingly do something stupid; (2) if we do something that hurts another person—even if we do it unknowingly. An example of a stupid act might be going through a severe initiation to get into a group that could easily turn out to be very uninteresting, or perhaps volunteering to write a counterattitudinal essay for very little reward. An example of a hurtful, guilt-producing action would be misleading a person by convincing him or her to do something you think might be harmful, saying cruel things to a person who has done you no harm, administering an electric shock to an innocent victim, and so on.

But these changes in the conceptualization of dissonance theory did not materialize out of thin air. They came gradually—partly as a result of external criticism. For example, twenty years ago I believed dissonance could exist between any two cognitions and the predicted results would inevitably follow. Mostly the results *did* follow because, without our realizing it, we dissonance theorists were designing our experiments in a manner such that a violation of the self-concept was almost always involved. That is, in our experiments, people were either knowingly committing themselves to stupid acts (like writing a counterattitudinal essay) or doing something immoral (like cheating or deceiving another person). Because we didn't realize these factors were involved, we were occasionally surprised when what seemed like a clear prediction did not turn out. For example, Milton Rosenberg[58] once performed an experiment similar to Arthur Cohen's experiment (reported on pp. 000–000) in which subjects were paid either a large reward or a small reward for writing an essay against their own beliefs. Rosenberg's results came out quite differently from Cohen's, with the subjects given a *large* reward showing a greater change in their own beliefs. This produced a great deal of confusion. Then, Darwyn Linder and his colleagues[59] focused attention on what had seemed to be a minor difference between the two experiments. The subjects in Cohen's experiment knowingly committed themselves to write an essay favoring the rather brutal actions of the New Haven police during a student demonstration, but they were informed at the outset they didn't have to do it if they didn't want to. Unlike the participants in Cohen's experiment, Rosenberg's subjects were not given a clear idea of what they were going to do before they agreed to do it. That is, while they were supposedly waiting to participate in one experiment, they were induced to commit themselves to help out another researcher. It wasn't until *after* they had been committed to the task that they realized they were going to have to write an essay that went against their own beliefs. It was too late to pull out. In this situation, it was easy for the subjects to remove their self-concept from the situation by saying in effect, "How was I supposed to know?"*

Intrigued by this difference, Linder and his associates then performed an experiment in which they systematically varied the subjects' freedom of choice. They found clear evidence: When the subjects knew what they were letting themselves in for in advance, there was a dissonance effect—those who wrote a counterattitudinal essay for a small reward changed their beliefs in the direction of their essay to a greater extent than those who did it for a large reward. When the subjects did not have this freedom of choice but committed themselves to an unknown task, the results were just the opposite. Thus, Linder's experiment and subsequent research[60] have clarified the limitations of dissonance effects and pointed to a new direction in the evolution of the theory.

Alternative Explanations of Dissonance Effects. Although the evolution of dissonance theory in terms of the self-concept has clarified the theory and has led to more precise predictions, the theory is still subject to challenge. For example, Daryl Bem[61] was not happy with the theory because it relied too heavily on the assumption of internal events that are difficult to measure. Bem made an earnest attempt to explain some of the phenomena discovered by dissonance theory in more concrete and readily observable terms. Briefly, his idea was to move away from a conceptual reliance on such internal states as "cognitions" and "psychological discomfort" and to replace such concepts with the more precise "stimulus-response" language of behaviorism. Bem concentrated his efforts on the area of counterattitudinal advocacy. Let's look at the situation through Bem's eyes.

Suppose you see a woman walk into a cafeteria, survey all of the desserts being offered, pick up a wedge of rhubarb pie, and begin to eat it. What would you conclude? Simple: "She

*Recall the two ways in which dissonance can be aroused through a violation of the self-concept: (1) knowingly doing something stupid, or (2) doing something that hurts another person. In the first situation, if it's easy to say, "How was I supposed to know?" there will be little dissonance. In the second situation, the fact that someone gets hurt makes it impossible to avoid dissonance simply by saying, "How was I supposed to know?"

must like rhubarb pie." Given the fact she has freedom of choice and a great many options, why else would she have chosen rhubarb pie? So far, so good. Now, suppose *you* walk into a cafeteria, select a wedge of rhubarb pie, and eat it. What would you conclude from your own actions? Simple: "I must like rhubarb pie—why else would I be eating it?" Bem applied this reasoning to an area the reader is very familiar with by now. Suppose you observe somebody writing an essay favoring the fierce actions of the New Haven police during a student demonstration, and you know he's being paid only fifty cents to do it. Wouldn't you conclude he must really believe that the actions of the New Haven police were right and reasonable? Why else would he say so? Surely not for the fifty cents. Suppose you find *yourself* writing an essay favoring the fierce actions of the New Haven police for a payment of fifty cents?

In short, Bem's notion is that many of the dissonance effects are nothing more than reasonable inferences people make about their attitudes based upon their perceptions of their own behavior. To test his notion, Bem has designed a method that is as simple as his theory. He merely describes an experimental procedure to his subjects—for example, Cohen's experiment on attitudes about the behavior of the New Haven police outlined above. He then asks his subjects to guess the real attitude of each of the subjects in the experiment he has just described—for example, how much did each of Cohen's essay writers *really* favor the actions of the New Haven police? Bem's results parallel those of the original experiment: His subjects guessed that the people who wrote essays for fifty cents favoring the actions of the New Haven police must have believed what they said to a greater extent than those who wrote similar essays for five dollars.

Bem's reasoning is elegant in its simplicity; his analysis is certainly more sparse than the traditional analyses of these data in terms of such hypothetical constructs as psychological discomfort, self-concept, and so on. In science, we strive for simplicity and parsimony; if two theories accurately account for a body of data, the simpler one is preferable. But does Bem's conceptualization account for these data as accurately as dissonance theory? It's difficult to be certain, but Bem's research seems to ignore a vital fact: The actor in a situation has more information than the observer. That is, when I write an essay favoring the brutal behavior of the New Haven police, chances are I *know* what my beliefs were before I wrote it; when you observe me writing an essay favoring the actions of the New Haven police, you *don't know* what my beliefs were beforehand. Both Russell Jones and his colleagues and Jane Piliavin and her colleagues[62] have demonstrated that, when observers know the prior beliefs of the actor in the situation, their statements no longer parallel those of the subjects in the original experiment—that is, Bem's results are not replicated. Does this mean Bem's analysis is inaccurate? Not necessarily. It is possible that, in many situations, even the *actors* are uncertain or ambivalent about their own prior beliefs and attitudes and thus utilize their observation of this behavior as a cue for determining what they are. Bem calls this concept a process of "self-reference" or "self-judgment." That is, it is conceivable that, prior to writing an essay favoring the actions of the New Haven police, Cohen's subjects may not have had a clear notion of how they felt about it—their behavior provided them with useful information. In the clearest examples of the operation of dissonance reduction, however, one's prior beliefs are well-defined; for example, subjects in the Festinger-Carlsmith experiment knew, initially, that the task they had performed was boring. It is when their behavior contradicts their beliefs and values—when they tell another person the task is interesting and fun—that dissonance is aroused and they begin striving to reduce it by altering their attitudes. Where the inconsistency between one's attitudes and behavior is significant and clear, recent research[63] supports dissonance theory over self-reference processes to explain and predict the resulting changes.

Dissonance as a State of Arousal. A crucial part of our statement of dissonance theory contends that a person's tendency to change his or her attitudes is motivated by an aversive state of arousal caused by the violation of the self-concept. It's difficult for me to believe that discomfort does not accompany dissonance. Like almost all investigators who have performed experiments testing hypotheses derived from dissonance theory, I am convinced that a person experiencing dissonance shows signs of being uncomfortable. Phenomenologically, when people encounter a dissonance-producing situation, their behavior does not seem to match the cool, calculated, objective, unemotional deduction game Bem describes. But such unsystematic perceptions by researchers do not, by themselves, constitute convincing data. Is there any independent evidence that people experiencing dissonance are in a state of discomfort? An experiment by Michael Pallak and Thane Pittman[64] lends support to the notion that psychological discomfort exists during a state of dissonance. Before describing their experiment, I should first mention a phenomenon discovered through research on the psychology of learning: Suppose you are performing a task that has several possible responses that compete for your attention (as opposed to a task in which there is one clear response). If you are in a state of high drive (that is, if you are very hungry, very thirsty, very sexy, or whatever), you will perform more poorly than if you are in a low-drive state. On the other hand, if the task is a clear and simple one, being in a high-drive state seems to energize a person without causing interference; hence, you will be more successful at such a task if you are in a high-drive state. Pallak and Pittman simply put some subjects in highly dissonant situation and others in a situation that produced very little dissonance. The low-dissonance subjects performed better than the high-dissonance subjects in a complex task (one with many competing responses), whereas the high-dissonance subjects performed better than the lows in a simple task (one with few competing responses). Thus, dissonance arousal seems to act like hunger or thirst.

An interesting experiment by Mark Zanna and Joel Cooper[65] provides further evidence that dissonance causes arousal. Participants in their study were given a *placebo*—a sugar pill having no physiological effect whatever. Some were told that the pill would arouse them and make them feel tense, while others were told the pill would relax them. Participants in a control condition were told the pill would not affect them. After ingesting a pill, each person voluntarily wrote a counterattitudinal essay (sound familiar?), thus creating dissonance. Zanna and Cooper found that participants in the control condition underwent considerable attitude change, as would be expected. Participants in the "aroused" condition, however, did not change their attitudes—they apparently attributed their discomfort to the pill, not the counterattitudinal essay. But the most exciting results occurred in the "relaxed" condition. These people changed their attitudes even *more* than control participants did. How come? There is only one reasonable explanation: They inferred that writing the counterattitudinal essay was *very* tension-producing, *very* inconsistent with their perception of themselves as "decent, good, and reasonable" because they experienced tension (due to the dissonance manipulation) even after taking a "relaxation" pill. Thus, their attitudes changed even more. Furthermore, in a recent experiment, Charles Bond[66] gave students a description of the Zanna and Cooper study; he then asked them to predict which groups would undergo the most and the least attitude change. Contrary to Bem's theory, these predictions were dissimilar to the actual behavior of Zanna and Cooper's subjects.

Taken together, these data indicate the presence of something akin to physiological discomfort during dissonance arousal. Accordingly, although Bem's explanation of dissonance phenomena is simple, straightforward, and useful, the analysis in terms of "discomfort produced by a violation of the self-concept" strikes me as being a richer and more accurate reflection of the dissonance phenomena.

Practical Applications of Dissonance Theory

One of the reasons the theory of cognitive dissonance has attracted such great interest and inspired so much research is its ability to explain and predict phenomena not readily explainable in common sense terms. Furthermore, as the reader has seen, dissonance theory has been applied to account for a great many phenomena ranging from how rumors are spread to major changes in important attitudes. It is exciting to use the theory as a way of understanding a number of events in contemporary society that otherwise might be puzzling indeed. For example, consider the Three Mile Island crisis in 1979, when an accident at the nuclear power plant caused an unstable condition in the reactor that lasted for several days, posing the threat of a meltdown that would result in catastrophic contamination of the surrounding area and endanger hundreds of thousands of people living in the vicinity. Common sense would suggest that the people living closest to the power plant would be the most frightened and, therefore, the most likely to take action. Dissonance theory makes a different prediction. Suppose you were living within a few miles of the plant at the time of the incident. Since radioactive steam escaped from the reactor during the initial stages of the accident, it is possible that you and your loved ones already have been contaminated. How will you respond? You can evacuate the area, but leaving your job and finding temporary lodging would be costly and fraught with hardship. Besides, even if you *do* evacuate, there is the likelihood that you have already been exposed to radiation. Many contradictory reports are circulating about the extent of the danger. Some of your neighbors have decided to leave; others are belittling the magnitude of the threat. After a time, the authorities from the Nuclear Regulatory Commission (NRC) arrive on the scene, issuing reassuring statements that the danger of leakage of radiation was minor and the probability of a serious disaster is minimal. How likely are you to believe these statements?

Our guess at the time was that people living closest to the power plant would be the most likely to latch on to these pronouncements and believe them, grasping at whatever reassurances they could find. If you were living near Three Mile Island, your cognition that you chose to live close enough to the nuclear power plant to absorb harmful radiation in case of an accident would be dissonant with your self-concept as smart, reasonable, prudent, and caring for your family. Therefore, regardless of whether or not you have evacuated, you would be eager to believe these reassurances. Even when the authorities changed their stance a couple of days later, advising that pregnant women *should* evacuate, the tendency of those living near the plant would be to trust the NRC spokesman when he said that they are merely being cautious and the danger is still minimal. Contrast this with the reaction of those living just outside the immediate danger zone. These people are also worried and scared, though they are threatened less directly and have not already been contaminated. Since they are not as deeply committed as those living in the immediate danger zone, they should be more able to express their skepticism and anger—indeed, it would be in their self-interest to do so, because they *would* be imperiled if the situation in the nuclear power plant deteriorated or if the crisis was more serious than what was being publicized. Our speculations, that residents nearest the Three Mile Island reactor would attribute more credibility to the pronouncements of the Nuclear Regulatory Commission than would those living further away, were confirmed by an extensive survey conducted shortly after the incident.[67] The data reveal that respondents closest to the plant were significantly more likely to say that the information conveyed by the NRC was extremely useful; those living further than 15 miles away were more inclined to say the information was totally useless. Anecdotal evidence also supports this conclusion: It was reported that the most dire rumors about the crisis came from as far away as California, and while the national media were filled with reports of the NRC's incompetence and inadequacy, the populace near Three Mile Island was said to have greeted the NRC "like cavalry riding to a nick-of-time rescue."[68]

Beyond its power to help us understand and predict a variety of phenomena, a theory is of particular value if it can be practically applied in ways that benefit people. Earlier in this chapter, we pointed out cognitive dissonance theory's relevance for educators wishing to instill intrinsic motivation for learning in their students, or for parents looking for a more effective means than severe punishment for helping their children learn moral and humane values. Institutions like the Marine Corps and college fraternities have long employed severe initiations to increase their members' commitment to the group. A recent experiment by Danny Axsom and Joel Cooper[69] provides a particularly compelling example of how dissonance theory can be used to help solve a difficult personal problem—obesity. Hypothesizing that expending a great deal of effort to reach an objective would increase a person's commitment to that goal, they induced a number of overweight women to volunteer for a weight control program and engaged them in intellectual activities requiring either a large or a small amount of effort but that were unrelated to losing weight. Over the four weeks of the program, only slight weight losses were observed in either group. But *six months and a year* later, when the experimenters contacted the women again, they discovered major differences: The women who had expended a great amount of effort had lost an average of eight pounds, while those who had performed tasks requiring little effort in the program had not lost any weight. Changing one's attitudes in order to justify one's behavior can not only have powerful effects but can initiate processes that are remarkably persistent over long periods of time.

Finally, dissonance theory has been used as a way of increasing our understanding of events that totally confound our imagination—like the Jonestown massacre. It goes without saying that the event was tragic in the extreme. In addition, it seems beyond comprehension that a single individual could have such power that, at his command, hundreds of people would kill their own children and themselves. How could this happen? The Jim Jones phenomenon is far too complex to be understood fully by a simple and sovereign analysis. But one clue does emanate from the *foot in the door* phenomenon discussed earlier in this chapter. Jones extracted great trust from his followers once step at a time. Indeed, close scrutiny reveals a chain of ever-increasing commitment on the part of his followers. While it is almost impossible to comprehend fully the final event, it becomes slightly more comprehensible if we look at it as part of a series. As I mentioned earlier in this chapter, once a small commitment is made, the stage is set for ever-increasing commitments.

Let us start at the beginning. It is easy to understand how a charismatic leader like Jones might extract money from the members of his church. Once they have committed themselves to donating a small amount of money in response to his message of peace and universal brotherhood, he is able to request and receive a great deal more; he induces people to sell their homes and turn over the money to the church. Soon, at his request, several of his followers pull up stakes, leaving their families and friends, to start life anew in the strange and difficult environment of Guyana. There, not only do they work hard (thus increasing their commitment), but they also are cut off from potential dissenting opinion, inasmuch as they are surrounded by true believers. The chain of events continues. Jones takes sexual liberties with the wives of several of his followers, who acquiesce, if reluctantly; Jones claims to be the father of their children. Finally, as a prelude to the climactic event, Jones induces his followers to perform a series of mock ritual suicides as a test of their loyalty and obedience. Thus, in a step-by-step fashion, the commitment to Jim Jones increases. Each step *in and of itself* is not a huge and ludicrous leap from the one preceding it.

Again, this is an admittedly oversimplified analysis. A great many events occurred among Jones' followers in addition to the gradual increases in commitment we have described. These contributed to the tragic outcome. At the same time, however, viewing the final outcome in the context of increasing commitment brought about by preceding events *does* shed a ray of light on a phenomenon that at first seems totally unfathomable.

"Man" Cannot Live by Consonance Alone

Near the beginning of this chapter, I made the point that people are capable of rational, adaptive behavior as well as dissonance-reducing behavior. Let's return to that issue. If individuals spend all of their time protecting their egos, they will never grow. In order to grow, we must learn from our mistakes. But if we are intent on reducing dissonance, we will not admit to our mistakes. Instead, we will sweep them under the rug, or, worse still, we will turn them into virtues. The autobiographical memoirs of former presidents are full of the kind of self-serving, self-justifying statements that can best be summarized as "if I had it all to do over again, I would not change a thing."[70]

On the other hand, people do frequently grow—people do frequently learn from their mistakes. How? Under what conditions? Ideally, when I make a mistake, it would be useful for me to be able to bring myself to say, in effect, "OK, I blew it. What can I learn from the experience so I will not end up in this position again?" This can come about in several ways:

1. Through an understanding of my own defensiveness and dissonance-reducing tendencies.
2. Through the realization that performing stupid or immoral actions does not necessarily mean I am an irrevocably stupid or immoral person.
3. Through the development of enough ego strength to tolerate errors in myself.
4. Through increasing my ability to recognize the benefits of admitting error in terms of my own growth and learning.

Of course, it is far easier to list these procedures than it is to accomplish them. How does a person get in touch with his or her defensiveness and dissonance-reducing tendencies? How can we come to realize that bright, moral people like ourselves can occasionally perform a stupid or immoral action? It is not enough to know it abstractly or superficially; in order to utilize this knowledge fully, a person must actually experience it and consciously practice it. A situation that encourages this kind of experience and practice will be discussed in Chapter 8.

5

Human Aggression

At the height of the war in Southeast Asia, I was watching Walter Cronkite broadcast the news on television. In the course of his newscast, he reported an incident in which American planes dropped napalm on a village in South Vietnam believed to be a Viet Cong stronghold. My oldest son, who was about ten at the time, asked brightly, "Hey, Dad, what's napalm?"

"Oh," I answered casually, "as I understand it, it's a chemical that burns people; it also sticks so that if it gets on your skin, you can't remove it." And I continued to watch the news.

A few minutes later, I happened to glance at my son and saw tears streaming down his face. Struck by my son's pain and

My thinking about the psychology of aggression has been influenced and enriched by a great many conversations with Dr. Leonard Berkowitz of the University of Wisconsin, while we were colleagues at the Center for Advanced Study in the Behavioral Sciences. I am pleased to acknowledge my indebtedness to him.

grief, I grew dismayed as I began to wonder what had happened to *me*. Had I become so brutalized that I could answer my son's question so matter-of-factly—as if he had asked me how a baseball is made or how a leaf functions? Had I gotten so accustomed to human brutality that I could be casual in its presence?

In a sense it is not surprising. We are living in an age of unspeakable horrors. During the past two decades, we have witnessed countless examples of man's inhumanity to man. In addition to the near random destruction of noncombatants in Vietnam, we have seen brutal civil wars in Central America, the mass execution of thousands of innocent civilians in Cambodia, Iran, and India, the induced suicide of over 900 people in Jonestown, and on and on and on . . . And yet, as tragic as these events were, occurrences of this kind are not peculiar to the present era. Many years ago, a friend showed me a very thin book—only ten or fifteen pages long—that purported to be a capsule history of the world. It was a chronological listing of the important events in recorded history. Can you guess how it read? Of course—one war after another, interrupted every now and then by a few non-violent events, such as the birth of Jesus and the invention of the printing press. What kind of species are we humans if the most important events in our brief history are situations in which people kill one another *en masse?*

We humans have shown ourselves to be an aggressive species. With the exception of certain rodents, no other vertebrates so consistently and wantonly kill members of their own kind. We have defined social psychology as the study of social influence—that is, one person's (or group's) influence on another. The most extreme form of aggression (physical destruction) can be considered the ultimate degree of social influence. Is aggression inborn—is it part of our very nature as human beings? Can it be modified? What are the social and situational factors that increase or decrease aggression?

Aggression Defined

It is difficult to present a clear definition of *aggression* because the term is used in so many different ways in common speech.

Clearly, the Boston Strangler, who made a hobby of strangling women in their apartments, was performing acts of aggression. But a football player making a tackle is also considered aggressive. A tennis player who charges the net is called aggressive. So, too, is a successful insurance salesperson who is "a real go-getter." The young girl who staunchly defends her own possessions against the encroachment of other children and the young girl who goes out of her way to clobber her brother are both considered aggressive. On a more subtle level, if a neglected husband sulks in the corner during a party, this may be an act of "passive aggression." Also, a child who wets the bed, a jilted boy friend who threatens suicide, or a student who doggedly attempts to master a difficult mathematical problem could conceivably be labeled as illustrations of an aggressive tendency in human beings. And what of the violence exerted by the state in its attempt to maintain law and order—and the less direct forms of aggression through which people of one race or religion humiliate and degrade people of different races or religions? If all these behaviors are to come under the blanket term *aggression*, the situation is indeed confused. As a way of increasing our understanding of aggression, we must cut through this morass and separate the "assertive" aspects of the popular definition from the destructive aspects. That is, a distinction can be made between behavior that harms others and behavior that does not harm others. Accordingly, the go-getting salesperson or the student doggedly sticking to the mathematical problem would not be considered aggressive, but the Boston Strangler, the clobbering child, the suicidal boy friend, and even the sulking, neglected husband would all be defined as aggressive.

But this distinction is not altogether satisfactory because, by concentrating on an outcome alone, it ignores the intention of the person perpetrating the act, and this is the crucial aspect of *aggression*. I would define an act of aggression as a behavior aimed at causing harm or pain. Thus, by definition, the football player is *not* considered to be performing an act of aggression if his aim is simply to bring down his opponent as efficiently as possible—but he *is* behaving aggressively if his aim is to cause pain or injury, whether or not he succeeds in doing so. To illustrate, suppose a three-year-old boy slaps at his father in anger. The slap may be totally ineffectual—it may even cause his father to laugh. But it is, nonetheless, an aggressive act. Similarly, the same child may, in total innocence, thrust a sharp elbow into his father's eye, causing severe pain and colorful contusions. Because its painful consequences were unintentional, this would not be defined as an act of aggression.

It might be useful to make one additional distinction regarding intentional aggression, namely, a distinction between aggression that is an end in itself and aggression that is instrumental in achieving some goal. The first we will call *hostile aggression;* the second we will call *instrumental aggression.* Thus, a football player might intentionally inflict an injury on the opposing quarterback in order to put him out of the game and thus increase his own team's probability of winning. This would be instrumental aggression. On the other hand, he might perform this action on the last play of the last game of the season to "pay back" the quarterback for some real or imagined insult or humiliation; this is hostile aggression since the aggressive act is an end in itself. Similarly, dropping a bomb on a ball-bearing factory in Munich in World War II can be considered an act of instrumental aggression, while shooting down defenseless women and children in a Vietnamese village can be considered an act of hostile aggression. The "hit man" working for the Mafia who guns down a designated victim is probably behaving instrumentally; thrill killers, such as members of the Manson family, probably are not.

Is Aggressiveness Instinctive?

Psychologists, physiologists, ethologists, and philosophers are in disagreement over whether aggressiveness is an innate, instinctive phenomenon or whether such behavior has to be learned. This is not a new controversy: it has been raging for centuries. For example, Jean-Jacques Rousseau's concept of the noble savage[1] (first published in 1762) suggested that man, in his natural state, is a benign, happy, and good creature and that a restrictive society forces aggressiveness and depravity upon him. Others have taken the view that man in his natural state is a brute and that only by enforcing the law and order of society can we curb or sublimate his natural instincts toward aggression. Sigmund Freud[2] is a good example of a proponent of this general position. Besides suggesting that humans are born with an instinct toward life, which he called *Eros*, Freud postulated that humans are also born with a death instinct, *thanatos*. When turned inward, the death instinct manifests itself in self-punishment, which in the extreme case, becomes suicide; when turned outward, this instinct manifests itself in hostility, destructiveness, and murder. "It is at work in every living being and is striving to bring it to ruin and to reduce life to its original condition of inanimate matter."[3] Freud believed this aggressive energy must come out somehow, lest it continue to build up and produce illness. This notion can be described as a "hydraulic" theory—that is, the analogy is one of water pressure building up in a container: Unless aggression is allowed to drain off, it will produce some sort of explosion. According to Freud, society performs an essential function in regulating this instinct and in helping people to sublimate it—that is, in helping people to turn the destructive energy into acceptable or useful behavior.

Taking the notion of innate aggressiveness one step further, some scholars believe humans in their natural state not only are killers but that their wanton destructiveness is unique among animals. Consequently, these scholars suggest that to call human behavior "brutal" is to libel nonhuman species. This point of view has been expressed eloquently by Anthony Storr:

> We generally describe the most repulsive examples of man's cruelty as brutal or bestial, implying by these adjectives that such behavior is characteristic of less highly developed animals than ourselves. In truth, however, the extremes of 'brutal' behavior are confined to man; and there is no parallel in nature to our savage treatment of each other. The sombre fact is that we are the cruellest and most ruthless species that has ever walked the earth; and that although we may recoil in horror when we read in the newspaper or history book of the atrocities committed by man upon man, we know in our hearts that each one of us harbours within himself those same savage impulses which lead to murder, to torture, and to war.[4]

There is a lack of definitive or even clear evidence on the subject of whether or not aggression is instinctive in humans. I suppose that is why the controversy still rages. Much of the evidence, such as it is, stems from observation of, and experimentation with, species other than humans. In one such study, for example, Zing Yang Kuo[5] attempted to explode the myth that cats will instinctively stalk and kill rats. His experiment was a very simple one. He raised a kitten in the same cage with a rat. Not only did the cat refrain from attacking the rat, but the two became close companions. Moreover, the cat refused either to chase or to kill other rats. It should be noted, however, that this experiment does not prove that aggressive behavior is not instinctive; it merely demonstrates that aggressive behavior can be inhibited by early experience. Thus, in an experiment reported by Irenaus Eibl-Eibesfeldt,[6] it was shown that rats raised in isolation (that is, without any experience in fighting other rats) will attack a fellow rat when one is introduced into the cage; moreover, the isolated rat uses the same pattern of threat and attack experienced rats use. Thus, although aggressive behavior can be modified by experience (as shown by Kuo's experiment), Eibl-Eibesfeldt showed that aggression apparently does not need to be learned. On the other hand, one should not conclude from this study that aggressiveness is necessarily instinctive, for, as John Paul Scott[7] has pointed out, in order to draw this conclusion, there must be physiological evidence of a spontaneous stimulation for fighting that arises from within the body alone. The stimulus in the above experiment came from the outside—that is, the sight of a new rat stimulated the isolated rat to fight. Scott concluded from his survey of the evidence that there is no inborn need for fighting: If an organism can arrange its life so there is no outside stimulation to fight, then it will not experience any physiological or mental damage as a result of not expressing aggression. This view contradicts Freud's contention and, in effect, asserts that there is no instinct of aggression.

The argument goes back and forth. Scott's conclusion has been called into question by the distinguished ethologist Konrad Lorenz.[8] Lorenz observed the behavior of certain cichlids, which are highly aggressive tropical fish. Male cichlids will attack other males of the same species apparently as an aspect of territorial behavior—that is, to defend their territory. In its natural environment, the male cichlid does not attack female cichlids, nor does he attack males of a different species—he only attacks males of his own species. What happens if all other male cichlids are removed from an aquarium, leaving only one male alone with no appropriate sparring partner? According to the hydraulic theory of instinct, the need to aggress will build up to the point where the cichlid will attack a fish that doesn't usually serve as an appropriate stimulus for attack; and that is exactly what happens. In the absence of his fellow male cichlids, he attacks males of other species—males he previously ignored. Moreover, if *all* males are removed, the male cichlid will eventually attack and kill females.

And the controversy continues. Leonard Berkowitz,[9] one of the world's leading experts on human aggression, believes humans are essentially different from nonhumans in that learning plays a more important role in their aggressive behavior. In humans, aggressiveness is a function of a complex interplay between innate propensities and learned responses. Thus, although it is true that many animals, from insects to apes, will attack an animal that invades their territory, it is a gross oversimplification to imply, as some popular writers have, that humans are likewise programmed to protect their territory and behave aggressively in response to specific stimuli. There is much evidence to support Berkowitz's contention that, among humans, innate patterns of behavior are infinitely modifiable and flexible. Human cultures vary dramatically on this dimension. For example take the primitive Tasaday tribe who until recently remained undiscovered, undisturbed, and uninfluenced by western civilization in a remote area of the Philippine Islands. They live in cooperative friendliness, both within their own tribe and in their relations with others. Acts of aggression are extremely rare—indeed, they have no word for war.[10] Similar observations have been made among the Lepchas of Sikkim, the Pygmies of Central Africa, and the Arapesh of New Guinea. Meanwhile, in more civilized society, it is estimated that in 1983 more than two billion dollars per *day* was spent on military projects. Even more striking is the observation that, within a given culture, changing social conditions can lead to changes in aggressive behavior. For example, the Iroquois Indians lived in peace for hundreds of years as a hunting nation. But in the 17th century, a growing trade with the newly arrived Europeans brought the Iroquois into direct competition with the neighboring Hurons over furs (to trade for manufactured goods). A series of wars developed—and the Iroquois became ferocious and successful warriors, not because of uncontrollable aggressive instincts, but because a *social* change produced increases in competition.[11]

There is even a good deal of evidence for such flexibility among nonhumans. For example, by electrically stimulating a certain area of a monkey's brain, one can evoke an aggressive response in the monkey. This area can be considered to be the neural center of aggression; but that does not mean that, when this area is stimulated, the monkey will always attack. If a male monkey is in the presence of other monkeys who are less dominant than he in their social hierarchy, he will indeed attack them when the appropriate area of his brain is stimulated; but, if the same area is stimulated while he is in the presence of monkeys who are *more* dominant than he, he will *not* attack, rather he will tend to flee the scene. Thus, the same physiological stimulation can produce widely different responses, depending upon learning. This appears to be true for humans. Our conclusion from reviewing these data is that, although aggressiveness may have an instinctual component in humans, the important point for the social psychologist is that it *is* modifiable by situational factors. How can it be modified? How much can it be modified? Should it be modified? Before getting to these questions, we must first understand what the situational factors are and how they operate.

Is Aggression Necessary?

Survival of the Fittest. We know that animals can be bred for aggression. For example, Kirsti Lagerspetz[12] observed the behavior of a group of normal mice. She then took those that were behaving most aggressively and allowed them to mate with one another. Similarly, she allowed the least aggressive to mate with one another. She then repeated this procedure for 26 generations—ending up with one group of extremely fierce mice and another group of extremely docile ones. Moreover, some investigators have suggested that certain kinds of aggression are useful and perhaps even essential. Konrad Lorenz,[13] for example, has argued that aggression is "an essential part of the life-preserving organization of instincts." Basing his argument on his observation of nonhumans, he sees aggressiveness as being of prime evolutionary importance, allowing the young animals to have the strongest and wisest mothers and fathers and enabling the group to be led by the best possible leaders. From their study of Old World monkeys, anthropologist Sherwood Washburn and psychiatrist David Hamburg concur.[14] They find that aggression within the same group of monkeys plays an important role in feeding, reproduction, and determining dominance patterns. The strongest and most aggressive male in a colony will assume a dominant position through an initial display of aggressiveness. This serves to reduce subsequent serious fighting within the colony (the other males know who's boss). Furthermore, because the dominant male dominates reproduction, the colony increases its chances of survival as the strong male passes on his vigor to subsequent generations.

A similar pattern is reported among elephant seals by Burney LeBoeuf.[15] Each year before mating season, pairs of males square off against each other and engage in ferocious blood battles for dominance. The strongest, most aggressive, and shrewdest male is not only number one in the dominance hierarchy among his fellows, but he becomes number one lovemaker in the group. For example, in one observation, the number one or "alpha" male in a particular rookery of 185 females and 120 males was responsible for half of the observed copulations. In smaller rookeries of 40 or fewer females, the alpha male is typically responsible for 100 percent of the copulations.

With these data in mind, many observers urge caution in attempting to control aggression in humans, suggesting that, as in lower animals, aggression is necessary for survival. This reasoning is based in part on the assumption that the same mechanism that drives one man to kill his neighbor drives another to "conquer" outer space, "sink his teeth" into a difficult mathematical equation, "attack" a logical problem, or "master" the universe.

But, as I argued earlier, this reasoning is based on an exaggerated definition of aggression. To equate high achievement and advancement with hostility and aggression is to confuse the issue. A problem or skill can be mastered without harming other people or even without attempting to conquer them. This is a difficult distinction for us to grasp, because the western mind—and perhaps the American mind in particular—has been trained to equate success with victory, to equate doing well with beating someone. M. F. Ashley Montagu[16] feels that an oversimplification and misinterpretation of Darwin's theory has given the average person the mistaken idea that conflict is necessarily the law of life. Ashley Montagu suggests that it was convenient during the industrial revolution for the wealthy industrialists, who were exploiting the workers, to justify their exploitation by talking about life being a struggle and it being natural for the fittest (and only the fittest) to survive. The danger is that this kind of reasoning becomes a self-fulfilling prophecy and can cause us to ignore or play down the survival value of nonaggressive and noncompetitive behavior. For example, Peter Kropotkin[17] concluded in 1902 that cooperative behavior and mutual aid have great survival value for many forms of life. There is ample evidence to support this conclusion. The cooperative behavior of certain social insects, such as termites, ants, and bees, is well known. Perhaps not so well known is a form of behavior in the chimpanzee that can only be described as altruistic. It goes something like this: Two chimpanzees are in adjoining cages. One chimp has food and the other doesn't. The foodless chimpanzee begins to beg. Reluctantly, the "wealthy" chimp hands over some of his food. In a sense, the very reluctance with which he does so makes the gift all the more significant. It indicates that he likes the food and would dearly enjoy keeping it for himself. Accordingly, it suggests the urge to share may have deep roots, indeed.[18] But Kropotkin's work has not been given much attention—in fact, it was largely ignored, perhaps because it did not fit the temper of the times or the needs of those who were profiting from the industrial revolution.

Let us look at our own society. As a culture, we Americans seem to thrive on competition; we reward winners and turn away from losers. For two centuries, our educational system has been based upon competitiveness and the laws of survival. With very few exceptions, we do not teach our kids to love learning—we teach them to strive for high grades. When sportswriter Grantland Rice said that what's important is not whether you win or lose but how you play the game, he was not *describing* the dominant theme in American life, he was *prescribing* a cure for our overconcern with winning. From the Little League ball player who bursts into tears after his team is defeated to the college students in the football stadium chanting "We're number one!;" from Lyndon Johnson, whose judgment during the Vietnam conflict was almost certainly distorted by his oft-stated desire not to be the first American president to lose a war to the third-grader who despises his classmate for a superior performance on an arithmetic test, we manifest a staggering cultural obsession with victory. Vince Lombardi, a very successful professional football coach, may have summed it all up with the simple statement "Winning isn't everything, it's the *only* thing." What is frightening about the acceptance of this philosophy is that it implies that the goal of victory justifies whatever means we use to win, even if it's only a football game—which, after all, was first conceived of as a recreational activity. An interesting and appalling footnote to Lombardi's statement involves the manner in which the residents of Green Bay, Wisconsin, treated his successor, Dan Devine, when, as coach of the Green Bay Packers in 1974, he had the misfortune to lead that team to a losing season. As a result, he was the target of physical threats, his family was insulted, his dog was shot in front of his house, people made obscene phone calls in the middle of the night, and false rumors spread that his daughters were the town sluts and his wife was an alcoholic.[19]

It may be true that, in the early history of human evolution, highly competitive and aggressive behavior were adaptive. Some writers have traced human aggressiveness to the time when our ancestors were hunters and gatherers who had to kill animals and forage widely to survive. On the other hand, recent archaeological evidence unearthed by Richard Leakey and his associates[20] indicates that this assumption may be invalid, that human aggressiveness grew much later, as people began to cultivate the land and became concerned with ownership and property. But in either case, as we look about and see a world full of strife, of international and interracial hatred and distrust, of senseless slaughter and political assassination, we feel justified in questioning the current survival value of this behavior. With the major powers in possession of enough nuclear warheads to destroy the world's population twenty-five times over, I wonder whether building still more warheads might not be carrying things a bit too far. Anthropologist Loren Eiseley paid tribute to our ancient ancestors but warned against imitating them when he wrote: "The need is now for a gentler, a more tolerant people than those who won for us against the ice, the tiger, and the bear."[21]

Catharsis. There is another sense in which it sometimes has been argued that aggressiveness serves a useful and perhaps a necessary function. I refer here to the psychoanalytic position. Specifically, as mentioned earlier, Sigmund Freud believed that, unless people are allowed to express themselves aggressively, the aggressive energy would be dammed up, pressure would build, and the energy would seek an outlet, either exploding into acts of extreme violence or manifesting itself as symptoms of mental illness. Is there any evidence to support this contention? The evidence, such as it is, suggests that *conflict about aggression* can lead to a state of high emotional tension in humans. This has led some investigators to the faulty conclusion that the inhibition of an aggressive response in humans produces either serious symptoms or intensely aggressive behavior. But there is no direct evidence for this conclusion.

"But still," one might ask, "can the expression of aggression be beneficial?" It is tempting to think so. Most of us, when frustrated or angry, have experienced something akin to a release of tension when we have "blown off steam" by yelling or cursing someone or perhaps even hitting someone. But does an act of aggression reduce the need for further aggression? Consider some of the ways in which aggressive energy can be discharged: (1) by expending it in the form of physical activity, such as games, running, jumping, punching a bag, and so on; (2) by engaging in a nondestructive form of fantasy aggression—like dreaming about hitting someone, or writing a violent story; and (3) by engaging in direct aggression—lashing out at someone, hurting him, getting him into trouble, saying nasty things about him, and the like.

Let us take the first one—engaging in socially acceptable aggressive behavior. There is widespread belief that this procedure works, and it is amply promoted by psychoanalytically oriented therapists. For example, the distinguished psychiatrist William Menninger has asserted that "competitive games provide an unusually satisfactory outlet for the instinctive aggressive drive."[22] It would seem reasonable to ask if there is any evidence that competitive games reduce aggressiveness. In his careful analysis of the existing data, Berkowitz[23] could find no simple, unequivocal findings to support the contention that intense physical activity reduces aggressiveness. In fact, a field study by Arthur Patterson[24] leads to quite the opposite conclusion. He measured the hostility of high school football players, rating them both one week before and one week after the football season. If it is true that the intense physical activity and aggressiveness that is part of playing football serves to reduce the tension caused by pent up aggressive urges, we would expect the players to exhibit a decline in hostility over the course of the season. Instead, the results of the measures showed a significant *increase*. Similarly, in an exhaustive study of college athletes, Warren Johnson[25] found no consistent evidence to support the notion of catharsis. He concluded that, not only is it absurd to argue that wars have been won on the playing fields of Eton, it is even more absurd to hope we can prevent them there. This is not to say that people do not get pleasure out of these games. They do. But engaging in these games does not decrease aggressiveness.

Even though engaging in competitive and aggressive games does not result in less aggressiveness, perhaps *watching* these kinds of games does. Gordon Russell,[26] a Canadian sports psychologist, measured the hostility of spectators at an especially violent ice hockey match. As the game progressed, the spectators became increasingly belligerent—their level of hostility did not return to the pregame level until after the game was over. Thus, *watching* a competitive activity not only fails to decrease aggressiveness—it temporarily increases it.

Let us examine the second form of aggression—fantasy. If

fantasy works to reduce subsequent aggression, attacking another person in fantasy would be a particularly beneficial way of relieving aggressive tensions; remember that, with fantasy aggression, no one actually gets hurt. There is some evidence that engaging in fantasy aggression can make people feel better and can even result in a temporary reduction in aggressiveness. In an interesting experiment by Seymour Feshbach,[27] students were insulted by their instructor; then, half of the students were given the opportunity to write imaginative stories about aggression, while the other half were not given this opportunity. There was also a control group who were not insulted. Feshbach's results showed that, immediately afterward, the people who had been given the opportunity to write stories about aggression were slightly less aggressive than were those who were not given this opportunity. It should be pointed out that both of these groups of insulted students were considerably more aggressive than a group of students who were not insulted at all. Thus, the utility of fantasy was limited: It did not reduce a great deal of aggressive energy. Indeed, an experiment by Jack Hokanson and Meredith Burgess[28] demonstrated that, when subjects were provoked by an experimenter, engaging in fantasy aggression against him reduced their arousal to a far lesser extent than did acts of direct aggression against their tormentor.

Let us now take a closer look at research on such acts of direct aggression: Do they reduce the need for further aggression? Although the evidence is not unequivocal, the overwhelming majority of experiments on the topic have failed to find such effects.[29] In fact, by far the most common finding resembles the research on watching violence cited above; namely, when people commit acts of aggression, such acts increase the tendency toward future aggression. For example, in an experiment by Russell Geen and his associates,[30] each subject was paired with another student, who was actually a confederate of the experimenters. First, the subject was angered by the confederate; during this phase, which involved the exchanging of opinions on various issues, the subject was given electric shocks when his partner disagreed with his opinion. Next, during a study of "the effects of punishment on learning" the subject acted as a teacher while the confederate served as learner. On the first learning task, some of the subjects were required to shock the confederate each time he made a mistake; other subjects merely recorded his errors. On the next task, all the subjects were given the opportunity to deliver shocks. If a cathartic effect was operating, we would expect the subjects who had previously shocked the confederate to administer fewer and less intense shocks the second time. This didn't happen; in fact, the subjects who had previously shocked the confederate expressed *more* aggression when given the subsequent opportunity to attack him. This phenomenon is not limited to the laboratory; the same tendency also has been observed systematically in naturally occurring events in the real world where verbal acts of aggression served to facilitate further attacks. In this "natural experiment," several technicians who had recently been laid off were provided with a chance to verbalize their hostility against their ex-bosses; later, when asked to describe that person, these technicians were much *more* punitive in their descriptions than those technicians who had not previously voiced their feelings.[31]

In summary, the weight of the evidence does not support the catharsis hypothesis. It appears to be a reasonable idea, in a limited way. That is, when somebody angers us, venting our hostility against that person does indeed seem to make us feel better. However, it does not reduce our hostility. What could be going on to contradict these predictions? With humans, aggression is not merely dependent on tensions—what one feels—but also on what a person *thinks*. Put yourself in the place of a subject in the previous experiments: After once shocking another person or expressing hostility against your old boss, it becomes easier to do so a second time. Aggressing the first time can reduce your inhibitions against committing other such actions; the aggression is legitimized, and it becomes easier to carry out such assaults. Furthermore, the main thrust of the research on this issue indicates that committing an overt act of aggression against a person changes one's feelings about that person, increasing one's negative feelings toward the target and therefore increasing the probability of future aggression against that person.

Why? As we have seen in the preceding chapter, when a person does harm to another, it sets cognitive processes in motion aimed at justifying that act of cruelty. Specifically, when we hurt another person, we experience cognitive dissonance. The cognition "I have hurt Sam" is dissonant with the cognition "I am a decent, reasonable, good person." A good way for me to reduce dissonance is somehow to convince myself that hurting Sam was not an indecent, unreasonable, bad thing to do. I can accomplish this by blinding myself to Sam's virtues and by emphasizing his faults, by convincing myself that Sam is a terrible human being who deserved to be hurt. This would especially hold if the target is an *innocent* victim of my aggression. Thus, in experiments by David Glass and by Keith E. Davis and Edward E. Jones[32] (discussed in the preceding chapter), the subject inflicted either psychological or physical harm on an innocent person who had done the subject no prior harm. The subjects then proceeded to derogate the victim, convincing themselves he was not a very nice person and therefore deserved what he got. This reduces dissonance, all right, and it also sets the stage for further aggression—once you have derogated a person, it makes it easier for you to hurt that person in the future.

But what happens if the victim isn't so innocent? What happens if he or she has done something to make you angry and therefore does indeed deserve retaliation? Here the situation becomes more complex and more interesting. One of several experiments performed to test this issue was a brilliantly conceived doctoral dissertation by Michael Kahn.[33] In Kahn's experiment, a medical technician, taking some physiological measurements from college students, made some derogatory remarks about these students. In one experimental condition, the subjects were allowed to vent their hostility by expressing their feelings about the technician to his employer—an action that looked as though it would get the technician into serious trouble, perhaps even cost him his job. In another condition, they were not provided with the opportunity to express any aggression against the person who had aroused their anger. What would psychoanalytic theory predict would occur? That's easy: the inhibited group would experience tension, a good deal of anger, and hostile feelings against the technician, while the group that expressed their feelings would feel relieved, relaxed, and not as hostile toward the technician. In short, according to psychoanalytic theory, expressing hostility would purge the insulted subjects of their hostile feelings. Being a good Freudian, Kahn expected these results. He was surprised and (to his credit) excited to find evidence to the contrary. Specifically, those who were allowed to express their aggression subsequently felt greater dislike and hostility for the technician than did those who were inhibited from expressing their aggression. In other words, expressing aggression did not inhibit the tendency to aggress, it tended to increase it—even when the target was not simply an innocent victim.

What Kahn's experiment illustrates is that, when people are made angry, they frequently engage in overkill. In this case, costing the technician his job is a serious overkill compared to the harm the technician perpetrated. The overkill produces dissonance in much the same way hurting an innocent person produces dissonance. That is, there is a discrepancy between what the person did to you and the force of your retaliation. That discrepancy must be justified—and just as in the "innocent victim" experiments, the justification takes the form of derogating the object of your wrath *after* you have hurt the person.

But what happens if you can arrange it so that retaliation is not allowed to run roughshod? That is, what if the degree of retaliation is reasonably controlled so it is not significantly more intense than the action that precipitated it? In such a circumstance, I would predict there would be little or no dissonance. "Sam has insulted me; I've paid him back; we're even. I have no need to retaliate further." And in fact, this is what was found in an experiment by Anthony Doob and Larraine Wood.[34] As in Kahn's experiment, Doob and Wood arranged things so their subjects were humiliated and annoyed by an accomplice. In one condition, they were given the opportunity to retaliate by administering a series of electric shocks to their tormentor. In this situation, once the score was evened, they had no further need to punish their tormentor. But those subjects who had not been given the opportunity to retaliate *did* choose to punish their tormentor subsequently. Thus, we have seen that retaliation can reduce the need for further aggression if something akin to equity has been restored. There is a major point here that must be underscored: Most situations in the real world are not as neat as the Doob and Wood situation where retaliation can be made functionally similar to the original act. In my opinion, the world is usually closer to the situation in Michael Kahn's experiment: Retaliation typically outstrips the original act by a great deal. For example, whatever the students at Kent State University might have been doing to the members of the Ohio National Guard (shouting obscenities, teasing, taunting), it hardly merited their being shot and killed. Moreover, most victims of massive aggression are totally innocent. In all these situations, the opposite of catharsis takes place. Thus, once I have shot dissenting students at Kent State, I will convince myself that they *really* deserved it, and I will hate dissenting students even more than I did before I shot them; once I have slaughtered women and children at My Lai, I will be even more convinced that Asians aren't really human than I was before I slaughtered them; once I have denied black people a decent education, I will become even more convinced that they are stupid and couldn't have profited from a good education to begin with. In most situations, violence does *not* reduce the tendency toward violence: violence breeds more violence.

If violence breeds more violence, then what are we to do with our angry feelings? There is an important difference between being angry and expressing that anger in a violent and destructive manner. To experience anger in appropriate circumstances is normal and harmless. Indeed, there is very little one can do to avoid anger. It is certainly possible to express that anger in a nonviolent manner; for example, by a forceful and simple statement: "I am very angry at you because of what you did." Indeed, such a statement in and of itself is a vehicle for self-assertion and probably serves to relieve tension and to make the angered person feel better. At the same time, because the target does not get hurt, such a response does not set in motion those cognitive processes that would lead the angered person to justify his or her behavior by ridiculing or derogating the target person. More will be said on this issue in Chapter 8.

Catharsis, Public Policy, and the Mass Media. What does all of this tell us about public policy? Consider the most extreme example of human aggression: war. In addition to hypothesizing that the death instinct worked on a personal level, Freud also theorized that it operated on a societal level as well, manifesting itself in battles between nations.[35] But do wars have cathartic effects, helping to provide an outlet for a society's aggressive tendencies? If so, we would expect that, in the years following a nation's involvement in war, there would be a decrease in violent crime among its citizens. Dane Archer and Rosemary Gartner[36] compared the crime rates for roughly 110 countries since 1900. They found that wars actually *encourage* domestic violence. Compared with similar nations that remained at peace, countries that fought wars exhibited substantial postwar increases in their homicide rates. Rather than reducing the tendency toward aggression, wars increase aggressive behavior by legitimizing it.

In spite of the mounting evidence against the catharsis hypothesis, it still seems to be widely believed by most people, including people who make important decisions that affect all of us. Thus, it is frequently argued that playing football[37] or watching people getting murdered on television[38] serves a valuable function in draining off aggressive energy. We have seen already that playing football fails to reduce general hostility and may even increase it. Furthermore, in a classic series of experiments, Albert Bandura and his associates[39] demonstrated that watching violence on television also failed to yield cathartic effects. Quite the contrary; simply seeing another person behave aggressively can *increase* the aggressive behavior of young children. The basic procedure in these studies was to have an adult knock around a plastic, air-filled "Bobo" doll (the kind that bounces back after it's been knocked down). Sometimes, the adult would accompany her physical aggression with verbal abuse against the doll. The kids were then allowed to play with the doll. In these experiments, not only did the children imitate the aggressive models, they also engaged in other forms of aggressive behavior after having witnessed the aggressive behavior of the adult. In short, the children did more than copy the behavior of an adult; seeing a person behave aggressively served as an impetus for them to engage in innovative aggressive behavior.

This evidence suggests that violence on television is potentially dangerous, in that it serves as a model for behavior—especially for children. And what do we see on television? For over fifteen years, George Gerbner and his associates have been conducting content analyses of television programming during prime time and on Saturday mornings. He has found that violence prevails in eight out of every ten programs. Moreover, the rate of violent incidents is about eight per program hour. Cartoons, which are the favorite viewing matter of most young children, contain the most violence—almost eighteen violent incidents per hour.[40]

Spokespersons for the major television networks have attempted to shrug off the Bandura experiments because they do not involve aggression against people. After all, who cares what a kid does to a "Bobo" doll? More recent experimental evidence demonstrates, however, that the effects of watching violence are *not* limited to walloping a "Bobo" doll: it induces kids to wallop each other as well. In one study, Liebert and Baron[41] exposed a group of subjects to a television production of "The Untouchables," an extremely violent cops-and-robbers program. In a control condition, a smilar group of children were exposed to a television production of a highly action-oriented sporting event for the same length of time. The children were then allowed to play in another room with a group of other children. Those who had watched the violent television program showed far more aggression against the other children than those who had watched the sporting event.

Ross Parke and his colleagues[42] have extended these findings to a more natural setting. They showed movies to boys living in juvenile detention facilities in the United States and Belgium, showing aggressive films to the boys living in some cottages within the facilities and showing nonviolent movies to those boys living in the other cottages. Both during and after the week of films, the boys who viewed the aggressive movies displayed more physical and verbal aggression against the other children. Further studies demonstrated that the effects could arise from seeing just *one* movie and that the increase in aggressive behavior was most pronounced in those boys who were initially *lower* in aggressiveness. In a longitudinal study, Leonard Eron and Rowell

Huesmann[43] found a high correlation between watching violence on television and aggressive behavior among eight-year-old boys. They then restudied 211 of these boys some eleven years later. Those nineteen-year-olds who had watched a great deal of TV violence at age eight were more aggressive than those who had not. Moreover, it was reasonably clear that TV viewing caused aggressive behavior (rather than *vise versa)* because the aggressive nineteen-year-olds who had watched a lot of violent TV at eight did not necessarily watch violent TV at age nineteen. In short, watching violence on television at age eight predicted subsequent aggressiveness; being aggressive at age eight did not predict subsequent violence-watching. The weight of the evidence led a select committee of the National Institute of Mental Health to conclude in 1982: "The consensus among most of the research community is that violence on television does lead to aggressive behavior by children and teenagers who watch the programs."[44]

In a related vein, Margaret Hanratty Thomas and her colleagues[45] have demonstrated that viewing television violence can subsequently numb the reactions of people when they are faced with real-life aggression. Thomas had children watch either a violent police drama or an exciting (but nonviolent) volleyball game. After a short break, the children observed a verbally and physically aggressive interaction between two preschoolers. Those children who had watched the police show responded less emotionally than did those who had watched the volleyball game. That is, viewing the initial violence *desensitized* the children to further acts of violence—they were not upset by an incident that, by all rights, should have upset them. While such a reaction may psychologically protect us from the debilitating effects of repeated violence, it also hardens us to the feelings of those who are the targets of aggression and may make it easier for us to commit violent acts on our own.

Thus far, we have focused much of our attention on children in discussing the effects of media violence. But the effect of media violence on violent behavior may not be limited to young children. The following news story was distributed by the Associated Press on November 23, 1971:

> Witnesses say a gunman armed with two rifles and dressed in Army fatigues yelled and laughed hysterically as he moved through a paint brush factory on a fatal shooting spree. Five workers died. Three other persons, including the alleged assailant and a policeman, were wounded. [The alleged assailant] . . . fired about a dozen shots. They killed two men. . . . Still firing, the gunman returned to a storage room where police later found two other bodies. Another man shot in the shipping department died en route to the hospital. . . . Police, unable to arrive at a motive for the rampage, were exploring possible parallels to a recent "Hawaii Five-0" television segment involving a multiple slaying. . . . Many characteristics, including the assailant's garb, method of operation and a bag of candy found in his pocket, resembled the television program. . . . Receipts found for one rifle and ammunition were dated shortly after the broadcast.

And this was not an isolated incident. Several years ago, a national magazine reported the following occurrences:

> In San Francisco, three teen-age girls lured two younger girls down a lonely path and sexually molested them. In Chicago, two boys attempted to extort $500 from a firm by means of a bomb threat. In Boston, a youthful gang set a woman on fire with gasoline. In all three cases police officials concluded that the crimes had been directly inspired by shows the adolescents had recently watched on prime-time television.

In fact, in a recent court case, it was argued that the producers and network that broadcast a television movie, "Born Innocent," should be held responsible for a brutal rape that replicated in detail an assault depicted in the film.

These incidents lend a macabre twist to Alfred Hitchcock's tongue-in-cheek statement, "One of television's great contributions is that it brought murder back into the home where it belongs." Indeed, it appears that Oscar Wilde was correct when he said that life imitates art. But surely those individuals who produce, package, and distribute violence on television and in films are aware of these data? What are they doing about it? Very little. Most of these individuals view themselves as merely responding to the needs and tastes of the public. For example, Samuel Arkoff, board chairman of American International Pictures (one of our leading manufacturers of violent films), said: "Maybe the need to view violence will someday be reduced by watching pro football."[46] Unfortunately, the data indicate this need is being increased, not satiated by people like Mr. Arkoff. How responsible are these people? "The effects on society?" asks Joe Wizan, another producer of violent films. "I don't give it a thought. Psychiatrists don't have the answers, so why should I?"[47]

In the face of the evidence, such an attitude would appear cynical in the extreme. It is reasonably clear that film producers believe that violent films bring people into the theaters and network executives believe that violence sells products. But, ironically, this may not be true. Edward Diener and Darlene DeFour[48] conducted an experiment in which college students were shown an adventure program *(Police Woman)* and then asked how much they liked it. Some students saw an uncut (violent) version and others saw an edited (nonviolent) version. Both groups liked the program they watched equally—that is, the inclusion of violence did nothing to enhance the program's popularity. While this one experiment is hardly conclusive, it *does* suggest the possibility that film and TV producers might be premature in leaping to the conclusion that Americans prefer violence to nonviolence. This experimental evidence is corroborated by the fact that an analysis of the ten top-rated television shows of 1982 reveals that only *one* showed a significant degree of violence—and that was *The Dukes of Hazzard*, where most of the violence is done to automobiles! The others on the list were: a quality news program *(Sixty Minutes)*, a relatively nonviolent soap opera *(Dallas)*, and a slew of situation comedies.

The Media, Pornography, and Violence Against Women. A particularly troubling aspect of aggression in this country is the apparent increase of violence expressed by some men against women—especially in the form of rape. In 1980 at least 82,000 American women are known to have been raped. That is one rape every six minutes . . . and the actual figures are probably higher since a great many rapes go unreported. According to the FBI, the number of reported rapes per year has doubled in the past twenty years. If, as we have suggested, the viewing of violence in films and on television plays a role in the incidence of violence, shouldn't it follow that viewing pornographic material would increase the incidence of rape? While this has been argued from both pulpit and lecturn, it is much too simplistic an assumption. It should be understood that rape is primarily an act of violence, *not* of sensuousness. And, indeed, after studying the available evidence, the Commission on Obscenity and Pornography concluded that explicit sexual material, *in and of itself*, did not contribute to sexual crimes, violence against women, or other antisocial acts.

The key phrase in the preceding sentence is "in and of itself." One might ask if there are undesirable effects of materials that combine sex with violence. During the past several years, Neil Malamuth has conducted a series of careful experiments to determine the effects, if any, of violent pornography. In one experiment,[49] male college students viewed one of two erotic films. One version portrayed two mutually-consenting adults engaged in lovemaking; the other version portrayed a rape incident. After viewing the film, the men were asked to engage in sexual fantasy. Those men who had viewed the rape version of the film created more violent sexual fantasies than those who had viewed the mutual-consent version. In another experiment,[50] Malamuth arranged for college students to watch either a violent-sexual feature-length film or a film with no violent or sexual acts. Several days later, the students filled out a Sexual Attitude Survey. For the male students, exposure to the violent-sexual film increased their acceptance of interpersonal violence against women. In addition, these males came to believe certain myths about rape—for example, that women provoke rape and actually enjoy being raped. For the female students, there was a tendency for those who were exposed to the violent-sexual film to be *less* accepting of violence against women and less accepting of myths about rape.

I should elaborate on this myth. Pamela Foa, a philosopher and feminist, gives us a clue as to how this might have developed.

> Every American girl . . . is well acquainted with the slippery-slope argument by the time she is ten. She is told that if she

> permits herself to become involved in anything more than a peck on the cheek, anything but the most innocent type of sexual behavior, she will inevitably become involved in behavior that will result in intercourse and pregnancy. And such behavior is wrong. That is, she is told that if she acquiesces to any degree to her feelings, then she will be doing something immoral. Meanwhile, every American boy is instructed, whether explicitly or not, that the girls have been given this argument (as a weapon) and that therefore, since everything that a girl says will be a reflection of this argument (and not of her feelings), they are to ignore everything that she says.[51]

There is a sense in which all of us have been victimized by a society which has ambivalent and even hypocritical attitudes toward adolescent sexuality. Foa is writing of the present situation. Her analysis is highly consistent with the experiences of my own adolescence. When I was a teenager (in the late 1940's and early 1950's), adolescent women were socialized to pretend that they were not interested in sex and that they didn't enjoy sex. The notion fostered by the adult world was that "nice girls" shouldn't enjoy sex until after they were safely married. Adolescent men were forever trying to "take liberties" and adolescent women were forever trying to push their hands away. But, over the course of time, say by the fourth date, as acquaintance and intimacy increased, the norms of "respectability" would allow for a limited degree of sexual behavior. The fact is, for a combination of biological and cultural reasons, young women in our society were—and still are—forced into the role of "line-drawers" and "limit-setters." That is, it is the woman who is at risk of becoming pregnant and it is the woman whose reputation might be damaged if she is considered promiscuous. But if a woman did become interested in a specific young man, she would allow greater intimacy over time. This sequence of increasing intimacy might have led some adolescent males to form the erroneous general belief that when women said "no," they often meant "maybe" or "later." Hollywood contributed to this belief and, in my opinion, magnified and generalized it. I wish I had a dollar for every film I've seen where the romantic hero takes the heroine in his arms and begins to kiss her. She fights him off—her hands push him away. But gradually she begins to succumb; the hands that were pushing him away begin to clasp him around the neck and slide sensuously through his hair. Her resistance yields to excitement, her excitement simmers into passion—all in the space of fifteen seconds! Such flim-flam might create the illusion that women are conflicted about sexuality and *want* to be taken forcefully.

It would be a tragic mistake to construe this analysis into a justification for either persistent sexual advances on the part of men in our society or for the erroneous belief that, deep down, women want to be taken forcefully. Such a construction would constitute a crass example of blaming the victim. While such behavior and beliefs are unjustifiable, the analysis does help us to gain some much-needed insight into where they may spring from. I should also point out that the belief in the rape myth is not limited to men. In a recent survey among university women, Malamuth and his colleagues found that while not a single woman felt that she, personally, would derive any pleasure from being overpowered sexually, a substantial percentage believed that some other women might.[52] Again, exposure to aggressive pornography tends to increase the tendency of men to believe the rape myth. Fortunately, there is substantial evidence that this myth is not part of a deep-seated belief system. For example, in one study, when college men were shown a pornographically aggressive film, their belief in the rape myth increased as predicted. But, after the film, when they were provided with an explanation of the experimental procedure, they became *less* accepting of the rape myth than a control group which neither viewed the film nor received the explanation.[53]

To sum up, the effect of violent pornography through the media seems to be remarkably similar to the effect of other violence in the media: The level of aggressiveness is increased. Viewing violence (pornographic or otherwise) does *not* serve a cathartic function but seems, rather, to stimulate aggressive behavior. These data raise complex policy issues involving censorship and First Amendment rights which extend beyond the scope of this book. While I personally am opposed to censorship, I think that an impartial reading of the research would lead media decision-makers to exercise some prudent self-restraint.

Aggression to Attract Public Attention. After the 1980 riot in the Liberty City section of Miami, no less a personage than the president of the United States came to the neighborhood and assurred residents that he was concerned and would provide federal aid. Do you think he would have dropped in for a friendly visit had there been no riot? In a complex and apathetic society like ours, aggressive behavior is often the most dramatic way for an oppressed minority to attract the attention of the powerful majority. No one can deny that the effects of the Watts and Detroit riots served to alert a large number of decent but apathetic people to the plight of black people in America. No one can doubt that bloodshed at Attica has led to increased attempts at prison reform. Are such outcomes worth the dreadful price in human lives? I cannot answer that question. But, as a social psychologist, what I can say (again and again) is that violence almost never ends simply with rectification of the conditions that brought it about. Violence breeds violence—not only in the simple sense of victim striking back against the enemy, but also in the infinitely more complex and insidious sense of attackers justifying their violence by exaggerating the evil of their enemies—and thereby increasing the probability that they will attack again (and again, and again . . .) There will never be a war to end all wars—quite the contrary: bellicose behaviors strengthen bellicose attitudes, which in turn increase the probability of bellicose behaviors. We must search for alternative solutions. A less aggressive form of instrumental behavior might redress social ills without producing an irreconcilable cycle of conflict. Consider Gandhi's success against the British in India during the 1930s. Strikes, boycotts, and other forms of civil disobedience eventually led to the end of British rule, without fostering a rapid escalation of hatred between citizens of the two countries. Such nonviolent strategies as sit-ins and boycotts also have been used effectively by Martin Luther King, Cesar Chavez, and others to awaken our own nation to real grievances. Accordingly, I echo Loren Eiseley's call for a gentler people but would add to it a call for a people more tolerant of their own differences and intolerant of injustice: a people who will love and trust one another, but who will yell, scream, strike, boycott, march, sit-in (and even vote) to eliminate injustice and cruelty. Violence cannot be turned on and off like a faucet. Research has repeatedly shown that the only solution is to find ways of reducing violence *while reducing the injustice that produces the frustrations that erupt in violent aggression.*

Frustration and Aggression

Aggression can be prompted by any unpleasant or aversive situation, such as anger, pain, boredom, and the like. Of these aversive situations, the major instigator of aggression is *frustration.* Imagine the following situation: You must drive across town for an important job interview. On your way to the parking lot you realize you are a bit late for your appointment, so you break into a fast trot. When you find your car you notice, to your dismay, that you have a flat tire. "Okay, I'll be twenty minutes late—that's not too bad," you say as you take the jack and lug wrench out of the trunk. After much tugging and hauling, you remove the old tire, put on the spare tire, tighten the lugs—and, lo and behold, the spare tire also is flat! Seething with frustration, you trudge back to your dorm and enter your room. Your roommate sees you standing there, resume in hand, sweaty and rumpled looking. Immediately sizing up the situation, he asks humorously, "How did the interview go?" Shouldn't he be prepared to duck?

If an individual is thwarted on the way to a goal, the resulting frustration will increase the probability of an aggressive response. This does not mean frustration *always* leads to aggression or that frustration is the *only* cause of aggression. There are other factors that will determine whether or not a frustrated individual will aggress—and there are other causes of aggression.

A clear picture of the relation between frustration and aggression emerges from a classic experiment by Roger Barker, Tamara Dembo, and Kurt Lewin.[54] These psychologists frustrated young children by showing them a roomful of very attractive toys, which they were then not allowed to play with. The children stood outside a wire screen looking at the toys, hoping to play with them—even expecting to play with them—

but were unable to reach them. After a painfully long wait, the children were finally allowed to play with the toys. In this experiment, a separate group of children were allowed to play with the toys directly without first being frustrated. This second group of children played joyfully with the toys. But the frustrated group, when finally given access to the toys, were extremely destructive. They tended to smash the toys, throw them against the wall, step on them, and so forth. Thus, frustration can lead to aggression.

Several factors can accentuate this frustration. Suppose you were about to bite into a thick, juicy hamburger, and somebody snatched it away. This would be more likely to frustrate you—and lead to an aggressive response—than if someone stopped you on your way to McDonald's. An analogue of this was demonstrated in a field study by Mary Harris.[55] She had students cut in front of people waiting in line for tickets, outside of restaurants, or to check out of a grocery store; sometimes they cut in front of the second person in line, other times in front of the twelfth person. As we would expect, the responses of the people standing behind the intruder were much more aggressive when the student cut into the second place in line. Frustration is increased when a goal is near and your progress toward it is interrupted. When the interruption is unexpected or when it seems illegitimate, the frustration is increased still further, as an experiment by James Kulik and Roger Brown points out.[56] Subjects were told they could earn money by telephoning for donations to charity and obtaining pledges. Some of them were led to expect a high rate of contributions, being informed that previous calls had been successful almost two-thirds of the time; others were led to expect far less success. When the potential donor refused to contribute, as all of them did (the subjects were actually calling confederates of the experimenters), the callers with the high expectations exhibited more aggression, speaking more harshly and slamming down the phone with more force. The experimenters also varied the reasons the confederates gave for refusing to contribute, sometimes making them sound legitimate ("I can't afford to contribute.") and sometimes having them sound arbitrary and illegitimate ("Charities are a waste of time and a rip-off."). The subjects who heard refusals that seemed unjustified displayed more aggression. As these experiments demonstrate, frustration is most pronounced when the goal is becoming palpable and drawing within reach, when expectations are high, and when it is blocked unjustifiably.

These factors help to point out the important distinction between frustration and deprivation. Children who simply don't have toys do not necessarily aggress. Rather, the earlier experiment indicates it was those children who had every reason to expect to play with the toys who experienced frustration when that expectancy was thwarted; this thwarting was what caused the children to behave destructively. In accord with this distinction, the psychiatrist Jerome Frank has pointed out that, in the 1960's, two of the most serious riots by American blacks in history did *not* take place in the geographical areas of greatest poverty; rather, they took place in Watts and Detroit, where things are not nearly so bad for blacks as they were in some other sections of the country. The point is, things *were* bad, relative to what "Whitey" had. Revolutions usually are not started by people whose faces are in the mud. They are most frequently started by people who have recently lifted their faces out of the mud, looked around, and noticed that other people are doing better than they are and that the system is treating them unfairly. Thus, frustration is not simply the result of deprivation; it is the result of *relative deprivation*. Suppose, after graduating from high school, I choose not to pursue a higher education and you choose to be educated; ten years later, if you have a better job than I do, I may be unhappy with my job but I will not experience frustration; I made a free choice and these are the reasonable consequences of my choice. But if we've both been educated, and you have a white collar job and I (because I'm black, or a Chicano, or a woman) am handed a broom, I *will* feel frustrated; or, if you find it easy to get an education, but, because I grew up in an impoverished ghetto, an education is denied me, I will also feel frustrated. This frustration will be exacerbated every time I turn on the TV and see all those beautiful houses white people live in and all those lovely appliances for sale to other people and all that gracious living and leisure I cannot share in. When you consider all the economic and social frustrations faced by minority groups in this affluent society, it is surprising there are so *few* riots. As Alexis de Tocqueville wrote some 130 years ago, "Evils which are patiently endured when they seem inevitable, become intolerable once the idea of escape from them is suggested." As long as there is hope that is unsatisfied, there will be frustrations that can result in aggression. Aggression can be reduced by satisfying that hope, or it can be minimized by eliminating it.

Hopeless people are apathetic people. The Ugandans, under the tyrannical, repressive, and wantonly violent dictatorship of Idi Amin, dared not dream of improving conditions or rebelling against Amin's rule. The South African blacks, and, to some extent, the blacks in the United States, did not revolt as long as they were prevented from hoping for anything better. Clearly, eliminating people's hope would be an undesirable means for reducing aggression. The saving grace of our nation is that—theoretically, at least—this is a land of promise. We teach our children, explicitly and implicitly, to hope, to expect, and to work to improve their lives. But unless this hope stands a reasonable chance of being fulfilled, turmoil will be inevitable.

Social Learning and Aggression

Although frustration and pain can be considered the major causes of aggression, there are many factors that can intervene either to induce aggressive behavior in a person who is suffering very little pain or frustration, or to inhibit an aggressive response in a person who is frustrated. These factors are the result of social learning. We have already seen how social learning can inhibit an aggressive response. Recall that, when we stimulate the area of a monkey's brain that characteristically produces aggressive behavior, the monkey will not aggress while in the presence of a monkey whom it *has learned* to fear. Another qualification based upon social learning is the intention attributed to an agent of pain or frustration. One aspect of behavior that seems to distinguish human beings from other animals is our ability to take the intentions of others into consideration. Consider the following situations: (1) a considerate person accidentally steps on your toe; (2) a thoughtless person you know doesn't care about you steps on your toe. Let us assume the amount of pressure and pain is exactly the same in both cases. My guess is that the latter situation would evoke an aggressive response, but the former would produce little or no aggression. Thus, I am suggesting that frustration and pain do not inexorably produce aggression. The response can be modified—and one of the primary things that can modify aggression is the intention attributed to the frustrator. This phenomenon was demonstrated in an experiment by Shabaz Mallick and Boyd McCandless[57] in which they frustrated third-grade school children by having another child's clumsiness prevent them from achieving a goal that would have resulted in a cash prize. Some of these children were subsequently provided with a reasonable and "unspiteful" explanation for the behavior of the child who fouled them up. Specifically, they were told he had been "sleepy and upset." The children in this condition directed much less aggression against the "thwarting" child than did children who were not given this explanation.

On the other side of the coin, certain stimuli can evoke aggressive behavior on the part of individuals who do not appear to be frustrated. In the "Bobo" doll experiments, Bandura and his associates showed that seeing another person behave aggressively increased the children's tendency to act aggressively. It is important to note, however, that the children did not confine their behavior to mere imitation but invented new and creative forms of aggression. This indicates that the effect of a model generalizes—it is not simply a matter of the children doing exactly what adults are doing—which means that children can be stimulated to perform a range of aggressive actions. Bandura and his co-workers also demonstrated that the outcome was important. If the aggressive models were rewarded for their aggressive behavior, the children who witnessed it were subsequently more aggressive than those who witnessed these models being punished for aggressing.

Carrying this one step further, Leonard Berkowitz and his colleagues have shown that, if an individual is angered or frustrated, the mere mention of a word or name associated with the provocation will increase that person's aggressiveness. In one experiment,[58] subjects were paired with another student (actually an accomplice of the experimenter) who was introduced either as a "college boxer" or as a "speech major." This accomplice provoked the subjects by shocking them; then, half of the angered subjects viewed a violent prize-fighting scene from a movie while the others watched an exciting but nonaggressive film clip. When subsequently given the chance to shock the confederate, the subject who had seen the violent movie segment administered more and longer shocks, as we would expect from the preceding discussion. Interestingly, however, among the subjects who had seen the prizefighting film, those paired with "the boxer" delivered more shocks to that target than those paired with "the speech major." In a similar experiment,[59] the accomplice was introduced to some subjects as "*Kirk* Anderson" and to others as "*Bob* Anderson." Again, the subjects watched one of the two film segments, and those watching the boxing sequence delivered greater shocks. But among those watching the fight scene, which was taken from the then-popular movie, "The Champion," which starred actor Kirk Douglas, those subjects who had been introduced to "*Kirk* Anderson" administered more shocks than those paired with "*Bob* Anderson." Apparently, the description or the name of a person can act as a cue to increase the aggressiveness directed against that target, even if it has nothing to do with what that person actually *did.*

Similarly, the mere presence of an object associated with aggression can also act as an aggressive cue. In another study,[60] college students were made angry: Some of them were made angry in a room in which a gun was left lying around (ostensibly from a previous experiment), and others in a room in which a neutral object (a badminton racket) was substituted for the gun. Subjects were then given the opportunity to administer some electric shocks to a fellow college student. Those individuals who had been made angry in the presence of the aggressive stimulus administered more electric shocks than did those made angry in the presence of the badminton racket. Again, certain cues associated with aggression act to increase a person's tendency to aggress. These studies point to an opposite conclusion from the slogan often seen on bumper stickers—"Guns don't kill people, people do." As Berkowitz puts it, "An angry person can pull the trigger of his gun if he wants to commit violence; but the trigger can also pull the finger or otherwise elicit aggressive reactions from him, if he is ready to aggress and does not have strong inhibitions against such behavior."[61]

One aspect of social learning that tends to *inhibit* aggression is the tendency most people feel toward taking responsibility for their actions. But what happens if this sense of responsibility is weakened? Philip Zimbardo[62] has demonstrated that persons who are anonymous and unidentifiable tend to act more aggressively than persons who are not anonymous. In Zimbardo's experiment, female students were required to shock another student (actually a confederate) as part of a "study of empathy." Some students were made "anonymous;" they were seated in a dimly-lit room, dressed in loose-fitting robes and large hoods, and never referred to by name. Other were easily identifiable; their room was brightly lit, no robes or hoods were used, and each woman wore a name tag. As expected, those students who were anonymous adminstered longer and more severe shocks. Zimbardo suggests that anonymity induces "deindividuation," a state of lessened self-awareness, reduced concern over social evaluation, and weakened restraints against prohibited forms of behavior. Such a process may explain the wild, impulsive acts of violence typically associated with riots, vigilante justice, and gang rape. When a person is part of a crowd, he or she is "faceless" and, therefore, takes less responsibility for his or her actions.

Toward the Reduction of Violence

So far, we have focused our discussion primarily on factors that serve to increase people's aggressiveness. If we believe, however, that the reduction of our propensity toward aggressiveness is a worthwhile goal, how should we proceed? It is tempting to search for simple solutions. In the last decade, no less an expert than a former president of the American Psychological Association suggested that we develop an anti-cruelty drug to be fed to people (especially national leaders) as a way of reducing violence on a universal scale.[63] The quest for such a solution is understandable and even somewhat touching; but it is extremely unlikely that a drug could be developed that would reduce cruelty without completely tranquilizing the motivational systems of its users. Chemicals cannot make the fine distinction that psychological processes can. Gentle, peace-loving people (like Albert Einstein) who are also creative, courageous, and resourceful are produced by a subtle combination of physiological and psychological forces, of inherited capacities and learned values. It is difficult to conceive of a chemical that could perform as subtly. Moreover, chemical control of human behavior has the quality of an Orwellian nightmare. Whom could we trust to use such methods?

There are probably no simple and foolproof solutions. But let's speculate about some complex and less foolproof possibilities based upon what we've learned so far.

Pure Reason. I am certain we could construct a logical, reasonable set of arguments depicting the dangers of aggression and the misery produced (not only in victims but in aggressors) by aggressive acts. I'm even fairly certain we could convince most people that the arguments were sound; clearly, most people would agree that war is hell and violence in the streets is undesirable. But such arguments probably would not significantly curtail aggressive behavior, no matter how sound, no matter how convincing. Even if convinced that aggression, in general, is undersirable, individuals will behave aggressively unless they firmly believe aggressiveness is undesirable *for them.* As Aristotle observed more than 2000 years ago, many people cannot be persuaded by rational behavior: "For argument based on knowledge implies instruction, and there are people whom one cannot instruct."[64] Moreover, because the problem of the control of aggression is one that first occurs in early childhood—that is, at a time when the individual is too young to be reasoned with—logical arguments are of little value. For these reasons, social psychologists have searched for alternative techniques of persuasion. Many of these have been developed with young children in mind but are adaptable to adults as well.

Punishment. To the average citizen, an obvious way of reducing aggression is to punish it. If one man robs, batters, or kills another, the simple solution is to put him in prison or, in extreme cases, to kill him. If a young girl aggresses against her parents, siblings, or peers, we can spank her, scream at her, remove her privileges, or make her feel guilty. The assumption here is that this punishment "will teach them a lesson," that they will "think twice" before they perform that activity again, and that the more severe the punishment, the better. But it is not that simple. Severe punishment has been shown to be effective temporarily, but, unless used with extreme caution, it can have the opposite effect in the long run. Observations of parents and children in the real world have demonstrated time and again that parents who use severe punishment tend to produce children who are extremely aggressive or children who, as adults, favor violent means of obtaining personal and political ends.[65] This aggressiveness usually takes place outside the home, where the child is distant from the punishing agent. But these naturalistic studies are inconclusive. They don't necessarily prove that punishment for aggression, in and of itself, produces aggressive children. Parents who resort to harsh punishment probably do a lot of other things as well—that is, they are probably harsh and aggressive people. Accordingly, it may be that their children are simply copying the general aggressive behavior of their parents. Indeed, it has been shown that if children are physically punished by an adult who had previously treated them in a warm and nurturant manner, they tend to comply with the adult's wishes even when the adult is absent from the scene. On the other hand, children who are physically punished by an impersonal, cold adult are far less likely to comply with the adult's wishes once the adult has left the room. Thus, there is some reason to believe that punishment can be useful if it is applied judiciously in the context of a warm relationship.

One other factor of great significance to the efficacy of punishment is its severity or restrictiveness. A severe or restrictive punishment can be extremely frustrating; because frustration is one of the primary causes of aggression, it would seem wise to avoid using frustrating tactics when trying to curb aggression. This point was demonstrated very nicely in a study by Robert Hamblin and his colleagues.[66] In this study, hyperactive boys were punished by their teacher by having privileges taken away from them. Specifically, the boys had earned some tokens exchangeable for a wide variety of fun things; but each time a boy aggressed, he was deprived of some of the tokens. During and after the application of this technique, the frequency of aggressive actions among these boys practically doubled. This was probably the result of an increase in frustration.

What about the prisons in our own country—institutions of punishment that are quite severe and restrictive? Though it may seem intuitively correct to think that putting a criminal in such a harsh environment would deter that person from committing crimes in the future, there is precious little evidence to support such an assumption.[67] As our analysis would predict, imprisonment may have the opposite effect. Determining its specific consequences is difficult, however; in most instances, it is impossible to isolate the effects of being incarcerated because too many other factors influence the person in that situation. Do many people incarcerated for years wind up returning to prison simply because they *are* criminal types? Are prisons oppressive and violent because prisoners are antisocial and immoral, and because guards are authoritarian and sadistic? While these possibilities usually are hard to test in the real world, two studies in particular provide evidence that prisons fail to deter crime among the inmates who are released and that their violent and dehumanizing nature is not merely due to the personalities of the prisoners and the guards. A Supreme Court decision provided the opportunity for the first study,[68] isolating the effects of imprisonment on recidivism. In 1963, after the *Gideon* v. *Wainwright* ruling that people could not be convicted of a felony without being provided with a lawyer, a number of the inmates in the Florida prisons were released before the end of their sentence. The only systematic difference between these prisoners and those remaining in jail was that the released prisoners had not previously been represented by counsel. Thus, researchers could compare two nearly identical groups of convicts—some had been prematurely released, and others had been punished and "rehabilitated" to the full extent of their term. In terms of recidivism, a startling difference emerged between the two groups: The prisoners who served their complete term were *twice* as likely to return to prison as those who were released early.

Turning to the second question, are the problems of prisons due to the kind of *people* in prison, or are they caused by the nature of the *environment?* The Stanford Prison Experiment,[69] the dramatic and frightening effects of which we quoted at the end of Chapter 1, points to the second conclusion. Philip Zimbardo and his associated created a simulated prison environment and filled it with *the most normal people they could select*, students that completed a battery of psychological tests and who were randomly assigned to the positions of prisoners and guards. Even with this careful selection process, placing these students in an authoritarian, oppressive *environment* resulted in the cruelty and dehumanization that Zimbardo described, causing the two-week experiment to be curtailed after just six days.

Further evidence along these lines indicates that, while severe punishment frequently results in compliance, it rarely produces internalization. In order to establish long-term nonaggressive behavior patterns, it is important to induce people when they are still children to internalize a set of values that denigrates aggressiveness. In two experiments discussed more fully in Chapter 4, both Merrill Carlsmith and I and Jonathan Freedman[70] demonstrated that, with young children, threats of mild punishment are far more effective than threats of severe punishment. Although these investigations dealt with toy preference in children, I would speculate that threats of mild punishment would curb aggression in the same way. Suppose a mother threatens to punish her young son in order to induce him to refrain, momentarily, from aggressing against his little sister. If she is successful, her son will experience dissonance. The cognition "I like to wallop my little sister" is dissonant with the cognition "I am refraining from walloping my little sister." If he were severely threatened, he would have an abundantly good reason for refraining—he would be able to reduce dissonance by saying, "The reason I'm not hitting my sister is that I'd get the daylights beaten out of me if I did—but I sure would like to." However, suppose his mother threatens to use a punishment that is mild rather than severe—a punishment just barely strong enough to get the child to stop his aggression. In this instance, when he asks himself why he's not hitting his infinitely hittable little sister at the moment, he can't use the threat as a way of reducing dissonance—that is, he can't easily convince himself he would be walloped if he hit his sister, simply because it's not true—yet he must justify the fact he's not hitting his sister. In other words, his external justification (in terms of the severity of the threat) is minimal; therefore, he must add his own justification in order to justify his restraint. He might, for example, convince himself he no longer enjoys hitting his little sister. This would not only explain, justify, and make sensible his momentarily peaceful behavior, but, more importantly, *it would decrease the probability of his hitting his little sister in the future.* In short, a counteraggressive value would have been internalized. He would have convinced *himself* that, for *him*, hitting someone is not a good or fun thing to do.

Although this process has been shown to work in several highly controlled laboratory experiments, it has one major drawback. Before it can be applied, it is essential that the parent know, for each child, exactly what sort of threat to use. It is important that it not be too severe, or else the child will have no need to seek additional justification for his lack of aggression. On the other hand, it must be severe enough for the child to refrain from aggressing momentarily. This is crucial because, if a parent administers a threat or a punishment that is not quite severe enough to get the child to desist momentarily, the entire process will backfire: The child will consciously decide not to stop his aggression, *even though* he knows he will be punished for it. This child experiences dissonance, too. The cognition "I am aggressing" is dissonant with the cognition "I will be punished for it." How does the child reduce dissonance? He does so by convincing himself it's worth it—that it's so enjoyable to hit his little sister he's willing to be punished for it. This reasoning serves to increase the long-term attractiveness of aggressive behavior. Thus, although threats of mild punishment can be an effective means of helping a child to become less aggressive, the technique cannot be used lightly or thoughtlessly. Careful consideration must be given to the precise intensity of the threat to be administered. This, of course, will vary somewhat from child to child. For some children, a stony stare from father may be too severe; for others, a hard spanking may not be severe enough. Again, the proper level can be found—but not easily. A threat not severe enough to bring about a momentary change in behavior will actually increase the attractiveness of the unwanted behavior.

Punishment of Aggressive Models. A variation on the theme of punishment involves punishing someone else. Specifically, it has been argued that it might be possible to reduce aggression by presenting the child with the sight of an aggressive model who comes to a bad end. The implicit theory here is that individuals who are exposed to this sight will in effect be vicariously punished for their own aggression and accordingly will become less aggressive. It is probable that, in our nation's past, public hangings and floggings were arranged by people who held this theory. Does it work? Gross data from the real world does not support the theory. For example, according to the President's Commission on Law Enforcement,[71] the existence and use of the death penalty does not decrease the homicide rate. Moreover, on the level of casual data, the mass media frequently depict aggressive people as highly attractive (Bonnie and Clyde, for example, or Butch Cassidy and the Sundance Kid), even though they are eventually punished. This tends to induce individuals to identify with these violent characters.

The evidence from controlled experiments presents a more precise picture. Typically, in these experiments, children watch a film of an aggressive person who subsequently is either rewarded or punished for acting aggressively. Later, the children are given an opportunity to be aggressive under circumstances similar to the ones shown in the film. The consistent finding is that the children who watched the film in which the aggressive person was punished display significantly less aggressive behavior than the children who watched the film of the person being rewarded.[72] As mentioned previously, there is also some evidence to indicate that the kids who watched the aggressive film character being punished displayed less aggressive behavior than did children who watched an aggressive film character who was neither rewarded nor punished. On the other hand—and this is most crucial to our discussion—seeing a model being punished for aggression did not decrease the general level of aggression below that of a group of children who were never exposed to an aggressive model. In other words, the major thrust of the research seems to indicate that seeing an aggressor rewarded will increase aggressive behavior in a child and that seeing an aggressor punished will *not increase* the child's aggressive behavior, but it's not clear that seeing an aggressor punished will *decrease* the child's aggressive behavior. It might be just as effective not to expose the child to aggressive models at all. The implications of this research for the portrayal of violence in the mass media have already been discussed.

Rewarding Alternative Behavior Patterns. Another possibility that has been investigated is to ignore a child when he or she behaves aggressively and to reward the child for nonaggressive behavior. This strategy is based in part on the assumption that young children (and perhaps adults as well) frequently behave aggressively as a way of attracting attention. For them, being punished is preferable to being ignored. Paradoxically, then, punishing aggressive behavior may actually be interpreted as a reward—"Hey, look, gang! Mommy pays attention to me every time I slug my little brother. I think I'll do it again." This idea was tested in an experiment conducted at a nursery school by Paul Brown and Rogers Elliot.[73] The nursery school teachers were instructed to ignore all aggressive behavior on the part of the kids. At the same time, the teachers were asked to be very attentive to the children and especially to give them a lot of attention when they were doing things incompatible with aggression—such as playing in a friendly manner, sharing toys, and cooperating with others. After a few weeks, there was a noticeable decline in aggressive behavior. In a more elaborate experiment, Joel Davitz[74] demonstrated that frustration need not necessarily result in aggression—rather, it *can* lead to constructive behavior, if such behavior has been made attractive and appealing by prior training. In this study, children were allowed to play in groups of four. Some of these groups were rewarded for constructive behavior, while others were rewarded for aggressive or competitive behavior. Then the kids were deliberately frustrated. This was accomplished by building up the expectation they would be shown a series of entertaining movies and be allowed to have fun. Indeed, the experimenters went so far as to begin to show a movie and to hand out candy bars to be eaten later. But then the frustration was administered. The experimenter abruptly terminated the movie at the point of highest interest and took the candy bars away. The children were then allowed to play freely. As you have learned, this is a setup for the occurrence of aggressive behavior. But those children who had been trained for constructive behavior displayed far more constructive activity and far less aggressive activity than those in the other group.

This research is encouraging indeed. It is unlikely that parents can ever succeed in building a frustration-free environment for their children. Even were this possible, it would not be desirable, because the world outside is full of frustrating situations, and a child who is sheltered from frustration will experience greater pain and turmoil when he or she is finally exposed to frustrating events. But it *is* possible to train children to respond to frustrating events in constructive and satisfying ways rather than in ways that are violent and destructive.

The Presence of Nonaggressive Models. An important curb to aggressive behavior is the clear indication that such behavior is inappropriate. And the most effective indicator is *social*—that is, the presence of other people in the same circumstances who are restrained and relatively unaggressive. For example, in a study by Robert Baron and Richard Kepner,[75] subjects were insulted by an individual and then observed that individual receiving electric shocks at the hands of a third person. The third person either delivered intense electric shocks or very mild electric shocks. There also was a control group in which subjects did not observe a model administering shocks. Subjects then were given the opportunity to shock their tormentor. Those who had witnessed a person delivering intense shocks delivered more intense shocks than those in the control condition; those who had witnessed a person delivering a mild shock delivered milder shocks then those in the control condition. Does this paradigm seem familiar? The reader can readily see that the expression of aggressive behavior, like the expression of *any* behavior, can be viewed as an act of conformity. Specifically, in an ambiguous situation, people look to other people for a definition of what is appropriate. Recall that in Chapter 2 we described the conditions under which you might belch at the dinner table of a Freedonian dignitary. Here we are suggesting that, if you and your friends are frustrated or made angry, and all around you people in your group are throwing snowballs at your tormentors, it will increase the probability you will throw snowballs; if they are merely talking forcefully, it will increase the probability you will talk forcefully; and, alas, if the people in your group are swinging clubs at the heads of their tormentors, it will increase the probability you will pick up a club and start swinging.

Building Empathy Toward Others. Picture the following scene. There is a long line of cars stopped at the traffic light of a busy intersection. The light turns green. The lead car hesitates for fifteen seconds. What happens? Of course. There is an eruption of horn-honking. Not simply a little toot designed to supply the lead car with the information that the light has changed, but prolonged and persistent blasting indicative of a frustrated group of people venting their annoyance on the hesitating driver. Indeed, in a controlled experiment, it was found that approximately 90 percent of the drivers of the second car tooted their horn in an aggressive manner. As part of the same experiment, a pedestrian crossed the street between the first and the second car *while the light was still red*, and was out of the intersection by the time the light turned green. Still, almost 90 percent of the second cars tooted their horn when the light turned green. But suppose the pedestrian were on crutches? Apparently, seeing a person on crutches evoked an emphathetic response; the feeling of empathy overwhelmed the desire to be aggressive—the percentage of people honking their horn decreased dramatically.[76]

Empathy is an important phenomenon. Seymour Feshbach notes that most people find it difficult to inflict pain purposely on another human being unless they can find some way of dehumanizing their victim. "Thus the policeman becomes a 'pig,' and the student a 'hippie.' The Asiatic becomes a 'Gook,' 'yellow people are treacherous,' and besides, 'we all know that life is cheap in the Orient.' "[77] As I have noted time and again in this book, the kind of rationalization that Feshbach has described not only makes it possible for us to aggress against another person but also guarantees that we will continue to aggress against that person. Recall the example of the schoolteacher living in Kent, Ohio, who, after the killing of four Kent State students by Ohio National Guardsmen, told author James Michener[78] that anyone who walks on the street barefoot deserves to die. This kind of statement is understandable only if we assume it was made by someone who had succeeded in dehumanizing the victims of this tragedy. We can deplore the process of dehumanization, but, at the same time, an understanding of the process can help us to reverse it. Specifically, if it is true that most individuals must dehumanize their victims in order to commit an extreme act of aggression, then, by building empathy among people, aggressive acts will become more difficult to commit. Indeed, Norma and Seymour Feshbach[79] have demonstrated a negative correlation between empathy and aggression in children: the more empathy a person has, the less he or she resorts to aggressive actions. More recently, Norma Feshbach has developed a method of teaching empathy and has tested its effects on aggressiveness.[80] Briefly, she taught primary school children how to see from the perspective of another. The children were trained to identify different emotions in people, they acted out roles in various emotionally charged situations, and they explored (in a group) their own feelings. These "empathy training activities" led to significant decreases in aggressive behavior, as compared to a control group that received no empathy training.

There are other ways to foster empathy among people, but we are not quite ready to discuss them at this point. First we must take a look at the other side of the question—dehumanization, the kind of dehumanization that occurs in prejudice, the kind of dehumanization that not only hurts the victim but hurts the oppressor as well. Read the first paragraph of the next chapter and you'll see what I mean.

6

Prejudice

> A white policeman yelled, "Hey boy! Come here!" Somewhat bothered, I retorted: "I'm no boy!" He then rushed at me, inflamed, and stood towering over me, snorting, "What d'ja say, boy?" Quickly he frisked me and demanded, "What's your name, boy?" Frightened, I replied, "Dr. Poussaint, I'm a physician." He angrily chuckled and hissed, "What's your first name, boy?" When I hesitated he assumed a threatening stance and clenched his fists. As my heart palpitated, I muttered in profound humiliation, "Alvin."
>
> He continued his psychological brutality, bellowing, "Alvin, the next time I call you, you come right away, you hear? You hear?" I hesitated. "You hear me, boy?"[1]

Hollywood would have had the hero lash out at his oppressor and emerge victorious. But in the real world, Dr. Poussaint simply slunk away, humiliated—or, in his own words, "psychologically castrated." The feeling of helplessness and powerlessness that is the harvest of the oppressed almost inevitably leads to a diminution of self-esteem that begins even in early childhood. Many years ago, Kenneth and Mamie Clark[2] demonstrated that black children, some of whom were only three years old, were already convinced being black was not a good thing—they rejected black dolls, feeling that white dolls were prettier and generally superior. This experiment suggests that educational facilities that are "separate but equal" are never equal because the separation itself implies to the minority children that they are being segregated because there is something wrong with them. Indeed, this experiment was specifically cited in the landmark Supreme Court decision (*Brown* v. *Board of Education*, 1954) that declared segregated schools to be unconstitutional.

This diminution of self-esteem is not limited to blacks; it affects other oppressed groups as well. In a study similar to the Clark and Clark experiment, Philip Goldberg[3] demonstrated that women have been taught to consider themselves the intellectual inferiors of men. In his experiment, Goldberg asked a number of female college students to read scholarly articles and to evaluate them in terms of their competence, style, and so on. For some students, specific articles were signed by male authors (for example, John T. McKay); and for others, the same articles were signed by female authors (for example, Joan T. McKay). The female students rated the articles much higher if they were "written" by a male author than if they were "written" by a female author. In other words, these women had "learned their place"—they regarded the output of other females as necessarily inferior to that of males, just as the black youngsters learned to regard black dolls as inferior to white dolls. This is the legacy of a prejudiced society.

The Clark and Clark experiment was conducted in the 1940's; the Goldberg experiment was conducted in the 1960's. Important changes have taken place in our society since then; indeed, more recent research has indicated that the earlier results no longer pertain.[4] While this is encouraging, we are not out of the woods yet—as we shall see.

Stereotypes and Attributions

Social scientists have defined prejudice in a variety of ways. Technically, there are positive and negative prejudices; I can be prejudiced against modern artists or prejudiced in favor of modern artists. This means that, before I am introduced to Sam Smear (who I've been told is a modern artist), I will be inclined to like or dislike him—and I will be inclined to expect to see certain characteristics in him. Thus, if I associate the concept "modern artist" with effeminate behavior, I would be filled with shock and disbelief if Sam Smear were to swagger through the door looking for all the world like the middle linebacker for the Green Bay Packers. If I associate the concept of "modern artist" with the radical end of the political spectrum, I would be astonished if Sam Smear were wearing a Ronald Reagan political button.

In this chapter, we will not be discussing situations that concern prejudice "in favor of" people; accordingly, the working definition of prejudice we will employ will be limited to negative attitudes. We will define prejudice as a hostile or negative attitude toward a distinguishable group based on generalizations derived from faulty or incomplete information. For example, when we say an individual is prejudiced against blacks, we mean he or she is oriented toward behaving with hostility toward blacks; the person feels that, with perhaps one or two exceptions, all blacks are pretty much the same. The characteristics he or she assigns to blacks are either totally inaccurate or, at best, based on a germ of truth that the person zealously applies to the group as a whole.

The generalization of characteristics or motives to a group of people is called *stereotyping*. To stereotype is to assign identical characteristics to any person in a group, regardless of the actual variation among members of that group. Thus, to believe blacks have a natural sense of rhythm, or Jews are materialistic, is to assume that virtually all blacks are rhythmic, or that virtually all Jews go around collecting possessions. We learn to assign identical characteristics at a very young age. In one study[5] fifty-grade and sixth-grade children were asked to rate their classmates in terms of a number of characteristics: cleanliness, attractiveness, and the like. The children of upper-class families were rated more positively than the children of lower-class families on *every* desirable quality. It seems the youngsters were unable to judge their classmates on an individual basis; instead, they had stereotyped them according to their social class.

Stereotyping is not necessarily an intentional act of abusiveness; it is frequently merely a way of simplifying our view of the world, and we all do it to some extent. Most of us have a specific picture in our mind when we hear the words "New York cab driver" or "Italian barber" or "high-school cheerleader." To the extent that the stereotype is based on experience and is at all accurate, it can be an adaptive, shorthand way of dealing with complex events. On the other hand, if the stereotype blinds us to individual differences within a class of people, it is maladaptive and potentially dangerous. Moreover, most stereotypes are not based upon valid experience, but are based on hearsay or images concocted by the mass media or are generated within our heads as ways of justifying our own prejudices and cruelty. Like the self-fulfilling prophecy discussed earlier in this book, it is helpful to think of blacks or Chicanos as stupid if it justifies depriving them of an education, and it is helpful to think of women as being biologically predisposed toward domestic drudgery if a male-dominated society wants to keep them tied to a vacuum cleaner. Likewise, it is useful to perceive individuals from the lower class as being unambitious, less intelligent, and prone to criminal behavior if we want to pay them as little as possible for doing menial work. In such cases, stereotyping is, indeed, abusive. It should be plain, moreover, that stereotyping can be painful to the target, even if the stereotype seems to be neutral or positive. For example, it is not necessarily negative to attribute "ambitiousness" to Jews or "a natural sense of rhythm" to blacks; but it is abusive, if only because it robs the individual Jewish or black person of the right to be treated as an individual with his or her own individual traits, be they positive or negative.

Stereotyping is a special case of the phenomenon of *attribution*. When an event occurs, there is a tendency among individuals to try to attribute a cause to that event. Specifically, if a person performs an action, observers will make inferences about what caused that behavior. Such casual inferences are called *attributions*. For example, if the tight end on your favorite football team drops an easy pass, there are many possible explanations: Perhaps the sun got in his eyes; maybe he was distracted by worry over the ill health of his child; maybe he dropped the ball on purpose because he bet on the other team; maybe he "heard footsteps"; or perhaps he just happens to be an untalented player. Note that each of the above attributions about the cause of the tight end's bobble has a very different set of ramifications. You would feel differently about the athlete if he were worried about his child's illness than if he had bet on the other team.

This need to find a cause for another person's behavior is part of a human tendency to go beyond the information given. It is often functional. For example, suppose you have just moved into a strange town where you have no friends and you are feeling very lonely. There is a knock on the door; it is Joe, a neighbor, who shakes your hand and welcomes you to the neighborhood. You invite him in. He stays for about twenty minutes, during which time you and he have an interesting conversation. You feel really good about the possibility of having discovered a new friend. As he gets up to leave, he says, "Oh, by the way, if you ever need some insurance, I happen to be in the business and I'd be happy to discuss it with you," and he leaves his card. Is he your friend who happens to be selling insurance, or is he an insurance salesman who is pretending to be your friend in order to sell you insurance? It is important to know, because you must decide whether or not to pursue a relationship with him. To repeat, in making attributions, the individual must go beyond the information given. We do not *know* the reason why the tight end dropped the pass; we do not *know* Joe's motivation for friendly behavior. We are guessing. Thus, the attributor's causal interpretations may be accurate or erroneous, functional or dysfunctional.

In the past several years, the phenomenon of attribution has been explored in a systematic manner by a number of investigators,[6] and their major findings have been loosely organized into a theory. Attribution theory deals with the rules most people use in attempting to infer the causes of the behavior they observe. The theory also deals with the different kinds of events that produce different kinds of attributions. In general, we tend to attribute our own blunders to the situation in which we find ourselves; conversely, we attribute other people's blunders to some personality defect or lack of ability in that person. Thus, if I lose money in a game of poker, I will tend to blame the losses on an unlucky succession of bad cards; if I see *you* lose, however, I am more prone to think it is because you are a poor poker player.[7]

Along these lines, there is a stock joke (which predates attribution theory) about two men, a Protestant and a Catholic, who happen to notice a priest entering a brothel. The Protestant clucks his tongue and smiles smugly as he reflects on the hypocrisy of the Catholic Church. The Catholic beams proudly as he reflects on the fact that, when a member of *his* church is dying, even in a brothel, he is entitled to the Holy Sacrament, and a priest will enter the brothel to administer it. What the joke illustrates, of course, is that, in an ambiguous situation, people tend to make attributions consistent with their beliefs or prejudices. Thomas Pettigrew has dubbed this "the ultimate attribution error."[8] If Mr. Bigot sees a well-dressed, white Anglo-Saxon Protestant sitting on a park bench sunning himself at three o'clock on a Wednesday afternoon, he thinks nothing of it. If he sees a well-dressed black man doing the same thing, he is liable to leap to the conclusion the man is unemployed—and he becomes infuriated, because he assumes his own hard-earned money is being taxed to pay that shiftless, good-for-nothing enough in welfare subsidies to keep him in fancy clothes. If Mr. Bigot passes Mr. Anglo's house and notices an overturned trash can and garbage strewn about, he is apt to conclude that a stray dog has been searching for food. If he passes Mr. Garcia's house and notices the same thing, he is inclined to become annoyed, and to assert that "those people live like pigs." Not only does prejudice influence his attributions and conclusions, his erroneous conclusions justify and intensify his negative feelings. Thus, the entire attribution process can spiral. Prejudice causes particular kinds of negative attributions or stereotypes that can, in turn, intensify the prejudice.[9]

The attribution process has been demonstrated most clearly in recent research on gender roles. For example, let's look at a well-controlled experiment by Shirley Feldman-Summers and Sara Kiesler.[10] When confronted with the phenomenon of a highly successful female physician, male undergraduates perceived her as being less competent and having had an easier path toward success than a successful male physician. Female undergraduates saw things a little differently. They did not see either the male physician or the female physician as being less competent, but they saw the male as having had an easier time of it. Both males and females attributed higher motivation to the female physician. It should be noted that attributing a high degree of motivation to a woman can be one way of implying she has less actual skill than her male counterpart. This possibility comes into focus when we examine a similar study by Kay Deaux and Tim Emsweiler[11] in which they showed that, if the sexual stereotype is strong enough, even members of the stereotyped group tend to buy it. Specifically, male and female students were confronted with a highly successful performance on a complex task by a fellow student and were asked to account for it. When it was a male who succeeded, both male and female students attributed his success to his ability; when it was a female who succeeded, both male and female students attributed her success to *luck*. Interestingly enough, the tendency for women to downplay the ability factor in a woman's success begins early in life and *might apply even to self-attributions*. John Nicholls[12] found that, while fourth-grade boys attributed their own successful outcomes on a difficult intellectual task to their ability, girls tended to derogate their own successful performance. Moreover, he found that, while boys had learned to protect their egos by attributing their own failures to bad luck, girls took more of the blame for failures on themselves.

This phenomenon of self-attribution may have some interesting ramifications. Suppose a male tennis player loses the first set in a best-of-three-sets match by the score of 6-2. What does he conclude? Probably that he didn't try hard enough or that he was unlucky—after all, his opponent *did* have that incredible string of lucky shots. Now suppose a female tennis player loses the first set. What does she conclude? Given Nicholl's data, she might think she is not as skilled a player as her opponent—after all, she did lose 6-2. Here comes the interesting part: The attributions a player makes about their failure in the first set may, in part, determine their success in subsequent sets. That is, men may try harder to "come from behind" and win the next two sets and the match. However, women may "give up," thus losing the second set and the match. This is, in fact, what happens. In a recent study,[13] the outcomes of 19,300 tennis matches where examined. In those matches where a player lost the first set, men were more likely than women to come back and win the second and third sets. Women were more likely to lose a match in straight sets. This phenomenon occurs even among professional tennis players—players who surely regard themselves as talented and able.

Recent research has shown gender-related attributions to be a double-edged sword. Kay Deaux and Janet Taynor[14] have shown that bias can cut both ways—that is, men are expected to succeed but, if they fail, they are treated more harshly than women who fail. In their experiment, Deaux and Taynor had subjects listen to a taped interview with a college student who was a candidate for a prestigious scholarship. If the candidate did well in the interview and was male, he was rated as more competent than a female who had done just as well. However, if the male candidate did poorly in the interview, he was seen as far more incompetent than a female candidate who had done as poorly.

Putting all this research together, it appears that men are expected to succeed in our society and are treated harshly when they do not. Women are *not* expected to succeed—when they do succeed, they are seen by others *(and by themselves)* either as the rare person with an extraordinarily high degree of motivation or as simply lucky. When they fail, they are treated more leniently.

Subtle and Unsubtle Stereotyping. In his classic book *The Nature of Prejudice*, Gordon Allport reported the following dialogue:

> Mr. X: The trouble with the Jews is that they only take care of their own group.

> Mr. Y: But the record of the Community Chest campaign shows that they gave more generously, in proportion to their numbers, to the general charities of the community, than did non-Jews.
> Mr. X: That shows they are always trying to buy favor and intrude into Christian affairs. They think of nothing but money; that is why there are so many Jewish bankers.
> Mr. Y: But a recent study shows that the percentage of Jews in the banking business is negligible, far smaller than the percentage of non-Jews.
> Mr. X: That's just it; they don't go in for respectable business; they are only in the movie business or run night clubs.[15]

This dialogue illustrates the insidious nature of prejudice far better than a mountain of definitions. In effect, the prejudiced Mr. X is saying, "Don't trouble me with facts; my mind is made up." He makes no attempt to dispute the data as presented by Mr. Y. He either distorts the facts in order to support his hatred of Jews, or he bounces off them, undaunted, to a new area of attack. A deeply prejudiced person is virtually immune to information at variance with his or her cherished stereotypes.

It is resonably safe to assume that all of us have some degree of prejudice—whether it is against an ethnic, national, or racial group, against specific geographical areas as places to live, or against certain kinds of food. Let's take food as an example: In this culture, we tend not to eat insects. Suppose someone (like Mr. Y) were to tell you that caterpillars, grasshoppers, or ants were a great source of protein and, when carefully prepared, extremely tasty. Would that convince you to eat them? Probably not. Like Mr. X, you would probably find some other reason for your prejudice, such as the fact that insects are ugly. After all, in this culture, we eat only aesthetically beautiful creatures—like lobsters!

Gordon Allport wrote his book in 1954; the dialogue between Mr. X and Mr. Y might seem somewhat dated to a reader in the 1980s. Do people really think that way? Is there anyone so simple-minded as to believe that old, inaccurate stereotype about Jewish bankers? Perhaps not. But as late as 1974, the most powerful military officer in the United States, General George S. Brown, Chairman of the Joint Chiefs of Staff, in a public speech referring to "Jewish influence in Congress," said, ". . .

it is so strong you wouldn't believe, now. . . . They own, you know, the banks in this country, the newspapers. Just look at where the Jewish money is."[16]

Not all prejudiced thinking is as obvious as that of Allport's Mr X or as blatantly misinformed as General Brown's statement about Jewish bankers. Many individuals who regard themselves as fair-minded, decent people are capable of more subtle forms of prejudice. A good example of this (perhaps) unconscious stereotyping was discussed by Meg Greenfield in her *Newsweek* column.[17] In Zimbabwe in 1983, a group of black tribesmen brutally slaughtered several of their white countrymen. Ms. Greenfield noted that some otherwise liberal journalists, in describing the massacre, allowed themselves a great deal of sighing and gasping which took the tone of "I-told-you-so, see-they-aren't-ready, this-is-a-descent-into-savagery." Greenfield went on to point out that such attributions are made only to the behavior of black Africans. They are not made by the press when similar atrocities are committed in other parts of the world—for example, the massacre of 3600 unfortunate Bangladesh citizens living in the Indian state of Assam, or the barbarous torture and murder of several innocents in Beverly Hills by members of the all-white Charles Manson family.

Similarly, it is not always easy for people who have never experienced prejudice to fully understand what it is like to be the target of prejudice. For relatively secure members of the dominant majority, empathy does not come easily. They may *sympathize* and wish that it weren't so, but frequently a hint of self-righteousness nevertheless creeps into their attitude, producing a slight tendency to lay the blame on the victim. This may take the form of the "well-deserved reputation." It goes something like this: "If the Jews have been victimized throughout their history, they must have been doing *something* wrong." Or, "If she got raped, she *must* have been doing something provocative." Or, "If those people (blacks, Hispanics, native Americans) don't *want* to get into trouble, why don't they just . . ." (stay out of the headlines, keep their mouths shut, don't go where they're not wanted, or whatever). Such a suggestion constitutes a demand that the outgroup conform to demands more stringent than those set for the majority.

Ironically, this tendency to blame victims for their victimization, attributing their predicaments to their own personalities and disabilities, is often motivated by a desire to see the world as just a place. As Melvin Lerner and his colleagues have shown,[18] people tend to assign responsibility for any inequitable outcome that is otherwise difficult to account for. For example, if two people work equally hard on the same task, and, by a flip of a coin, one receives a sizable reward and the other receives nothing, observers show a strong tendency to rate the unlucky person as having worked less hard. Apparently, people find it scary to think about living in a world where hard workers can get no pay—therefore, they decide the unpaid worker must not have worked very hard, even though they saw the reward was determined by a mere flip of a coin. By the same token, if six million Jews get butchered for no apparent reason, it is somehow comforting to believe they might have done something to deserve it.*

Prejudice and Science

Scientists are supposedly an objective, fair-minded lot. But even they can be influenced by the prevailing atmosphere. Louis Agassiz, one of the great American biologists of the nineteenth century, argued that God had created blacks and whites as separate species.[19] In a similar vein, in 1925 Karl Pearson, a distinguished British scientist and mathematician, concluded his study of ethnic differences by stating: "Taken on the average and regarding both sexes, this alien Jewish population is somewhat inferior physically and mentally to the native [British] population."[20] On the basis of his findings, Pearson argued against allowing the immigration of East European Jews into Great

*The astute reader may have noticed that this is a milder form of our tendency to derogate a person *we* have victimized. In Chapters 4 and 5, we saw that, when one person hurts another, the aggressor tends to derogate the target, turn the victim into a nonperson, and hurt that person again. Now we see that, if one person notices another has gotten the short end of the stick, he or she somehow feels the victim must have done something to deserve it.

Britain. Most contemporary scientists are now sophisticated enough to demand more valid arguments than those put forward by Agassiz and Pearson. For example, we are sophisticated enough to view most standard IQ tests as prejudiced instruments that unintentionally discriminate in favor of white, middle-class suburbanites by stating examples in terms and phrases more familiar to children reared in the suburbs than to children reared in the ghetto or on the farm. Thus, before we conclude it was stupidity that caused a black person, a Chicano, or the resident of a rural community to do poorly on an IQ test, we demand to know whether or not the IQ test was culture-free.

But we can take this one step further. The fact that we live in a society with racist and sexist overtones can have subtle but important effects on the behavior of the dominant majority, as well as the behavior of women and minority group members. A good deal of this behavior occurs without our awareness. In an important set of experiments, Carl Word and his associates[21] first trained white Princeton students to interview applicants for a job. Their observation of the behavior of the interviewers revealed huge differences between black and white applicants: When the applicant was black, the interviewer unwittingly sat slightly further away, made more speech errors, and terminated the interview 25 percent sooner than when the applicant was white. Do you suppose this had an effect on the performance of the job applicants? In a second experiment, Word and his colleagues trained their interviewers to treat white students in the same manner that the interviewers had treated either the white applicants or the black applicants in the previous experiment. The experimenters videotaped the students being interviewed. Independent judges rated those who had been treated like the black applicants as being more nervous and less effective than those treated like the white applicant. The results of this experiment strongly lead us to suspect that when women or minority group members are interviewed by a white Anglo-Saxon male their performance may suffer, not because there is anything wrong with them but because, without necessarily intending to, the interviewer is likely to behave in a way that makes them uncomfortable.

Confessions of a Male Chauvinist. The traps that well intentioned people can fall into in a sexist society can be very subtle. Let me offer a personal example. In the first edition of this book, while discussing individual differences in persuasibility, I made the point that women seem to be more persuasible than men. This statement was based on a well-known experiment by Irving Janis and Peter Field.[22] A close inspection of this experiment, however, suggests it was weighted unintentionally against women in much the same way IQ tests are weighted against rural and ghetto residents. The topics of the persuasive arguments included civil defense, cancer research, von Hindenberg, and so on—topics the culture trains men and boys to take a greater interest in than women and girls. Thus, the results may simply indicate people are more persuasible on topics they don't care about or don't know about. Indeed, these speculations were confirmed by a more recent series of experiments by Frank Sistrunk and John McDavid.[23] In their studies, they used a variety of topics, some of greater interest to men and others applying more to women's interests and expertise. Their results were clear: While women were more persuasible on the masculine-oriented topics, men were more persuasible on the topics that appealed to women. Of course, the mere fact that women and men are raised not to be interested in certain topics is in and of itself an unfortunate consequence of sex discrimination.

In 1970, when I was writing the first edition of this book, I was unaware of the possible weakness in the experiment by Janis and Field until it was called to my attention (gently but firmly) by a friend who happens to be both a feminist and a social psychologist. The lesson to be gained from this example is a clear one: When we are reared in a prejudiced society, we often accept those prejudices uncritically. It is easy to believe women are gullible because that is the stereotype held by the society. Thus, we tend not to look at supporting scientific data critically and, without realizing it, we use the data as scientific support for our own prejudice.

Daryl and Sandra Bem[24] suggest that the prejudice against women in our society is an example of a *nonconscious ideology*—that is, a set of beliefs we accept implicitly but of which we are unaware because we cannot even conceive of alternative conceptions of the world. In this culture, for example, we are socialized in such a way that it becomes difficult for us to imagine a woman going out to work as a truck driver or a custodian while her husband stays home taking care of the kids, mending socks, and cleaning house. When we hear of such a situation, many of us leap to the conclusions that something is wrong with that couple. Why? Because such an arrangement is not held to be a real option in our society. Much as a fish is unaware its environment is wet, we don't even notice the existence of this ideology because it is so totally prevalent.

Recall the example in Chapter 1 in which little Mary received a Suzie Homemaker set ("complete with her own little oven") for her birthday. By the time she was nine, she was conditioned to know her place was in the kitchen. This conditioning was so thorough that her father was convinced "housewifery" was genetic in origin. This is no mere fantasy. As we mentioned, even the first picture books very young children read tend to transmit these role stereotypes.[25] Indeed, studies by Ruth Hartley[26] indicate that, by age *five*, children have already developed clearly defined notions of what constitutes appropriate behavior for women and men. This nonconscious ideology can have important consequences for society. For example, Jean Lipman-Blumen[27] reports that the vast majority of women who, in early childhood, acquired a traditional view of their gender role (that is, "a woman's place is in the home") opted not to seek advanced education; on the other hand, those women who had acquired a more egalitarian view of gender roles showed a much stronger tendency to aspire to advanced education.

Current trends in the direction of raising women's consciousness are proving to be beneficial to women. Extrapolating from Lipman-Blumen's findings, my guess is that, as traditional gender-role stereotypes continue to crumble, there will be an increase in the number of women who seek advanced education. In fact, this is already beginning to happen: For the first time, women undergraduates outnumbered men on the nation's college campuses during the 1979-1980 academic year. The elevation of women's consciousness also is proving beneficial to men. As women widen their interests and enter new occupations, the role prescriptions for men are becoming less restrictive. On a more personal level, the above example of my own unconscious chauvinism is instructive. To the extent that my friends are able to help me see my own blind spots, they help me to become a better scientist and a less biased person.

Let us broaden this example. In recent years, our society has become increasingly aware of the discrimination and stereotyping that occurs as a result of differential gender roles. The notion of gender roles, or roles appropriate to one's biological sexual identity, is useful in understanding the pressures society places on both men and women. Generally, males are expected to be the breadwinners, the initiators, and the aggressors, all the while hiding their softer emotions and their vulnerabilities. Traditionally, femininity has consistently been correlated with high anxiety, low self-esteem, and low social acceptance.[28] Women are seen as warmer and more expressive but less competent and decisive.[29] The female role has been centered around the home, children, and marriage, with limited access to higher status or more differentiated jobs. And this gender-role stereotyping has serious consequences. In an interesting experiment, Natalie Porter and Florence Geis showed that, compared to their male counterparts, even female graduate students were not given much credit for intellectual leadership. College students were shown a picture of either a group of men or a group of women sitting around a table. The picture was described as a group of graduate students working on a research project. They were asked to guess which member contributed most to the group. Their strong tendency was to choose the person sitting at the head of the table. In another condition, college students were shown a picture of a mixed-gender group (two men and three women) sitting around a table. When a man was at the head of the table, the subjects overwhelmingly named him as the greatest contributor. When a woman was pictured at the head of the table, she was hardly chosen at all. Indeed, each of the men in the picture received more "votes" than all three of the women combined. The results of this experiment provide an excellent example of what we mean by a nonconscious ideology inasmuch as the results were similar for male and female subjects; moreover, the women were severely underchosen by feminists as well as non-feminists.

The gender-role socialization process has led many people to regard the roles of females and males as characteristically rigid and limiting. Researchers in this domain find such traditional labeling antithetical to a rich and full growth process. For example, Sandra Bem advocates that people reduce this gender-role stereotyping by becoming more "androgynous": according to Bem, both men and women "should be encouraged to be both instrumental and expressive, both assertive and yielding, both masculine and feminine—depending upon the situational appropriateness of these various behaviors."[30] To illustrate, when asking for a pay raise, assertiveness is an adaptive, desirable action—for men and women alike. Behaving in a coy, passive, or timid manner probably will not get you your raise. When reconciling after an argument, however, yielding is an adaptive, desirable action—for men and women. Assertiveness may serve to increase the tension.

But the road to adrogynous behavior is not an easy one. Women, like the members of many minorities, are often rewarded for actions tending to support the prevailing cultural stereotype—that they are inferior, passive, dependent, and neurotic. Consequently, the self-fulfilling prophecy is in effect: If a woman were to attempt to view herself as different from the socially accepted norm, she would inevitably experience some discomfort because her behavior would be discrepant from the self-concept she had been developing since childhood. For example, as mentioned earlier, if a male truck driver and a housewife were to change roles, much dissonance would be aroused, especially when interacting with their peers. In this manner, a socially conditioned stereotype tends to be perpetuated. If a woman attempts to deviate from her rigid gender role by being assertive or by seeking an unconventional job, she is risking the loss of friendships and may be evoking even more prejudiced feelings in others. Accordingly, if individuals need to compare themselves to similar others, stepping out of an accepted role is less likely to occur.

Gender role socialization has many consequences. In a series of experiments in the late 1960s and early 1970s, Matina Horner[31] found that women actually *fear* success, especially when it seems inappropriate to the expectations of their role. In her studies, when female undergraduates were asked to write a story about "Anne, [who] finds herself at the top of her medical school class," the women were likely to describe Anne's future as an unhappy one, with the character either trying to minimize her own achievement or suffering negative consequences as a result of her success. Interestingly enough, more recent experiments[32] have demonstrated the same thing happens to men—if they experience success in a nontraditional setting. Specifically, men who were told that "John" was at the top of his *nursing* school class anticipated more negative consequences than did women who were told that "Anne" was at the top of her nursing school class. Thus, the "fear-of-success" phenomenon is similar to the "persuasibility" phenomenon; both men and women exhibit behaviors symptomatic of this effect—when and how depends on the situation.

I think two important lessons can be learned here. First, although there are undeniable differences between men and women, many of these differences can be traced to the different situations that men and women find themselves in. That is, women initially may seem more persuasible or afraid of success because they are being evaluated according to the rules of a man's game. Lo and behold, when men are evaluated according to *women's* rules, *they* seem more persuasible, afraid of success, or whatever. Thus, before we conclude that one sex is inferior to the other, we must carefully examine the context within which the behavior occurs. Remember Aronson's first law: People who do crazy things are not necessarily crazy. Likewise, people who do *inferior* things are not necessarily inferior. The second lesson has to do with the realization that all of us—men, women, boys, girls, blacks, Chicanos, Asians, whites, rich, poor—all of us are the victims of confining stereotyped roles. While it would be naive to miss the obvious fact that some roles are more restricting and debilitating than others, it would be foolish to fail to realize that one group's efforts to free itself from the chains of prejudice indirectly benefits us all. As we learn to accept others' out-of-role behavior, so too will our own out-of-role behavior become increasingly accepted—and all of us will become freer to fulfill our potential as human beings.

Causes of Prejudice

As we have seen, one determinant of prejudice in a person is a need for self-justification. In the last two chapters, for example, we have shown that, if we have done something cruel to a person or a group of people, we derogate that person or group in order to justify our cruelty. If we can convince ourselves a group is unworthy, subhuman, stupid, or immoral, it helps *us* to keep from feeling immoral if we enslave members of that group, deprive them of a decent education, or murder them. We can then continue to go to church and to feel like good Christians, because it isn't a fellow human we've hurt. Indeed, if we're skillful enough, we can even convince ourselves that the barbaric slaying of old men, women, and children is a Christian virtue—as the crusaders did when, on the way to the holy land, they butchered European Jews in the name of the Prince of Peace. Again, as we have seen, this act of self-justification serves to intensify subsequent brutality.

Of course, there are other human needs in addition to self-justification. For example, there are status and power needs. Thus, an individual who is low on the socioeconomic hierarchy may need the presence of a downtrodden minority group in order to be able to feel superior to somebody. Several studies have shown that a good predictor or prejudice is whether or not a person's social status is low or declining. Regardless of whether it is prejudice against blacks[33] or against Jews,[34] if a person's social status is low or declining, that individual is apt to be more prejudiced than someone whose social status is high or rising. It has been found that people who are at or near the bottom in terms of education, income, and occupation not only are the highest in their dislike of blacks but also are the ones most likely to resort to violence in order to prevent the desegregation of schools.[35]

These findings raise some interesting questions. Are people of low socioeconomic and educational status more prejudiced because (1) they need someone to feel superior to, (2) they most keenly feel competition for jobs from minority group members, (3) they are more frustrated than most people and, therefore, more aggressive, or (4) their lack of education increases the probability of their taking a simplistic stereotypical view of the world? It is difficult to disentangle these variables, but it appears that each of these phenomena contributes to prejudice. Indeed, there is no single cause of prejudice. Prejudice is determined by a great many factors. Let's look at some of the major determinants of prejudice.

In this chapter, we will discuss four basic causes of prejudice: (1) economic and political competition or conflict, (2) displaced aggression, (3) personality needs, and (4) conformity to existing social norms. These four causes are not mutually exclusive—indeed, they may all operate at once—but it would be helpful to determine how important each cause is, because any action we are apt to recommend in an attempt to reduce prejudice will depend on what we believe to be the major cause of prejudice. Thus, for example, if I believe bigotry is deeply ingrained in the human personality, I might throw my hands up in despair and conclude that, in the absence of deep psychotherapy, the majority of prejudiced people will always be prejudiced. This would lead me to scoff at attempts to reduce prejudice by reducing competitiveness or by attempting to counteract the pressures of conformity.

Economic and Political Competition. Prejudice can be considered to be the result of economic and political forces. According to this view, given that resources are limited, the dominant group might attempt to exploit or derogate a minority group in order to gain some material advantage. Prejudiced attitudes tend to increase when times are tense and there is conflict over mutually exclusive goals. This is true whether the goals are economic, political, or ideological. Thus, prejudice has existed between Anglo and Mexican-American migrant workers as a function of a limited number of jobs, between Arabs and Israelis over disputed territory, and between Northerners and Southerners over the abolition of slavery. The economic advantages of discrimination are all too clear when one looks at the success certain craft unions have had, over the years, in denying membership to women and members of ethnic minorities, thus keeping them out of the relatively high-paying occupations they control. For example, the decade between the mid-fifties and the mid-sixties was one of great political and legal advancement for the civil rights movement. Yet in 1966 only 2.7 percent of union-controlled apprenticeships were filled with black workers—an increase of only one percent over the preceding ten years. Moreover, in the mid-sixties, the U.S. Department of Labor surveyed four major cities in search of minority-group members serving as apprentices among union plumbers, steamfitters, sheetmetal workers, stone masons, lathers, painters, glaziers, and operating engineers. In the four cities, they failed to find a single black person thus employed. Clearly, prejudice pays off for some people,[36] While the 1970s and 1980s have produced significant changes in many of these statistics, they also show that the situation remains far from equitable for minority groups.

Discrimination, prejudice, and negative stereotyping increase sharply as competition for scarce jobs increases. In one of his classic early studies of prejudice in a small industrial town, John Dollard documented the fact that, although there was initially no discernible prejudice against Germans in the town, it came about as jobs became scarce:

> Local whites largely drawn from the surrounding farms manifested considerable direct aggression toward the newcomers. Scornful and derogatory opinions were expressed about these Germans, and the native whites had a satisfying sense of superiority toward them . . . The chief element in the permission to be aggressive against the Germans was rivalry for jobs and status in the local woodenware plants. The native whites felt definitely crowded for their jobs by the entering German groups and in case of bad times had a chance to blame the Germans who by their presence provided more competitors for the scarcer jobs. There seemed to be no traditional pattern of prejudice against Germans unless the skeletal suspicion against all outgroupers (always present) can be invoked in this place.[37]

Similarly, the prejudice, violence, and negative stereotyping directed against Chinese immigrants in the United States fluctuated wildly throughout the 19th century—spurred largely by changes in economic competition. For example, when the Chinese were attempting to mine gold in California, they were described as "depraved and vicious . . . gross gluttons . . . bloodthirsty and inhuman."[38] However, just a decade later, when they were willing to accept dangerous and arduous work building the transcontinental railroad—work that Caucasian Americans were unwilling to undertake—they were generally regarded as sober, industrious, and law-abiding. Indeed, Charles Crocker, one of the western railroad tycoons, wrote . . ."They are equal to the best white men . . . They are very trusty, very intelligent and they live up to their contracts."[39] After the completion of the railroad, however, jobs became more scarce; moreover, when the Civil War ended, there was an influx of former soldiers into an already tight job market. This was immediately followed by a dramatic increase in negative attitudes toward the Chinese: The stereotype changed to "criminal," "conniving," "crafty," and "stupid."

These data indicate that competition and conflict breed prejudice. Moreover, this phenomenon transcends mere historical significance—it seems to have enduring psychological effects as well. In a survey conducted in the 1970s, most antiblack prejudice was found in groups that were just one socioeconomic rung above the blacks. And, as we would predict, this tendency was most pronounced in situations in which whites and blacks were in close competition for jobs.[40] At the same time, there is some ambiguity in interpreting the data, because in some instances, the variables of competition are intertwined with such variables as educational level and family background.

In order to determine whether competition causes prejudice in and of itself, an experiment is needed. But how can we proceed? Well, if conflict and competition lead to prejudice, it should be possible to produce prejudice in the laboratory. This can be done by the simple device of (1) randomly assigning people of differing backgrounds to one of two groups, (2) making those two groups distinguishable in some arbitrary way, (3) putting those groups into a situation in which they are in competition with each other, and (4) looking for evidence of prejudice. Such an experiment was conducted by Muzafer Sherif and his colleagues[41] in the natural environment of a Boy Scout camp. The subjects were normal, well-adjusted, twelve-year-old boys who were randomly assigned to one of two groups, the *Eagles* and the *Rattlers*. Within each group, the youngsters were taught to cooperate. This was largely done through arranging activities that made each group highly intradependent. For example, within each group, individuals cooperated in building a diving board for the swimming facility, preparing group meals, building a rope bridge, and so on.

After a strong feeling of cohesiveness developed within each group, the stage was set for conflict. The researchers arranged this by setting up a series of competitive activites in which the two groups were pitted against each other in such games as football, baseball, and tug-of-war. In order to increase the tension, prizes were awarded to the winning team. This resulted in some hostility and ill will during the games. In addition, the investigators devised rather diabolical devices for putting the groups into situations specifically designed to promote conflict. In one such situation, a camp party was arranged. The investigators set it up so that the *Eagles* were allowed to arrive a good deal earlier than the *Rattlers*. In addition, the refreshments consisted of two vastly different kinds of food: About half the food was fresh, appealing, and appetizing; the other half was squashed, ugly, and unappetizing. Perhaps because of the general competitiveness that already existed, the early arrivers confiscated most of the appealing refreshments, leaving only the less interesting, less appetizing, squashed, and damaged food for their adversaries. When the *Rattlers* finally arrived and saw how they had been taken advantage of, they were understandably annoyed—so annoyed they began to call the exploitive group rather uncomplimentary names. Because the *Eagles* believed they deserved what they got (first come, first served), they resented this treatment and responded in kind. Name-calling escalated into food-throwing, and, within a very short time, a full-scale riot was in progress.

Following this incident, competitive games were eliminated and a great deal of social contact was initiated. Once hostility had been aroused, however, simply eliminating the competition did not eliminate the hostility. Indeed, hostility continued to escalate, even when the two groups were engaged in such benign activities as sitting around watching movies. Eventually, the investigators succeeded in reducing the hostility. Exactly how this was accomplished will be discussed later in this chapter.

The "Scapegoat" Theory of Prejudice. In the preceding chapter, I made the point that aggression is caused, in party, by frustration and such other unpleasant or aversive situations as pain or boredom. In that chapter, we saw that there is a strong tendency for a frustrated individual to lash out at the cause of his or her frustration. Frequently, however, the cause of a person's frustration is either too big or too vague for direct retaliation. For example, if a six-year-old boy is humiliated by his teacher, how can he fight back? The teacher has too much power. But this frustration may increase the probability of his aggressing against a less-powerful bystander—even if the bystander had nothing to do with his pain. By the same token, if there is mass unemployment, who is the frustrated, unemployed worker going to strike out against—the economic system? The system is much too big and much too vague. It would be more convenient if the unemployed worker could find something or someone less vague and more concrete to blame. The President? He's concrete, all right, but also much too powerful to strike at with impunity.

The ancient Hebrews had a custom that is noteworthy in this context. During the days of atonement, a priest placed his hands on the head of a goat while reciting the sins of the people. This symbolically transferred the sin and evil from the people to the goat. The goat was then allowed to escape into the wilderness, thus cleansing the community of sin. The animal was called a scapegoat. In modern times the term *scapegoat* has been used to describe a relatively powerless innocent who is made to take the blame for something that is not his or her fault. Unfortunately, the individual is not allowed to escape into the wilderness but is usually subjected to cruelty or even death. Thus, if people are unemployed, or if inflation has depleted their savings, they can't very easily beat up on the economic system—but they can find a scapegoat. In Nazi Germany, it was the Jews; in 19th century California, it was Chinese immigrants; in the rural South, it was black people. Several years ago, Carl Hovland and Robert Sears[42] found that, in the period between 1882 and 1930, they could predict the number of lynchings in the

South in a given year from a knowledge of the price of cotton during that year. As the price of cotton dropped, the number of lynchings increased. In short, as people experienced an economic depression, they probably experienced a great many frustrations. The frustrations apparently resulted in an increase in lynchings and other crimes of violence.

Otto Klineberg,[43] a social psychologist with a special interest in the cross-cultural aspects of prejudice, describes a unique scapegoating situation in Japan. The Eta or Burakumin are a group of two million outcasts, scattered throughout Japan. They are considered unclean and fit only for certain undesirable occupations. As you might imagine, the Eta usually live in slum areas. Their IQ scores are, on average, 16 points lower than those of other Japanese. Eta children are absent from school more often and their delinquency rate is three times higher than other Japanese children. For a non-Eta to marry an Eta is taboo, although there is some "passing." For an Eta to "pass" is relatively easy because there are *no inherited racial or physical differences* between the Eta and other Japanese. The Eta are an invisible race—an outgroup defined more by social class than physical characteristics. They can only be identified because of their distinctive speech pattern (which has developed from years of nonassociation with other Japanese) and their identity papers. Although the historic origins of the Eta are unclear, they probably occupied the lower rungs of the socioeconomic ladder until an economic depression led to their complete expulsion from Japanese society. Now the Japanese consider the Eta to be "innately inferior," thus justifying further scapegoating and discrimination.

It is difficult to understand how the lynching of blacks or the mistreatment of the Eta could be due only to economic competition. There is a great deal of emotion in these actions which suggests the presence of deeper psychological factors in addition to economics. Similarly, the zeal with which Nazis carried out their attempt to erase all members of the Jewish ethnic group (regardless of economic status) strongly suggests the phenomenon was not exclusively economic or political, but was (at least in part) psychological.[44] Firmer evidence for the existence of psychological processes comes from a well-controlled experiment by Neal Miller and Richard Bugalski.[45] Individuals were asked to state their feelings about various minority groups. Some of the subjects were then frustrated by being deprived of an opportunity to attend a film and were given an arduous and difficult series of tests instead. They were then asked to restate their feelings about the minority groups. These subjects showed some evidence of increased prejudicial responses following the frustrating experience. A control group that did not go through the frustrating experience did not undergo any change in prejudice.

Additional research has helped to pin down the phenomenon even more precisely. In one experiment,[46] white students were instructed to administer a series of electric shocks to another student as part of a learning experiment. The subjects had the prerogative to adjust the intensity of the shocks. In actuality, the learner was an accomplice of the experimenter who (of course) was not really connected to the apparatus. There were four conditions: The accomplice was either black or white; he was trained to be either friendly or insulting to the subject. When he was friendly, the subjects administered slightly *less* intense shocks to the black student; when he insulted them, they administered far more intense shocks to the black student than to the white student. In another experiment, college students were subjected to a great deal of frustration. Some of these students were highly anti-Semitic; others were not. The subjects were then asked to write stories based on pictures they were shown. For some subjects, the characters in these pictures were assigned Jewish names; for others, they were not. There were two major findings: (1) after being frustrated, anti-Semitic subjects wrote stories that directed more aggression toward the Jewish characters than did people who were not anti-Semitic; and (2) there was no difference between the anti-Semitic students and the others when the characters they were writing about were not identified as Jewish. In short, frustration or anger leads to a specific aggression—aggression against an outgroup member.

The laboratory experiments help to clarify factors that seem to exist in the real world. The general picture of scapegoating that emerges is that individuals tend to displace aggression onto groups that are disliked, that are visible, and that are relatively powerless. Moreover, the form the aggressiveness takes depends on what is allowed or approved by the ingroup in question: In society, lynchings of blacks and pogroms against Jews are not frequent occurrences, unless they are deemed appropriate by the dominant culture or subculture.

The Prejudiced Personality. As we have seen, the displacement of aggression onto scapegoats may be a human tendency, but not all people do it to a like degree. We have already identified socioeconomic status as a cause of prejudice. Also, we have seen that people who dislike members of a particular outgroup are more apt to displace aggression onto them than are people who do not dislike members of that outgroup. We can now carry this one step further. There is some evidence to support the notion of individual differences in a general tendency to hate. In other words, there are people who are predisposed toward being prejudiced, not solely because of immediate external influences, but because of the kind of people they are. Theodor Adorno and his associates[47] refer to these individuals as "authoritarian personalities." Basically, authoritarian personalities have the following characteristics: They tend to be rigid in their beliefs; they tend to possess "conventional" values; they are intolerant of weakness (in themselves as well as in others); they tend to be highly punitive; they are suspicious; and they are respectful of authority to an unusual degree. The instrument developed to determine authoritarianism (called the *F* scale) measures the extent to which each person agrees or disagrees with such items as these:

1. Sex crimes such as rape and attacks on children deserve more than mere imprisonment; such criminals ought to be publicly whipped, or worse.
2. Most people don't realize how much our lives are controlled by plots hatched in secret places.
3. Obedience and respect for authority are the most important virtues children should learn.

A high degree of agreement with such items indicates authoritarianism. The major finding is that people who are high on authoritarianism do not simply dislike Jews or dislike blacks, but, rather, they show a consistently high degree of prejudice against *all* minority groups.

Through an intensive clinical interview of people high and low on the *F* scale, Adorno and his colleagues have traced the development of this cluster of attitudes and values to early childhood experiences in families characterized by harsh and threatening parental discipline. Moreover, people high on the *F* scale tend to have parents who use love and its withdrawal as their major way of producing obedience. In general, authoritarian personalities, as children, tend to be very insecure and highly dependent on their parents; they fear their parents and feel unconscious hostility against them. This combination sets the stage for the emergence of an adult with a high degree of anger, which, because of fear and insecurity, takes the form of displaced aggression against powerless groups, while the individual maintains an outward respect for authority.

Although research on the authoritarian personality has added to our understanding of the possible dynamics of prejudice, it should be noted that the bulk of the data are correlational. That is, we know only that two variables are related—we cannot be certain what causes what. Consider, for example, the correlation between a person's score on the *F* scale and the specific socialization practices he or she was subjected to as a child. Although it is true adults who are authoritarian and highly prejudiced had parents who tend to be harsh and to use "conditional love" as a socialization technique, it is not necessarily true that this is what *caused* them to develop into prejudiced people. It turns out that the parents of these people tend, themselves, to be highly prejudiced against minority groups. Accordingly, it may be that the development of prejudice in some people is due to conformity through the process of *identification*, as described in Chapter 2. That is, a child might consciously pick up beliefs about minorities from his or her parents because the child identifies with them. This is quite different from, and much simpler than, the explanation offered by Adorno and his colleagues, which is based on the child's unconscious hostility and repressed fear of his or her parents.

This is not to imply that, for some people, prejudice is not rooted in unconscious childhood conflicts. Rather, it is to suggest that many people may have learned a wide array of prejudices on Mommy's or Daddy's knee. Moreover, some people may conform to prejudices that are limited and highly specific, depending upon the norms of their subculture. Let's take a closer look at the phenomenon of prejudice as an act of conformity.

Prejudice Through Conformity. It is frequently observed that there is more prejudice against blacks in the South than in the North. This often manifests itself in stronger attitudes against racial integration. For example, in 1942, only four percent of all Southerners were in favor of the desegregation of transportation facilities, while 56 percent of all Northerners were in favor of it.[48] Why? Was it because of economic competition? Probably not; there is more prejudice against blacks in those southern communities in which economic competition is low than in those northern communities in which economic competition is great. Are there relatively more authoritarian personalities in the South than in the North? No. Thomas Pettigrew[49] administered the *F* scale widely in the North and in the South and found the scores about equal for Northerners and Southerners. In addition, although there is more prejudice against blacks in the South, there is *less* prejudice against Jews in the South than there is in the nation as a whole; the prejudiced personality should be prejudiced against everybody—the Southerner isn't.

How then do we account for the animosity toward blacks that exists in the South? It could be due to historical causes: The blacks were slaves, the Civil War was fought over the issue of slavery, and so on. This could have created the climate for greater prejudice. But what sustains this climate? One possible clue comes from the observation of some rather strange patterns of racial segregation in the South. One example, a group of coal miners in a small mining town in West Virginia, should suffice. The black miners and white miners developed a pattern of living that consisted of total and complete integration while they were under the ground, and total and complete segregation while they were above the ground. How can we account for this inconsistency? If you truly hate someone, you want to keep away from him—why associate with him below the ground and not above the ground?

Pettigrew has suggested that the explanation for these phenomena is *conformity*. In this case, people are simply conforming to the norms that exist in their society (above the ground!) The historical events of the South set the stage for greater prejudice against blacks, but it is conformity that keeps it going. Indeed, Pettigrew believes that, although economic competition, frustration, and personality needs account for some prejudice, the greatest proportion or prejudiced behavior is a function of unthinking conformity to social norms.

How can we be certain that conformity is responsible? One way is to determine the relation between a person's prejudice and that person's general pattern of conformity. For example, a study of interracial tension in South Africa[50] showed that those individuals who were most likely to conform to a great variety of social norms also showed a higher degree of prejudice against blacks. In other words, if conformists are more prejudiced, the suggestion is that prejudice may be just another thing to conform to. Another way to determine the role of conformity is to see what happens to people's prejudice when they move to a different area of the country. If conformity is a factor in prejudice, we would expect individuals to show dramatic increases in their prejudice when they move into areas in which the norm is more prejudicial, and to show dramatic decreases when they are affected by a less prejudicial norm. And that is what happens. In one study, Jeanne Watson[51] found that people who had recently moved to New York City and had come into direct contact with anti-Semitic people became more anti-Semitic themselves. In another study, Pettigrew found that, as Southerners entered the army and came into contact with a less discriminatory set of social norms, they became less prejudiced against blacks.

The pressure to conform can be relatively overt, as in the Asch experiment. On the other hand, conformity to a prejudicial norm might simply be due to the unavailability of accurate evidence and a preponderance of misleading information. This can lead people to adopt negative attitudes on the basis of hearsay. Examples of this kind of stereotyping behavior abound in literature. For example, consider Christopher Marlowe's *The Jew of Malta* or William Shakespeare's *The Merchant of Venice*. Both of these works depict the Jew as a conniving, money-hungry, bloodthirsty, cringing coward. We might be tempted to conclude Marlowe and Shakespeare had had some unfortunate experiences with unsavory Jews, which resulted in these bitter and unflattering portraits—except for one thing: The Jews had been expelled from England some 300 years before these works were written. Thus, it would seem the only thing with which Marlowe and Shakespeare came into contact was a lingering stereotype. Unfortunately, their works not only reflected the stereotype but undoubtedly contributed to it as well.

Bigoted attitudes can also be fostered intentionally by a bigoted society through institutionally supporting these attitudes. For example, a society that supports the notion of segregation through law and custom is supporting the notion that one group is inferior to another. A more direct example: one investigator[52] interviewed white South Africans in an attempt to find reasons for their negative attitudes toward blacks. He found the typical white South African was convinced that the great majority of crimes were committed by blacks. This was erroneous. How did such a misconception develop? The individuals reported they saw a great many black convicts working in public places—they never saw any white convicts. Doesn't this prove blacks are convicted of more crimes than white? No. In fact, the rules forbade white convicts from working in public places! In short, a society can *create* prejudiced beliefs by its very institutions. In our own society, forcing blacks to ride in the back of the bus, keeping women out of certain clubs, preventing Jews from staying at exclusive hotels are all part of our recent history—and create the illusion of inferiority or unacceptability.

The media play an important institutional role. Until recently, newspapers tended to identify the race of a nonwhite criminal or suspect but never bothered to mention the wrongdoer's race if he or she happened to be white. This has undoubtedly contributed to a distorted picture of the amount of crime committed by nonwhites. Again, until very recently, it was rare to see a black face on television in a nonstereotypic role or in a commercial. Indeed, it is still unusual to see a Hispanic playing a major role in a television show. These practices create the illusion that blacks and Hispanics are inconsequential members of our society—people who don't use aspirin or shaving cream, who don't have real problems or human emotions. Moreover, if the participation of blacks is limited to stereotypic roles like the characters in "Amos 'n Andy" or the song-and-dance man on a variety show, the stereotype that blacks are stupid, shiftless, lazy, and have a natural sense of rhythm is strengthened. Likewise, if Hispanics are portrayed consistently as illegal aliens or gang members, another ethnic stereotype is strengthened. In the past several years, black athletes have been appearing on TV screens with greater frequency; I would guess that whites from rural northern towns who do not have much direct contact with blacks would be surprised to learn there actually are blacks who are unable to run the 100-meter dash in less than 11 seconds!

Of course, the same problems affects the portrayal of women. When the media portray women in situation comedies, advertisements, or picture books, they are not, in general, seen as authority figures, intellectuals, or adventurous people. Instead, they are frequently viewed as attractive but simple minded "girls" who worry excessively about which laundry detergent to use and who depend on men for guidance on important issues. Indeed, an analysis of 14,378 magazine ads published between 1959 and 1971 found that women were most often portrayed as: (1) sexual objects, (2) physically beautiful and (3) dependent on men.[53] Similarly, a content analysis of award-winning children's picture books found that, although the number of female pictures and characters had increased between 1967 and 1979, the portrayals and characterizations of women had not improved over that same time span. Women were overwhelmingly depicted as dependent and passive, as working in the home or not working at all, and as preferring indoor activities.[54] This finding is echoed by TV: Men outnumber women by a factor of 3 to 1; most women do not work outside the home and are significantly younger than the men they work with.[55] We tend to believe or accept things we see with great frequency—unless there are powerful reasons against doing so. Moreover, it is very difficult for us to account for what is not represented. Thus, if we hardly ever see women in powerful roles or enjoying outdoor activities, it is easy to conclude that they are incapable of using power effectively or that they don't enjoy camping and fishing.

Stateways Can Change Folkways

In 1954 the United States Supreme Court declared that separate but equal schools were, by definition, unequal. In the words of Chief Justice Earl Warren, when black children are separated from white children on the basis of race alone, it "generates a feeling of inferiority as to their status in the community that may affect their hearts and minds in a way unlikely ever to be undone." Without our quite realizing it, this decision launched our nation into one of the most exciting, large-scale social experiments ever conducted.

In the aftermath of this historic decision, many people were opposed to integrating the schools on "humanitarian" grounds. They predicted a holocaust if the races were forced to mingle in schools. They argued that you cannot legislate morality—meaning that, although you can force people to attend the same school, you cannot force people to like and respect each other. This echoed the sentiments of the distinguished sociologist William Graham Sumner, who, years earlier, had stated "stateways don't change folkways." What Sumner meant, of course, is you can't legislate morality; you can force people to desegregate, but you can't force them to like one another. A great many people urged that desegregation be delayed until attitudes could be changed.

Social psychologists at the time, of course, believed the way to change behavior is to change attitudes. Thus, if you can get bigoted adults to become less prejudiced against blacks, then they will not hesitate to allow their children to attend school with blacks. Although they should have known better, many social scientists were relatively confident they could change bigoted attitudes by launching information campaigns. They took a "16-millimeter" approach to the reduction of prejudice: If prejudiced people believe blacks are shiftless and lazy, then all you have to do is show them a *movie*—a movie depicting blacks as industrious, decent people. The idea is that you can combat misinformation with information. If Shakespeare believes Jews are conniving bloodsuckers because he has been exposed to misinformation about Jews, expose him to a more accurate range of information about Jews, and his prejudice will fade away. If most South Africans believe blacks commit virtually all the crimes, show them the white convicts, and they'll change their beliefs. Unfortunately, it is not quite that simple. Whether prejudice is largely a function of economic conflict, conformity to social norms, or deeply rooted personality needs, it is not easily changed by an information campaign. Over the years, most people become deeply committed to their prejudicial behavior. To develop an open, accepting attitude toward minorities when all of your friends and associates are still prejudiced is no easy task. A mere movie cannot undo a way of thinking and a way of behaving that has persisted over the years.

As the reader of this book has learned, where important issues are involved, information campaigns fail, because people are inclined not to sit still and take in information that is dissonant with their beliefs. Paul Lazarsfeld,[56] for example, described a series of radio broadcasts presented in the early forties designed to reduce ethnic prejudice by presenting information about various ethnic groups in a warm and sympathetic manner. One program was devoted to a description of Polish-Americans, another was devoted to Italian-Americans, and so forth. Who was listening? The major part of the audience for the program about Polish-Americans consisted of Polish-Americans. And guess who made up the major part of the audience for the program on Italian-Americans? Right. Moreover, as we have seen, if people are compelled to listen to information uncongenial to their deep-seated attitudes, they will reject it, distort it, or ignore it—in much the same way Mr. X maintained his negative attitude against Jews despite Mr. Y's information campaign, and in much the same way the Dartmouth and Princeton students distorted the film of the football game they watched. For most people, prejudice is too deeply rooted in their own belief systems, is too consistent with their day-to-day behavior, and receives too much support and encouragement from the people around them to be reduced by a book, a film, or a radio broadcast.

The Effects of Equal-Status Contact. Although changes in attitude might induce changes in behavior, as we have seen, it is often difficult to change attitudes through education. What social psychologists have long known, but have only recently begun to understand, is that *changes in behavior can affect changes in attitudes.* On the simplest level, it has been argued that, if blacks and whites could be brought into direct contact, prejudiced individuals would come into contact with the reality of their own experience, not simply a stereotype; eventually, this would lead to greater understanding. Of course, the contact must take place in a situation in which blacks and whites have equal status; throughout history many whites have always had a great deal of contact with blacks, but typically in situations in which the blacks played such menial roles as slaves, porters, dishwashers, shoe-shine boys, washroom attendants, and domestics. This kind of contact serves only to increase stereotyping by whites and thus adds fuel to their prejudice against blacks. It also serves to increase the resentment and anger of blacks. Until recently, equal-status contact has been rare, both because of educational and occupational inequities in our society and because of residential segregation. The 1954 Supreme Court decision was the beginning of a gradual change in the frequency of equal-status contact.

Occasionally, even before 1954, isolated instances of equal-status integration had taken place. The effects tended to support the notion that behavior change will produce attitude change. In a pioneering study, Morton Deutsch and Mary Ellen Collins[57] examined the attitudes of whites toward blacks in public housing projects. Specifically, in one housing project, black and white families were assigned to buildings in a segregated manner—that is, they were assigned to separate buildings in the same project. In another project, the assignment was integrated—black and white families were assigned to the same building. Residents in the integrated project reported a greater positive change in their attitudes towards blacks subsequent to moving into the project than did residents of the segregated project. From these findings, it would appear that stateways *can* change folkways, that you *can* legislate morality—not directly, of course, but through the medium of equal-status contact. If diverse racial groups can be brought together under conditions of equal status, they stand a chance of getting to know each other better. This can increase understanding and decrease tension, *all other things being equal*.*

The Vicarious Effects of Desegregation. It wasn't until much later that social psychologists began to entertain the notion that desegregation can affect the values of people who do not even have the opportunity to have direct contact with minority groups. This can occur through the mechanisms we have referred to in Chapter 4 as the *psychology of inevitability*. Specifically, if I know that you and I will inevitably be in close contact, and I don't like you, I will experience dissonance. In order to reduce dissonance, I will try to convince myself you are not as bad as I had previously thought. I will set about looking for your positive characteristics and will try to ignore, or minimize the importance of, your negative characteristics. Accordingly, the mere fact that I know I must at some point be in *close contact* with you will force me to change my prejudiced attitudes about you, *all other things being equal*. Laboratory experiments have confirmed this prediction: For example, children who believed they must inevitably eat a previously disliked vegetable began to convince themselves the vegetable wasn't as bad as they had previously thought.[58] Similarly, college women who knew they were going to spend several weeks working intimately with a woman who had several positive and negative qualities developed a great fondness for that woman before they even met her; this did not occur when they were *not* led to anticipate working with her in the future.[59]

Admittedly, it's a far cry from a bowl of vegetables to relations between blacks, Hispanics, and whites. Few social psychologists are so naive as to believe that deep-seated racial intolerance can be eliminated if people reduce their dissonance simply through coming to terms with what they believe to be inevitable events. I would suggest that, under ideal conditions,

*The study alluded to in this paragraph took place in public housing projects rather than in private residential areas. This is a crucial factor that will be discussed in a moment.

such events *can* begin to unfreeze prejudiced attitudes and produce a *diminution* of hostile feelings in *most* individuals. I will discuss what I mean by "ideal conditions" in a moment; but first, let us put a little more meat on those theoretical bones. How might the process of dissonance reduction take place?

Turn the clock back to the late 1950s. Imagine a 45-year-old white male whose 16-year-old daughter attends a segregated school. Let us assume he has a negative attitude toward blacks, based in part on his belief that blacks are shiftless and lazy and that all black males are oversexed and potential rapists. Suddenly, the edict is handed down by the Justice Department: The following autumn, his fair-haired, nubile daughter must go to an integrated school. State and local officials, while perhaps not liking the idea, clearly convey the fact that there's nothing that can be done to prevent it—it's the law of the land and it must be obeyed. The father might, of course, refuse to allow his child to obtain an education, or he could send her to an expensive private school. But such measures are either terribly drastic or terribly costly. So he decides he must send her to an integrated school. His cognition that his fair-haired young daughter must inevitably attend the same school with blacks is dissonant with his cognition that blacks are shiftless rapists. What does he do? My guess is he will begin to re-examine his beliefs about blacks. Are they *really* all that shiftless? Do they *really* go around raping people? He may take another look—this time, with a strong inclination to look for the good qualities in blacks rather than to concoct and exaggerate bad, unacceptable qualities. I would guess that, by the time September rolls around, his attitude toward blacks would have become unfrozen and would have shifted in a positive direction. If this shift can be bolstered by positive events *after* desegregation—for example, if his daughter has pleasant and peaceful interactions with her black schoolmates—a major change in the father's attitudes is likely to result. Again, this analysis is admittedly oversimplified. But the basic process holds. And look at the advantages this process has over an information campaign. A mechanism has been triggered that *motivated* the father to alter his negative stereotype of blacks.

My analysis strongly suggests that a particular kind of public policy would be most potentially beneficial to society—a policy exactly opposite of what has been generally recommended. As mentioned previously, following the 1954 Supreme Court decision there was a general feeling that integration must proceed slowly. Most public officials and many social scientists believed that, in order to achieve harmonious racial relations, integration should be delayed until people could be re-educated to become less prejudiced. In short, the general belief in 1954 was that the behavior (integration) must *follow* a cognitive change. My analysis suggests the best way to produce eventual interracial harmony would be to launch into behavioral change. Moreover, *and most important*, the sooner the individuals realize integration is inevitable, the sooner their prejudiced attitudes will begin to change. On the other hand, this process can be (and has been) sabotaged by public officials through fostering the belief that integration can be circumvented or delayed. This serves to create the illusion that the event is not inevitable. In such circumstances, there will be no attitude change; the result will be an increase in turmoil and disharmony. Let's go back to our previous example: If the father of the fair-haired daughter is led (by the statements and tactics of a governor, a mayor, a school-board chairman, or a local sheriff) to believe that there's a way out of integration, he will feel no need to reexamine his negative beliefs about blacks. The result is apt to be violent opposition to integration.

Consistent with this reasoning is the fact that, as desegregation has spread, favorable attitudes toward desegregation have increased. In 1942, only 30 percent of the whites in this country favored desegregated schools; by 1956, the figure rose to 49 percent; in 1970, 75 percent. Finally, in 1980, as it became increasingly clear school desegregation was inevitable, the figure approached 90 percent.[60] The change in the South alone is even more dramatic. In 1942, only two percent of the whites in the South favored integrated schools; in 1956, while most Southerners still believed the ruling could be circumvented, only 14 percent favored desegregation; but by 1970, as desegregation continued, just under 50 percent favored desegregation—and the figures continued to climb in the '80s. Of course, such statistical data do not constitute absolute proof that the reason people are changing their attitudes toward school desegregation is that they are coming to terms with what is inevitable—but the data are highly suggestive.

In a careful analysis of the process and effects of school desegregation, Thomas Pettigrew raised the question of why, in the early years of desegregation, violence occurred in some communities, such as Little Rock and Clinton, and not in others, such as Norfolk and Winston-Salem. His conclusion, which lends further support to my reasoning, was that "violence has generally resulted in localities where at least some of the authorities give prior hints that they would gladly return to segregation if disturbances occurred; peaceful integration has generally followed firm and forceful leadership."[61] In other words, if people were not given the opportunity to reduce dissonance, there was violence. As early as 1953, Kenneth B. Clark[62] observed the same phenomenon during the desegregation in some of the border states. He discovered that immediate desegregation was far more effective than gradual desegregation. Moreover, violence occurred in those places where ambiguous or inconsistent policies were employed or where community leaders tended to vacillate. The same kind of thing happened when military units began to desegregate during World War II: Trouble was greatest where policies were ambiguous.[63]

But All Other Things Are Not Always Equal. In the preceding section, I presented an admittedly oversimplified view of a very complex phenomenon. I did this intentionally as a way of indicating how things *can* proceed theoretically under ideal conditions. But conditions are seldom ideal. There are almost always some complicating circumstances. Let us now look at some of the complications and then proceed to discuss how these complications might be eliminated or reduced.

When I discussed the fact that prejudice was reduced in an integrated housing project, I made special note of the fact it was a *public* housing project. Some complications are introduced if it involves privately owned houses. Primarily, there is a strong belief among whites that, when blacks move into a neighborhood, real-estate values decrease. This belief introduces economic conflict and competition, which mitigate against the reduction of prejudiced attitudes. Indeed, systematic investigations in integrated *private* housing show an increase in prejudiced attitudes among the white residents.[64]

Moreover, as I mentioned, the experiments on the psychology of inevitability were done in the laboratory where the dislikes involved in the studies were almost certainly not as intense or as deep-seated as racial prejudice is in the real world. Although it is encouraging to note these findings were paralleled by the data from actual desegregation efforts, it would be naive and misleading to conclude that the way to desegregation will always be smooth as long as individuals are given the opportunity to come to terms with inevitability. Frequently, trouble begins once desegregation starts. This is often due, in part, to the fact that the contact between white and minority group children (especially if it is not begun until high school) is usually not equal-status contact. Picture the scene: A tenth-grade boy from a poor black or Chicano family, after being subjected to a second-rate education, is suddenly dropped into a learning situation in a predominately white middle-class school taught by white middle-class teachers, where he finds he must compete with white middle-class students who have been reared to hold white middle-class values. In effect, he is thrust into a highly competitive situation for which he is unprepared, a situation in which the rules are not his rules and payoffs are made for abilities he has not yet developed. He is competing in a situation that, psychologically, is far removed from his home turf. Ironically enough, these factors tend to produce a diminution of his self-esteem—the very factor that influenced the Supreme Court decision in the first place.[65] In his careful analysis of the research on desegregation, Walter Stephan[66] found *no* studies indicating significant increases in self-esteem among black children, while 25 percent of the studies he researched showed a significant *drop* in their self-esteem following desegregation. In addition, prejudice was not substantially reduced. Stephan found it increased in almost as many cases as it decreased.

With these data in mind, it is not surprising to learn that a newly integrated high school is typically a tense place. It is natural for minority group students to attempt to raise their self-esteem. One way of raising self-esteem is to stick together, lash out at whites, assert their individuality, reject white values and white leadership, and so on.[67]

Let me sum up the discussion thus far: (1) Equal-status contact under the ideal conditions of no economic conflict can and does produce increased understanding and a diminution of prejudice.[68] (2) The psychology of inevitability can and does set up pressures to reduce prejudiced attitudes, and can set the stage for smooth, nonviolent school desegregation, *under ideal conditions.* (3) Where economic conflict is present (as in integrated neighborhoods of private domiciles) there is often an increase in prejudiced attitudes. (4) Where school desegregation results in a competitive situation, especially if there are serious inequities for the minority groups, there is often an increase in hostility of blacks or Chicanos toward whites that is at least partially due to an attempt to regain some lost self-esteem.

Interdependence—A Possible Solution. School desegregation can open the door to increased understanding among students but, by itself, is not the ultimate solution. The issue is not simply getting youngsters of various races and ethnic backgrounds into the same school—it's what happens after they get there that is crucial. As we have seen, if the atmosphere is a highly competitive one, whatever tensions exist initially might actually be increased as a result of contact. The tension that is frequently the initial result of school desegregation reminds me somewhat of the behavior of the young boys in the summer camp experiment by Muzafer Sherif and his colleagues.[69] Recall that hostility was produced between two groups by placing them in situations of conflict and competition. Once the hostility was established, it could no longer be reduced simply by removing the conflicts and the competition. As a matter of fact, once distrust was firmly established, bringing the groups together in equal-status, noncompetitive situations served to *increase* the hostility and distrust. For example, the children in these groups had trouble with each other even when they were simply sitting near each other watching a movie.

How did Sherif eventually succeed in reducing the hostility? By placing the two groups of boys in situations in which they were mutually interdependent—situations in which they had to cooperate with each other in order to accomplish their goal. For example, the investigators set up an emergency situation by damaging the water-supply system. The only way the system could be repaired was if all the children cooperated immediately. On another occasion, the camp truck broke down while the boys were on a camping trip. In order to get the truck going again, it was necessary to pull it up a rather steep hill. This could be accomplished only if all the youngsters pulled together—regardless of whether they were *Eagles* or *Rattlers*. Eventually, there was a diminution of hostile feelings and negative stereotyping. The boys made friends across groups, began to get along better, and began to cooperate spontaneously.

The key factor seems to be *mutual interdependence*—a situation wherein individuals need one another and are needed by one another in order to accomplish their goal. Several researchers have demonstrated the benefits of cooperation in well-controlled laboratory experiments. Morton Deutsch,[70] for example, has shown that problem-solving groups are both friendlier and more attentive when a cooperative atmosphere is introduced than when a competitive atmosphere prevails.

Unfortunately, cooperation and interdependence are not characteristic of the process that exists in most school classrooms, even at the elementary level. We have already alluded to the competitive nature of the process; let us take a closer look at it. First, let's define "process." Whenever people interact, two things exist simultaneously. One of these things is the content and the other is the process. By content, we simply mean the substance of their encounter; by process, we mean the dynamics of the encounter. In a classroom, for example, the content could be arithmetic, geography, social studies, or music; the process is the manner in which these lessons are taught. It goes without saying that the content is of great importance. However, the importance of the process is frequently underestimated. But it is through the process that pupils learn a great deal about the world they live in. Indeed, I would even go so far as to say that, in some respects, the process is a more important source of learning than the content itself.

I was provided with a golden opportunity to observe classroom process several years ago when I was called in as a consultant to the Austin, Texas school system. Desegregation had just taken place; this was followed by a great deal of turmoil and a number of unpleasant incidents. My colleagues and I entered the system, not to smooth over the unpleasantness but, rather, to see if there was anything we might do to help desegregation achieve some of the positive goals envisioned for it. The first thing we did was systematically observe the process. We tried to do this with fresh eyes—as if we were visitors from another planet—and the most typical process we observed was this: The teacher stands in front of the class, asks a question, and waits for the children to indicate that they know the answer. Most frequently, six to ten youngsters strain in their seats and wave their hands to attract the teacher's attention. They seem eager to be called upon. Several other students sit quietly with their eyes averted, as if trying to make themselves invisible. When the teacher calls on one of the students, there are looks of disappointment, dismay, and unhappiness on the faces of those students who were eagerly raising their hands but were not called on. If the student who is called upon comes up with the right answer, the teacher smiles, nods approvingly, and goes on to the next question. This is a great reward for the child who happens to be called on. At the same time the fortunate student is coming up with the right answer and being smiled upon by the teacher, an audible groan can be heard coming from the children who were striving to be called upon but were ignored. It is obvious they are disappointed because they missed an opportunity to show the teacher how smart and quick they are.

Through this process, students learn several things. First, they learn there is one and only one expert in the classroom: the teacher. They also learn that there is one and only one correct answer to any question the teacher asks—namely, the answer the teacher has in mind. The students' task is to figure out which answer the teacher expects. The students also learn that the payoff comes from pleasing the teacher by actively displaying how quick, smart, neat, clean, and well-behaved they are. If they do this successfully, they will gain the respect and love of this powerful person, who will then be kind to them and will tell their parents what wonderful children they are. There is no payoff for them in consulting with their peers. Indeed, their peers are their enemies—to be beaten. Moreover, collaboration is frowned upon by most teachers; if it occurs during class time it is seen as disruptive, and if it takes place during an exam it is called "cheating."

The game is very competitive and the stakes are very high—because, in an elementary-school classroom, the youngsters are competing for the respect and approval of one of the two or three most important people in their world (important for most students, anyway). If you are a student who knows the correct answer and the teacher calls on one of your peers, it is likely you will sit there hoping and praying he or she will come up with the wrong answer so you will have a chance to show the teacher how smart you are. Those who fail when called upon, or those who do not even raise their hands and compete, have a tendency to resent those who succeed. Frequently, the "losers" become envious and jealous of the successful students; perhaps they tease them or ridicule them by referring to them as "teacher's pets." They might even use physical aggression against them in the school yard. The successful students, for their part, often hold the unsuccessful students in contempt; they consider them to be dumb and uninteresting. The upshot of this process—which takes place, to a greater or lesser extent, in most classrooms—is that friendliness and understanding are not promoted among *any* of the children in the same classroom. Quite the reverse. The process tends to create enmity, even among children of the same racial group. When ethnic or racial unfamiliarity is added, or when tension brought about by forced busing flavors the stew of an already unhappy process, the situation can become extremely difficult and unpleasant.

Although competitiveness in the classroom is typical, it is not inevitable. In my research, I found that many classroom teachers were eager to try more cooperative techniques. Accordingly, my colleagues and I developed a simple method wherein children were put into interdependent learning groups; we systematically compared their performance, satisfaction, and liking for one another with that of children in more traditional, competitive classroom situations.[71] We called our method the *jigsaw* technique because it works very much like a jigsaw puzzle. An example will clarify: In our initial experiment, we entered a fifth-grade classroom of a newly desegregated school. In this classroom, the children were studying biographies of famous Americans. The upcoming lesson happened to be a biography of Joseph Pulitzer, the famous publisher. First, we constructed a biography of Joseph Pulitzer consisting of six paragraphs. Paragraph one was about Joseph Pulitzer's ancestors and how they came to this country; paragraph two was about Joseph Pulitzer as a little boy and how he grew up; paragraph three was about Joseph Pulitzer as a young man, his education, and his early employment; paragraph four was about his middle-age and how he founded his newspaper; and so forth. Each major aspect of Joseph Pulitzer's life was contained in a separate paragraph. We mimeographed our biography of Joseph Pulitzer, cut each copy of the biography into six one-paragraph sections, and gave every child in each of the six-person learning groups one paragraph about Joseph Pulitzer's life. Thus, each learning group had within it the entire biography of Joseph Pulitzer, but each individual child had no more than one-sixth of the story. Like a jigsaw puzzle, each child had one piece of the puzzle, and each child was dependent on the other children in the group for the completion of the big picture. In order to learn about Joseph Pulitzer, each child had to master a paragraph and teach it to the others. Each student took his paragraph and went off by himself where he could learn it. In learning the paragraph, the child was free to consult with his counterpart in one of the other learning groups. That is, if Johnnie had been dealt Joseph Pulitzer as a young man, he might have consulted with Christina, who was in a different learning group and had also been dealt Pulitzer as a young man. They could use each other to rehearse and clarify for themselves the important aspects of that phase of Joseph Pulitzer's life. A short time later, the students came back into session with their six-person groups. They were informed they had a certain amount of time to communicate their knowledge to one another. They were also informed that, at the end of the time (or soon thereafter), they were going to be tested on their knowledge.

When thrown on their own resources, the children eventually learned to teach and to listen to one another. The children gradually learned that none of them could do well without the aid of each person in the group—and that each member had a unique and essential contribution to make. Suppose you and I are children in the same group. You've been dealt Joseph Pulitzer as a young man; I've been dealt Pulitzer as an old man. The only way I can learn about Joseph Pulitzer as a young man is to pay close attention to what you are saying. You are a very important resource for me. The teacher is no longer the sole resource—he or she isn't even an important resource; indeed, the teacher isn't even in the group. Instead, every kid in the circle becomes important to me. I do well if I pay attention to other kids; I do poorly if I don't. I no longer get rewarded for trying to please the teacher at your expense. It's a whole new ball game.

But cooperative behavior doesn't happen all at once. Typically, it requires several days before children use this technique effectively. Old habits are difficult to break. The students in our experimental group had grown accustomed to competing during all of their years in school. For the first few days, most of the youngsters tried to compete—even though competitiveness was dysfunctional. Let me illustrate with an actual example, typical of the way the children stumbled toward the learning of the cooperative process. In one of our groups there was a Mexican-American boy, whom we will call Carlos. Carlos was not very articulate in English, his second language. He had learned over the years how to keep quiet in class because frequently, when he had spoken up in the past, he was ridiculed. In this instance, he had a great deal of trouble communicating his paragraph to the other children; he was very uncomfortable about it. He liked the traditional way better. This is not surprising, because, in the system we introduced, Carlos was forced to speak, whereas before he could always deindividuate himself and keep a low profile in the classroom. But the situation was even more complex than that—it might even be said that the teacher and Carlos had entered into a conspiracy, that they were in collusion. Carlos was perfectly willing to be quiet. In the past, the teacher had called on him occasionally; he would stumble, stammer, and fall into an embarrassed silence. Several of his peers would make fun of him. The teacher had learned not to call on him anymore. The decision probably came from the purest of intentions—the teacher simply did not want to humiliate him. But, by ignoring him, she had written him off. The implication was that he was not worth bothering with—at least the other kids in the classroom got that message. They believed there was one good reason why the teacher wasn't calling on Carlos—he was stupid. Indeed, even Carlos began to draw this conclusion. This is part of the dynamic of how desegregation, when coupled with a competitive process, can produce unequal-status contact and can result in even greater enmity between ethnic groups and a loss of self-esteem for members of disadvantaged ethnic minorities.[72]

Let us go back to our six-person group. Carlos, who had to report on Joseph Pulitzer's young manhood, was having a very hard time. He stammered, hesitated, and fidgeted. The other kids in the circle were not very helpful. They had grown accustomed to a competitive process and they responded out of this old, overlearned habit. They knew what to do when a kid stumbles—especially a kid whom they believed to be stupid. They ridiculed him, put him down, and teased him. During our experiment, it was Mary who was observed to say: "Aw, you don't know it, you're dumb, you're stupid. You don't know what you're doing." In our initial experiment, the groups were being loosely monitored by a research assistant who was floating from group to group. When this incident occurred, our assistant made one brief intervention: "OK, you can do that if you want to. It might be fun for you, but it's *not* going to help you learn about Joseph Pulitzer's young manhood. The exam will take place in an hour." Notice how the reinforcement contingencies have shifted. No longer does Mary gain much from putting Carlos down—in fact, she now stands to lose a great deal. After a few days and several similar experiences, it began to dawn on the students in Carlos' group that the *only* way they could learn about Joseph Pulitzer's young manhood was by paying attention to what Carlos had to say. Gradually, they began to develop into pretty good interviewers. Instead of ignoring or ridiculing Carlos when he was having a little trouble communicating what he knew, they began asking probing questions—the kind of questions that made it easier for Carlos to communicate what was in his head. Carlos began to respond to this treatment by becoming more relaxed; with increased relaxation came an improvement in his ability to communicate. After a couple of weeks, the other children concluded Carlos was a lot smarter than they had thought he was. They began to see things in him they had never seen before. They began to like him. Carlos began to enjoy school more and began to see the Anglo students in his group not as tormentors but as helpful and responsible people. Moreover, as he began to feel increasingly comfortable in class and started to gain more confidence in himself, his academic performance began to improve. The vicious cycle had been reversed; the elements that had been causing a downward spiral were changed—the spiral now began to move upward.

We have now replicated this experiment in scores of classrooms with thousands of students. The results are clear-cut and consistent. Children in the interdependent, jigsaw classrooms grow to like each other better, develop a greater liking for school, and develop greater self-esteem than children in traditional classrooms. The increase in liking among children in the jigsaw classroom crosses ethnic and racial boundaries.[73] The exam performance of members of ethnic minorities is higher in the jigsaw classroom than in the traditional classrooms. For example, in one study[74] my colleagues and I found that, within two weeks of participating in the jigsaw groups, minority group children increased their performance almost an entire letter grade, without any cost to the performance of the other children. Finally, teachers enjoyed using the technique and found it to be effective. Most of the teachers who agreed to use the jigsaw method as part of the our experiment continued to use it *after* the experiment was over.

One of the crucial factors underlying the positive effects of the jigsaw technique is the development of empathy. In the preceding chapter, I mentioned that increasing a person's empathy—the ability to put oneself in another's position—is beneficial to human relations, enhancing helping behavior and decreasing aggressiveness. In the classroom, the best way to maximize learning—especially in the jigsaw situation—is to pay close attention to the child who is speaking. For example, if I am in a jigsaw group with Carlos and want to learn what he knows, not only must I listen attentively to him, in addition, I must put myself in his shoes in order to ask him questions in a clear and non-threatening manner. In the process, I learn a lot not only about the subject, and not only about Carlos, but about the process of seeing the world through another person's eyes. In a fascinating experiment, Diane Bridgeman demonstrated the positive effects of participating in the jigsaw classroom on the child's ability to take another person's perspective.[75] She administered a series of cartoon sequences to ten-year-old children, half of whom had spent eight weeks participating in jigsaw classes. The cartoons are aimed at measuring a child's ability to empathize. In one sequence of cartoons, for example, a little boy looks sad as he says good-bye to his father at the airport. In the next frame, a mailman delivers a package to the child. When the boy opens it, he finds a toy airplane—and promptly bursts into tears. When Bridgeman asked the children why the little boy cried, almost all of the children told her the reason: The airplane reminded the child of being separated from his father, which made him sad. So far so good. Now for the crucial part. Bridgeman asked the childred what *the mailman* who delivered the package was thinking. Most children that age make a consistent error, based on the egocentric assumption that their own knowledge is universal; specifically, they erroneously assume the mailman would know the boy was sad because the gift reminded him of his father leaving. The responses of the children who had participated in the jigsaw classes followed a different pattern, however. Because of their jigsaw experience, they were better able to take the mailman's perspective; they knew he was not privy to the same information they were and that he wasn't aware of the scene at the airport. Accordingly, the jigsaw children realized the mailman would experience *confusion* at the sight of a little boy crying over receiving a nice present. In sum, participation in jigsaw groups has a general impact on a child's ability to see the world through another person's eyes; this seems to be a major cause of the beneficial effects we described above.

One of the most encouraging ramifications of this increase in empathy is that the usual tendency people have of giving themselves the benefit of the doubt can now be extended to other people, including people who aren't members of their own ethnic or racial group. Let me explain. You will recall that in making attributions about the cause of failure, people tend to give themselves the benefit of the doubt—but rarely extend that benefit to others. Thus, if I do poorly on an exam, I tend to conclude that I was sleepy or that the questions were unfair; but if *you* do poorly on an exam, I would tend to conclude that you were stupid or lazy. In a series of experiments,[76] my colleagues and I corroborated this finding: We found that, in a competitive situation, not only do children attribute their rivals' failures to lack of ability, they also attribute their rivals' successes to luck. But here is the interesting part: We also found that, in a *cooperative* situation (like jigsaw), children are as generous with their partners as they are with themselves; they attribute their partner's success to skill and failure to an unlucky break. This is exciting because, when we can begin to think of members of other races and ethnic groups with the same generosity we extend to ourselves, the ultimate attribution error breaks down and prejudice is being reduced at a deep level.

Although interdependence—especially through the jigsaw technique—is clearly a promising strategy, it is not a perfect solution. For example, while jigsaw does produce beneficial effects with high school students,[77] it works *best* with young children, before prejudiced attitudes have an opportunity to become deeply ingrained. Moreover, prejudice is a complex phenomenon; no one solution is *the* solution. As we have seen, many aspects of our society are changing simultaneously—more equitable exposure of ethnic minorities via the mass media, greater educational opportunities, and so on. It is a slow process, and equity is still a long distance away. Yet prejudice is on the wane, and this is encouraging. Recall that, at one time, it was argued that desegregation would be impossible without prior attitude change. It was once generally believed that a good deal of prejudice is generally the result of a deeply rooted personality disorder that must be cured before desegregation can proceed. The evidence indicates that, for the vast majority of individuals, this is not true. The first wedge in the diminution of prejudice is desegregation. In the words of Thomas Pettigrew, one of our most tireless investigators in this area:

> Some cynics have argued that successful racial desegregation in the South will require an importation of tens of thousands of

> psychotherapists, and therapy for millions of bigoted southerners. Fortunately for desegregation, psychotherapists, and southerners, this will not be necessary; a thorough repatterning of southern interracial behavior will be sufficient therapy in itself.[78]

Although Pettigrew may have been overly optimistic, it seems we are beginning to learn how prejudice can be reduced.

In the next two chapters, we will broaden the base of our discussion on prejudice and prejudice reduction. In Chapter 7, we will look at the positive or negative feelings a person can have for another and investigate why some individuals like each other and some dislike each other. In Chapter 8, we will look at a technique aimed at increasing interpersonal understanding through honest, face-to-face communication.

7

Attraction: Why People Like Each Other

Early in this book I described several situations, both in the laboratory and the real world, in which people turned their backs on the needs of their fellow human beings. I mentioned incidents in which people watched someone being killed without attempting to help; in which people walked casually by, around, and over a woman with a broken leg lying on a Fifth Avenue sidewalk; in which people, hearing a woman in the next room apparently fall off a stepladder and injure herself, did not so much as ask if she needed assistance. I also described a situation in which people went a step further by apparently causing a person to suffer severe pain: A large number of individuals, in blind obedience to the commands of an authority figure, continued to administer severe electric shocks to another human being even after the person screamed in pain, pounded on the door, begged to be released, and then fell into ominous silence. Finally, we saw how people, through fear, hate, and prejudice, can deprive one another of their civil rights, rob one another of their freedom, and even destroy one another.

With all of these events in mind, I asked if there is any way to diminish aggression and to encourage people to take responsibility for the welfare of their fellow human beings. In this chapter, I will ask this question in a more formal manner: What do we know about the factors that cause one person to like another?

The question is almost certainly an ancient one. The first amateur social psychologist, who must have lived in a cave, undoubtedly wondered what he could do to make the fellow in a nearby cave like him more or dislike him less—or, at least, to make him refrain from clubbing him on the head. Perhaps he bared his teeth as a means of showing his neighbor he was tough and might bite a chunk out of the latter's leg, if the neighbor behaved aggressively. As luck would have it, this simple gesture worked, and the baring of teeth, now called a smile, gradually evolved into a social convention—a way of getting people not to hurt us and perhaps even to like us. Charles Darwin presents an interesting discussion of this phenomenon in a little book called *The Expression of Emotions in Man and Animals.*[1]

After several thousand years, people are still speculating about the antecedents of attraction—how to behave so the person at the next desk, in the next house, or in the next country likes us more, or at least refrains from putting us down or trying to destroy us. What do we know about the causes of attraction? When I ask my friends why they like some of their acquaintances better than others, I get a wide variety of responses. The most typical responses are that people like most (1) those whose beliefs and interests are similar to their own; (2) those who have some skills, abilities, or competencies; (3) those with some pleasant or "admirable" qualities, such as loyalty, reasonableness, honesty, and kindness; and (4) those who like them in return.

These reasons make good sense. They are also consistent with the advice given by Dale Carnegie in a book with the chillingly manipulative title *How to Win Friends and Influence People.*[2] Manipulative title notwithstanding, this recipe book for interpersonal relations seems to have been exactly what people were looking for—it proved to be one of the best sellers of all time. That's not surprising. Americans seem to be deeply concerned with being liked and making a good impression. A series of polls conducted among high school students during the 1940s and 1950s[3] indicated that their most important concern was the way others reacted to them—and their overwhelming desire was for people to like them more. There is no reason to believe this concern has changed in the last 35 years. Such concerns may be greatest during adolescence when the peer group assumes enormous importance, but the desire to be liked is certainly not limited to American adolescents. The search for a simple formula to attract others seems universal. Dale Carnegie's book was translated into thirty-five different languages and was avidly read around the globe. Carnegie's advice is deceptively simple: If you want people to like you, be pleasant, pretend you like them, feign an interest in things they're interested in, "dole out praise lavishly," and be agreeable.

Is it true? Are these tactics effective? To a limited extent they *are* effective, at least in the early stages of the acquaintance process. Data from well-controlled laboratory experiments indicate we like people with pleasant characteristics more than those with unpleasant characteristics;[4] we like people who agree with us more than people who disagree with us; we like people who like us more than people who dislike us; we like people who cooperate with us more than people who compete with us; we like people who praise us more than people who criticize us; and so on. These aspects of interpersonal attraction can be gathered under one sweeping generalization: We like people whose behavior provides us with maximum reward at minimum cost.[5]

A general reward theory of attraction covers a great deal of ground. It allows us to explain why we like people who are pretty more than people who are homely, because pretty people bring us "aesthetic" rewards.[6] At the same time, it allows us to predict we will like people with opinions similar[7] to ours because, when we run into such people, they reward us by providing us with consensual validation for our beliefs—that is, by helping us to believe our opinions are "correct." Moreover, as we learned in the preceding chapter, one way prejudice and hostility can be reduced is by changing the environment in such a way that individuals cooperate with each other rather than compete. Another way of stating this relation is that cooperation leads to attraction. Thus, whether the environment is a summer camp, as in Muzafer Sherif's experiments,[8] or a classroom situation, as in the experiments I performed with my colleagues,[9] there is an increase in mutual attraction if people spend some time cooperating with each other. Cooperative behavior is clearly rewarding by definition—a person who cooperates with us is giving us aid, listening to our ideas, making suggestions, and sharing our load.

A general reward-cost theory can explain a great deal of human attraction, but not all of it—the world is not that simple. For example, a reward-cost theory would lead us to suspect that, all other things being equal, we would like people who live in close proximity to us, because we can get the same reward at less cost by traveling a short distance than we can by traveling a great distance. Indeed, it does tend to be true that people have more friends who live close by than friends who live far away; but this does not necessarily mean it is their physical proximity that makes them attractive. Their physical proximity may simply make it easier to get to know them, and once we get to know them, we tend to like them. Moreover, as we pointed out earlier in this book, individuals also like things or people for which or for whom they have suffered. For example, recall the experiment I did in collaboration with Judson Mills[10] in which we found that people who went through an unpleasant initiation in order to become members of a group liked that group better than did those who became members by paying a smaller price in terms of time and effort. Where is the reward? The reduction of suffering? The reduction of dissonance? How does the reward become attached to the group? It is not clear.

Moreover, simply knowing that something is rewarding does not necessarily help us to predict or understand a person's behavior. For example, recall that, in Chapters 2, 3, and 4, we analyzed why people conform and why they change their attitudes, and we discussed several reasons: out of a desire to win praise, to be liked, to avoid ridicule; out of a desire to identify with someone whom they respect or admire; out of a desire to be right; or out of a desire to justify their own behavior. In some way, all of these behaviors make sense, or feel good, or both, and therefore can be considered rewards. But simply to label them as rewards tends to obscure the important differences among them. Although both the desire to be right and the desire to avoid ridicule produce a state of satisfaction when gratified, the behaviors a person must employ to gratify these needs frequently are opposite in kind. For example, in judging the size of a line, a person might conform to group pressure out of a desire to avoid ridicule, but that same person might deviate from the unanimous opinion of the other group members out of a desire to be right. Little understanding is gained by covering both behaviors with the blanket term "reward." For the social psychologist, a far more important task is to determine the conditions under which one or the other course of action will be taken. This point will become clearer as we discuss some of the research on interpersonal attraction.

The Effects of Praise and Favors

Recall that Dale Carnegie advised us to "dole out praise lavishly." This seems like good old-fashioned common sense: Surely we can "win friends" by praising our teachers' ideas or our employees' efforts. Indeed, several experiments have been done showing, in general, that we like people who evaluate us positively far more than those who evaluate us negatively.[11] But does it *always* work? Let's take a closer look. Common sense also suggests there are situations in which criticism might be more useful than praise. For example, suppose you are a brand-new college instructor lecturing to a class full of graduate students and presenting a theory you are developing. In the rear of the classroom are two students. One of these people is nodding and smiling and looks as though he is in rapture. At the close of your presentation, he comes up and tells you that you are a genius and your ideas are the most brilliant he's ever heard. It feels good to hear that, of course. In contrast, the other student shakes her head and scowls occasionally during your presentation, and afterward, she comes up and tells you there are several aspects of your theory that don't make sense. Moreover, she points these out in some detail and with a note of disdain in her voice. That evening, while ruminating on what was said, you realize that the remarks made by the second student, although somewhat extreme and not completely accurate, did contain some valid points and forced you to rethink a few of your assumptions. This eventually leads you to a significant modification of your theory. Which of these two people will you like better? I don't know. Although praise is clearly rewarding, disagreement that leads to improvement may carry its own rewards. Because I am, at this point, unable to predict which of these behaviors is more rewarding, it is impossible to be sure which of the two students you will like better.

The relative impact of praise and criticism is even more complicated—and more interesting. Recent research shows that, all other things being equal, a negative evaluation generally increases the admiration we feel for the evaluator—so long as he or she is not evaluating *us!* In this experiment, Theresa Amabile[12] asked college students to read excerpts from two reviews of novels which had appeared in the *Sunday New York Times* book review section. Both reviews were similar in style and quality of writing—but one was extremely favorable, and the other, extremely unfavorable. Students considered the negative reviewer to be considerably more intelligent, competent, and expert than the positive reviewer—but less likable!

Let us take a different example, one involving the attribution of ulterior motives to the praiser. Suppose Nancy is an engineer and she produces an excellent set of blueprints. Her boss says, "Nice work, Nancy." That phrase will almost certainly function as a reward, and Nancy's liking for her boss will probably increase. But suppose Nancy is having an off day and produces a sloppy set of blueprints—and knows it. The boss comes along and emits the same phrase in exactly the same tone of voice. Will that phrase function as a reward in this situation? I am not sure. Nancy *may* interpret the statement as her boss's attempt to be encouraging and nice, even in the face of a poor performance; because of the boss's display of considerateness, Nancy may come to like him even more than she would have had she, in fact, done a good job. On the other hand, Nancy may attribute all kinds of characteristics or ulterior motives to her boss:

She may conclude her boss is being sarcastic, manipulative, dishonest, nondiscriminating, patronizing, seductive, or stupid—any one of which could reduce Nancy's liking for him. A general reward-cost theory loses a good deal of its value if our definition of what constitutes a reward is not clear. As situations become complex, we find that such general notions decrease in value, because a slight change in the social context in which the reward is provided can change a "reward" into a punishment.

Research in this area indicates that, although people like to be praised and tend to like the praiser,[13] they also dislike being manipulated. If the praise is too lavish, if it seems unwarranted, or (most important) if the praiser is in a position to benefit from the ingratiating behavior, then he or she is not liked very much. Edward E. Jones and his students[14] have carried out a great deal of research on this problem. In a typical experiment, an accomplice watched a young woman being interviewed, and then proceeded to evaluate her. The evaluations were prearranged so some women heard a positive evaluation, some heard a negative evaluation, and some heard a neutral evaluation. In one experimental condition, the evaluator was ascribed an ulterior motive. In this condition, subjects were informed in advance that the evaluator was a graduate student who needed subjects for her own experiment and would be asking her (the subject) to volunteer. The results showed that the students liked the evaluators who praised them better than those who provided them with a negative evaluation—but there was a sharp drop in how much they liked the praiser with the ulterior motive. Thus the old adage "flattery will get you nowhere" is clearly wrong. As Jones puts it, "flattery will get you *somewhere*"—but not everywhere.

By the same token, we like people who do us favors. Favors can be considered rewards, and we do tend to like people who provide us with this kind of reward. For example, in a classic study by Helen Hall Jennings,[15] it was shown that, among young women in a reformatory, the most popular were those who performed the most services for others—specifically, those who initiated new and interesting activities and helped others become a part of the activities. Our liking for people who do us favors extends even to situations in which these favors are not intentional. This was demonstrated by Albert and Bernice Lott[16] in an experiment with young children. The researchers organized children into groups of three for the purpose of playing a game that consisted of choosing various pathways on a board. Those who were lucky enough to choose the safe pathways won the game; making the wrong choice led to disaster. The children were, in effect, walking single file in an imaginary mine field, whose mines remained active even after they exploded. If the child at the front of the line chose the wrong path, that player was "blown up" (out of the game), and the child next in line would, of course, choose a different path. Leaders who happened to choose correctly led the others to a successful completion of the game. The results indicated those children who were rewarded (by arriving safely at the goal) showed a greater liking for their teammates (who, of course, had been instrumental in helping them achieve the reward) than did those children who did not reach the final goal. In short, we like people who contribute to our victory more than those who do not—even if they had no intention of doing us a favor.

But, as with those who praise us, we do not always like people who do favors for us; specifically, we do not like people whose favors seem as though they may have some strings attached to them. Such strings constitute a threat to the freedom of the receiver. People do not like to receive gifts if a gift is expected in return; moreover, people do not like to receive favors from individuals who are in a position to benefit from that favor. Recall the example I mentioned in a previous chapter: If you were a teacher, you might enjoy receiving gifts from your students. On the other hand, you might be made pretty uncomfortable if a borderline student presented you with an expensive gift just before you were about to grade his or her term paper. Strong support for this reasoning comes from an experiment by Jack Brehm and Ann Cole.[17] In this experiment, college students were asked to participate in a study (which the experimenters characterized as important) in which they would be giving their first impressions of another person. As each subject was waiting for the experiment to begin, the "other person" (actually a stooge) asked permission to leave the room for a few moments. In one condition, he simply returned after a while and resumed his seat.

In the other condition, he returned carrying a soft drink, which he immediately gave to the subject. Subsequently, each subject was asked to help the stooge perform a dull task. Interestingly enough, those students who had *not* been given the drink by the stooge were more likely to help him than those who *had* been given the drink.

The upshot of this research is that favors and praise are not universal rewards. For a starving rat or a starving person, a bowl of dry cereal is a reward—it is a reward during the day or during the night, in winter or in summer, if offered by a male or by a female, and so on. Similarly, for a drowning person, a rescue launch is a reward under all circumstances. That is, such rewards are "transsituational." But praise, favors, and the like are not transsituational: Whether or not they function as rewards depends on minor situational variations, some of which can be extremely subtle. Indeed, as we have seen, praise and favors can even function to make praisers or favor-doers less attractive than they would have been had they kept their mouths shut or their hands in their pockets. Thus, Dale Carnegie's advice is not always sound. If you want someone to like you, doing a favor as a technique of ingratiation is indeed risky.

Getting someone to do *you* a favor is a more certain way of using favors to increase your attractiveness. Recall that, in Chapter 4, I described a phenomenon we called "the justification of cruelty." Briefly, I pointed out that, if individuals cause harm to a person, they will attempt to justify their behavior by derogating the victim. We also analyzed how the justification process could work in the opposite direction: The "foot-in-the-door" technique can be used to make people more likely to do large favors by first getting them to do a small favor. Not only can this increase people's tendency to help; if we do someone a favor, we can also justify this action by convincing ourselves that the recipient of this favor is an attractive, likable, deserving person. In effect, we will say to ourselves, "Why in the world did I go to all of this effort (or spend all of this money, or whatever) for Sam? Because Sam is a wonderful person, that's why!"

This notion is not new—indeed, it seems to be a part of folk wisdom. One of the world's greatest novelists, Leo Tolstoy [18] in 1869 wrote: "We do not love people so much for the good they have done us, as for the good we have done them." Similarly, in 1736 Benjamin Franklin utilized this bit of folk wisdom as a political strategy—with apparent success. Franklin, disturbed by the political opposition and apparent animosity of a member of the Pennsylvania state legislature, set out to win him over:

> I did not . . . aim at gaining his favour by paying any servile respect to him but, after some time, took this other method. Having heard that he had in his library a certain very scarce and curious book I wrote a note to him expressing my desire of perusing that book and requesting he would do me the favour of lending it to me for a few days. He sent it immediately and I return'd it in about a week with another note expressing strongly my sense of the favour. When we next met in the House he spoke to me (which he had never done before), and with great civility; and he ever after manifested a readiness to serve me on all occasions, so that we became great friends and our friendship continued to his death. This is another instance of the truth of an old maxim I had learned, which says, "He that has once done you a kindness will be more ready to do you another than he whom you yourself have obliged."[19]

While Benjamin Franklin was clearly pleased with the success of his maneuver, as a scientist I am not totally convinced. It is not entirely clear whether Franklin's success was due to this strategy or to any one of many charming aspects of his personality. In order to be certain, a well controlled experiment is necessary. Just such an experiment was conducted by Jon Jecker and David Landy,[20] over two hundred and forty years after Benjamin Franklin's more casual experiment. In this experiment, students participated in a concept-formation task that enabled them to win a rather substantial sum of money. After the experiment was over, one-third of the subjects were approached by the experimenter, who explained that he was using his own funds for the experiment and was running short—which would mean he might be forced to stop the experiment. He asked, "As a special favor to me, would you mind returning the money you won?" Another one-third of the subjects were approached, *not* by the experimenter, but by the departmental secretary, who asked them if they would return the money as a special favor to the psychology department's research fund, which was running low. The remaining subjects were not asked to return their winnings. Finally, all of the subjects were asked to fill out a questionnaire, which included an opportunity to rate the experimenter. Those subjects who had been cajoled into doing a special favor for the experimenter found him most attractive—they had convinced themselves he was a decent, deserving fellow.

Similar results were obtained in an experiment by Melvin Lerner and Carolyn Simmons,[21] in which groups of subjects were allowed to observe a student who appeared to be receiving a series of electric shocks as part of an experiment in learning. After watching for a while, some groups of subjects were allowed to vote (by private ballot) on whether or not the "victim" should continue to receive electric shocks. Other groups of subjects were not allowed to vote on this procedure. All subjects who were allowed to vote did, indeed, vote for the termination of the shocks; but some groups of voting subjects were successful in effecting a termination of the shocks, while others were not. It turned out that the subjects who were successful at stopping the shocks rated the victim as significantly more attractive than did those who were not allowed to vote, or those whose vote was ineffective. Thus, doing a favor for someone will increase your liking for that person, but only if the effort you expend results in a successful outcome.

Personal Attributes

As I have already mentioned, there are several personal characteristics that play an important role in determining the extent to which a person will be liked.[22] Thus, people tend to like others who are sincere, competent, intelligent, energetic, and so on. Most of these studies were done in the manner of a public opinion poll—that is, people were simply asked to describe the attributes of people they like and those of people they dislike. In studies of this sort, it is difficult to establish the direction of causality: Do we like people who have pleasant attributes, or do we tend to convince ourselves that our friends tend to have these pleasant attributes? Chances are that causality flows in both directions. In order to be *sure* people with certain positive personal attributes are liked better than others, however, it is necessary to examine this relation under more controlled conditions than exists in the opinion poll. In this section, we will examine closely two of the most important personal attributes: competence and physical attractiveness.

Competence. It would seem obvious that, all other things being equal, the more competent an individual is, the more we will like that person. This is probably because people have a need to be right; we stand a better chance of being right if we surround ourselves with highly able, highly competent people. But, as we continue to learn in this chapter, factors that determine interpersonal attraction are often complex; they cannot always be spelled out in simple terms. As for competence, there is a great deal of apparently paradoxical evidence in the research literature demonstrating that, in problem-solving groups, the participants who are considered the most competent and to have the best ideas tend *not* to be the ones who are best liked.[23] How can we explain this apparent paradox? One possibility is that, although we like to be around competent people, a person who has a great deal of ability may make us uncomfortable. That person may seem unapproachable, distant, superhuman. If this were true, we might like the person more were he or she to show some evidence of fallibility. For example, if Sam were a brilliant mathematician as well as a great basketball player and a fastidious dresser, I might like him better if, every once in a while, he misadded a column of numbers, blew an easy layup, or appeared in public with a gravy stain on his tie.

Several years ago, I was speculating about this phenomenon when I chanced upon some startling data from a Gallup poll: When John Kennedy was President, his personal popularity actually increased immediately after his abortive attempt to invade Cuba at the Bay of Pigs in 1961. This was startling, in view of the fact that this attempted invasion was such a phenomenal blunder it was immediately dubbed (and is still commonly known as) "the Bay of Pigs fiasco." What can we make of it? This was a situation in which a president committed one of our country's greatest blunders (up until that time, that is) and, miraculously, people came to like him more for it. Why? One possibility is that John Kennedy may have been "too perfect."

In 1961 John Kennedy stood very high in personal popularity. He was a character of almost storybook proportions. Indeed, his regime was referred to as Camelot. Kennedy was young, handsome, bright, witty, charming, and athletic; he was a voracious reader, the author of a best seller, a master political strategist, a war hero, and an uncomplaining endurer of physical pain; he was married to a talented and beautiful woman (who spoke several foreign languages), had two cute kids (one boy and one girl), and was part of a commendable, close-knit family. Some evidence of fallibility (like being responsible for a major blunder) could have served to make him more human in the public eye and, hence, more likable.

Alas, this is only one of several possible explanations, and (as the reader knows all too well by now) the real world is no place to test such a hypothesis. In the real world, there are too many things happening simultaneously, any one of which could have increased Kennedy's popularity. For example, after the fiasco occurred, President Kennedy did not try to make excuses or to pass the buck; rather he bravely accepted full responsibility for the blunder. This selfless action could have done much to make him more attractive in the eyes of the populace. In order to test the proposition that evidence of fallibility in a highly competent person may make that person better liked, an experiment was needed. One of the great advantages of an experiment is that it eliminates or controls extraneous variables (such as the selfless assumption of responsibility) and allows us, therefore, to assess more accurately the effect of one variable on another.

I performed such an experiment in collaboration with Ben Willerman and Joanne Floyd.[24] The subjects were college men at the University of Minnesota. Each subject listened to a simple audiotape recording featuring one of four stimulus persons: (1) a nearly perfect person, (2) a nearly perfect person who commits a blunder, (3) a mediocre person, and (4) a mediocre person who commits a blunder. In preparation, each subject was told he would be listening to a person who was a candidate for the then-popular "College Bowl" quiz show, and that he would be asked to rate one of the candidates by the kind of impression he made, by how likable he seemed, and so forth. Each tape consisted of an interview between a young man (stimulus person) and an interviewer and contained a set of extremely difficult questions posed by the interviewer; the questions were like those generally asked on "College Bowl." On one tape, the stimulus person showed a high degree of competence—indeed, he seemed to be virtually perfect, answering 92 percent of the questions correctly—and, in the body of the interview, when asked about his activities in high school, he modestly admitted he had been an honor student, the editor of the yearbook, and a member of the track team. On another tape, the stimulus person (actually the same actor using the same tone of voice) was presented as a person of average ability: He answered only 30 percent of the questions correctly, and, during the interview, he admitted he had received average grades in high school, had been a proofreader on the yearbook staff, and had tried out for the track team but had failed to make it. On the other two recordings (one of the "superior" young man and one of the "average" young man), the stimulus person committed an embarrassing blunder. Near the end of the interview, he clumsily spilled a cup of coffee all over himself. This "pratfall" was created by making a tape recording that included sounds of commotion and clatter, the scraping of a chair, and the anguished voice of the stimulus person saying, "Oh my goodness, I've spilled coffee all over my new suit." To achieve maximum control, the tape of the incident was reproduced, and one copy was spliced onto a copy of the tape of the superior person, while the other copy was spliced onto a tape of the average person. This gave us four experimental conditions: (1) a person of superior ability who blundered, and (2) one who did not; and (3) a person of average ability who blundered, and (4) one who did not.

The superior person who committed a blunder was rated most attractive; the average person who committed the same blunder was rated least attractive. The perfect person (no blunder) was second in attractiveness, and the mediocre person (no blunder) finished third. Clearly, there was nothing inherently attractive about the simple act of spilling a cup of coffee. Although it did serve to add an endearing dimension to the perfect person, making him more attractive, the same action served to make the mediocre person appear that much more mediocre and, hence, less attractive. This experiment presents stronger evidence to support our contention that, although a high degree of competence does make us appear more attractive, some evidence of fallibility increases our attractiveness still further. This phenomenon has been dubbed "the pratfall effect."

More complex experiments have since produced some interesting refinements of this general finding. Basically, the pratfall effect holds most clearly when, within the head of the observer, there is some implicit threat of competition with the stimulus person. Thus, an experiment by Kay Deaux[25] demonstrates that the pratfall effect applies most strongly to males. She found that, although most males in her study preferred the highly competent man who committed a blunder, women showed a tendency to prefer the highly competent nonblunderer, regardless of whether the stimulus person was male or female. Similarly, my colleagues and I found that males with a moderate degree of self-esteem are most likely to prefer the highly competent person who commits a blunder, while males with low self-esteem (who apparently feel little competitiveness with the stimulus person) prefer the highly competent person who *doesn't* blunder.[26]

It should be emphasized that no sizable proportion of people—regardless of their own level of self-esteem—preferred the mediocre person. I want to take special pains to make this point because of a bizarre political event. In the early 1970s, when former president Richard Nixon was at the height of his popularity, he tried, in vain, to appoint to the Supreme Court two strikingly mediocre lower-court judges. In defending these nominees, Senator Roman Hruska argued (seriously, I'm afraid), that while it was true these men were mediocre, the mediocre citizens of the country needed someone on the Supreme Court to represent them too! Again, our data do not support that argument.

Physical Attractiveness. Imagine you are on a blind date. It is near the end of the evening and you are wondering whether or not you want to go out with this person again. Which of your partner's characteristics will weigh most heavily: Warmth? Sensitivity? Intelligence? Compassion? *How about good looks?* You guessed it!

Most of us tend to be both incredulous and appalled by such a suggestion. We don't want this to be true. We would like to believe that beauty is only skin deep and, therefore, a trivial determinant of liking. Also, it seems so unfair; why should something like physical attractiveness—which is largely beyond a person's control—play an important role? Indeed, when asked what they looked for in a potential date, most college students put "physical attractiveness" at the very bottom of the list.[27] But I'm afraid this reflects only what students think they *ought* to believe—for, in studies of their actual behavior, college students overwhelmingly go for physical attractiveness. In one study, for example, Elaine Hatfield Walster and her associates[28] randomly matched incoming students at the University of Minnesota for a blind date. The students previously had been given a battery of personality tests. Which of their many characteristics determined whether or not they liked each other? It was not their intelligence, masculinity, femininity, dominance, submission, dependence, independence, sensitivity, sincerity, or the like. The *one* determinant of whether or not a couple liked each other and actually repeated their date was their physical attractiveness. If a handsome man was paired with a beautiful woman, they were most likely to desire to see each other again.

This general phenomenon is not limited to a blind date. Gregory White[29] studied relatively long-term relationships among young couples at UCLA. Like Walster and her colleagues, White found that physical attractiveness was a very important factor; but in this situation it was the *similarity* of the attractiveness of the members of the couple that was crucial in determining whether or not a relationship had staying power. Specifically, some nine months after the couples started dating, those pairs who were well matched in terms of rated physical attractiveness were more deeply involved with each other than where the members differed from each other in physical attractiveness.

What is clear from these studies of dating couples is that, in one way or another, physical attractiveness plays an important role in determining who likes whom in both the short run and the long run. Moreover, these studies indicate that there are clear cultural standards for physical attractiveness—at least among college students in the United States. Judges had no difficulty rating people on physical attractiveness. And the judges agreed with one another—that is, the ratings were highly *reliable*. Moreover, all other things being equal, people's physical attractiveness not only helps us predict whether or not others will want to date them, it also influences a wide range of attributions. For example, in one study, Karen Dion and her colleagues[30] showed college students photographs of three college-age people. The photos were especially selected for differing degrees of attractiveness: one was attractive, one average, and one unattractive. The subjects were asked to rate each of the people depicted in these photographs on twenty-seven different personality traits, and were asked to predict their future happiness. The physically attractive people were assigned by far the most desirable traits and the greatest prognosis for happiness. This was true whether it was men rating men, men rating women, women rating men, or women rating women.

Does it surprise you to learn that most people seem to agree on both the physical characteristics and the concomitant personality traits of so called "beautiful" people? Perhaps it shouldn't. From early childhood experiences we learn that a specific definition of beauty is associated with goodness. Walt Disney's movies and the illustrators of children's books have taught us that gentle and charming heroines like Snow White, Cinderella, and Sleeping Beauty—as well as the princes who woo and win them—all look alike. They all have regular features, small pert noses, big eyes, shapely lips, blemish-free complexions, and slim athletic bodies. They all look like Barbie and Ken dolls. Indeed, so do Barbie and Ken dolls! And how are the wicked stepmothers, stepsisters, and queens depicted?

In addition, television sustains these cultural standards; actors who fit the American stereotype of beauty are carefully selected to play the heroes and heroines of adventure dramas such as *Charlie's Angels* and *Magnum, P.I.* And then there are the commercials. Anyone who watches a fair amount of television is subjected to a continuous flow of propaganda aimed at selling the idea of beauty in a bottle. Shampoo, skin lotion, deodorant, toothpaste—all are peddled by promoting the conviction that these products will make us beautiful and ultimately successful. And exposure to this kind of thing *does* have an impact. For example, in one recent experiment,[31] young women between the ages of 16 and 18 were systematically exposed to some fifteen TV commercials extolling the virtues of beauty preparations. In a control group, teenagers were shown fifteen commercials unrelated to "beauty" products. Some time later all of the young women were asked to rank the relative importance of ten attributes—for example, sex appeal, intelligence, a pretty face, industriousness, and so on. The young women who had been shown the beauty ads were more likely than the control group to consider beauty-oriented attributes more important than other qualities.

One of the implications of our discussion is that cultural standards of beauty are learned early. If we learn about beauty by looking at the pictures in story books, or from Walt Disney movies, or from watching television, then it should follow that even young children are affected by these norms. And so they are. In a striking study, Karen Dion and Ellen Berscheid[32] found that, even as early as nursery school, children are responsive to the physical attractiveness of their peers. In their study, Dion and Berscheid first had several independent judges (graduate students) rate the physical attractiveness of the nursery-school children. Then they determined who liked whom among the children themselves. They found that physical attractiveness was very important. The clearest results were obtained for the males: The physically attractive boys were liked better than the physically unattractive boys. Moreover, unattractive boys were considered to be more aggressive than their attractive counterparts and, when the children were asked to name the classmates that "scared them," they tended to nominate the unattractive children. Of course, it might have been the case that the less attractive children actually *behaved* more aggressively. The researchers did not observe the actual behavior of the children in the nursery school so they could not test that possibility. But there is independent evidence that people do tend to attribute less blame to physically attractive children, regardless of the facts. This finding emerges from another study by Karen Dion.[33]

Women were asked to examine reports of rather severe classroom disturbances, apparently written by a teacher. Attached to each report was a photo of the child who was said to have initiated the disturbance. In some instances, the photo was that of a physically attractive boy or girl; in others, the photo was that of a less attractive boy or girl. The women tended to place more blame on the less attractive children and to infer that this was typical of their everyday behavior. When the child was pictured as physically attractive, however, these women tended to excuse the disruptive behavior. As one of the women put it, "She plays well with everyone, but like anyone else, a bad day can occur. Her cruelty . . . need not be taken seriously." When a physically *un*attractive girl was pictured as the culprit in exactly the same situation described in exactly the same way, a typical respondent said, "I think the child would be quite bratty and would probably be a problem to teachers. She would probably try to pick a fight with other children her own age. . . . All in all, she would be a real problem." Thomas Baglan[34] examined this phenomenon in adults. He found that the *atypical* (unexpected) behavior of an attractive person was attributed externally—to the situation. But the *typical* (expected) behavior of the same attractive person was attributed internally—to stable dispositions. Thus, it seems attractive people are given the benefit of the doubt. Their desirable actions are attributed to them, but their undesirable actions are attributed to the effects of the situation, other people, or an unfortunate accident.

In a different vein, Harold Sigall and I[35] demonstrated that attractive women have more impact on men than less attractive women—for better or for worse. In this experiment, a woman was made to appear either physically attractive or unattractive. This was accomplished by taking a naturally beautiful woman and, in the unattractive condition, providing her with loose, baggy, unflattering clothing, fitting her with a frizzy blond wig that did not quite match her skin coloring, and making her complexion look oily and unwholesome. Then, posing as a graduate student in clinical psychology, she interviewed several college men. At the close of the interview, she gave each student her own personal, clinical evaluation of him. Half of the students received highly favorable evaluations, and half received unfavorable evaluations. We found that, when the evaluator was made to look unattractive, the men didn't seem to care much whether they received a good evaluation or a poor evaluation from her—in both situations, they liked her a fair amount. When she was beautiful, however, they liked her a great deal when she gave them a favorable evaluation, but, when she gave them an unfavorable evaluation, they disliked her more than in any of the other conditions. Interestingly enough, although the men who were evaluated negatively by the attractive woman said they didn't like her, they did express a great desire to return in order to interact with her in a future experiment. It seems the negative evaluations from the beautiful woman were so important to the subjects that they wanted the opportunity to return so as to induce her to change her evaluations of them.

Similarly, Harold Sigall and Nancy Ostrove[36] showed that people tend to favor a beautiful woman unless they suspect her of misusing her beauty. Both male and female college students were allowed to read an account of a criminal case in which the defendant was clearly guilty of a crime. Each subject then "sentenced" the defendant to a prison term he or she considered appropriate. The results showed that, when the crime was unrelated to attractiveness (burglary), the sentences were much more lenient when the defendant was physically attractive. When the crime was related to her attractiveness (a swindle in which the defendant induced a middle-aged bachelor to invest some money in a nonexistent corporation), the sentences were much harsher for the physically attractive defendant. These results paralleled those of Sigall and Aronson (described above) inasmuch as both experiments indicate that a woman's physical attractiveness can have a powerful impact on the way she is treated—for better or worse—depending exactly on how that attractiveness is used.

The effects of a person's physical attractiveness go beyond how we evaluate or how much we are influenced by *that* person; it can also change our perceptions about the people with whom he or she is associated. An experiment by Harold Sigall and David Landy[37] demonstrated that, when seen in the company of a beautiful woman, a man is perceived differently from when he is seen with an unattractive woman. In their study, subjects who met a man seated next to an extremely attractive woman tended to like him more and to rate him as friendlier and more self-confident than did subjects who met the same man when he was seated beside an unattractive woman.

Taking all of this research into consideration, it is clear that beauty is more than skin deep. We are affected by physically attractive people, and unless we are specifically abused by them, we tend to like them better. Moreover, in situations involving trouble and turmoil, beautiful people tend to be given the benefit of the doubt—they receive more favorable treatment than less attractive people. This begins at a very young age. The disconcerting aspect of these data is the strong possibility that such preferential treatment contains the seeds of a self-fulfilling prophecy: We know that the way people are treated affects the way they come to think of themselves. Some evidence for this phenomenon comes from an ingenious experiment conducted by Mark Snyder, Elizabeth Decker Tanke, and Ellen Berscheid.[38] Put yourself in the place of a typical male undergraduate in their experiment: You have volunteered to participate in an investigation of "how people become acquainted with each other," and you have been paired with a female student who is located in another room, ostensibly because the two of you are assigned to the "no nonverbal communication" condition of the study. Though you haven't seen your partner, you have been given a packet of information, which contains a Polaroid snapshot. When you proceed to have a conversation with this woman over an intercom, do you think the physical attractiveness of the woman in the photo will influence your impressions of her? Snyder, Tanke, and Berscheid found it did. As the reader might suspect, the snapshot viewed by the male subject did not depict his actual partner. For half of the subjects, it pictured a very attractive woman; for the others, it pictured a relatively unattractive woman. But the snapshot did have an effect. The subjects who thought they were talking with an attractive partner rated her as more poised, humorous, and socially adept than did those who thought they were talking with a less attractive woman. This is not very surprising. But what *was* startling was this: When independent observers were allowed to listen to a tape recording of only the woman's half of the conversation (without looking at a photograph), they were far more impressed by the woman whose male partner thought she was physically attractive. In short, since the male partner thought he was talking to an attractive woman, he spoke to her in a way that brought out her best and most sparkling qualities. When these independent observers listened to her conversation, they rated her as more attractive, more confident, more animated, and warmer than the woman whose partner thought her to be less beautiful. Thus, physically attractive people may come to think of themselves as "good" or lovable because they are continually treated that way. Conversely, homely people may begin to think of themselves as "bad" or unlovable because they are continually treated that way—even as children. Ultimately, people may begin to behave in a way consistent with this self-concept—a way that is consistent with how they were treated to begin with.

Please note that, for the most part, our discussion of beauty has focused on "visual" beauty. But there are other kinds of beauty. Our visual perceptual mechanisms exercise a terribly conservative influence on our feelings and behavior. We are wedded to our eyes—especially as a means of determining physical attractiveness. And, as we have seen, once we have categorized a person as pretty or homely, we tend to attribute other qualities to that person—for example, pretty people are likely to strike us as being more warm, sexy, exciting, and delightful than homely people. In the next chapter, I will be discussing sensitivity-training groups. Some of these groups allow people to engage in nonvisual sensory experiences. For example, one such experience enables people to "turn off their eyes" and become acquainted with each other solely through the sense of touch. After participating in one of these exercises, group members typically report a dramatic diminution of their prior stereotypes. Basically, individuals find there is little "homeliness" in a non-visual situation. Moreover, participants are frequently astonished to learn that, for example, the incredibly warm, gentle, and sensitive person they had been having a nonvisual encounter with is, "in reality," the funny-looking guy with the pimples. I doubt that, after even one such nonvisual encounter with him, a person would ever relate to him again as merely a funny-looking guy with pimples. To the extent such experiences can enable people to become aware of the nonvisual aspects of beauty, some of the unfairness due to the inequitable distribution of physical beauty may be reduced.

Similarity and Attraction

Lynne goes to a cocktail party and is introduced to Suzanne. While they chat for only a few moments, it turns out they agree completely on several issues, including the inequity of the income-tax structure, the status of Douglas MacArthur in world history, and the importance of a liberal arts education. Upon returning home, Lynne tells her husband she likes Suzanne a great deal and considers her a wonderful and intelligent person. Literally dozens of tightly controlled experiments by Donn Byrne and his associates[39] have shown over and over again that, if all you know about a person are his or her opinions on several issues, the more similar those opinions are to yours, the more you like the person.

Why is agreement important? There are at least two possibilities. First, people who share our opinion on an issue provide us with a kind of social validation for our beliefs—that is, they provide us with the feeling we are right. This is rewarding; hence, we like those who agree with us. If a person disagrees with us, the possibility that we may be wrong is introduced. This possibility is punishing; hence, we don't like people who disagree with us. Second, it is likely we make certain negative inferences about the character of a person who disagrees with us on a substantive issue, not simply because such disagreement is wrong, but, rather, because we suspect the individual's opinion on that issue is indicative of the kind of person we have found in the past to be unpleasant, immoral, or stupid. For example, suppose you believe the penalties for using drugs are too severe. You meet a woman who tells you that drug users should be put away for several years. I then come along, ask you if you liked that woman, and you say, "No." Am I to conclude (1) you didn't like her because hearing her state her belief suggested to you that your belief might be wrong, or (2) you didn't like her because, in your experience, people who favor harsh punishments for drug users tend to be unpleasant, immoral, inhuman, bigoted, harsh, cruel, conventional, punitive, and stupid?

Both of these factors undoubtedly play a role. There is some evidence to suggest that the second factor may be of less importance. This stems from Harold Sigall's brilliant investigation of the psychological effects of conversion.[40] Sigall showed that, if people are highly involved with an issue, they prefer a "disagreer" to an "agreer" if they can succeed in converting that person to their way of thinking. In short, Sigall demonstrated that people like converts better than loyal members of the flock. Apparently, the competence people feel when they induce someone to convert overcomes any tendency they might have to actively dislike the other person for being the sort who would hold an "awful" opinion to begin with.

One additional factor must be mentioned here: We humans are so certain of the relationship between attitude similarity and liking that if we like someone, we will assume that his or her attitudes must be similar to ours. Thus, causality works in both directions: All other things being equal, we like people whose attitudes are similar to ours; *and* if we like someone, we attribute attitudes to him or her that are similar to ours.[41]

Liking, Being Liked, and Self-Esteem

There is still another reason why we tend to like people who hold opinions similar to ours. It may be that, all other things being equal, if we learn that a person's opinion is similar to our own, we might be prone to believe he or she will really like us, if and when that person gets to know us. This can be very important because, as it turns out, the single most powerful determinant of whether one person will like another is whether the other likes that person.

Several investigators have demonstrated that being liked indeed does make the heart grow fonder.[42] Furthermore, the greater our insecurity and self-doubt, the fonder we will grow of the person who likes us. In a fascinating experiment by Elaine Hatfield Walster,[43] female college students, while waiting to receive the results of personality tests they had taken previously, were approached by a rather smooth, good-looking, well-dressed young man who was, in fact, an accomplice in the employ of the experimenter. The smooth young man struck up a conversation with the subject, indicated he liked her, and proceeded to make a date. At this point, the experimenter entered and led the young woman into an office to be informed of the results of her tests. In the course of this procedure, the young woman was allowed to read an evaluation of her own personality. Half of the young women received highly positive descriptions, designed expressly to raise their self-esteem temporarily. The other women received somewhat negative descriptions, designed to lower their self-esteem temporarily. Finally, as part of the experiment, the women were asked to rate how much they liked a wide variety of people—a teacher, a friend, ". . . and since we have one space left, why don't you rate that fellow you were waiting with?" Those women who received unfavorable information about themselves (from the personality test) showed far more liking for their male admirer than did those who received favorable information about themselves. In short, we like to be liked—and the more insecure we feel, the more we like someone who likes us.

One of the implications of this experiment is that people who are secure about themselves are less "needy"—that is, they are less likely to accept overtures from just any person who comes along. Just as a starving person will accept almost any kind of food and a well-fed person can be more selective, so too will an insecure person accept almost anyone who expresses interest, while a secure person will be more selective. Moreover, a person who feels insecure may even seek out a less attractive person in order to diminish the possibility of being rejected. This implication was tested in an interesting experiment by Sara Kiesler and Roberta Baral,[44] who led male college students to believe they had done either very well or very poorly in a test of intellectual achievement. They then took a break and the experimenter joined the student for a cup of coffee. As they entered the coffee shop, the experimenter "recognized" a female student seated alone at a table, joined her, and introduced the male subject to her. Of course, the female student was a confederate, intentionally planted there. Half of the time the confederate was made up to look attractive; the other half of the time she was made to look somewhat less attractive. The investigators observed the degree of romantic interest displayed by the male subjects—whether they asked to see her again, offered to pay for her coffee, asked for her phone number, tried to get her to stay longer, and so on. Interestingly enough, those induced to feel secure about themselves (that is, led to believe they had performed well on the test) showed more romantic interest toward the "attractive" woman; those induced to feel insecure showed more romantic interest toward the "unattractive" woman. In a related vein, Joel Grube and his colleagues[45] found that males with low self-esteem are attracted more to a "traditional" woman, but that males with high self-esteem tend to be attracted more to a "nontraditional" woman—that is, a woman who expresses "feminist" values. Grube suggests that male prejudice against feminists and other nontraditional women may be, in part, an attempt to bolster one's self-esteem in the face of perceived threat. That is, a nontraditional woman is usually seen as more assertive and independent than her more traditional counterpart. These traits may threaten the feelings of control and autonomy of a man with low self-esteem; thus he derogates the nontraditional woman in order to protect his own self-image. A man with high self-esteem, however, is, by definition, more secure and less easily threatened. Thus, he has no need to derogate an assertive, independent woman.

There are a great many factors that can influence a person's self-esteem and therefore have an important effect on his or her selectivity in the interpersonal marketplace. As the reader knows, one of these factors is physical attractiveness—people who are physically attractive tend to be treated better by others and this is almost certain to raise self-esteem. How does physical attractiveness affect selectivity? In a study reported by Zick Rubin,[46] a number of women were asked to complete a questionnaire about their dating preferences; the young women were also surreptitiously rated on the dimension of their own physical attractiveness. When rating their dating preferences, all of the women found men in the high-status occupations (physicians and lawyers, for example) to be acceptable dates, and rejected those in low-status jobs (janitors, bartenders). However, when it came to judging the acceptability of those men more towards the middle of the status hierarchy (electricians, bookkeepers, plumbers), differences emerged according to the attractiveness of the women—the more attractive women were more selective, finding such men to be unacceptable dates, while the less attractive women reported they would go out with men in these occupations.

The Relation Between Similarity and Being Liked. If we like people who hold opinions similar to ours, and if we like people who like us, shouldn't it follow that we will like a person particularly well if we learn he or she is *both* similar *and* he or she likes us? While this seems like common sense, the answer is no; the evidence suggests these two factors are not additive. In an experiment I performed in collaboration with Edward Jones and Linda Bell,[47] we showed that, although it is nice to be liked by someone who shares our values and opinions, it is far *more* exciting to be liked by someone who doesn't. Each of the college women in this experiment had a brief conversation with another woman in which she discovered that they either agreed or disagreed on a number of issues. After the conversation, the subject was allowed to eavesdrop on a conversation the other woman (actually a stooge) was having with a third person. During this conversation, the other woman discussed her feelings about the subject. In one condition, she indicated she liked her; in another condition, she indicated she disliked her. How did this affect the subject's feelings about the stooge? The subjects expressed the greatest liking for people with *dissimilar* attitudes who *liked* them. Thus, although we generally like people who have attitudes similar to our own, if we encounter someone who likes us *in spite* of the fact our opinions differ, we are inclined to infer there must be something special and unique about us that she finds attractive. In short, people tend to suspect that, where opinions differ, "That person likes me for myself—not for my opinions." Because this realization is especially gratifying, we tend to like that individual more.

And Opposites Do Attract—Sometimes. The old adage seems to be true: Birds of a feather do tend to flock together. That is, people who share similar opinions tend to like each other. As we have just learned, however, it is far more complicated than that: If someone likes us, we like that individual better if he or she is *different* from us. These data are consistent with some of the findings of investigators who have studied relationships more enduring than those produced in the sociopsychological laboratory. Robert Winch,[48] for example, who has done exhaustive studies of the personality characteristics of several engaged and married couples, finds that, under certain limited conditions, opposites attract—that is, people tend to choose people who have needs and characteristics that complement (rather than coincide with) their own needs and characteristics.

The reader will note I used the term "under certain limited conditions," because it turns out there are contradictory data in this research area. Some investigators find that married couples tend to have complementary need systems; others find married couples tend to have similar need systems. My guess is that whether birds of a feather flock together or whether opposites attract depends on which personality characteristics are under consideration. Imagine a person who values neatness and tidiness. Such a person would be disinclined to marry someone who was casual to the point of slovenliness. Similarly, the slob would not be too happy with an overly neat person. It seems reasonable that neat birds would flock with other neat birds and slobs would flock with slobs. By the same token, a person who was extroverted might not get along too well with an introverted person whose idea of a good time was to sit home watching TV. It is also true that people who are similar in wealth, intelligence, religious preference, attractiveness, education, and height do tend to flock together—especially in enduring relationships.[49] On the other hand, if we look at a different set of characteristics—say, nurturance and dependency—then a different picture emerges. A man who is very nurturant might be miserable if he found himself in a relationship with a highly independent woman—and *vice versa*. By the same token, what could be better for a dependent man than to live out his life on the bosom of someone who really enjoyed being nurturant? The same holds true for masculinity-femininity, assertiveness-passivity, and dominance-submissiveness. And, in a somewhat more facetious vein, what union could be happier than that of a sadist and a masochist?

In a long-term relationship, sociological factors also combine with need complementarity to play a sizable role in determining the extent to which two people will be attracted to each other and stay together. Society sets forth certain "role norms" for married couples. For example, in most of the world, society expects husbands to be relatively dominant and wives to be relatively submissive. If the complementarity of the needs of a couple coincide with the role norms set forth by society, the chances of marital happiness are increased. It should also be noted that, although the notion of need complementarity and the notion of opinion similarity frequently lead to opposite predictions about attraction, this is not necessarily true. People with certain complementary personality needs can be in complete agreement in their opinions about a given issue. To use an example just mentioned, it seems likely a dominant male and a submissive female will share the same opinions concerning sex roles in marriage—that a man should be dominant and a woman submissive. Obviously, these role norms can and do change. My own guess (and hope) is that, as men and women come to place more value on androgyny, the nineteenth-century role norms of the dominant husband and submissive wife will continue to change.

The Gain and Loss of Esteem

We have seen that our being liked by a person increases the likelihood we will like him or her. Let us take a closer look at this relation. Imagine that, at cocktail party, you meet a young woman for the first time and have an animated conversation with her. After a while, you excuse yourself to refill your glass. You return and find her back to you; she is deep in conversation with another person—and she's talking about you. So, naturally, you pause to listen. Clearly, the things she says about you will have an impact on how you feel about her. It is obvious she has no ulterior motives; indeed, she doesn't even know you are eavesdropping. Thus, if she tells her partner that she was impressed by you, that she liked you, that she found you bright, witty, charming, gracious, honest, and exciting, my guess is that this disclosure would have a positive effect on your liking for her. On the other hand, if she indicates that she was unimpressed, that she disliked you, that she found you dull, boring, dishonest, stupid, and vulgar, my guess is that this revelation would have a negative effect on your liking for her.

So far so good. But I'm sure that's not very interesting to you; you've always known that the more good things we hear about ourselves, the better we like the speaker (unless that speaker is trying to con us), and the more bad things we hear about ourselves, the more we dislike the person who says them. Everybody knows that—*but it happens to be untrue.* Imagine this: You have attended seven consecutive cocktail parties and, miracle of miracles, the same general event has occurred each time. You chat with a person for several minutes, you leave and when you come back you overhear her talking about you. It's the same person each time. Her responses might remain constant throughout her seven encounters with you, or they might vary. There are four possibilities that are particularly interesting to me: (1) you overhear the person saying exclusively positive things about you on all seven occasions; (2) you overhear her saying exclusively negative things about you on all seven occasions; (3) her first couple of evaluations are negative, but they gradually become increasingly positive until they equal her statements in the exclusively positive situation, and then level off; and (4) her first couple of evaluations are positive, but they gradually become more negative until they equal her statements in the exclusively negative situation, and then level off. Which situation would render the person most attractive to you?

According to a simple reward-cost idea of liking, you should like the person most in the first situation, in which she says exclusively positive things, and you should like her least (or dislike her most) in the second situation, in which she says exclusively negative things. This seems obvious. Because positive statements are rewarding, the more the better; because negative statements are punishing, the more the worse.

A few years ago, I developed a theory of interpersonal attraction, called the gain-loss theory, that makes a rather different prediction.[50] My theory is a very simple one. It suggests that *increases* in a positive, rewarding behavior from another person have more impact on an individual than constant, invariant reward from that person. Thus, if we take being liked as a reward, a person whose liking for us increases over time will be liked better than one who has always liked us. This would be true even if the *number* of rewards was greater from the latter person. Similarly, *losses* in rewarding behavior have more impact than constant punitive behavior from another person. Thus, a person whose esteem for us decreases over time will be disliked more than someone who has always disliked us—even if the number of punishments were greater from the latter person. To return to the cocktail party for a moment, I would predict you would like the individual most in the *gain* situation (where she begins by disliking you and gradually increases her liking) and you would like her least in the *loss* condition (where she begins by liking you and gradually decreases her liking for you).

In order to test my theory, I needed an experimental analogue of the cocktail-party situation—but for reasons of control, I felt it would be essential to collapse the several events into a single long session. In such an experiment, it is important that the subject be absolutely certain that the evaluator is totally unaware that she (the evaluator) is being overheard. This eliminates the possibility of the subject's suspecting the evaluator of intentionally flattering him when she says positive things. This situation presents a difficult challenge for the experimentalist. The central problem in devising a way to perform the experiment was one of credibility: How can I provide a believable situation in which, in a relatively brief period of time, the subject (1) interacts with a preprogrammed confederate, (2) eavesdrops while the preprogrammed confederate evaluates him or her to a third party, (3) engages in another conversation with the confederate, (4) eavesdrops again, (5) converses again, (6) eavesdrops again, and so on, through several pairs of trials. To provide any kind of a cover story would indeed be difficult; to provide a sensible cover story that would prevent subjects from becoming suspicious would seem impossible. But, in collaboration with Darwyn Linder, I did devise such a situation.[51] The devices we used to solve these problems are intricate, and they provide a unique opportunity to look behind the scenes of an unusually fascinating sociopsychological procedure. Accordingly, I would like to describe this experiment in some detail, in the hope it will provide the reader with an understanding of some of the difficulties and excitements involved in conducting experiments in social psychology.

> When the subject (a female college student) arrived, the experimenter greeted her and led her to an ovservation room connected to the main experimental room by a one-way window and an audio-amplification system. The experimenter told the subject that two women were scheduled for that hour: One would be the subject and the other would help perform the experiment—and because she had arrived first, she would be the helper. The experimenter asked her to wait while he left the room to see if the other woman had arrived. A few minutes later, through the one-way window, the subject was able to see the experimenter enter the experimental room with another female student (a paid confederate). The experimenter told the confederate to be seated for a moment and he would return shortly to explain the experiment to her. He then reentered the observation room and began the instructions to the real subject (who believed *herself* to be the confederate). The experimenter told her she was going to assist him in performing a verbal conditioning experiment on the other student; that is, he was going to reward the other student for certain words she used in conversation. He told the subject these rewards would increase the frequency with which the other woman would use these words. He went on to say that his particular interest was "not simply in increasing the output of those words that I reward; that's already been done. In this experiment, we want to see if the use of rewarded words generalizes to a new situation from the person giving the reward when the person is talking to a different person who does not reward those specific words." Specifically, the experimenter explained he would try to condition the other woman to increase her output of plural nouns by subtly rewarding her with an "mmmm hmmm" every time she said a plural noun. "The important question is: Will she continue to use an abundance of plural nouns when she talks to you, even though you will not be rewarding her?" The real subject was then told her tasks were: (1) to listen in and record the number of plural nouns used by the woman while the latter was talking to the experimenter, and (2) to engage her in a series of conversations (in which the use of plural nouns would

not be rewarded) so the experimenter could listen and determine whether generalization occurred. The experimenter then told the subject they would alternate in talking to the woman (first the subject, then the experimenter, then the subject) until each had spent seven sessions with her.

The experimenter made it clear to the subject that the other woman must not know the purpose of the experiment, lest the results be contaminated. He explained that, in order to accomplish this, some deception must be used. The experimenter said that, as much as he regretted the use of deception, it would be necessary for him to tell the "subject" the experiment was about interpersonal attraction. ("Don't laugh, some psychologists are actually interested in that stuff.") He said the woman would be told she was to carry on a series of seven short conversations with the subject and that, between each of these conversations, both she and the subject would be interviewed—the woman by the experimenter and the subject by an assistant in another room—to find out what impressions they had formed. The experimenter told the subject this "cover story" would enable the experimenter and the subject to perform their experiment on verbal behavior, because it provided the woman with a credible explanation for the procedure they would follow.

The major variable was introduced during the seven meetings the experimenter had with the confederate. During their meetings, the subject was in the observation room, listening to the conversation and dutifully counting the number of plural nouns used by the confederate. Because she had been led to believe that the confederate thought the experiment involved impressions of people, it was quite natural for the experimenter to ask the confederate to express her feelings about the subject. Thus, the subject heard herself being evaluated by a fellow student on seven successive occasions.

Note how, by using a cover story that *contains* a cover story involving "interpersonal attraction," we were able to accomplish our aim without arousing suspicion—only four of eight-four subjects were suspicious of this procedure.

There were four major experimental conditions: (1) positive—the successive evaluations of the subject made by the confederate were all highly positive; (2) negative—the successive evaluations were all highly negative; (3) gain—the first few evaluations were negative, but they gradually became more positive, reaching a level equal to the level of the positive evaluations in the positive condition; and (4) loss—the first few evaluations were positive, but they gradually became negative, leveling off at a point equal to the negative evaluations in the negative condition.

The results confirmed our predictions: The subjects in the gain condition liked the confederate significantly better than the subjects in the positive condition. By the same token, the subjects in the loss condition had a tendency to dislike the confederate more than the subjects in the negative condition. Recall that a general reward-cost theory would lead us to a simple algebraic summation of rewards and punishments and, accordingly, would have led to somewhat different predictions. The results are in line with our general theoretical position: A gain has more impact on liking than a set of events that are all positive, and a loss tends to have more impact than a set of events that are all negative. The philosopher Baruch Spinoza may have had something like this in mind when, about 300 years ago, he observed:

> Hatred which is completely vanquished by love passes into love, and love is thereupon greater than if hatred had not preceded it. For he who begins to love a thing which he was wont to hate or regard with pain, from the very fact of loving, feels pleasure. To this pleasure involved in love is added the pleasure arising from aid given to the endeavor to remove the pain involved in hatred accompanied by the idea of the former object of hatred as cause.[52]

Two important conditions are necessary for the gain-loss effect to be operative. First, it is not just any sequence of positive or negative statements that constitute a gain or loss; there must be an integrated sequence implying a change of heart. In other words, if you indicate that you think I'm stupid and insincere, and later you indicate you think I'm generous and athletic, this does not constitute a gain according to my definition—or Spinoza's. On the other hand, if you indicate I'm stupid or insincere and subsequently indicate that you've changed your mind—that you now believe me to be smart and sincere—this is a true gain because it indicates a reversal, a replacement of a negative attitude with its opposite. David Mettee and his colleagues[53] performed an experiment that demonstrated this distinction. A gain effect occurred only when a change in heart was made explicit. Second, the change in attitude must be gradual. The reason for this should be clear: An abrupt about-face is viewed by the stimulus person with confusion and suspicion—especially if it occurs on the basis of very little evidence. If Mary thinks Sam is stupid after three encounters, but brilliant after the fourth encounter, such a dramatic shift is bound to arouse suspicion on Sam's part. A gradual change, on the other hand, makes sense; it does not produce suspicion and hence produces an intensification of the person's liking for his or her evaluator.[54]

The Care and Feeding of Friendship

One of the possible implications of the gain-loss theory is that, in the words of the well-known ballad, "You always hurt the one you love." That is, once we have grown certain of the rewarding behavior of a person, that person may become less potent as a source of reward than a stranger. We have demonstrated that a gain in liking is a more potent reward than a constant level of liking; accordingly, a close friend (or a mother, a brother, or a mate) probably is behaving near ceiling level and, therefore, cannot provide us with a gain. To put it another way, because we have learned to expect love, favors, and praise from a friend, such behavior is not likely to represent a gain in that friend's esteem for us. By the same token, the good friend has great potential as a punisher. The closer the friend and the greater the past history of invariant esteem and reward, the more devastating is the withdrawal of that person's esteem. In effect, then, the friend has power to hurt the one he or she loves—but very little power to offer an important reward.

An example may help to clarify this point. After twenty years of marriage, a doting husband and his wife are getting dressed to attend a formal dinner party. He compliments her on her appearance: "Gee, honey, you look great." She hears his words, but they may not fill her with delight. She already knows her husband thinks she's attractive; she will not turn cartwheels at hearing about it for the thousandth time. On the other hand, if the doting husband (who in the past was always full of compliments) were to tell his wife he had decided she was losing her looks and he found her quite unattractive, this would cause her a great deal of pain, because it represents a loss of esteem.

Is she doomed to experience either boredom or pain? No, because there are other people in the world. Suppose Mr. and Mrs. Doting arrive at a party and a total stranger engages Mrs. Doting in conversation. After a while, he says, with great sincerity, that he finds her very attractive. My guess is she would not find this at all boring. It represents a distinct gain for her, it makes her feel good, and it increases the attractiveness of the stranger.

This reasoning is consistent with previous experimental findings. O. J. Harvey[55] found a tendency for subjects to react more positively to strangers than to friends when each were designated as the sources of relatively positive evaluations of the subjects. Moreover, subjects tended to react more negatively to friends than to strangers when each were designated as the sources of negative evaluations of subjects. Similarly, several experiments have shown that strangers have more impact on the behavior of young children than either parents or other familiar adults.[56] Most children are accustomed to receiving approval from parents and other adults with whom they are familiar. Therefore, additional approval from them does not represent much of a gain. However, approval from a stranger *is* a gain and, according to gain-loss theory, should result in a greater improvement in performance.

These results and speculations suggest a rather bleak picture of the human condition—we seem to be forever seeking favor in the eyes of strangers while, at the same time, we are being hurt by friends and other familiar people. Before we jump to this conclusion, however, let us take a few steps backward and look at the impact that gain or loss of esteem has on the behavior of individuals—quite aside from its effect on the perceived attractiveness of the evaluator. One study is highly pertinent in this respect. Joanne Floyd[57] divided a group of young children into pairs, so each child was either with a close friend or with a stranger. One child in each pair was then allowed to play a game in which he or she earned several trinkets. The child was then instructed to share these with the assigned partner. The perceived stinginess of the sharer was manipulated by the experimenter. Some children were led to believe the friend (or stranger) was treating them generously, and others were led to believe the friend (or stranger) was treating them in a stingy manner. Each "receiving" child was then allowed to earn several trinkets, and was instructed to share them with his or her partner. As expected, the children showed the most generosity in the gain and loss conditions—that is, they gave more trinkets to generous strangers and stingy friends. In short, they were relatively stingy to stingy strangers (and why not? the strangers behaved as they might have been expected to behave) and to generous friends ("Ho-hum, my friend likes me—so what else is new?"). But when it looked as though they might be gaining a friend (the generous stranger), they reacted with generosity; likewise, when it looked as though they might be *losing* one (the stingy friend), they also responded with generosity. Although it appears true "you always hurt the one you love," the hurt person appears to be inspired to react kindly—rather than "in kind"—in an attempt to re-establish the positive intensity of the relationship. This suggests the comforting possibility that individuals are inclined to behave in a way that will preserve stability in their relations with others.

Let us return to Mr. and Mrs. Doting for a moment. Although Mr. Doting has great power to hurt his wife by criticizing her, Mrs. Doting is apt to be very responsive to such criticism and will likely strive to make some changes in order to regain his interest. The reverse is also true: If Mrs. Doting suddenly were to change her high opinion of Mr. Doting, he could—and chances are he would—take action to regain her approval. A relationship becomes truly creative and continues to grow when both partners strive to grow and change in creative ways—and in all of this, "authenticity" assumes great importance. Carrying this reasoning a step further, I would suggest that the more honest and authentic a relationship, the less the possibility of reaching the kind of dull and deadening plateau on which the Dotings appear to be stuck. What I am suggesting is that a relationship in which marriage partners or close friends are the ones *least* likely to provide us with gains in esteem is almost certain to be a relationship in which the partners are not open and honest with each other. In a closed relationship, people tend to suppress their annoyances and to keep their negative feelings to themselves. This results in a fragile plateau that appears stable and positive but that can be devastated by a sudden shift in sentiment. Unfortunately, this may be a common kind of relationship in this country.

In an open, honest, authentic relationship, one in which people are able to share their true feelings and impressions (even their negative ones), no such plateau is reached. Rather, there is a continuous zigzagging of sentiment around a point of relatively high esteem. Indeed, recent research[58] has shown that marriage partners who use an intimate, nonaggressive, yet *confrontative* method of conflict resolution report higher levels of marital satisfaction. In a relationship of this sort, the partners are reasonably close to the gain condition of the gain-loss experiment. Similarly, a great deal of research has shown that an exchange of intimate and important aspects of *oneself*—both positive and negative—is necessary for the development of close relationships.[59] Moreover, it has been found that, all other things being equal, we like a person better after *we* have disclosed something important about ourselves—even if it is unsavory. We also tend to like other people better when they honor us by revealing something intimate and negative about themselves; this is especially true when the person is ordinarily reserved and, therefore, the behavior implies that there is something special about us that made him or her feel like opening up.

In summary, it is clear that Dale Carnegie's formula for winning friends is not only manipulative, it is also far too simplistic to be of much general value. Moreover, it is my best guess that, over the course of a long-term relationship, *no* formula for impression management—not even a subtle and complex one—will be very effective if it is applied in a calculated, manipulative way *in order to* induce a positive response from another person. To illustrate: The reader will recall that Benjamin Franklin was successful in *opening the door* to an important friendship with his legislative colleague by inducing the latter to do him a favor;

however, it is my contention that this friendship almost certainly would have withered and died if Franklin had continued to use such manipulative tactics indefinitely.

This is not to deny or minimize the importance of the early stages of the acquaintance process. First impressions are important; relationships must begin before they can develop and mature, as Benjamin Franklin aptly demonstrated. But as a relationship ripens toward greater intimacy, what becomes increasingly important is authenticity—our ability to give up trying to make a good impression and begin to reveal things about ourselves that are honest even if unsavory. In addition, we must be willing to communicate a wide range of feelings to our friends under appropriate circumstances and in ways that reflect our caring. Thus, to return again to the Dotings, if two people are genuinely fond of each other, they will have a more satisfying and exciting relationship over a longer period of time if they are able to express both positive and negative feelings than if they are completely "nice" to each other at all times. But the communication of feelings is no easy matter—as we shall see in the next chapter. Read the next three or four pages and you'll see what I mean.

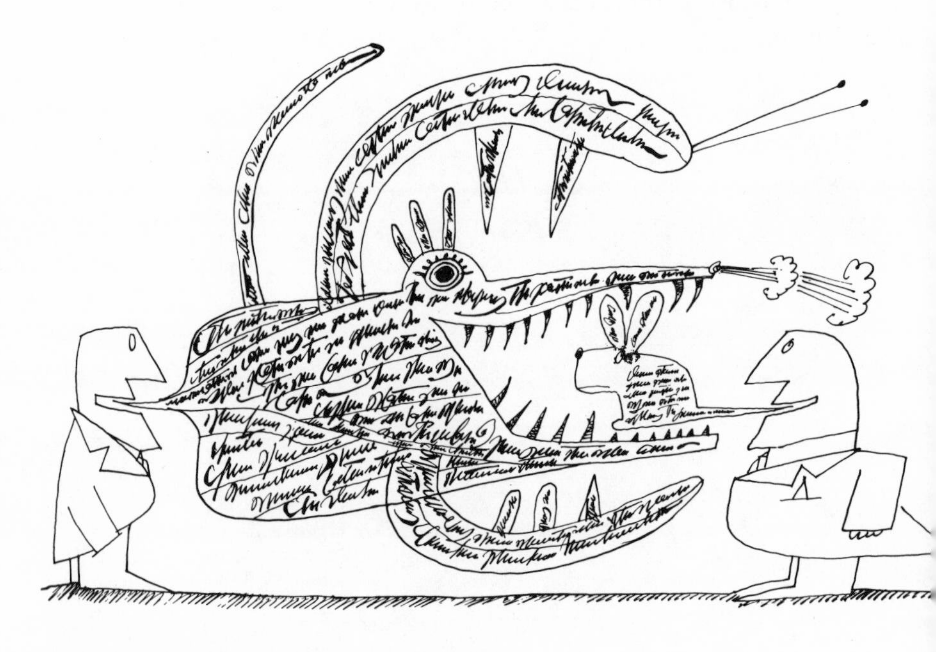

8

Interpersonal Communication and Sensitivity

Phil and Alice Henshaw are washing the dishes. They have had some friends over for dinner, the friends have left, and Phil and Alice are cleaning up. During the evening Alice was her usual charming, witty, vivacious self. But Phil, who is usually delighted by her charm, is feeling hurt and a little angry. It seems that, during a political discussion, Alice had disagreed with his position and sided with Tom. Moreover, she seemed to express a great deal of warmth toward Tom in the course of the evening. In fact, her behavior could be considered mildly flirtatious.

Phil is thinking: "I love her so much. I wish she wouldn't do things like that. Maybe she's losing interest in me. God, if she ever left me, I don't know what I'd do. Is she really attracted to Tom?" Phil actually says: "You sure were throwing yourself at Tom tonight. Everybody noticed it. You really made a fool of yourself."

Alice cares a great deal about Phil. She felt that she had said some very bright things—especially during the political discussion—and felt that Phil didn't acknowledge her intellectual contribution. "He thinks I'm just a housewife."

> Alice: "I don't know what you're talking about. You're just mad because I happened to disagree with you about the president's tax proposal. Tom saw it my way. I think I was right."
> Phil: "He saw it *your* way! Are you kidding? What else could he do? You were practically sitting in his lap. The other guests were embarrassed."
> Alice (teasing): "Why, Phil, I do believe you're jealous!"
> Phil: "I'm *not* jealous! I really don't give a damn . . . if you want to act like a slut, that's your business."
> Alice (angrily): "Boy, are you old-fashioned. You're talking like some Victorian, for God's sake! You're always doing that!"
> Phil (coldly): "That just shows how little you know about me. Other people find me up to date—even dashing."
> Alice (sarcastically): "Yes, I'm sure you cut quite a figure with all the little secretaries at your office!"
> Phil: "Now, what's *that* supposed to mean?"

Alice falls into a stony silence. Phil makes several attempts to get a response from her, fails, then storms out of the room, slamming the door. What is going on? Here are two people who care about each other. How did they get into such a vicious, hurtful, spiteful argument?

One of the major characteristics of humans that separates us from other organisms is our unique ability to communicate complex information through the use of a highly sophisticated language. The subtlety of communication that is possible among humans as compared to that among other animals is truly awesome. And yet misunderstandings among people are frequent. Moreover, misunderstandings typify even those relationships that are close and caring. Though hypothetical, the argument between the Henshaws is not at all unrealistic; rather, it is typical of hundreds of such conversations I have heard as a consultant trying to help straighten out dyadic communications that are garbled, indirect, and misleading.

It would be relatively easy to analyze the argument between

Phil and Alice. Each had a major concern that was being threatened. Neither was able or willing to state in a clear, straightforward way what that concern was. For Alice, the major concern seemed to be her intellectual competence. She was afraid Phil thought she was dumb; her major *implicit* complaint in this argument was that Phil didn't acknowledge the cogency of her statements during the political discussion, and he seemed to be implying that the only reason Tom paid attention to her or seemed to be interested in her statements was because of lust or sexual flirtation. This hurt her, threatened her self-esteem, and made her angry. She didn't express the hurt. She expressed the anger, but not simply by revealing it; rather, she took the offensive and attacked Phil by implying that he is stodgy and uninteresting.

Phil's major concern seemed to be a feeling of insecurity. While he enjoys Alice's vivacity, he appears to be afraid of the possibility that, with increasing age, he may be losing his own attractiveness as a man. Thus, he assumed that Alice's agreeing with Tom is akin to her siding with Tom against him—and he attached sexual connotations to it because of his own insecurities. When Alice called him "old-fashioned," he seemed mostly to hear the "old"—and he quickly defended his masculinity and sex appeal, which Alice, driven by her *own* anger, promptly ridiculed.

This kind of argument is a familiar one among people living in close relationships. There are important feelings and concerns. Instead of being discussed openly and honestly, the feelings are allowed to escalate into hostility, which only exacerbates the hurt and insecurity that initiated the discussion. As the divorce rate continues to soar in America, it seems reasonable to ask seriously why this happens. It would be silly to proclaim that all anger, disagreement, hurt, and hostility between people who supposedly care about each other is a function of poor or inadequate communication. Often there are conflicts between the needs, values, desires, and goals of people in close relationships. These produce stresses and tensions, which must either be lived with or resolved by compromise, yielding, or the dissolution of the relationship.

But frequently, the problem *is* largely one of communication. How might Phil have communicated differently? Pretend for the moment you are Phil. And Alice, a person you care about, approaches you and makes the following statement in a tone of voice that was nonblaming and nonjudgmental:

> "I'm feeling insecure about my intelligence—or at least the way people view me on that dimension. Since you are one of the most important people in my world, it would be particularly gratifying to me if you would acknowledge statements of mine that you think are intelligent or worthwhile. When we disagree on a substantive issue and you speak harshly or become impatient with me, it tends to increase my feelings of insecurity. Earlier this evening, during our political discussion, I would have been delighted if you had complimented me on some of my ideas and insights."

Imagine, now, that you are Alice, and Phil had opened the after-dinner discussion in the following way:

> "This is difficult to say. I don't know what it is with me lately, but I was feeling some jealousy tonight. This isn't easy to say . . . but here goes: You and Tom seemed kind of close—both intellectually and physically—and I was feeling hurt and lonely. I've been worried lately about middle age. This may seem silly, but I've been slowing down, feeling tired, developing a paunch. I need some reassurance you still find me attractive. I would love it if you'd look at me the way you seemed to be looking at Tom this evening."

My guess is most people would be receptive and responsive to that kind of *straight talk.* By *straight talk*, I mean a person's clear statement of his or her feelings and concerns without accusing, blaming, judging, or ridiculing the other person. As we shall see, straight talk is effective, precisely because it enables the recipient to listen nondefensively.

Straight talk seems so simple, and it obviously is effective. Why don't people use it more often? The main reason is that it is not as easy as it appears. In the course of growing up in a competitive society, most of us have learned how to protect ourselves by making ourselves relatively invulnerable. Thus, when we are hurt, we have learned not to show it. Rather, we have learned either to avoid the person who hurt us or to lash out at him or her with anger or ridicule. As we have seen, this will usually result in either a defensive response or a counter-attack, and the argument escalates.

In short, the general lesson of our society is never to reveal your vulnerabilities. This strategy may be useful and in some situations even essential, but in many circumstances it is inappropriate, dysfunctional, and counterproductive. It is probably wise not to reveal your vulnerability to someone who is your sworn enemy. But it is almost certainly unwise to conceal your vulnerability from someone who is your friend and cares about you. Thus, if Alice and Phil had known about the other's insecurity, they each could have acted in ways that would have made the other feel more secure. Because each of them had overlearned the societal lesson of "attack rather than reveal," they inadvertently placed themselves on a collision course.

It would be extraordinarily useful if we could teach people how to communicate more effectively. But, as you can see, it is not as simple as learning a set of rules or guidelines. People need to learn to overcome their fear of making themselves vulnerable. This cannot be readily done by taking a course or reading a book.

Moreover, the problem is even more complicated than the one depicted in our example. Alice and Phil seem to have some idea of what their concerns are and what their feelings are. They got into serious conflict primarily because they had difficulty communicating their insecurity and hurt feelings with each other. But, in many situations, people are not fully aware of their own needs, wants, and feelings. Instead, there may be a vague feeling of discomfort or unhappiness that the person can't easily pinpoint. Often there is misattribution; that is, Phil may feel uncomfortable, and he could attribute the discomfort to embarrassment over Alice's alleged flirtatious behavior rather than to his own underlying insecurities about advancing middle age. Thus, if we are not in touch with our own feelings and cannot articulate them clearly to ourselves, how in the world can we communicate them to another person?

The key issue is sensitivity. Can we learn to be more sensitive to our own feelings? Can we learn to be sensitive to others so that, when people *do* make themselves vulnerable, we treat that vulnerability with care and respect?

These skills *can* be learned. But they are best learned through experience. This experiential learning is most effective if it takes place in a relatively safe, protected social environment where people can practice straight talk without fear that others will take advantage of their vulnerability.

In many respects, the kind of social environment we have in mind is almost the exact opposite of many of the situations described thus far in this book. For example, in Chapter 2, we described a scene in which a group of people were passing judgments on the size of a line. This was the setting of Solomon Asch's classic experiment on conformity. As you recall, the behavior of most of the people in that group was inauthentic—that is, they were making statements quite different from their real perceptions. They had an agenda in mind, and it was hidden from one of the individuals in the group. Their agenda was to attempt to influence or manipulate that person's behavior. In this chapter, I will focus on a very different kind of group. In this group, from ten to twenty people are sitting around in a circle. Unlike the group in the line-judging experiment, this group has no specific task agenda. Typically, the members have no intention of solving any specific problem. The intent of the group is not to manipulate anyone. Quite the contrary—the intent is to be authentic and to talk straight. The group I am describing is usually referred to as an encounter group, sensitivity-training group, or human relations training group (*T-group*, for short). The various terms are often used interchangeably, but in fact they do connote differences in orientation and technique.

Broadly speaking, the term *T-group* refers to the more conservative, more traditional group, in which the primary emphasis is on verbal behavior, and group discussions are almost exclusively confined to the here and now. It is associated with East Coast centers, principally the National Training Laboratories in Bethel, Maine and Washington, D.C. The term *encounter group* is most often associated with the more radical wing of the human potential movement; the activities of such groups often include such nonverbal procedures as touching, body movement, dance, and massage. Although they tend to be associated with such West Coast centers as Esalen Institute, encounter groups may be found throughout the United States. I will use the term *T-group* throughout this chapter; the groups I will be describing are more toward the traditional end of the spectrum, although they may use some of the more recent innovations usually associated with the encounter group.

The first T-group was an accident. But, like most productive accidents, it occurred in the presence of a brilliant and creative person who was quick to appreciate the importance and potential utility of what he had stumbled upon. In 1946 Kurt Lewin, perhaps the greatest innovator and theorist in the brief history of social psychology, was asked to conduct a workshop to explore the use of small group discussions as a way of addressing some of the social problems of the day. The participants were educators, public officials, and social scientists. They met during the day in small groups. The small groups were observed by several of Lewin's graduate students, who met in the evenings to discuss their interpretation of the dynamics of the group discussions they had observed during the day.

One evening, a few of the participants asked if they could sit in and listen while the graduate students discussed their observations. Lewin was a little embarrassed by the request, but, much to the surprise of his graduate students, he allowed the visitors to sit in. As it happened, one of the educators joined the group just as the observers were discussing and interpreting an episode that she had participated in the preceding morning. She became very agitated and said the observer's interpretation was all wrong. She then proceeded to give her version of the episode. The discussion proved very exciting. The next night, all fifty of the participants showed up and gleefully joined the discussion, frequently disagreeing with the observations and interpretations of the trained observers. The session was both lively and illuminating.

Lewin and his students were quick to grasp the significance of that event: A group engaged in a problem-solving discussion can benefit enormously by taking time out to discuss its own dynamics or "group process" without special training as observers. Indeed, the participants themselves are much better observers of their own process because each is privy to his or her own intentions—something not easily available to outside observers—no matter how astute and well-trained they are. After a time, what evolved was the agenda-less group: The group could meet with maximum benefit if it had no formal agenda and no problems to discuss other than its own dynamics.

Interest in T-groups has grown rapidly since 1946. They are conducted in all sections of the country, and their members include individuals from all walks of life. There have been specialized groups consisting solely of college students, high school teachers, corporation presidents, police officers, members of the State Department, and delinquents; there have been confrontation groups of blacks and whites, managers and their employees, and other groups in conflict. But most groups have been heterogeneous—the same group might contain a lawyer, a laborer, a nun, a housewife, a bank teller, a college student, and a smattering of male and female business executives, teachers, and drop-outs. T-groups, in large part, were a phenomenon of the sixties and seventies—they received wide (and often sensational) publicity. They often were treated with an uncritical, cultish, almost religious zeal by some of their proponents; and they were castigated by the right wing as an instrument of the devil, as a subversive form of brainwashing that was eating away at the moral fabric and soul of the nation. The heyday of the T-group has passed and so too have most of the excessive reactions to them—both positive and negative. What remains is a solid core of an experiential methodology for learning communication skills and gaining knowledge about interpersonal relationships. In various forms, T-groups can be found in establishment institutions like big business and public education. Such widespread acceptance demonstrates that T-groups are neither the panacea nor the menace they frequently were made out to be. When properly used, they can be enormously useful as a means of increasing self-awareness and enriching human relations. With this in mind, the distinguished psychotherapist Carl Rogers characterized the T-group as "the most significant social invention of the century,"[1] and the social historian William Thompson considered the T-group "a rehearsal for the complete transformation of human nature and civilization."[2] When abused, they can be a waste of time—or, in extreme cases, they might even provide people with some very painful experiences, whose effects can persist long beyond the termination of the group.

The primary focus in this chapter will be on the sensitivity-training group as an instrument of communication. Although there are all kinds of groups, I will discuss only the traditional T-groups. I will attempt to describe them from within and from without and discuss what happens in a group, what gets learned, and what the inherent problems might be.

The Content and Process of a T-Group

A T-group experience is educational, but educational in a different way from what most of us have grown accustomed to. It is different both in the *content* of the material learned and in the *process* by which learning takes place.

The Content: What Gets Learned. Generally, individuals in a T-group learn things about themselves and their relations with other people. It can be said that, in a college psychology course, I learn how people behave; in a T-group, I learn how *I* behave. But I learn much more than that. I also learn how others see me, how my behavior affects them, and how I am affected by other people.

The primary purpose of T-groups is to learn how to communicate effectively, to listen carefully, and to understand one's own feelings and those of other people. In addition, many people are motivated to participate in a T-group because they believe there may be something missing in their lives. People may feel alienated from their work, their family, and other people. They may feel that life is going by too quickly. They may feel they want something more out of life than waking up in the morning, eating breakfast, going to work, coming home, watching television, and going to sleep. In short, many people are searching for greater self-awareness and greater enrichment of their lives through these groups. This does not mean a person has to be in the middle of an existential crisis in order to join a group; many people join because they have specific confusions and are searching for specific answers: "Why do I have trouble getting along with my children (or my employees, or the opposite sex)?" "Why do other people make friends easily, while I tend to be alone?" "Why do I have difficulty opening up to people?" "What is there about people that makes them so untrustworthy?" "How can I handle my anger?" "What do I do that turns people off?" "Why is it that, when I meet a guy, all he wants to do is take me to bed?"

Interacting with other people in a competently-led T-group *can*, and frequently *does*, provide individuals with answers to specific questions like these. But, more generally, the T-group provides the first step toward the achievement of a number of goals and forms the basis for the clarification of a wide range of confusions. Among the major goals of a T-group are:

1. To develop ways of communicating that are clear, straight, and nonattributional.
2. To develop a spirit of inquiry and a willingness to examine one's own behavior and to experiment with one's role in the world.
3. To develop an awareness of more things about more people.
4. To develop greater authenticity in interpersonal relations; to feel freer to be oneself and not feel compelled to play a role.
5. To develop the ability to act in a collaborative and mutually dependent manner with peers, superiors, and subordinates rather than in an authoritarian or submissive manner.
6. To develop the ability to resolve conflicts and disputes through problem solving rather than through coercion or manipulation.

The Process: How Things Are Learned. The single most important distinguishing characteristic of a T-group is the method by which people learn. Again, a T-group is not a seminar or a lecture course. Although a great deal of learning *does* occur, it's not the kind of learning that can be easily transmitted verbally in a traditional teacher-student relationship. It is learning through doing, learning through experience. In a T-group, people learn by trying things out, by paying attention to their feelings, by expressing those feelings, and by listening carefully to other people. "Trying things out" not only helps individuals understand their own feelings, it also allows them the opportunity of benefiting from learning about how their behavior affects other people. If I want to know whether or not people find me to be a cold, aloof, unemotional person, I simple *behave*—and then others in the group will tell me how my behavior makes them feel.

An implicit assumption underlying these groups is that very little can be gained if someone tells us how we are *supposed* to feel, how we are *supposed* to behave, or what we are *supposed* to do with our lives. A parallel assumption is that a great deal can be gained if we understand *what* we're feeling, if we understand the kinds of interpersonal events that trigger various kinds of feelings, if we understand how our behavior is read and understood by other people, and if we understand the wide variety of options available to us. The role of the T-group leader is not to present us with answers but simply to help establish an atmosphere of trust and intensive inquiry in which we are willing to look closely at our own behavior and the behavior of others.

It is in this sense that a T-group is not a therapy group. The leader does not attempt to interpret our motives or probe into our experiences outside the group; in addition, he or she tends to discourage other group members from doing this. Instead, the leader simply encourages us to behave and to react to the behavior of others. It is a social psychological situation rather than a clinical-therapeutic situation.

The Cultural Island. As we race through life, we frequently are distracted. Thoughts about the work we must do compete for our attention with the person we are supposedly listening to now; thoughts about the person we must see during the *next* hour distract us from the work we are trying to do now; as we stand at the cocktail party, balancing a drink in one hand and holding a cigarette in the other, "listening" to the pompous fellow in the flashy suit, we glance over his shoulder to see who else is at the party, and we begin to wonder why we didn't go to that other party instead. This kind of distraction is minimized in a T-group, because there is literally no alternative to paying attention. Here, we are in a room—on a "cultural island"—with several other people for two weeks (or ten days, or a weekend) with nothing to do and no agenda and no one directing us toward any specific action. We are meeting for ten to sixteen hours a day—

there's nothing else happening. Initially, this can be somewhat frightening, as we realize how difficult it is to interact with people in the absence of conversational crutches (the weather, have you seen any good films lately, and so on). Then, as we learn to pay attention to others, to listen, to look, we begin to pick up nuances of speech and behavior that we didn't think we were capable of noticing. We also begin to listen to ourselves more, to pay attention to those rumblings in our gut and to try to make sense out of them in the context of what is going on in the room, *outside* our gut.

OK, but what happens? How do people get started? What is there to talk about? Typically, the group begins with the leader (sometimes called the "trainer" or "facilitator") outlining the "housekeeping" schedule—when meals will be served, how long each session will last before it breaks, and so on. She may or may not proceed to outline her philosophy of groups and the limits of her own participation. She may or may not discuss the "contract"—what the participants do *not* have to do. In any case, she soon falls into silence. Minutes pass. They seem like hours. The group members may look at each other or out the window. We are not accustomed to being left to our own devices by people in leader-teacher roles. Typically, the participants will look to the leader for guidance or direction. None is forthcoming. After several minutes, someone might express his discomfort. This may or may not be responded to. Eventually, in a typical group, someone will express some annoyance at the leader: "I'm getting sick of this. This is a waste of time. How come you're not doing your job? What the hell are we paying you for? Why don't you tell us what we're supposed to do?" There may be a ripple of applause in the background. But someone else might jump in and ask the first person why he's so bothered by a lack of direction—does he need someone to tell him what to do? And the T-group is off and running.

Learning from Each Other

How does learning occur? How can we learn from people who are not experts? We learn through communicating. There are many ways for communications to become distorted. Occasionally, in our everyday lives, when we think we are communicating something to a person, that person is hearing something entirely different. Suppose, for example, that Fred has warm feelings for Jack, but, out of shyness or out of fear of being rejected, he finds it difficult to express these feelings directly. As is common among males in our culture, Fred may choose to communicate those warm feelings by engaging in a teasing, sarcastic kind of banter. Jack may not understand this as warmth, however; indeed, the sarcasm might hurt him. As I indicated earlier, in our culture, it is difficult to communicate hurt feelings, because it indicates weakness and vulnerability. So Jack keeps quiet. Thus, Fred, oblivious to the fact that his behavior is disturbing to Jack, continues to express his warmth via sarcastic jocularity—continuing to hurt the person he likes—until he succeeds in driving Jack away. Not only does Fred lose out on what could have been a warm friendship, but he may also fail to learn from this experience and may continue to go through life alienating the very people toward whom he feels most warmly.

It may be useful to view the interaction between two people as a chain of events, as illustrated in the figure in page 332. The Person (P) has some feelings about the Recipient (R). He intends to communicate a particular feeling. This manifests itself in some kind of behavior—some words, a gesture, a smile, a look, or whatever. The Recipient perceives this behavior in his own way, based upon his own needs, feelings, past history, opinions about P, and so on. This perception of P's behavior evokes a feeling in R (warmth, anger, annoyance, love, fear, or whatever). This feeling is quickly translated into an interpretation of what P's intentions were, which in turn flows into an evaluation of what kind of person P is.

There are possibilities for error or distortion along any point in the links of this chain. Thus, to return to our example, Fred (P) has some warm feelings (P_1) toward Jack. He intends to communicate these (P_2), but he does it in an oblique, noncommittal, self-protective way: He teases Jack, makes fun of his clothes, is jocular and sarcastic (P_3). Jack perceives this sarcasm and teasing (R_1); it causes him pain (R_2); and he decides that

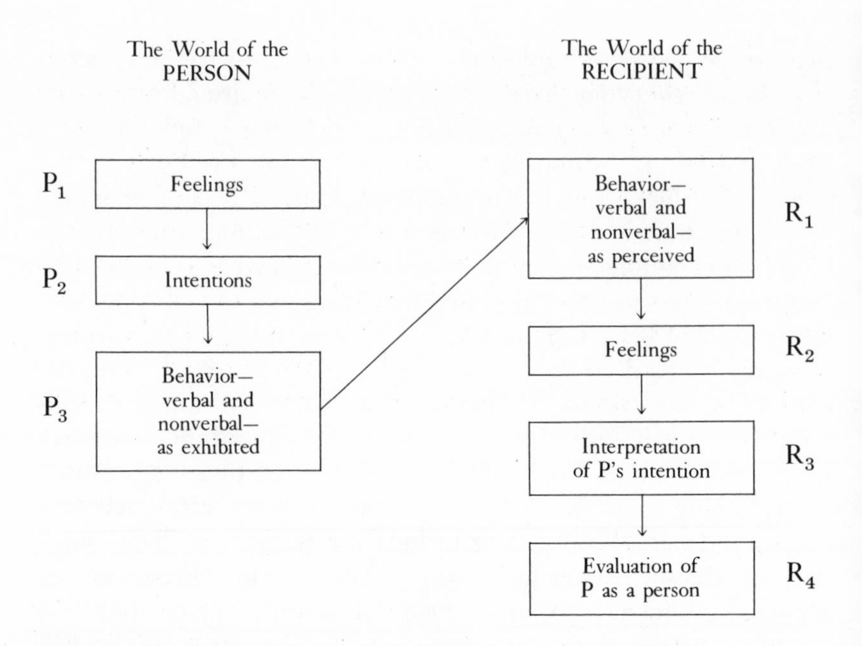

Fred was trying to put him down (R_3). He concludes, therefore, that Fred is a cruel, aggressive, unfriendly person (R_4).

Error can occur in a different part of the chain. Imagine a totally new situation in which Fred is completely direct and honest, but Jack is suspicious. Suppose Fred expresses his warmth directly—by putting his arm around Jack's shoulder, by telling Jack how much he likes him, and so on. But, in this case, such behavior may be too fast for Jack. Accordingly, Jack may feel uncomfortable, and, instead of simply admitting his discomfort, he may interpret Fred's behavior as manipulative in intent. He may evaluate Fred as an insincere, political, manipulative person.

The process described above may be familiar to readers of this book. It has been discussed in Chapter 6 under the term *attribution*. If we see a person behaving in a particular way, we have a strong tendency to attribute some motive or personality disposition to the person on the basis of that behavior. If this process can be explored and examined, there is a great deal of potential learning in the encounter for both Fred and Jack. Is Fred too scared to display his warm feelings openly? Is Jack too suspicious to accept genuine warmth without vilifying Fred? These are important questions whose answers can produce a lot of insight, *but the opportunity for gaining this insight rarely occurs in the real world.* This learning can occur only if Fred and Jack share their feelings with each other. The T-group provides an atmosphere in which these feelings can be expressed and worked through. The group accomplishes this by encouraging the participants to stay with their feelings and to avoid "short-circuiting" the process by skipping from Fred's behavior (P_3) all the way to Jack's attribution (R_3) and ultimately to Jack's evaluation of Fred (R_4) without exploring the preceding and intervening events.

Openness and the Need for Privacy

Basically then, a T-group is a setting in which people are provided with the opportunity to talk straight to each other—and to listen straight. The emphasis is on the *here and now*, rather than on past history. Thus, a participant is *not* encouraged, for example, to explain to everyone the kind of person she is, nor is she encouraged to reveal her childhood experiences, her job anxieties, or the intricacies of her sex life. She *may* talk about these things if she chooses, but she usually learns more if she simply allows events to happen, reacts to the events openly as she experiences them, and allows others to respond to her as she *is* rather than as she describes herself to be. "Openness" is the key aspect of behavior in a T-group. Some critics of T-groups have reacted against the emphasis on openness, because they believe it violates the individual's dignity and need for privacy. But, in this context, openness does not mean detailed self-revelation; it simply means straight talk between two or more people. In a competently conducted T-group, a norm is established that provides each member with the right to as much physical and emotional privacy as that person desires. Participants are encouraged to resist any pressure to make them reveal things they would rather hold private. But if a member does wish to express something in a group, he or she is helped to learn how to express it directly rather than obliquely. For example, if

Debbie is angry at Ralph, it is her right to keep that anger to herself, if she so chooses. But if she chooses to express her anger, it is much more useful (for Debbie, for Ralph, and for everyone else concerned) if she expresses it directly by telling Ralph about her feelings than it is if she expresses it by any one of a number of indirect means—such as making snide remarks or sarcastic statements, grunting whenever Ralph talks, making fun of Ralph covertly, or lifting her eyes to the ceiling, so that everyone can be made aware of her contempt for Ralph. If Debbie makes a snide remark, the leader or a member of the group will almost invariably ask her if she has any feelings about Ralph that she wants to share with the group. She is not coerced into sharing her feelings—but she is discouraged from talking in riddles and encouraged to translate the muddy language of sarcasm into straight talk.

This is not to deny that, in some groups, a great deal of coercion is used to make people reveal things they might prefer not to reveal. Sigmund Koch, a vocal and erudite critic of group encounter, provides a graphic description of some of the more lurid and extreme examples of coercive groups. But he goes beyond that and asserts that *all* T-groups constitute a threat to human dignity and "a challenge to any conception of the person that would make life worth living."[3] Koch has sounded a warning siren worth heeding. Personally, I would choose not to participate in a group that invaded my privacy and pressured me to make self-revealing statements against my better judgment; I believe such groups are not only invasive but also potentially dangerous. However, I believe Koch's condemnation of all T-groups on these grounds is based on a misunderstanding of the term "openness" and an overgeneralization of his limited exposure to the goings on in "far-out" groups. At the same time, I would agree with Koch to the extent of advising people to steer clear of encounter groups unless they are competently conducted and unless they practice the value that no one has to do anything he or she does not want to do. More will be said about this near the end of the chapter.

Characteristics of Effective Feedback

The Importance of Immediacy. As I mentioned previously, members of T-groups are encouraged to express their feelings directly and openly. When the participants abide by this norm, they receive immediate feedback on how people interpret what they say and do. In this way, we are able to gain insight into the impact that our actions and statements have on other people. Once we gain this insight, we are free to do whatever we want with it. That is, people are not advised to perform only those actions that no one finds objectionable; rather, they are allowed to see the consequences of their behavior and to decide whether the price they are paying is worth it. They are also given the opportunity of discovering that there are almost always more options available to them than they may have realized. To illustrate, suppose I perform an act that angers my best friend, who also happens to be my wife. If she doesn't express this anger, I may never become aware of the fact that the action I've performed makes her angry. On the other hand, suppose she gives me immediate feedback; suppose she tells me how these actions on my part make her feel angry. Then, I have at least two options: I can continue to behave in that way, or I can stop behaving in that way—the choice is mine. The behavior may be so important that I don't want to give it up. Conversely, my wife's feelings may be so important that I choose to give up the behavior. In the absence of any knowledge of how my behavior makes her feel, I don't have a choice. Moreover, knowing exactly how she feels about a particular set of actions may allow me to explore a *different* set of actions that may satisfy my needs as well as her needs.

The value of feedback is not limited to the recipient. Frequently, in providing feedback, people discover something about themselves and their own needs. If a woman feels, for example, that it's always destructive to express anger, she may block out her awareness of this feeling. When the expression of such feelings is legitimized, she has a chance to bring them out in the open, to look at them, and to become aware that her expression of anger has not caused the world to come to an end. Moreover, the direct expression of a feeling keeps the encounter on the up-and-up and thus helps to prevent the escalation of negative feelings. For example, if my wife has learned to express her anger directly, it keeps our discussion on the issue at hand. If she suppresses the anger, but it leaks out in other ways—at different times and in different situations—I do not know where her hostility is coming from and I become confused, hurt, or angry.

For example, suppose we are at a party and I begin to tell a "hilarious" story. When I am midway through my story, my wife says, "Oh, come on, now—I'm sure no one is interested in that tired old joke you keep telling," and she abruptly changes the subject. I am stunned, because I have no idea that her need to put me down is a result of some anger she felt toward me for something I had done two weeks earlier—some anger she was unwilling or unable to express at the time. Indeed, by this time, she herself may be unaware of what caused her to interrupt my "hilarious" story. My response to the put-down might be to become self-righteous about being abused for no apparent reason. This makes me angry, and the argument escalates.

Feelings Versus Evaluations. People often need some coaching in how to provide feedback. We often do it in a way that angers or upsets the recipient, thereby causing more problems than we solve. Indeed, one of the aspects of T-groups that sometimes frightens and confuses people who have never been in a properly conducted group is that their prior experiences with providing and receiving feedback have not always been pleasant. This is one of the reasons why it is so difficult to communicate what happens in a T-group to people who have never experienced one. Specifically, when we describe this aspect of a T-group, we are describing behavior of a sort that all of us have experienced—much of it unpleasant. And yet, we're trying to say that such behavior can be productive in a T-group. To say this, however, may make the group seem to be a magical, mystical thing, which it is not. The way this can happen is better illustrated than described in the abstract. I will do this by providing an example of dysfunctional feedback and of how people can be taught to modify their method of providing feedback (without modifying its quality) in order to maximize communication and understanding. This example is an actual event that occurred in a T-group I was leading several years ago.

In the course of the group meeting, one of the members (Sam) looked squarely at another member (Harry) and said, "Harry, I've been listening to you and watching you for a day and a half, and I think you're a phony." Now that's quite an accusation. How can Harry respond? He has several options: He can (1) agree with Sam; (2) deny the accusation and say he's not a phony; (3) say, "Gee, Sam, I'm sorry you feel that way;" (4) get angry and call Sam some names; or (5) feel sorry for himself and go into a sulk. Taken by themselves, none of these responses is particularly productive. In the "real world" it is unlikely Sam would have come out with this statement; if he had come out with it, there almost certainly would have been trouble. But doesn't Sam have the right to express this judgment? After all, he's only being open.

This sounds like a dilemma: T-groups encourage openness, but openness can hurt people. The solution to this apparent dilemma is rather simple: It is possible to be open and and, at the same time, to express oneself in a manner that causes a minimum of pain. The key rests in the term *feeling;* Sam was not expressing a feeling, he was expressing a judgment. As I mentioned previously, openness in a T-group means the open expression of feelings. The term "feeling" has several meanings. In this context I don't mean "hunch" or "hypothesis." By *feeling*, I mean, specifically, anger or joy, sadness or happiness, annoyance, fear, discomfort, warmth, hurt, envy, excitement, and the like. In the terms of the figure on page 332, Sam has leapt to R_4, instead of sharing R_1 and R_2.

How was this encounter handled in the T-group? In this situation, the group leader intervened by asking Sam if he had any *feelings* about Harry. In our society, people are not accustomed to expressing feelings. It is not surprising, then, that Sam thought for a moment and then said, "Well, I *feel* that Harry is a phony." Of course, this is not a feeling, as defined above. This is an opinion or a judgment expressed in the terminology of feelings. A judgment is nothing more or less than a feeling that is inadequately understood or inadequately expressed. Accordingly, the leader probed further by asking Sam *what* his feelings were. Sam still insisted he felt Harry was a phony. "And what does that do to you?" asked the leader. "It annoys the hell out of me," answered Sam. Here, another member of the group intervened and asked for data: "What kinds of things has Harry done that annoyed you, Sam?" Sam, after several minutes of probing by various members of the group, admitted he got annoyed whenever Harry showed affection to some of the women in the group. On further probing, it turned out Sam perceived Harry as being very attractive to women. What eventually emerged was that Sam owned up to a feeling of jealousy and envy—that Sam wished he had Harry's charm and popularity with women. Note that Sam had initially masked this feeling of envy; rather, he had discharged his feelings by expressing disdain, by saying Harry was a phony. This kind of expression is ego-protecting: Because we live in a competitive society, Sam had learned over the years that, if he had admitted to feeling envious, it might have put him "one down" and put Harry "one up." This would have made Sam vulnerable—that is, it would have made him feel weak in relation to Harry. By expressing disdain, however, Sam succeeded in putting *himself* "one up." Although his behavior was successful as an ego-protecting device, it didn't contribute to Sam's understanding of his own feelings and of the kinds of events that caused those feelings; and it certainly didn't contribute to Sam's understanding of Harry or to Harry's understanding of Sam (or, for that matter, to Harry's understanding of himself). In short, Sam was communicating ineffectively. As an ego-defensive measure, his behavior was adaptive; as a form of communication, it was extremely maladaptive. Thus, although it made Sam vulnerable to admit he envied Harry, it opened the door to communication; eventually, it helped them to understand each other. Moreover, a few other men also admitted they felt some jealousy about Harry's behavior with women. This was useful information for Harry, in that it enabled him to understand the effects his behavior had on other men.

As we know, Harry has several options: He can continue to behave as he always has and let other people continue to be jealous and perhaps express their jealousy in terms of hostility, or he can modify his behavior in any one of a number of ways in order to cause other people (and ultimately, himself) less difficulty. *The decision is his.* Should he decide that his "enviable" behavior is too important to give up, he has still gained from his encounter with Sam in the T-group. Specifically, if a similar situation occurs in the real world, Harry, who now knows the effect his behavior may have on other men, will not be surprised by their responses, will be more understanding, will be less likely to overreact, and so forth.

But who needs a group? Couldn't Sam and Harry have done just as well by themselves? No. First of all, they probably would not have discussed the issue directly. Sam would either have avoided Harry or he would have found some covert way of punishing him for being attractive to women. If Sam did confront Harry directly by calling him a phony, they almost certainly would have ended simply by calling each other names, hurting each other's feelings, and making each other angry in much the same fashion Alice and Phil did in the example at the opening of this chapter. It is not easy to talk straight. But suppose they had the benefit of a trained counselor in human relations—wouldn't that be as good as a group? Probably not. One of the great advantages and excitements about the T-group is that we don't deal with expert opinion (in the traditional sense). Rather, each person is considered an expert on his or her own feelings. By sharing their feelings, the other members of the group can be enormously helpful to Sam and Harry. Specifically, the other group members contributed to the data Harry was gathering by expressing their own feelings about Harry's behavior.

Indeed, if the other members of the group do not spontaneously express their feelings, the group leader might specifically ask them to do so. Why is this important? Let's take two opposite cases. First, let us assume that Sam was the only person in the room who felt envious. In that case, it would have been relatively safe to conclude that the situation was largely Sam's problem, and he could then work on it. Sam would have gained the understanding that he is inordinately jealous or envious of people who do particular things, as evidenced by the fact no one else experienced such feelings toward Harry. On the other hand, if it came out (as it did in reality) that several people also felt envious of Harry, it would be clear the problem was one that Harry himself might want to face up to.

This is another reason why it is important for the group that each member be honest and open in expressing feelings. If all the members of the group actually experienced envy of Harry, but (out of kindness, or fear, or shyness) none of them admitted it, then it would have left Sam with the feeling that he was an extraordinarily envious person. If, on the other hand, very few of the other members felt this envy, but they wanted to support Sam and did so by claiming this feeling of enviousness, then this would have left Harry with the erroneous belief that his behavior was causing a lot of negative feelings in other people. It would also leave Sam with the erroneous belief that his behavior was not extraordinary. Thus, a desire to protect Sam would certainly not be doing him any good—it would be protecting him from an understanding of himself.

Of course, the preceding example was a relatively easy one to deal with. It ended with Sam feeling envy for Harry—which is, in fact, a form of admiration. But what if Sam hates Harry—should he express his hatred? What if Sam believes that Harry is an evil person—should he express that belief? Here again, we can see the difference between a feeling and an evaluation. It would be useful if Sam would express the feelings underlying his judgments and evaluations. Did Harry do something that hurt Sam and made him angry? Is this why Sam hates Harry and thinks he's an evil person? Sam will not get very far by discussing Harry's evilness. *Sam:* "I hate you, Harry; you are evil." *Harry:* "No I'm not." *Sam:* "Well, that is the way I see it; I'm just giving you feedback like we're supposed to do in here." *Harry:* "That's your problem—besides, you're not so great yourself." By calling Harry names, Sam sets up the situation in a way that invites Harry to defend himself and to counterattack rather than to listen. But if Sam were to lead with his own feelings ("I am hurt and angry"), it would invite Harry into a discussion about what he (Harry) did to hurt and anger Sam. This is not to say that it is pleasant to hear someone say he is angry at us or hurt by us—it's not. But it helps us to pay attention and to try to deal with the problem at hand.

Why is it tempting for Sam to call Harry evil rather than to talk about his own hurt? The reasons for this behavior should be clear by now. Being hurt puts us "one down"—it makes us vulnerable. In this society, we tend to glide through life protecting ourselves; in effect, each of us wears a suit of behavioral armor, so that other people can't hurt us. This results in a lot of inauthentic behavior—that is, we mask our true feelings from other people. This is often accomplished through the process of short-circuiting. Sometimes, we are so successful at it that we mask our feelings from ourselves as well.

In summary, then, feedback expressed in terms of feelings is a lot easier for the recipient to listen to and deal with than feedback in the form of judgments and evaluations. This is true for two major reasons: First, a person's opinions and judgments about another person are purely a matter of conjecture. Thus, Sam's opinions about Harry being a phony and about Harry being an evil person may reflect reality, or they may, just as likely, not—they are merely Sam's theories about Harry. Only Harry knows for sure whether he's being a phony: Sam is only guessing. But Sam's statement that he is feeling envious or angry is not a guess or a theory—it is an absolute fact. Sam is not guessing about his feelings—he knows them; indeed, he is the only person in the world who knows them for sure. Harry may or may not care about Sam's intellectual theories or pontifical judgments, but, if he is desirous of interacting with Sam, he is probably very interested in knowing about Sam's feelings and what role he (Harry) plays in triggering those feelings.

The second major reason why feedback expressed in terms of feelings is preferable to feedback expressed in terms of judgments is that, when Sam states an opinion or a judgment about Harry, he is saying something about Harry only, but when he states a *feeling* evoked by Harry's behavior, he is revealing something about himself as well. Indeed, in this instance, Sam's primary statement *is* about himself. Thus, the statement of feeling is a gift. Metaphorically, it is Sam opening the door to his home and letting Harry in. When Sam states a judgment about Harry, however, he is storming Harry's barricades and accusing him or something on the basis of inadequate evidence. Harry has good reason to resist this, because Sam has no right to be in his home without an invitation. Harry can let him in by telling him what his feelings are; likewise, Sam can let Harry in by telling him what *his* feelings are.[4]

Feelings and Intentions. Frequently, in our everyday life, one person will say or do something that hurts another. If the recipient (R) *does* get to the point of expressing his hurt, the person (P) may insist that hurting wasn't her intention. It is important that P expresses her intention, but it is even more important to move beyond it. If P says, "Oh, I'm sorry, I didn't mean to hurt you—I really like you," and R answers by saying, "Oh, that's fine, I feel better about it now," that may smooth things over and make things tolerable. Much of the time, all we are after is interpersonal relations that are tolerable. But, ultimately, we want more than that—we want to learn something about ourselves and the other person. We accomplish this by moving beyond our tendency to cover over events such as this—by moving toward an exploration of the process: "Why is it I hurt people when I don't intend to?" or "Why am I so easily hurt?"

If P does not *intend* to hurt R, there is often a tendency for her to deny the legitimacy of R's hurt, saying, in effect, "What right do you have to be hurt, now that you know I didn't intend to hurt you?" Again, this kind of attitude neither increases P's learning nor helps R feel cared for. If I spilled a cup of hot tea on my friend's lap, the fact that I did not intend to hurt him does not completely remove the hurt. I may want to reach out to my friend and express concern that he's hurt—and then examine my own clumsiness to try to learn from it so that the probability of my doing it in the future will be reduced. At the same time, it may be that the tea wasn't all that hot. Perhaps my friend has a tendency to overreact to minor events. As we have seen, the exploration of the nuances of such an apparently simple interaction can be extremely difficult. But in a T-group, people can learn the basic skills required and apply them outside the group. In a T-group, the other members may be useful in helping my friend and me explore the dynamics of this complex relationship—not to decide who is right and who is wrong, but to help us understand ourselves, each other, and the nature of our relationship. In a T-group, people do not attempt to decide who is right and who is wrong; rather, an attempt is made to determine what can be learned. If a person is misunderstood, it is not enough for him to sulk and say, "Alas, nobody understands me." It is far more productive if he tries to find out why it is that people don't understand him and what he can do to increase the probability that he will be understood in the future. In order to accomplish this, each individual must assume some part of the responsibility for what happens to him or her.

The Role of the Group Leader

The leader* or "trainer" of a T-group is neither therapist nor teacher. Typically, group leaders do not offer depth interpretations of the behavior of the members of the group, nor do they spend much time in delivering lectures to the participants. They are, first and foremost, members of the group they are leading. That means that, as group leader, my feelings are as much a part of the group process as the feelings of any other member of the group. I do not hold myself aloof from the group, and my feelings are not hidden from the group. Unlike most therapists, I am not in an asymmetrical relationship to the group, doing all the listening and none of the disclosing. As a member, it is also appropriate for me to receive feedback from the participants. This can be an extremely important function, for the manner in which I give and receive feedback serves as a model for the other participants. If I give feedback openly and without evaluation and receive feedback without being defensive, my group will learn more quickly and thoroughly than otherwise.

But, of course, I am also a professional who has had more experience in such matters than the other participants; although

*In this section, my aim was to describe the behavior of a typical group leader—but alas, there is no such animal. There is a wide range of acceptable behavior, and there are a great many stylistic differences among competent group leaders. Accordingly, I find that I must settle for a description of my own behavior while leading a group. I hasten to add that my style is anything but idiosyncratic—indeed, during the past 15 years, I have benefited greatly from having collaborated with many gifted co-leaders who will recognize aspects of their style and philosophy throughout this section. These include Vera Aronson, Jev Sikes, Michael Kahn, David Bradford, Mathew Snapp, and the late Ann Dreyfus.

I will disclose my own feelings, I do other things as well. I may underscore what is going on so that important events do not slide by. I may occasionally make a "group-level" intervention, describing where the group seems to be headed in terms of its own dynamics. I will help individuals work through their encounters, helping the participants to discuss their feelings (rather than their judgments), until such time as the group members themselves learn to do this for one another. Again, this learning is facilitated by the way I discuss my own feelings. I also lend support to those group members who are taking risks and making themselves vulnerable, until the participants learn to support one another. This is an extremely important function of the leader. It is through the leader's attitude and behavior that a general atmosphere of caring and supportiveness develops. Thus, a well-run T-group is not run in an atmosphere of tugging and shouting (as is frequently implied by the mass media); rather, it is led in a highly democratic manner where people are encouraged to proceed at their own pace, where a member's reluctance to go along with the group is supported by the leader, where attempts at coercion are dealt with openly and fairly. Indeed, it is the climate of safety (created by the leader) that makes it possible for the participants to try things out, risk making themselves vulnerable (if they so choose), and, ultimately, learn about themselves.

This does not mean the leader is wishy-washy or bland. As a leader, I will express a wide range of emotions—including anger, fear, warmth, and envy—if I experience them in the course of the group sessions. The leader's ability to express anger as well as warmth helps establish an atmosphere of authenticity as well as safety in the group.

The leader's job is not to protect participants from experience. At the same time the leader has a responsibility to intervene if someone is being made the scapegoat, bullied, coerced, or unfairly criticized. For example, when Sam called Harry a phony, Harry was left in a very difficult and painful position. He was being attacked, but he didn't know what he had done to elicit the attack and Sam wasn't about to tell him. What could Harry do? Recall that I intervened by taking the spotlight (momentarily) off of Harry and focusing it on Sam, where it properly belonged. This intervention served to protect Harry from the pain and embarrassment of an unjust attack without protecting him from learning something important from Sam, once Sam was able to rephrase his statement in a fair and useful manner. It is this kind of intervention that helps create a feeling of psychological safety: The group learned that none of them would be subjected to an ambush. At the same time, Sam (who did the ambushing!) was not punished or humiliated for his action. Rather, he was gently (but *persistently*) helped to encounter Harry in a fair and authentic manner. Thus, confrontation was not discouraged—only attack was discouraged.

There are some situations in which it is imperative, in my opinion, for a leader to intervene (as in the above example). But the leader should not do all the work: Maximal learning occurs when the group eventually learns to do its own work. Thus, from the leader's perspective, in many situations, an act of nonintervention can be more helpful than an act of intervention—no matter how "brilliant" that act of intervention might be. While experience helps the leader decide when and how to intervene in a variety of situations, it also helps the leader to determine when *not* to intervene. Thus, during a confrontation, two or more participants might become entangled in a communication which seems at an impasse. It is natural for them to look to the leader for help. But, if the group is far enough along, the leader will be well advised *not* to intervene—for the ultimate goal of experiential learning of this sort is for the participants to learn to disentangle their own communications, so they can apply this skill outside the group without the aid of a facilitator.

Although not a therapist, the leader is in a unique and powerful position in the group. This means she sometimes must use caution, lest she have *too much* impact on the group members. For example, even when an event produces strong feelings in the leader, she will be wise to delay expressing those feelings until after others have had the opportunity to express theirs. Otherwise, participants whose feelings differ from the leader's might hesitate to express "dissenting" emotions. In addition, because of the role and power of the leader, it is likely that some members of the group will be reminded of their relations with other powerful figures in their lives; given the permissive atmosphere of the group, they may choose the leader as the target of some of their hostile feelings toward others as the target of some of their hostile feelings toward others in positions of authority. Frequently, this takes the form of an attack on the leader which is not justified on the basis of his or her behavior. A skillful leader will not be too quick to disclaim responsibility. It frequently is useful to allow events to unfold before exploring with the group and with the particular member the extent to which the leader's behavior may have elicited the hostility and the extent to which the hostility may have been a response to the leader's role. In any event, leaders must learn to come to terms with their own power; it is tempting to ignore it or to pretend it isn't there, but such a pretense is always dysfunctional.

The Application of T-group Learning to the World Outside

Throughout this chapter, we have made a distinction between the T-group and the "real world." This can be misleading. In most respects, the T-group is a real-world situation. The people in these groups do not play games with each other; their interactions are real, their emotions are real, the difficulties they get into with other people are real. There is one major difference between human interactions in the T-group and human interactions elsewhere. In the T-group, a norm of openness is quickly established; accordingly, the participants are oriented toward making themselves vulnerable and learn *not* to take advantage of one another's vulnerability. This is not true outside the T-group; we cannot expect others to express the kinds of feelings that would make them vulnerable, nor can we be certain that others will not take advantage of our vulnerability. For this reason, I consider the T-group to be the safest social environment on earth. My ultimate goal is to try to make more of my social environments approach the safety of a competently led T-group.

Let me illustrate: When two or more people are engaged in some sort of relationship, whether in a T-group or in the outside world, they usually have some feelings about each other.

If these feelings are not understood, they can get in the way of the task at hand. But let us take the situation outside the T-group: Suppose you and I are members of a six-member committee to raise funds for underprivileged children. Suppose you are intelligent, creative, athletic, wealthy, and personable. I'm feeling competitive with you; I want the other committee members to like and admire me more than they like and admire you. Because of those feelings, if you propose an idea for raising funds, I might be prone to find fault with it, to ridicule it, to argue it down, even if it's a good idea—*especially* if it's a good idea.

But suppose I have had some experience in a T-group. How does that help me? Would I immediately stand up, cross over to where you are sitting, put my hand on your shoulder and say, "I'm feeling jealous and competitive; but you have great ideas and are a terrific guy—I want to support your ideas"? I doubt it. First of all, I'd be frightened to do that. Because we are not in the relatively protected environment of a T-group, you may not be inclined to interact according to the norm of openness. Left vulnerable by my confession, I am an easy target should you decide to take advantage of my position and put me down. There is no group of people to rally around us and help us work through our confrontation. There isn't an experienced leader to intervene in order to help me salvage the pieces of my shattered ego.

Furthermore, because you have not agreed to be in my impromptu T-group, I have no business using my openness as a means of coercing you to make yourself vulnerable to me. If there is one thing that sensitivity training should have taught me, it is to be sensitive to you and your style, so as not to coerce you into being more open that you feel like being. An excellent example of half-baked sensitivity training on the rampage was portrayed in the film *Bob, Carol, Ted and Alice*. In one scene, the heroine, fresh from a weekend encounter and feeling self-righteously open, is about to leave a restaurant when the headwaiter says he hopes she enjoyed the meal. "Do you really mean that?" she asks. This kind of question is boorish in the extreme. It is an apt caricature of half-baked sensitivity training in action.

Well, then, if these specific techniques are not transferable to the outside world, is T-group training of any value? Yes! The important learning is more than mere techniques—and such learning *is* transferable. Specifically, I can apply any insights I may have had about myself in the T-group and any communication skills (talking and listening) I learned in the T-group. To illustrate, let us go back to the committee meeting: When you propose a good idea, I feel awful. I also feel a compulsion to find fault with your idea. But if, in the T-group, I had learned to confront my feelings of envy and competitiveness, I may stop and think about whether your idea was *really* a bad one, or whether I'm just being competitive again. If I can be aware of my jealousy and my need to compete, I have a good chance of being able to curb these feelings and thereby become a more productive committee member. Subsequently, if I get to know you better and begin to trust you, I may decide to share with you (in private) my prior feelings of competitiveness. Perhaps I can do it in a way that will serve to invite you into a closer, more honest relationship, without attempting to *force* you into one. As this develops with more and more of my acquantances, my social environment *does* become increasingly safer, more open, more relaxed, more exciting, and more conducive to learning and growth.

Research on T-Groups: Do They Really Work?

Most people who have participated in a competently conducted T-group *know* that something important happens there. They know it because they have experienced important changes in themselves and have seen others change. Moreover, nearly all T-group leaders can show you a great many letters from "satisfied customers." Carl Rogers, one of the better known group leaders, has published a typical response from a participant.

> I am more open, spontaneous. I express myself more freely. I am more sympathetic, empathetic and tolerant. I am more confident. I am more religious in my own way. My relations with my family, friends, and co-workers are more honest and I express my likes and dislikes and true feelings more openly. I ad-

> mit ignorance more readily. I am more cheerful. I want to help others more.[5]

Although it is encouraging and gratifying to know that individuals feel better about themselves and their relations with others, these spontaneous testimonials do not, of course, constitute scientific data. The problem is that only a small percentage of the participants send spontaneous letters. What about the others? It is possible that little of importance happened to them.

One step beyond examining unsolicited letters, in terms of scientific rigor, is distributing questionnaires. With a questionnaire study, we can get responses from a random sample of participants and not simply from those who choose to write letters. Several studies have been done in which questionnaires were mailed to the individuals after their participation in a T-group. Almost all these studies show that the vast majority of participants feel they've benefited a great deal from their experience. But still, this is not totally satisfying.

What are the specific benefits participants felt they were gaining from their experiences in T-groups? What is the baseline for change? In the absence of specifiable objectives for T-group participants, and without a control condition against which to compare their achievement, it is impossible to get meaningful results about what really happened. These problems were solved nicely in a study by Nancy Adler and Daniel Goleman.[6] These investigators tested the hypothesis that participation in a T-group would be beneficial in helping individuals achieve whatever goals they set for themselves. For example, an individual might want to become less shy and more assertive; would participation in a T-group facilitate this change? The answer appears to be yes. High-school students who participated in a T-group reported making more progress in accomplishing their own goals than those who had not participated in a T-group. While this study is an improvement over many of the earlier studies, it suffers from a major flaw: Somehow, the self-report of a participant does not seem very objective. After all, the "good" outcome reported by a person may be nothing more than a subtle bit of self-deception. The participants spent a lot of time and effort in that group; if the experience was worthless, they would feel absurd. It is always possible they convinced themselves it was an important event, in much the same way the young women did in the initiation experiment that Judson Mills and I conducted (pp. 152–153).

On the other hand, it is not my intention to minimize the importance of people's awareness of their own feelings and their beliefs about the accomplishment of their goals. If people feel better about themselves because they have gone through a T-group, this is not to be brushed off simply because they are not clear about the exact antecedents of this change. Indeed, in my opinion, if just one T-group experience results in a person's feeling more sensitive, more understanding, more tolerant, and all those other things reported by the participant in Carl Rogers' group, then that is ample justification for the existence of T-groups. Moreover, if these effects persist for several months (as reported by most participants), then it is hard to argue against its being a significant event in the individual's life—regardless of whether we, as scientists, fully understand the phenomenon. These two sides of the question do not exclude each other. We humanists can continue to revel in the impact that group experiences have on participants without necessarily denigrating the scientist who is trying to determine whether the effects extend beyond the self-reports of the participants; we scientists can continue to try to find out "if" and "why" in precise ways without disparaging T-groups simply because the phenomenon is difficult to investigate in as precise a manner as we would like.

Why are T-groups so hard to investigate? As we have seen, one reason is the difficulty in measuring whether the participants actually change and benefit from their experience in the groups. After determining that changes do occur, however, the scientist also wants to isolate the exact causes of those changes. But in the T-group, it is difficult for the scientist to control and manipulate the variables that supposedly produce the outcomes. So many things are happening at once in a T-group that, after it is over, it is impossible to know what factors were crucial in making a person feel good. If some of the events in the group had been different, would the same results have occurred? Unless we know for sure "what causes what," the hard-headed scientist might be tempted to control things by having the leader act in a certain way by planting a couple of stooges in a T-group and telling them to behave in a predetermined manner. The scientist could then measure the effects this would have on the other participants. Such a procedure would encompass the controls and the impact that constitute the kind of experiment that has played such a major role in increasing our understanding of the social animal. But this kind of experiment is simply not feasible. The T-group is one of the few sanctuaries of honesty and authenticity left on this planet. The implicit (and often explicit) assumption of the participants is that people are at least *trying* to be honest. For the experimental social psychologist to bring deception into this environment would be a serious violation of this implicit contract.

What we are left with is some kind of compromise. Most of the research done on T-groups lacks the control and precision of the laboratory experiments we've been discussing throughout this volume. It remains difficult to be certain about what causes what. At the same time, after surveying the research literature, I am compelled to draw the conclusion, albeit tentatively, that important changes do take place in T-groups and that these changes are demonstrable beyond the individual's own self-report. In several studies, for example, it has been shown that other people outside of the T-group can see changes in participants that are consistent with the stated goals of the T-group and the individual's own self-report.[7] Basically, here's how these studies were done: An industrial organization allowed a few of its managers to participate in a T-group. Several weeks later, the back-home colleagues of those individuals were asked if they had noticed any changes in their on-the-job behavior. As a control, the same respondents were also asked to rate any changes in the on-the-job behavior of managers who had *not* been in a T-group. By and large, the data show a tendency for managers who had participated in T-groups to be viewed by their associates as having changed more than managers who had not. Specifically, th T-groupers were seen to be more sensitive, to have more communication skills and more leadership skills, and to be more considerate of others. Thus, these effects are not simply a matter of self-deception on the part of the participants; they indicate that real changes occur that can be perceived by other people. These findings are encouraging, but not perfect. It is always possible that some of the raters were aware of which of their colleagues had or had not been to a T-group; if this were true, it could conceivably have influenced their rating. Again, in the natural environment of an industrial organization, it is difficult to eliminate this possibility.[8]

In a different setting, however, an experiment by Jerry Shapiro and Robert Ross[9] indicates that participating in T-groups can have beneficial effects that are noticeable even to observers who are *not* aware of the participants' activity. One-third of the guards at a women's correctional facility participated in groups, meeting twice weekly over three months. Following this experience, not only did the participants report significant increases in self-confidence and enhanced self-esteem, but the inmates (who were unaware of the program) verified these effects, seeing improvements in those guards who participated in the groups while finding that the behavior of the nonparticipating guards had worsened. Moreover, these effects were long lasting; in a follow-up study,[10] Shapiro and Ross found they were still apparent one year later.

Several experiments using a different strategy have yielded interesting and reliable data. For example, Irwin Rubin[11] assessed the effects of a T-group on reducing ethnic prejudice. We have seen that people coming out of a T-group are generally more accepting of themselves and feel more sensitive, more empathetic, more tolerant, and so forth. If this general feeling of self-acceptance, sensitivity, and tolerance is more than an empty self-assessment, it should result in a person's being less prejudiced against minority groups. Rubin simply administered a test designed to measure ethnic prejudice to a large group of people. Half of those people then went through a T-group experience. He then remeasured the ethnic prejudice of all the individuals. Those who had gone through the T-group showed a sharp reduction in ethnic prejudice; those who had not gone through the T-group showed no significant change.

Research has demonstrated that T-groups also can have other beneficial effects. An experiment by Michael Diamond and Jerry Shapiro[12] demonstrated that participants developed a greater *internal locus of control* than subjects in a nonparticipating condition. That is, they came to perceive themselves as having more personal control over the events of their lives. This orientation is associated with a greater willingness to remedy personal problems as well as more self-confidence, insight, and achievement. Further experiments have shown conclusively that, after participating in a sensitivity-training group, people become more hypnotizable.[13] At first glance, it may seem that susceptibility to hypnotism is not a very desirable outcome—but consider what it means: Several researchers have demonstrated that people who are less suspicious and more trusting than others are more easily hypnotized. The fact that participating in a T-group increases the ease with which a person can be hypnotized suggests strongly that T-groups foster a sense of trust in their participants. These are exciting findings for two reasons: (1) generally, it is not easy to help people to learn to trust each other using other techniques; and (2) from a scientific point of view, susceptibility to hypnosis is a very convincing outcome—far more convincing than a person's own self-assessment of his or her increase in trust.

In another experiment, Marvin Dunnette[14] organized and set up ten separate T-groups. Some of these groups were led by well-trained, highly competent leaders; others were led by leaders having only a little prior experience. In addition, three groups of a different sort were set up; these were run as discussion groups in which the participants talked about current events, played games, solved puzzles, and so on. Before the groups started, and again after several sessions, the members were measured for their empathy with other people in their group—specifically, on how well they could predict the preferences of the members of their own group for various activities, occupations, and the like. The members of the T-groups showed a greater increase in empathy than the members of the other groups. Moreover, within the T-groups themselves, the greatest eventual empathy occurred in those groups having the more competent leaders and showing more member interaction.

This last experiment is of interest not only for its results and for its methodological soundness, but, in addition, because it was conducted by an experimenter who was seriously skeptical about

T-groups. Just a year earlier, Marvin Dunnette (along with John Campbell) wrote a highly critical review of research on T-groups. After performing his own experiment, Dunnette wrote:

> These results seem to me to be firm evidence that T-groups may be accomplishing what their advocates claim for them. . . . It appears from these meager but provocative results that T-groups may truly be a medium for getting to know others better—that the Quest for Love may properly be sharpened, focused, and guided by the T-group experience.[15]

What constitutes a Good or a Bad Outcome?

T-groups have been criticized because occasionally, following a group experience, an individual may seek psychological counseling. What does this mean? Is it a good outcome or a bad outcome? It's hard to be certain. It could be the individual was hurt by the T-group experience. It might also indicate that, as a result of the T-group experience, certain emotional problems *that were always there* came into clear focus, and the individual was able to see for the first time the need for therapy. Alternatively, it might mean the group provided the individual with the courage to seek out the therapy that he or she already knew was needed. Or, it might simply mean the person wanted therapy and tried to get it more cheaply in a T-group; when this failed, he or she sought the therapy from a more appropriate source. With this in mind, it is instructive to compare two recent articles on T-groups by psychiatrists. In one, Ralph Cranshaw[16] cited three cases of individuals who needed psychiatric hospitalization following their experiences in sensitivity-training groups. He considered this a tragic outcome, and he laid the blame for it on the groups, implying that the sensitivity-training movement was experimenting irresponsibly with human beings. In another article in the same journal, James Cadden and his associates[17] reported on a sensitivity program for incoming medical students. These investigators found the program had a beneficial effect—it helped some of their students become aware of a need for psychiatric counseling. Moreover, the number of serious psychiatric crises among these students was lower than that for similar groups in previous years. This was attributed to the fact that the T-group enabled the individuals to handle their crises more effectively.

Some Dangers of Group Encounter—Let the Buyer Beware

The dynamics of a T-group are powerful. This means a group encounter can be an exciting, exhilarating, enriching experience in which a great many emotions are felt and in which a lot of learning takes place. But, as with any powerful situation, there are some dangers. Individuals frequently experience anger and frustration, physical or emotional attraction for another member of the group, and intense joy or sadness. These experiences can produce understanding and growth, if they are discussed and worked through. However, if they are ignored or mishandled by the group, they can produce upset, pain, humiliation, and loss of dignity, which could persist long after the group encounter has terminated.

Suppose you are a person who is interested in joining a group. Has the preceding paragraph frightened you? Good! Has it scared you out of considering a group experience? I hope not. The occurrence of serious disturbances in groups run by well-trained professional leaders is extremely small. After a thorough study of groups conducted under the auspices of the National Training Laboratories, Charles Seashore stated: "The incidence of serious stress and mental disturbance during sensitivity training is difficult to measure but it is estimated to be less than one percent of participants and in almost all cases occurs in persons with a history of prior disturbances."[18] More recent studies[19] have found similar results. After extensive research, Cary Cooper concluded that the alarms expressed about the dangers of T-groups have not been verified when subjected to careful scientific scrutiny. In fact, there is evidence that more common experiences, like university examinations, are far more stressful.

The question to be asked is: "How do I maximize the probability of having a good experience and minimize the probability of having a bad one?" Basically, there are two ways: First, make certain you do not join a group unless it is being conducted by a skilled, experienced, competent leader; and second, make certain that the philosophy and techniques of the group are consistent with your own values. I will address the remainder of this section to those readers who are thinking about joining a group. The rest of you can skip to the next section, "The T-group and Empathy Formation."

The Competence of the Trainer. During the sixties and seventies, with the burgeoning of interest in group encounter, the demand for groups exceeded the supply of competent leaders. Into this breech jumped the well-meaning individual who, fresh from an exciting experience as a participant in a T-group, decided to make this experience available to others by becoming a group leader. *Stay Away!* No matter how good their intentions may be, they are almost certainly not equipped to handle a group. The vast majority of "bad trips" we hear and read about have occurred in just such a group. Leading a group is a very subtle business that requires a great deal of training, experience, and sensitivity as well as a strong sense of responsibility. Don't trust it to amateurs! Moreover, even a psychologist with a Ph.D., licensed and accredited to do therapy, may not be an appropriate group leader if he or she has not had the requisite training. There are a few centers in the country that offer training and internships in group leadership to qualified individuals. The most well established is the National Training Laboratory (NTL) in Washington, D. C. They have an extensive and rigorous screening and evaluation system. This minimizes the possibility of finding an incompetent leader in a workshop sponsored by NTL.

Types of Groups. In this chapter, we have been describing relatively conservative groups—groups in which there is maximum freedom, minimum coercion, and few "far-out" procedures. This happens to be the kind of group I am most comfortable with. It also produces the greatest positive outcome and the lowest risk.[20] But, as we have indicated, there are all kinds of groups. Let's look at a couple of extreme examples. Some groups are conducted in the nude. A lot of learning can take place in such a group—for example, people have a chance to overcome excessive modesty, hang-ups about their bodies, and so on. It *can* be a freeing experience. But if *you* don't feel ready for such an experience, you should make certain you don't wander into this kind of group by accident. There are also groups in which a great deal of screaming, yelling, and physical pushing and shoving is encouraged. This may have some value for some people; if you're *not* one of these people, however, you shouldn't stumble into such a group. In short, you should do everything you can to inform yourself of the nature of the group before agreeing to participate.

In general, you might want to steer clear of groups that do not allow you to say "no." As Michael Kahn[21] puts it, no one should be forced to do something that he or she does not want to do. Indeed, in a study of outcomes of encounter groups, Morton Lieberman and his associates[22] found that groups conducted by coercive, forceful leaders have a tendency to produce more casualties than other kinds of groups. They produce less long-term learning as well. Often a forceful, dynamic, coercive leader can "make things happen," and, by so doing, can produce temporary "highs" in some of the participants. But the ultimate goal of a group is not to get "high" but to learn some things about group dynamics and about oneself that can be important outside of the group situation. And learning is most likely to occur if the individual participant takes the initiative without the stage managership of an overly active, coercive trainer. Lieberman and his colleagues also found that the groups producing the most enduring positive outcomes were those conducted by leaders who were competent, supportive, and charismatic without being coercive or domineering.

In his analysis of the T-group, Kahn makes the point that coercion can be subtle—it need not be a function of a forceful leader but can be a norm that develops gradually and undramatically within the group itself. He therefore suggests that the word *no* should be actively supported by the leader—in this way, the freedom *not* to comply becomes the norm. This does not mean it's always good for group members to avoid situations that look frightening or painful—sometimes, important growth is possible in those situations—but the individual should be the one to make the decision. A person should be encouraged to try only when that person feels ready—and equally encouraged to decline if the feeling of readiness is not present. Growth is an exciting (and often painful) experience—but no one person can "grow" another. Individuals indicate they are ready to grow when they take that first step *on their own*, and not because they are coerced.

The T-Group and Empathy Formation

In the chapters devoted to aggression and prejudice, the point was made that it is a lot easier for us to hurt or kill other people if we have succeeded in dehumanizing them. When we think of South Vietnamese peasants as "gooks," we feel less guilty about putting the torch to their houses or killing their children. When we think of a police officer as a "pig" or a student as a "long-haired weirdo," it keeps *us* from hurting as we proceed to hurt them. One of the most exciting aspects of T-groups is the potential to reverse this process. Indeed, this potential was demonstrated to be a reality following a tense period of confrontation between police and students on the Stanford University campus in 1970. After the invasion of Cambodia sparked demonstrations at colleges across the United States—including the tragedy at Kent State—Stanford suffered the worst disorder in its history. Following a week of violent clashes, both the police and the students harbored intense feelings against each other, which threatened to erupt into renewed violence. At that point, a "Police-Student Depolarization" program was initiated, which involved small groups of police and students meeting together for T-group sessions, police-student dinners, or students riding along in squad cars accompanying police officers on routine duties. As the research we have discussed in this chapter indicates, when individuals are in a situation in which they are talking straight and listening to each other, they begin to gain mutual understanding. Police officers and students who participated in the communication activities exhibited less polarized attitudes, and more willingness to interact with each other nonviolently, with those participating in the T-group exercises showing the greatest changes.[23]

It should be emphasized that I am not suggesting that people use T-groups as a way of obscuring important political or ideological differences or as a way of preventing people from speaking out forcefully and emphatically when faced with a situation that appears unjust or stupid. What I *am* suggesting is that not only are violence and name-calling unnecessary, they often are counterproductive in that they lead to greater violence, a movement away from problem solving, and a decrease in mutual understanding. Increasing understanding does not always lead to agreement: The police officers and students still had *different* attitudes, though they were less extreme than before their meetings. Similarly, understanding does not always lead to attraction: I may understand you and decide you are not *my kind* of person, but I would have difficulty concluding you are not *a person*. Accordingly, I might choose not to be your friend or never to associate with you, but it would be very difficult for me to choose to hurt you without anticipating a great deal of guilt and emotional pain.

In my experience with groups, I have seen this happen on countless occasions. I have seen blacks and whites (or members of the Establishment and rebellious youngsters) enter with some sullen suspicion, gradually bring some of their feelings of animosity and distrust out in the open, and occasionally yell at each other in exasperation, frustration, and anger. But, in almost all cases, they eventually began to listen to each other and to process their own feelings honestly and openly. Rarely did they end up by flinging themselves into each other's arms; but rarely did they leave without a major increase in their awareness of the other person *as a person*. At the beginning of this chapter, I said that T-groups were not the panacea that their extreme advocates occasionally make them out to be. I repeat that statement here: T-groups are not going to save the world. But, when properly used, they offer a viable technique for increasing self-awareness and promoting understanding among people.

E
F
A
B
G
H
C
D

9

Social Psychology as a Science

The distinguished Soviet psychologist Pavel Semenov once observed that humans satisfy their hunger for knowledge in two ways: (1) they observe their environment and try to organize the unknown in a sensible and meaningful way (this is science); and (2) they reorganize the known environment in order to create something new (this is art). From my own experience, I would add the observation that in social psychology, the two are often blended: The experimentalist uses art to enrich science. In this chapter, I will try to communicate how this happens.

In Chapter 2, I described an incident at Yosemite National Park. Briefly, what happened was this: When awakened by sounds of distress, a great many campers rushed to the aid of

Many of the ideas contained in this chapter first saw the light of day several years ago in an article I wrote for *The Handbook of Social Psychology* in collaboration with J. Merrill Carlsmith. I am pleased to acknowledge Dr. Carlsmith's important contribution to my thinking on this topic.

the person who needed help. Because the behavior of these campers was decidedly different from the behavior of witnesses to the Genovese murder (thirty-eight people watched a woman being stabbed to death without attempting to help in any way), I speculated about what may have caused this difference in behavior in the two situations. But no matter how clever and adroit my speculations might have been, no amount of thinking and cognition could make us certain these speculations were correct. There are literally dozens of differences between the Yosemite campground situation and the Genovese murder case. How can we be certain that the factor I mentioned constitutes a crucial difference—the difference that made the difference?

We ran into a similar problem in Chapter 7. In that chapter, we mentioned the almost unbelievable fact that, while John Kennedy was president, his personal popularity increased immediately after he committed a great blunder. After Kennedy's tragic miscalculation known as the Bay of Pigs fiasco, a Gallup poll showed people liked him better than they had just before that incident. We speculated about what could have caused that shift toward greater popularity, suggesting that committing a blunder might have made Kennedy seem more human, thus making people feel closer to him. But, because there were many factors involved in Kennedy's behavior, it was impossible to be certain my speculation was accurate. In order to get some definitive evidence supporting the proposition that blunders can humanize people who appear to be perfect, it was necessary to go beyond observation. We had to design an experiment that allowed us to control for extraneous variables and test the effects of a blunder on attraction in a less complex situation.

This is why social psychologists perform experiments. Although some experiments in social psychology are exciting and interesting in form and content, the process of designing and conducting experiments in social psychology is not fun and games. It is time-consuming and laborious work, and it almost always puts the experimenter in an ethical bind. Moreover, in striving for control, the experimenter must often bring her ideas into the laboratory; this tyipcally entails concocting a situation bearing little resemblance to the real-world situation that originally inspired the idea. In fact, a frequent criticism is that laboratory experiments are unrealistic and contrived imitations of human interaction that don't reflect the "real world" at all. But is this true?

Perhaps the best way to answer this question is to examine one laboratory experiment closely, considering its advantages and disadvantages, as well as an alternative, more realistic approach that might have been used to study the same issue. The initiation experiment I performed in collaboration with Judson Mills[1] suits our purpose. The reader may recall that, in this experiment, we showed that people who expended great effort (by undergoing a severe initiation) to gain membership into a group liked the group more than did people who became members with little or no effort.

Here's how the experiment was performed: Sixty-three college women who initially volunteered to participate in several discussions on the psychology of sex were subjects of the study. Each student was tested individually. At the beginning of the study, I explained that I was studying the "dynamics of the group-discussion process." I said the actual topic of the discussion was not important to me, but, because most people are interested in sex, I selected that topic in order to be certain of having plenty of participants. I also explained I had encountered a major drawback in choosing sex as the topic: Specifically, because of shyness, many people found it difficult to discuss sex in a group setting. Because any impediment to the flow of the discussion could seriously invalidate the results, I needed to know if the subjects felt any hesitancy to enter a discussion about sex. When the subjects heard this, each and every one indicated she would have no difficulty. These elaborate instructions were used to set the stage for the important event to follow. The reader should note how the experimenter's statements tend to make the following material believable.

Up to this point, the instructions had been the same for each subject. Now it was time to give each of the people in the various experimental conditions a different experience—an experience the experimenters believed would make a difference. This is called the *independent variable.*

Subjects were randomly assigned in advance to one of three conditions: (1) one-third of them would go through a severe initiation, (2) one-third of them would go through a mild initiation, and (3) one-third would not go through any initiation at all. For the no-initiation condition, subjects were simply told they could now join the discussion group. For the severe and mild-initiation conditions, however, I told each subject that, because it was necessary to be positive she could discuss sex openly, I had developed a screening device, a test for embarrassment, which I then asked her to take. This test constituted the initiation. For the severe-initiation condition, the test was highly embarrassing. It required the subject to recite, in my presence, a list of twelve obscene words and two detailed descriptions of sexual activity taken from current novels. (This may not seem terribly embarrassing to today's reader, but remember, this was in 1959!) The mild-initiation subjects had only to recite a list of words related to sex that were not obscene.

After the initiation, each subject was allowed to eavesdrop on a group discussion being conducted by members of the group she had just joined. In order to control the content of this material, a tape recording was used; but the subjects were led to believe it was a live discussion. Thus, all subjects—regardless of whether they had gone through a severe initiation, a mild initiation, or no initiation—listened to the same group discussion. The group discussion was about as dull and as boring as possible; it involved a halting, inarticulate analysis of the secondary sex characteristics of lower animals—changes in plumage among birds, intricacies of the mating dance of certain spiders, and the like. The tape contained long pauses, a great deal of hemming and hawing, interruptions, incomplete sentences, and so on, all designed to make it boring.

At the end of the discussion, I returned with a set of rating scales and asked the subject to rate how interesting and worthwhile the discussion had been. This is called the *dependent variable,* because, quite literally, the response is assumed to be "dependent" on which of the experimental conditions the subject had been assigned to.

The results supported the hypothesis: Women who went through a mild initiation, or no initiation at all, saw the group discussion as relatively dull. But those who suffered in order to be admitted to the group thought it was really an exciting discussion. Remember, all the students were rating *exactly the same discussion*.

Judson Mills and I spent several hundred hours designing

this experiment, creating a credible situation, writing a script for the tape recording of the group discussion, rehearsing the actors who played the roles of group members, constructing the initiation procedures and the measuring instruments, recruiting volunteers to serve as subjects, pilot-testing the procedure, running the subjects through the experiment, and explaining the true purpose of the experiment to each subject (the reason for the deception, what it all meant, and so forth). What we found was that people who go through a severe initiation in order to gain entry into a group tend to like that group better than people who go through a mild initiation (or no initiation at all). Surely there must be a simpler way! The reader may have noticed a vague resemblance between the procedure used by Mills and me and other initiations, such as those used by primitive tribes and those used by some college fraternities and other exclusive clubs or organizations. Why, then, didn't Judson Mills and I take advantage of the real-life situation, which is not only easier to study but also far more dramatic and realistic? Let's look at the advantages. Real-life initiations would be more severe (that is, they would have more impact on the members); we would not have had to go to such lengths to design a group setting the participants would find convincing; the social interactions would involve real people, rather than mere voices from a tape recording; we would have eliminated the ethical problem created by the use of deception and the use of a difficult and unpleasant experience in the name of science; and, finally, it could all have been accomplished in a fraction of the time the experiment consumed.

Thus, when we take a superficial look at the advantages of a natural situation, it appears Mills and I would have had a much simpler job if we had studied existing fraternities. Here is how we might have done it. We could have rated each group's initiation for severity and later interviewed the members to determine how much they liked their group. If the members who had undergone a severe initiation liked their fraternities more than the mild- or no-initiation fraternity members, the hypothesis would be supported. Or would it? Let's take a closer look at why people bother to do experiments.

If we were to ask people to name the most important characteristic of a laboratory experiment, the great majority would say "control." And this *is* a major advantage. Experiments have the advantage of controlling the environment and the variables so the effects of each variable can be precisely studied. By taking our hypothesis to the laboratory, Mills and I eliminated a lot of the extraneous variation that exists in the real world. The severe initiations were all equal in intensity; this condition would have been difficult to match if we had used several "severe-initiation" fraternities. Further, the group discussion was identical for all subjects; in the real world, however, fraternity members would have been rating fraternities that were, in fact, different from each other. Assuming we had been able to find a difference between the "severe-initiation" fraternities and the "mild-initiation" fraternities, how would we have known whether this was a function of the initiation rather than of the differential likableness that already existed in the fraternity members themselves? In the experiment, the *only* difference was the severity of the initiation, so we know that any difference was due to that procedure.

The Importance of Random Assignment

Control *is* a very important aspect of the laboratory experiment, but it is not the major advantage of this procedure. A still more important advantage is that subjects can be randomly assigned to the different experimental conditions. This means that each subject has an equal chance to be in any condition in the study. Indeed, the random assignment of subjects to conditions is the crucial difference between the experimental method and nonexperimental approaches. And the great advantage of the random assignment of people to conditions is this: Any variables not thoroughly controlled are, in theory, distributed randomly across the conditions. This means it is extremely unlikely such variables would affect our results in a systematic fashion. An example might help to clarify this point: Suppose you are a scientist and you have the hypothesis that marrying intelligent women makes men happy. How do you test this hypothesis? Let us say you proceed to find a thousand men who are married to intelligent women and a thousand men who are married to not so intelligent women, and you give them all a "happiness" questionnaire. Lo and behold, the men married to intelligent women *are* happier than the men married to less intelligent women. Does this mean being married to an intelligent woman makes men happy? No. Perhaps happy men are sweeter, more good-humored, and easier to get along with, and that, consequently, intelligent women seek these men out and marry them. So it may be that being happy *causes* men to marry intelligent women. The problem doesn't end there. It is also possible there is some third factor that causes *both* happiness *and* being married to an intelligent woman. One such factor could be money: It is conceivable that being rich helps make men happy and that their being rich is what attracts the intelligent women. So it is possible that neither causal sequence is true—it is possible that happiness does not cause men to marry intelligent women and that intelligent women do not cause men to be happy.

The problem is even *more* complicated. It is more complicated because we usually have no idea what these third factors might be. In the case of the happiness study, it could be wealth; it could also be that a mature personality causes men to be happy and also attracts intelligent women; it could be social grace, athletic ability, power, popularity, using the right toothpaste, being a snappy dresser, or any of a thousand qualities the poor researcher does not know about and could not possibly account for. But if the researcher performs an experiment, he or she can randomly assign subjects to various experimental conditions. Although this procedure does not eliminate differences due to any of these variables (money, social grace, athletic ability, and the like), it neutralizes them by distributing these characteristics *randomly* across various experimental conditions. That is, if subjects are randomly assigned to experimental conditions, there will be approximately as many rich men in one condition as in the others, as many socially adept men in one condition as in the others, and as many athletes in one condition as in the others. Thus, if we do find a difference between conditions, it is unlikely this would be due to individual differences in any single characteristic, because *all* of these characteristics had equal (or nearly equal) distribution across all of the conditions.

Admittedly, the particular example of happy men and their

intelligent wives does not easily lend itself to the confines of the experimental laboratory. But let us fantasize about how we would do it if we could. Ideally, we would take fifty men and randomly assign twenty-five to intelligent wives and twenty-five to less intelligent wives. A few months later, we could come back and administer the happiness questionnaire. If the men assigned to the intelligent wives are happier than the men assigned to the less intelligent wives, we would know what caused their happiness—*we* did! In short, their happiness couldn't easily be attributed to social grace, or handsomeness, or money, or power—these were randomly distributed among the experimental conditions. It almost certainly was caused by their wives' characteristics.

To repeat, this example is somewhat fantastic—even social psychologists must stop short of arranging marriages for scientific purposes. But this does *not* mean we cannot test important, meaningful, relevant events under controlled laboratory conditions. This book is loaded with such examples. Let's look at one of these examples as a way of clarifying the advantages of the experimental method. In Chapter 5, I reported a correlation between the amount of time children spend watching violence on television and their tendency to choose aggressive solutions to their problems. Does this mean watching aggression on television causes youngsters to become aggressive? Not necessarily. It might. But it might also mean aggressive youngsters simply like to watch aggression and they would be just as aggressive if they watched "Sesame Street" all day long. But then, as we saw, some experimenters came along and proved that watching violence increases violence.[2] How? By randomly assigning some children to a situation in which they watched an episode of "The Untouchables"—a television series in which people beat, kill, rape, bite, and slug each other for fifty minutes per episode. As a control, the experimenters randomly assigned some other children to a situation in which they watched an athletic event for the same length of time. The crucial point: Each child stood *an equal chance* of being selected to watch "The Untouchables"; therefore, any differences in character structure among the children in this experiment were neutralized across the two experimental conditions. Thus, the finding that youngsters who watched "The Untouchables" showed more aggressiveness afterward than those who watched the athletic event suggests quite strongly that watching violence can lead to violence.

Let us return to the initiation experiment. If we conducted a survey and found that members of severe-initiation fraternities find each other more attractive than do members of mild-initiation fraternities, than we would have evidence that severity of initiation and liking for other members of the fraternity are *positively correlated.* By "positively correlated" we mean that the more severe the initiation, the more a member will like his fraternity brothers. No matter how highly correlated the two variables are, however, we cannot conclude, from our survey data alone, that severe initiations *cause* liking for the group. All we can conclude from such a survey is that these two factors are associated with each other.

It is possible that the positive correlation between severe initiation and liking for other members of a fraternity exists not because severe initiations *cause* members to like their groups more but for just the opposite reason. It could be that high attractiveness for the group causes severe initiations. If group members see themselves as highly desirable, they may try to keep the situation that way by maintaining an elite group. Thus, they might require a severe initiation in order to discourage people from joining, unless those people have a high desire to do so. From our survey data alone, we cannot conclude that this explanation is false and severe initiations really do lead to liking. The data give us no basis for making this choice, because they tell us nothing about cause and effect. Moreover, as we have seen in our previous example, there could be a third variable that causes both severe initiations *and* liking. Who would like to give and receive a severe initiation? Why, people with strong sadomasochistic tendencies, of course. Such people may like each other not because of the initiation but because "birds of a feather" tend to like each other. Although this may sound like an outlandish explanation, it is certainly possible. What is more distressing for the researcher are the countless other explanations he or she can't even think of. The experimental method, based as it is on the technique of random assignment to experimental conditions, eliminates all of these in one fell swoop. The sadomasochists in the experiment have just as much chance of being assigned to the no-initiation condition as to the severe-initiation condition. In the real-world study, alas, most of them would most certainly *assign themselves* to the severe-initiation condition, thus making the results uninterpretable. Sorrow

The Challenge of Experimentation in Social Psychology

Control Versus Impact. All is not so sunny in the world of experimentation. There are some very real problems connected with doing experiments. I mentioned that control is one of the major advantages of the experiment; yet it is impossible to exercise complete control over the environment of human subjects. One of the reasons why many psychologists work with rats, rather than people, is that researchers are able to control almost everything that happens to their subjects from the time of their birth until the experiment ends—climate, diet, exercise, degree of exposure to playmates, absence of traumatic experiences, and so on. Social psychologists do not keep human subjects in cages in order to control their experiences. Although this makes for a happier world for the subjects, it also makes for a slightly sloppy science.

Control is further limited by the fact that individuals differ from one another in countless subtle ways. We try to make statements about what *people* do. By this we mean, of course, what most people do most of the time under a given set of conditions. To the extent that unmeasured individual differences are present in our results, our conclusions may not be precise for all people. Differences in attitudes, values, abilities, personality characteristics, and recent past experiences can affect the way people respond in an experiment. Thus, even with our ability to control the experimental situation itself, the same situation may not affect each person in exactly the same way.

Furthermore, when we do succeed in controlling the experimental setting so it is exactly the same for every person, we run the real risk of making the situation so sterile that the subject is inclined not to take it seriously. The word "sterile" has at least two meanings: (1) germ-free, and (2) ineffective or barren. The experimenter should strive to make the experimental situation as "germ-free" as possible without making it barren or "unlifelike" for the subject. If subjects do not find the events of an experiment interesting and absorbing, chances are their reactions will not be spontaneous and our results, therefore, will have little meaning. Thus, in addition to control, an experiment must have an impact on the subjects. They must take the experiment seriously and become involved in it, lest it not affect their behavior in a meaningful way. The difficulty for social psychologists is that these two crucial factors, impact and control, often work in opposite ways: As one increases, the other tends to decrease. The dilemma facing experimenters is how to maximize impact on the subjects without sacrificing control over the situation. Resolving this dilemma requires considerable creativity and ingenuity in the design and construction of experimental situations. This leads us to the problem of realism.

Realism. Early in this chapter, I mentioned that a frequent criticism of laboratory experiments is that they are artificial and contrived imitations of the world, that they aren't "real." What do we mean by *real?* Several years ago, Merrill Carlsmith and I tried to pinpoint the definition of *real.* We reasoned an experiment can be realistic in two separate ways: If an experiment has an impact on the subjects, forces them to take the matter seriously, and involves them in the procedures, we can say it has achieved *experimental realism.* Quite apart from this is the question of how similar the laboratory experiment is to the events that frequently happen to people in the outside world. This can be termed *mundane realism.* Often, a confusion between experimental realism and mundane realism is responsible for the criticism that experiments are artificial and worthless because they don't reflect the real world.

Perhaps the difference between the two realisms can be illustrated by an example of a study high in experimental realism but low in mundane realism. Recall the experiment by Stanley Milgram[3] discussed in Chapter 2, in which each subject was asked to deliver a series of shocks, of increasing intensity, to another person who was supposedly wired to an electrical apparatus in an adjoining room. Now, honestly, how many times in our everyday life are we asked to deliver electric shocks to people? It's unrealistic—but unrealistic only in the mundane sense. Did the procedure have experimental realism—that is, were the subjects wrapped up in it, did they take it seriously, did it have an impact on them, was it part of *their* real world at that moment? Or were they merely play-acting, not taking it seriously, going through the motions, ho-humming it? Milgram reports his subjects experienced a great deal of tension and discomfort. But I'll let Milgram describe, in his own words, what a typical subject looked like:

> I observed a mature and initially poised businessman enter the laboratory smiling and confident. Within 20 minutes he was reduced to a twitching, stuttering wreck, who was rapidly approaching a point of nervous collapse. He constantly pulled on his earlobe, and twisted his hands. At one point he pushed his fist onto his forehead and muttered: "Oh God, let's stop it." And yet he continued to respond to every word of the experimenter, and obeyed to the end.[4]

This hardly seems like the behavior of a person in an unrealistic situation. The things happening to Milgram's subjects were *real*—even though they didn't happen to them in their everyday existence. Accordingly, it would seem safe to conclude that the results of this experiment are a reasonably accurate indication of the way people would react if a similar set of events *did* occur in the real world.

Deception. The importance of experimental realism can hardly be overemphasized. The best way to achieve this essential quality is to design a setting that will be absorbing and interesting to the subjects. At the same time, it is frequently necessary to disguise the true purpose of the study. This puts the social psychologist in the position of a film director who's setting the stage for action but not telling the actor what the play is all about. Such settings are called *cover stories* and are designed to increase experimental realism by producing a situation in which the subject can act naturally, without being inhibited by knowing just which aspect of behavior is being studied. For example, in the

Aronson-Mills initiation study, subjects were told they were taking a test for embarrassment in order to screen them for membership in a group that would be discussing the psychology of sex—this was the cover story. In reality, they were being subjected to an initiation to see what effect, if any, this would have on their liking for the group. If the subjects had been aware of the true purpose of the study before their participation, the results would have been totally meaningless. Researchers who have studied this issue have shown that, if subjects know the true purpose of an experiment, they do *not* behave naturally but either try to perform in a way that puts themselves in a good light, or try to "help out" the experimenter by behaving in a way that makes the experiment come out as predicted. Both of these outcomes are disastrous for the experimenter. The experimenter can usually succeed in curbing the subject's desire to be "helpful," but the desire to "look good" is more difficult to curb. Most people do not want to be thought of as weak, abnormal, unattractive, stupid, or crazy. Thus, if given a chance to figure out what the experimenter is looking for, most people will try to make themselves look good or "normal." For example, in an experiment designed specifically to elucidate this phenomenon,[5] when we told subjects a particular outcome indicated they possessed a "good" personality trait, they exhibited the behavior necessary to produce that outcome far more often than when we told them it reflected a negative trait. Although this behavior is understandable, it does interfere with meaningful results. For this reason, experimenters find it necessary to deceive subjects about the true nature of the experiment.

To illustrate, let's look again at Solomon Asch's classic experiment on conformity.[6] Recall that, in this study, a student was assigned the task of judging the relative size of a few lines. It was a simple task. But a few other students (who were actually accomplices of the experimenter) purposely stated an incorrect judgment. When faced with this situation, a sizable number of the subjects yielded to the implicit group pressure and stated an incorrect judgment. This was, of course, a highly deceptive experiment. The subjects thought they were participating in an experiment on perception, but, actually, their conformity was being studied. Was this deception necessary? I think so. Let's play it back without the deception: Imagine yourself a subject in an experiment in which the experimenter said, "I am interested in studying whether or not you will conform in the face of group pressure," and then he told you what was going to happen. My guess is you wouldn't conform. My guess is almost *no one* would conform—because conformity is considered a weak and unattractive behavior. What could the experimenter have concluded from this? That people tend to be nonconformists? Such a conclusion would be erroneous and misleading. Such an experiment would be meaningless.

Recall Milgram's experiments on obedience. He found that 62 percent of the average citizens in his experiment were willing to administer intense shocks to another person in obedience to the experimenter's command. Yet, each year, when I describe the experimental situation to the students in my class and ask them if *they* would obey such a command, only one percent indicate they would. Does this mean my students are nicer people than Milgram's subjects? I don't think so. I think it means people, if given half a chance, will try to look good. Thus, unless Milgram had used deception, he would have come out with results that simply do not reflect the way people behave when they are led to believe they are in real situations. If we were to give people the opportunity to sit back, relax, and make a guess as to how they would behave if . . . , we would get a picture of how people would like to be rather than a picture of how people are.

Ethical Problems. Using deception may be the best (and perhaps the *only*) way to get useful information about the way people behave in most complex and important situations, but it *does* present the experimenter with a serious ethical problem. Basically, there are three problems:

1. It is simply unethical to tell lies to people. This takes on even greater significance in the post-Watergate era, when it has been revealed that government agencies have bugged citizens illegally, that presidents tell outright lies to the people who elected them, and that all matter of dirty tricks, fake letters, forged documents, and so on have been used by people directly employed

by the president. Can social scientists justify adding to the pollution of deception that currently exists?
2. Such deception frequently leads to an invasion of privacy. When people serving as subjects do not know what the experimenter is really studying, they are in no position to give their informed consent. For example, in Asch's experiment, it is conceivable some students might not have agreed to participate had they known in advance that Asch was interested in examining their tendency toward conformity rather than their perceptual judgment.
3. Experimental procedures often entail some unpleasant experiences, such as pain, boredom, anxiety, and the like.

Do the ends justify the means? This is a debatable point. Some argue that, no matter what the goals of this science are and no matter what the accomplishments, they are not worth it if people are deceived or put through some discomfort. On the opposite end of the spectrum, others insist that social psychologists are finding things out that may have profound benefits for humankind, and, accordingly, almost any price is worth paying for the results.

My own position is somewhere in between. I believe the science of social psychology is important, and I also believe experimental subjects should be protected at all times. When deciding whether a particular experimental procedure is ethical or not, I believe a cost-benefit analysis is appropriate. That is, how much "good" will derive from doing the experiment and how much "bad" will happen to the experimental subjects? Put another way, the benefits to society are compared with the costs to the subjects, and this ratio is entered into the decision calculus. Unfortunately, such a comparison often is difficult to make because, typically, neither the benefit to society nor the harm to subjects is known or calculable. Furthermore, even the anticipated result of an experiment may alter our evaluation of its ethicality. Would we question the ethics of the Milgram procedure if none of the subjects had administered shocks beyond the "Moderate Shock" level? Apparently not. A recent study[7] found that individuals' ratings of the "harmfulness" of the Milgram procedure varied according to the type of outcome they believed to have happened. That is, individuals who were told that a high proportion of the subjects were obedient rated the procedure as more harmful than individuals who were told that a low proportion were obedient.

Thus my decision to do an experiment depends on the particular costs and benefits associated with the research at hand. There are, however, five guidelines I subscribe to at all times:

1. Procedures that cause intense pain or discomfort should be avoided. If experimenters exercise a great deal of ingenuity and caution, they can usually succeed in testing their hypotheses without using extreme methods. Although a less intense procedure usually produces less clear results, experimenters should choose to sacrifice some clarity in the interests of protecting their subjects.
2. Experimenters should be ever alert to alternative procedures to deception. If some other viable procedure can be found, it should be used.
3. Experimenters should provide their subjects with the real option of quitting the experiment if their discomfort becomes too intense.
4. Experimenters should spend considerable time with each subject at the close of the experimental session, carefully explaining the experiment, its true purpose, the reasons for the deception, and so on. They should go out of their way to protect the dignity of subjects, to avoid making them feel stupid or gullible about having "fallen for" the deception. They should make certain that subjects leave the scene in good spirits—feeling good about themselves and their role in the experiment. This can be accomplished by any earnest experimenter who is willing to take the time and effort to repay each subject (with information and consideration) for the very important role that subject has played in the scientific enterprise.
5. Finally, experimenters should not undertake an experiment that entails deception or discomfort "just for the hell of it." Before entering the laboratory, experimenters should be certain their experiment is sound and important—that they are seeking the answer to an interesting question and seeking it in a careful and well-organized manner.

Most experimenters in social psychology are extremely sensitive to the needs of their subjects. Although many experiments entail procedures that cause some degree of discomfort, the vast majority of these procedures contain many safeguards for the protection of subjects. For example, from the point of view of subject discomfort, most readers would agree that Stanley Milgram's experiment on obedience is one of the most difficult studies reported in this book. There has been considerable debate as to whether or not the experiment should have been conducted. Yet it is evident that Milgram worked hard after the experiment to turn the overall experience into a useful and exciting one for his subjects. It is also clear that his efforts achieved a high degree of success: Several weeks after the experiment, 84 percent of the participants reported they were glad to have taken part in the study; 15 percent reported neutral feelings; and only 1 percent stated they were sorry they had participated. (We should view these findings with caution, however. Our discussion of cognitive dissonance in Chapter 4 has taught us that people sometimes justify their behavior by changing their previously-held attitudes.) More convincing evidence comes from a follow-up study: One year after the experimental program was completed, a university psychiatrist interviewed a sample of the subjects and found no evidence of injurious effects—rather, the typical response was that their participation was instructive and enriching.

The Postexperimental Session. The postexperimental session, sometimes called debriefing, is an extremely important part of the experiment. Not only is it of great value as a means of undoing some of the discomfort and deceptions that occurred during the experimental session, it also gives the experimenter an opportunity to provide additional information about the topic so the experiment can become an educational experience for the participants. In addition, the experimenter can determine the extent to which the procedure worked—and find out from the one person who knows best (the subject) how the procedure might be improved. In short, the prudent experimenter regards subjects as colleagues—not as objects. For those of you who have never had a first-hand experience with a debriefing session, a description of exactly what is involved and how subjects are treated may provide a more complete understanding of the experimental technique.

At first, the experimenter encourages the subject to give his overall reaction to the experiment and to ask any questions to clear up any existing confusion. She then tries to determine why the subject responded as he did and whether he interpreted the procedures the way they were intended. If deception occurred, was the subject suspicious of the cover story? If the subject was suspicious, the experimenter must decide whether his suspicions were great enough to have affected his behavior. If so, then the subject's responses cannot be included in the data of the experiment. Because the experimenter is interested in how subjects spontaneously behave, any responses motivated by suspicions cannot be spontaneous and are most likely invalid. If more than a few subjects must be discarded for reasons of suspiciousness, the entire experiment must be scrapped.

Throughout this first part of the debriefing, the experimenter probes to try to learn as precisely as possible what the subjects' reactions were, and whether they were suspicious. She then informs him of the deception. The pace should be gradual and the manner gentle, so subjects are not suddenly confronted with the information. I can picture Lucy (in the "Peanuts" comic strip) as the world's worst experimenter. How might she break the news to Charlie Brown? "You've been fooled; we've been lying to you and you fell for it—ha! ha!" Clearly, this kind of approach must be avoided.

Every experimenter has his or her own technique for debriefing. I will discuss my own procedure in some detail. I begin by asking subjects whether the experiment was perfectly clear—if they have any questions about either the purpose or the procedure. I usually ask some open-ended questions—for example, I might simply ask them to tell me frankly how the experiment struck them. Because people do react differently, it helps me to know their feelings. I then begin zeroing in by asking the subject if any part of the procedure seemed odd, confusing, or disturbing. If there are any suspicions, they will probably be revealed by this procedure, or at least I will see signs that indicate the need for further probing; but if not, I continue toward greater specificity and ask if he or she thinks there may be more to the experiment than meets the eye. This is a giveaway. It tells the subject, in effect, that there *was* more than met the eye. Many subjects will indicate they do think so. This does not necessarily mean they had strong and definite suspicions; it means, rather, that some people know deception is frequently a part of certain psychology experiments and they are vaguely suspicious that this experiment may have been one of those. My own questioning may have helped confirm these suspicions. It is important to overtly recognize the subject's lack of gullibility. It is also important to communicate that being fooled by the procedure is not a matter of stupidity or gullibility but that it is a function of the procedure—because if it's a good experiment, *virtually everyone* gets fooled. This is crucial: Being "taken in" hurts only if it leads us to conclude we are extraordinarily stupid or gullible. But this is not true with these experiments. If the experiment is a good one, *everyone* will be "taken in." Accordingly, it is imperative that the experimenter take the time and trouble to make this clear to the subject. This one factor is frequently the crucial determinant of whether the subject goes home feeling good or feeling like a fool. Any experimenter who does not take special care with this part of the experiment has no business in a psychological laboratory.

Any subjects who voice specific suspicions are invited to specify how these might have affected their behavior. The answer to this question is crucial. If the subject does have some clear suspicions (right or wrong), and if these might have affected his or her behavior, I will discard the data for that subject. Obviously, this decision is made in ignorance of whether or not the data from this subject supported the hypothesis! If the subjects' suspicions are not on target, I will tell them it was reasonable to be suspicious, that there *is* more to the experiment, and I will then proceed to describe what I am studying and the reasons for using deception. I try to level with subjects by sharing my own discomfort about using deception. I also try hard to explain why I think the results of the experiment might be important.

If an occasional subject is feeling uncomfortable, or angry, or disdainful, I want to know so I can be of assistance. But most subjects are polite. To help subjects build up the courage to tell me off (if they feel like it), I try to share my own questions and criticisms about the procedure and its impact, in the hope of removing any resistance they may feel in talking about their skepticism, their feeling that the whole experiment seemed trivial and meaningless, their annoyance, their discomfort, or the fact the procedure had *more* of an impact on them than I had intended. Subjects are usually eager to help me improve the experiment and frequently have provided me with many valuable suggestions.

To close the session, I ask that subjects try to keep their laboratory experiences secret. If future subjects know the study's purpose in advance, their reactions will be invalid and could lead to our drawing incorrect conclusions about the results. To avoid this waste of time, experimenters need to secure the help of each person participating in the study. I have been successful at maintaining secrecy by emphasizing the great harm that would be done to the scientific community if sophisticated subjects provided me with results that falsely supported my hypothesis.[8]

In this chapter, I have discussed the advantages of the experimental method, and shown how complex and challenging it is to design a laboratory experiment in social psychology. In addition, I have shared some of the excitement I feel in overcoming difficulties and explored the ways I attempt to insure the wellbeing, as well as the learning, of my subjects. Experimental subjects have contributed a great deal to our understanding; we are in their debt. The knowledge, information, and insights described in the first eight chapters of this book are based on the techniques and procedures discussed in this chapter, as well as on the cooperation of our experimental subjects. Ultimately, our understanding of human beings in all their complexity rests on our ingenuity in developing techniques for studying behavior that are well-controlled and impactful without violating the essential dignity of those individuals who contribute to our understanding by serving as experimental subjects.

The Morality of Discovering Unpleasant Things

There is one additional ethical consideration—a rather knotty one: the moral responsibility of the scientist for what he or she discovers. Throughout this book, I have been dealing with some extremely powerful antecedents of persuasion. This was particularly true in Chapter 4, in which I discussed techniques of self-persuasion, and in some of the subsequent chapters, in which I discussed applications of these techniques. Self-persuasion is a powerful force because, in a very real sense, the persuaded never know what hit them. They come to believe that a particular thing is true, not because J. Robert Oppenheimer or T. S. Eliot or Joe "The Shoulder" convinced them it is true, but because they have convinced *themselves* the thing is true. What's more, they frequently do not know why or how they came to believe it. This renders the phenomenon not only powerful but frightening. As long as I know why I came to believe X, I am relatively free to change my mind; but if all I know is that X is true—and that's all there is to it—I am far more likely to cling to that belief, even in the face of a barrage of disconfirming evidence.

The mechanisms I described can be used to get people to brush their teeth, to stop bullying smaller people, to reduce pain, or to love their neighbors. Many people might consider these good outcomes; but they are manipulative just the same. Moreover, the same mechanisms can also be used to get people to buy particular brands of toothpaste and perhaps to vote for particular political candidates. Isn't it immoral to uncover ways of manipulating people?

As the reader of this volume must know by this time, as a real person living in the real world, I have a great many values—and have made no effort to conceal them; they stick out all over the place. For example, I would like to eliminate bigotry and cruelty. If I had the power, I would employ the most humane and effective methods at my disposal in order to achieve those ends. I am equally aware that, once these methods are developed, others might use them to achieve ends I might not agree with. This causes me great concern. I am also aware that you may not share my values—therefore, if you believe these techniques are powerful, *you* should be concerned.

At the same time, I should hasten to point out that the phenomena I have been describing are not new. It was not a social psychologist who got Mr. Landry hooked on Marlboros, and it was not a social psychologist who induced Lt. Calley to wantonly kill Vietnamese civilians. They did what they did on their own. Social psychologists are attempting to understand these phenomena and scores of others that take place in the world every day, phenomena that have been occurring since the first two people on earth began interacting. By understanding these phenomena, the social psychologist may be able to help people refrain from a particular kind of behavior when they themselves decide it is maladaptive.

But the mere fact that we working social psychologists know that the phenomena we are working with are not of our own creation does not free us from moral responsibility. Our research often crystallizes these phenomena into highly structured, easily applicable techniques. There is always the possibility that some individuals may develop these techniques and use them for their own ends. In the hands of a demagogue, these techniques could conceivably turn our society into an Orwellian nightmare. It is not my intention to preach about the responsibilities of social psychologists. What I am most cognizant of are what I believe to be *my own* responsibilities. Briefly, they are to educate the public about how these techniques might be used and to remain vigilant against their abuse as I continue to do research aimed at furthering our understanding of the social animal—how we think and how we behave. Frankly, I can think of no endeavor more interesting or more important.

Notes

Chapter 1. What is Social Psychology?

1. James Michener, *Kent State: What Happened and Why* (New York: Random House, 1971).
2. Kenneth Clark and Mamie Clark, "Racial Identification and Preference in Negro Children," in *Readings in Social Psychology*, ed. T. M. Newcomb and E. L. Hartley (New York: Holt, 1947), pp. 169–178.
3. Jonathan Harris, *Hiroshima: A Study in Science, Politics, and the Ethics of War* (Menlo Park, Calif.: Addison-Wesley, 1970).
4. Michener, *op. cit.*
5. Ellen Berscheid; personal communication.
6. Philip Zimbardo, *The Psychological Power and Pathology of Imprisonment* (a statement prepared for the U. S. House of Representatives Committee on the Judiciary; Subcommittee No.

3: Hearings on Prison Reform, San Francisco, Calif., October 25, 1971), p. 3.

Chapter 2. Conformity

1. Copyright © 1933, 1961 by James Thurber. From "The Day the Dam Broke," in *My Life and Hard Times* (New York: Harper, 1933), pp. 41, 47. (Originally printed in *The New Yorker*.)
2. Stanley Schachter, "Deviation, Rejection, and Communication," *Journal of Abnormal and Social Psychology*, 46 (1951): 190–207.
3. Albert Speer, *Inside the Third Reich: Memoirs*, tr. Richard Winston and Clara Winston (New York: Macmillan, 1970).
4. *Playboy*, January, 1975, p. 78.
5. Solomon Asch, "Effects of Group Pressure upon the Modification and Distortion of Judgment," in *Groups, Leadership and Men*, ed. M. H. Guetzkow (Pittsburgh: Carnegie, 1951), pp. 117–190. Solomon Asch, "Studies of Independence and Conformity: A Minority of One Against a Unanimous Majority," *Psychological Monographs*, 70 (1956): No. 9, Whole No. 416.
6. Robert Wolosin, Steven Sherman, and Arnie Cann, "Predictions of Own and Other's Conformity," *Journal of Personality*, 43 (1975): 357–378.
7. Morton Deutsch and Harold Gerard, "A Study of Normative and Informational Social Influence upon Individual Judgment," *Journal of Abnormal and Social Psychology*, 51 (1955): 629–636.
8. Jane Moulton, Robert Blake, and Joseph Olmstead, "The Relationship Between Frequency of Yielding and the Disclosure of Personal Identity," *Journal of Personality*, 24 (1956): 339–347.
9. Michael Argyle, "Social Pressure in Public and Private Situations," *Journal of Abnormal and Social Psychology*, 54 (1957): 172–175.
10. Solomon Asch, "Opinions and Social Pressure," *Scientific American*, 193 (5) (1955): 31–35. William Morris and Robert Miller, "The Effects of Consensus-Breaking and Consensus-Preempting Partners on Reduction of Conformity," *Journal of Experimental Social Psychology*, 11 (1975): 215–223. Ehor Boy-

anowsky, Vernon Allen, Barry Bragg, and John Lepinski, "Generalization of Independence Created By Social Support," *Psychological Record,* 31 (1981): 475–488.

11. Vernon Allen and John Levine, "Social Support and Conformity: The Role of Independent Assessment of Reality," *Journal of Experimental Social Psychology,* 7 (1971): 48–58.
12. Deutsch and Gerard, *op. cit.*
13. Bernard Mausner, "The Effects of Prior Reinforcement of the Interaction of Observer Pairs," *Journal of Abnormal and Social Psychology,* 49 (1954): 65–68. Bernard Mausner, "The Effect on One's Partner's Success in a Relevant Task on the Interaction of Observed Pairs," *Journal of Abnormal and Social Psychology,* 49 (1954): 557–560. Solomon Goldberg and Ardie Lubin, "Influence as a Function of Perceived Judgment Error," *Human Relations,* 11 (1958): 275–281. David Wiesenthal, Norman Endler, Teresa Coward, and Jean Edwards, "Reversibility of Relative Competence as a Determinant of Conformity Across Different Perceptual Tasks," *Representative Research in Social Psychology,* 7 (1976): 35–43.
14. Stanley Milgram, "Nationality and Conformity," *Scientific American,* 205 (5) (1961): 45–51. Robert Frager, "Conformity and Anticonformity in Japan," *Journal of Personality and Social Psychology,* 15 (1970): 203–210.
15. Eleanor Maccoby and Carol Jacklin, *The Psychology of Sex Differences* (Stanford, CA: Stanford University Press, 1974), pp. 268–272. Harris Cooper, "Statistically Combining Independent Studies: A Meta-Analysis of Sex Differences in Conformity Research," *Journal of Personality and Social Psychology,* 37 (1979): 131–146.
16. Alice Eagly and Linda Carli, "Sex of Researchers and Sex-typed Communications as Determinants of Sex Differences in Influenceability: A Meta-analysis of Social Influence Studies," *Psychological Bulletin,* 90 (1981): 1–20. Gregory Javornisky, "Task Content and Sex Differences in Conformity," *Journal of Social Psychology,* 108 (1979): 213–220. Shirley Feldman-Summers, Daniel Montano, Danuta Kasprzyk, and Beverly Wagner, "Influence Attempts When Competing Views Are Gender-related: Sex as Credibility," *Psychology of Women Quarterly,* 5 (1980): 311–320.
17. Frank Schneider, "Conforming Behavior of Black and White

Children," *Journal of Personality and Social Psychology*, 16 (1970): 466–471.

18. Gordon Allport, *The Nature of Prejudice* (Cambridge, MA: Addison-Wesley, 1954), pp. 13–14.
19. James Dittes and Harold Kelley, "Effects of Different Conditions of Acceptance Upon Conformity to Group Norms," *Journal of Abnormal and Social Psychology*, 53 (1956): 100–107.
20. Leon Festinger, "A Theory of Social Comparison Processes," *Human Relations*, 7 (1954): 117–140.
21. Elliot Aronson and Michael O'Leary, "The Relative Effectiveness of Models and Prompts on Energy Conservation: A Field Experiment in a Shower Room," *Journal of Environmental Systems*, (1982–83).
22. Stanley Schachter and Jerome Singer, "Cognitive, Social, and Physiological Determinants of Emotional State," *Psychological Review*, 69 (1962): 379–399.
23. William James, *Principles of Psychology* (New York: Smith, 1890).
24. Herbert Kelman, "Processes of Opinion Change," *Public Opinion Quarterly*, 25 (1961): 57–78.
25. Charles Kiesler, Mark Zanna, and James De Salvo, "Deviation and Conformity: Opinion Change as a Function of Commitment, Attraction, and Presence of a Deviate," *Journal of Personality and Social Psychology*, 3 (1966): 458–467.
26. Roger Vogler, Theodore Weissbach, John Compton, and George Martin, "Integrated Behavior Change Techniques for Problem Drinkers in the Community," *Journal of Consulting and Clinical Psychology*, 45 (1977): 267–279. Carolin Kuetner, Edward Lichtenstein, and Hayden Mees, "Modification of Smoking Behavior: A Review," *Psychological Bulletin*, 70 (1968): 520–533.
27. Stanley Milgram, "Behavioral Study of Obedience," *Journal of Abnormal and Social Psychology*, 67 (1963): 371–378. Stanley Milgram, "Some Conditions of Obedience and Disobedience to Authority," *Human Relations*, 18 (1965): 57–76. Stanley Milgram, *Obedience to Authority* (New York: Harper and Row, 1974).
28. Wesley Kilham and Leon Mann, "Level of Destructive Obedience as a Function of Transmitter and Executant Roles in

the Milgram Obedience Paradigm," *Journal of Personality and Social Psychology*, 29 (1974): 696–702. Mitri Shanab and Khawla Yahya, "A Behavioral Study of Obedience in Children," *Journal of Personality and Social Psychology*, 35 (1977): 530–536. Francisca Bonny Miranda, Rosa Bordes Caballero, Maria Garcia Gomez, and Maria Martin Zamorano, "Obedience to Authority," *Psiquis: Revista de Psiquiatria, Psicoloqia y Psicosomatica*, 2 (1981): 212–221. David Mantell, "The Potential for Violence in Germany," *Journal of Social Issues*, 27 (1971): 101–112.

29. Stanley Milgram, *Obedience to Authority* (New York: Harper and Row, 1974). Charles Sheridan and Richard King, "Obedience to Authority With an Authentic Victim," Paper presented at the American Psychological Association convention, 1972.
30. Stanley Milgram, "Liberating Effects of Group Pressure," *Journal of Personality and Social Psychology*, 1 (1965): 127–134.
31. Stanley Milgram, "Some Conditions of Obedience and Disobedience to Authority," *Human Relations*, 18 (1965): 57–76.
32. Stanley Milgram, "Liberating Effects of Group Pressure," *Journal of Personality and Social Psychology*, 1 (1965): 127–134.
33. A. M. Rosenthal, *Thirty-Eight Witnesses* (New York: McGraw-Hill, 1964).
34. Charles Korte and Nancy Kerr, "Response to Altruistic Opportunities in Urban and Nonurban Settings," *Journal of Social Psychology*, 95 (1975): 183–184. J. Philippe Rushton, "Urban Density and Altruism: Helping Strangers in a Canadian City, Suburb, and Small Town," *Psychological Reports*, 43 (1978): 987–990.
35. John Darley and Bibb Latane, "Bystander Intervention in Emergencies: Diffusion of Responsibility," *Journal of Personality and Social Psychology*, 8 (1968): 377–383. Bibb Latane and John Darley, "Group Inhibition of Bystander Intervention in Emergencies," *Journal of Personality and Social Psychology*, 10 (1968): 215–221. Bibb Latane and Judith Rodin, "A Lady in Distress: Inhibiting Effects of Friends and Strangers on Bystander Intervention," *Journal of Experimental Social Psychology*, 5 (1969): 189–202.
36. Bibb Latane and Steve Nida, "Ten Years of Research on Group Size and Helping," *Psychological Bulletin*, 89 (1981): 308–324.
37. Latane and Rodin, *op. cit.*

38. Darley and Latane, *op. cit.*

39. Irving Piliavin, Judith Rodin, and Jane Piliavin, "Good Samaritanism: An Underground Phenomenon?" *Journal of Personality and Social Psychology*, 13 (1969): 289–299.

40. Leonard Bickman, "Social Influence and Diffusion of Responsibility in an Emergency," *Journal of Experimental Social Psychology*, 8 (1972): 438–445.

41. Leonard Bickman, "The Effect of Another Bystander's Ability to Help on Bystander Intervention in an Emergency," *Journal of Experimental Social Psychology*, 7 (1971): 367–379. Leonard Bickman, "Social Influence and Diffusion of Responsibility in an Emergency," *Journal of Experimental Social Psychology*, 8 (1972): 438–445.

42. Jane Piliavin and Irving Piliavin, "The Effect of Blood on Reactions to a Victim," *Journal of Personality and Social Psychology*, 23 (1972): 353–361.

43. John Darley and C. Daniel Batson, " 'From Jerusalem to Jericho': A Study of Situational and Dispositional Variables in Helping Behavior," *Journal of Personality and Social Psychology*, 27 (1973): 100–108.

44. Russell Clark III and Larry Word, "Why Don't Bystanders Help? Because of Ambiguity?" *Journal of Personality and Social Psychology*, 24 (1972): 392–400. Linda Solomon, Henry Solomon, and Ronald Stone, "Helping as a Function of Number of Bystanders and Ambiguity of Emergency," *Personality and Social Psychology Bulletin*, 4 (1978): 318–321.

45. Robert A. Baron, "Magnitude of Model's Apparent Pain and Ability to Aid the Model as Determinants of Observer Reaction Time," *Psychonomic Science*, 21 (1970): 196–197.

46. Peter Suedfeld, Stephen Bochner, and Deanna Wnek, "Helper-Sufferer Similarity and a Specific Request for Help: Bystander Intervention During a Peace Demonstration," *Journal of Applied Social Psychology*, 2 (1972): 17–23.

Chapter 3. Mass Communication, Propaganda and Persuasion

1. *Newsweek*, June 2, 1974, p. 79. John J. O'Connor, "They Sell All Kinds of Drugs on Television," *The New York Times*, March 10, 1974, p. D15.

2. Kenneth Bollen and David Phillips, "Imitative Suicides: A National Study of the Effects of Television News Stories," *American Sociological Review*, 47 (1982): 802–809.
3. Mark Levy, quoted in *Time*, Oct. 1, 1979, p. 83.
4. Philip Mann and Ira Iscoe, "Mass Behavior and Community Organization: Reflections on a Peaceful Demonstration," *American Psychologist*, 26 (1971): 108–113.
5. *St. Petersburg* (Florida) *Times*, October 21, 1982. *The* (Nashville) *Tennesseean*, October 31, 1982.
6. *Newsbank*, October 1982, vol. 19, p. 1.
7. Joe McGinness, *The Selling of the President: 1968* (New York: Pocket Books, 1970), p. 160.
8. Jack Lyle and Heide Hoffman, "Explorations in Patterns of Television Viewing by Preschool-Age Children," in *Television and Social Behavior*, eds. J. P. Murray, E. A. Robinson, and G. A. Comstock (Rockville, Md.: National Institutes of Health, 1971), Vol. 4, pp. 257–344.
9. Jack Lyle and Heidi Hoffman, "Children's Use of Television and Other Media," in *Television and Social Behavior*, eds. J. P. Murray, E. A. Robinson, and G. A. Comstock (Rockville, Md.: National Institutes of Health, 1971), Vol. 4, pp. 129–256.
10. Daryl Bem, *Beliefs, Attitudes, and Human Affairs* (Belmont, Calif.: Brooks/Cole, 1970).
11. Robert Zajonc, "The Attitudinal Effects of Mere Exposure," *Journal of Personality and Social Psychology, Monograph Supplement*, 9 (1968): 1–27.
12. Joseph Grush, Kevin McKeough, and Robert Ahlering, "Extrapolating Laboratory Exposure Re Research to Actual Political Elections," *Journal of Personality and Social Psychology*, 36 (1978): 257–270.
13. Philip Zimbardo, Ebbe Ebbesen, and Christina Maslach, *Influencing Attitudes and Changing Behavior*, 2nd edition (Reading, Mass.: Addison-Wesley, 1977).
14. Aristotle, "Rhetoric," tr. W. Rhys Roberts, in *Aristotle, Rhetoric and Poetics* (New York: Modern Library, 1954), p. 25.
15. Carl Hovland and Walter Weiss, "The Influence of Source Credibility on Communication Effectiveness," *Public Opinion Quarterly*, 15 (1951): 635–650.

16. Elliot Aronson and Burton Golden, "The Effect of Relevant and Irrelevant Aspects of Communicator Credibility on Opinion Change," *Journal of Personality*, 30 (1962): 135–146.

17. *The New York Times*, February 17, 1974.

18. Elaine Walster (Hatfield), Elliot Aronson, and Darcy Abrahams, "On Increasing the Persuasiveness of a Low Prestige Communicator," *Journal of Experimental Social Psychology*, 2 (1966): 325–342.

19. Alice Eagly, Wendy Wood, and Shelly Chaiken, "Causal Inferences About Communicators and Their Effect on Opinion Change," *Journal of Personality and Social Psychology*, 36 (1978): 424–435.

20. Elaine Walster (Hatfield) and Leon Festinger, "The Effectiveness of 'Overheard' Persuasive Communications," *Journal of Abnormal and Social Psychology*, 65 (1962): 395–402.

21. Judson Mills and Elliot Aronson, "Opinion Change as a Function of Communicator's Attractiveness and Desire to Influence," *Journal of Personality and Social Psychology*, 1 (1965): 173–177.

22. Alice Eagly and Shelly Chaiken, "An Attribution Analysis of the Effect of Communicator Characteristics on Opinion Change: The Case of Communicator Attractiveness," *Journal of Personality and Social Psychology*, 32 (1975): 136–144.

23. George Hartmann, "A Field Experience on the Comparative Effectiveness of 'Emotional' and 'Rational' Political Leaflets in Determining Election Results," *Journal of Abnormal and Social Psychology*, 31 (1936): 336–352.

24. Howard Leventhal, "Findings and Theory in the Study of Fear Communications," in *Advances in Experimental Social Psychology*, Vol. 5, ed. L. Berkowitz (New York: Academic Press, 1970), pp. 119–186.

25. *The New York Times Magazine*, July 4, 1982, pp. 14–17, 31–39.

26. *The Bulletin of the Atomic Scientists*, August/September 1982, pp. 3–5.

27. Richard Nisbett, Eugene Borgida, Rick Crandall, and Harvey Reed, "Popular Induction: Information is Not Always Informative," in J. S. Carroll and J. W. Payne (Eds.), *Cognition and Social Behavior*. (Hillsdale, NJ: Erlbaum, 1976), pp. 227–

236. Richard Nisbett and Lee Ross, *Human Inference: Strategies and Shortcomings of Social Judgment* (Englewood Cliffs, NJ: Prentice-Hall, 1980). Ruth Hamill, Timothy DeCamp Wilson, and Richard Nisbett, "Insensitivity to Sample Bias: Generalizing from Atypical Cases," *Journal of Personality and Social Psychology*, 39 (1980): 578–589. Shelley Taylor, a cognitive social psychologist, argues that the "vividness" effect is not supported by a majority of the experimental findings. For a discussion of this issue, see Shelley Taylor and Suzanne Thompson, "Stalking the Elusive 'Vividness' Effect," *Psychological Review*, 89 (1982): 155–181.

28. Carl Hovland, Arthur Lumsdain, and Frederick Sheffield, *Experiments on Mass Communications* (Princeton: Princeton University Press, 1949).

29. Norman Miller and Donald Campbell, "Recency and Primacy in Persuasion as a Function of the Timing of Speeches and Measurements," *Journal of Abnormal and Social Psychology*, 59 (1959): 1–9.

30. Philip Zimbardo, "Involvement and Communication Discrepancy as Determinants of Opinion Conformity," *Journal of Abnormal and Social Psychology*, 60 (1960): 86–94.

31. Carl Hovland, O. J. Harvey, and Muzafer Sherif, "Assimilation and Contrast Effects in Reaction to Communication and Attitude Change," *Journal of Abnormal and Social Psychology*, 55 (1957): 244–252.

32. Elliot Aronson, Judith Turner, and J. Merrill Carlsmith, "Communication Credibility and Communication Discrepancy as Determinants of Opinion Change," *Journal of Abnormal and Social Psychology*, 67 (1963): 31–36.

33. Miriam Zellner, "Self-Esteem, Reception, and Influenceability," *Journal of Personality and Social Psychology*, 15 (1970): 87–93.

34. Irving L. Janis, Donald Kaye, and Paul Kirschner, "Facilitating Effects of 'Eating-While-Reading' on Responsiveness to Persuasive Communication," *Journal of Personality and Social Psychology*, 1 (1965): 181–186.

35. R. Glen Hass and Kathleen Grady, "Temporal Delay, Type of Forewarning, and Resistance to Influence," *Journal of Experimental Social Psychology*, 11 (1975): 459–469.

36. Jonathan Freedman and David Sears, "Warning, Distraction, and Resistance to Influence," *Journal of Personality and Social Psychology*, 1 (1965): 262–266.

37. Jack Brehm, *Explorations in Cognitive Reactance* (New York: Academic Press, 1966).

38. Madeline Heilman, "Oppositional Behavior as a Function of Influence Attempt Intensity and Retaliation Threat," *Journal of Personality and Social Psychology*, 33 (1976): 574–578.

39. Richard Petty and John Cacioppo, "Forewarning, Cognitive Responding and Resistance to Persuasion," *Journal of Personality and Social Psychology*, 35 (1977): 645–655.

40. Leon Festinger and Nathan Maccoby, "On Resistance to Persuasive Communications," *Journal of Abnormal and Social Psychology*, 68 (1964): 359–366.

41. Lloyd Sloan, Robert Love, and Thomas Ostrom, "Political Heckling: Who Really Loses?" *Journal of Personality and Social Psychology*, 30 (1974): 518–525.

42. William McGuire and Dimitri Papageorgis, "The Relative Efficacy of Various Types of Prior Belief-Defense in Producing Immunity Against Persuasion," *Journal of Abnormal and Social Psychology*, 62 (1961): 327–337.

43. Alfred McAlister, Cheryl Perry, Joel Killen, Lee Anne Slinkard, and Nathan Maccoby, "Pilot Study of Smoking, Alcohol and Drug Abuse Prevention," *American Journal of Public Health*, 70 (1980): 719–721.

44. B. Pryor and T. Steinfatt, "The Effects of Initial Belief Level on Inoculation Theory and Its Proposed Mechanisms," *Human Communications Research*, 4 (1978): 217–230.

45. Lance Canon, "Self-Confidence and Selective Exposure to Information," in *Conflict, Decision, and Dissonance*, ed. L. Festinger (Stanford: Stanford University Press, 1964), pp. 83–96.

46. A. C. Nielsen Co., *The Television Audience: 1975* (Chicago: A/C Nielsen, 1975).

47. Robert Leibert, testimony before the Subcommittee on Communications of the House Committee on Interstate and Foreign Commerce, July 16, 1975.

48. *San Francisco Chronicle*, August 25, 1979, p. 15. *San Francisco*

Sunday Examiner and Chronicle, August 26, 1979, p. 2. *San Jose Mercury-News*, February 11, 1982, p. A2.

49. Leslie McArthur and Beth Resko, "The Portrayal of Men and Women in American Television Commercials," *Journal of Social Psychology*, in press.

50. Lenore Weitzman, Deborah Eifler, Elizabeth Hokada, and Catherine Ross, "Sex-Role Socialization in Picture Books for Preschool Children," *American Journal of Sociology*, 77 (1972): 1125–1150.

51. George Gerbner and Nancy Signorielli, "Women and Minorities in Television Drama, 1969–1978," The Annenberg School of Communications, University of Pennsylvania, October 1979. Michael Morgan, "TV Professions and Adolescents' Career Choices." In *Promise and Performance: Broadcasting for Young Adolescents*, an Action for Children's Television Resource Guide, September 1980. George Gerbner, Larry Gross, Nancy Signorielli, and Michael Morgan, "Aging with Television: Images on Television Drama and Conceptions of Social Reality," *Journal of Communication*, 30 (Winter 1980): 37–47. George Gerbner, Larry Gross, Michael Morgan, and Nancy Signorielli, "The 'Mainstreaming' of America: Violence Profile No. 11," *Journal of Communication*, 30 (Summer 1980): 10–29. *Newsweek*, December 6, 1982, pp. 136–141.

52. Quoted in *Newsweek*, December 6, 1982, p. 140.

53. Craig Haney and John Manzolati, "Television Criminology: Network Illusions of Criminal Justice Realities," in *Readings about the Social Animal*, 3rd. edition (San Francisco: W. H. Freeman, 1981), pp. 125–136.

54. Karen Hennigan, Linda Heath, J. D. Wharton, Marlyn DelRosario, Thomas Cook, and Bobby Calder, "Impact of the Introduction of Television on Crime in the United States: Empirical Findings and Theoretical Implications," *Journal of Personality and Social Psychology*, 42 (1982): 461–477.

55. David Ronis, Michael Baumgardner, Michael Leippe, John Cacioppo, and Anthony Greenwald, "In Search of Reliable Persuasion," *Journal of Personality and Social Psychology*, 35 (1977): 548–569.

Chapter 4. Self-Justification

1. Jamuna Prasad, "A Comparative Study of Rumors and Reports in Earthquakes," *British Journal of Psychology*, 41 (1950): 129–144.
2. Durganand Sinha, "Behavior in a Catastrophic Situation: A Psychological Study of Reports and Rumours," *British Journal of Psychology*, 43 (1952): 200–209.
3. Leon Festinger, *A Theory of Cognitive Dissonance* (Stanford: Stanford University Press, 1957).
4. Harold Kassarjian and Joel Cohen, "Cognitive Dissonance and Consumer Behavior," *California Management Review*, 8 (1965): 55–64.
5. Renata Tagliacozzo, "Smokers' Self-Categorization and the Reduction of Cognitive Dissonance," *Addictive Behaviors*, 4 (1979): 393–399.
6. *Austin American*, November 18, 1971, p. 69.
7. Albert Hastorf and Hadley Cantril, "They Saw a Game: A Case Study," *Journal of Abnormal and Social Psychology*, 49 (1954): 129–134.
8. Lenny Bruce, *How to Talk Dirty and Influence People* (Chicago: Playboy Press, and New York: Pocket Books, 1966), pp. 232–233.
9. *Newsweek*, Letter to the Editor, June 18, 1973.
10. Edward Jones and Rika Kohler, "The Effects of Plausibility on the Learning of Controversial Statements," *Journal of Abnormal and Social Psychology*, 57 (1959): 315–320.
11. Charles Lord, Lee Ross, and Mark Lepper, "Biased Assimilation and Attitude Polarization: The Effects of Prior Theories on Subsequently Considered Evidence," *Journal of Personality and Social Psychology*, 37 (1979): 2098–2109.
12. Danuta Ehrlich, Isaiah Guttman, Peter Schonbach, and Judson Mills, "Postdecision Exposure to Relevant Information," *Journal of Abnormal and Social Psychology*, 54 (1957): 98–102.
13. Jack Brehm, "Postdecision Changes in the Desirability of Alternatives," *Journal of Abnormal and Social Psychology*, 52 (1956): 384–389.
14. Leon Festinger and Nathan Maccoby, "On Resistance to Per-

suasive Communication," *Journal of Abnormal and Social Psychology*, 68 (1964): 359–366.

15. Elie Wiesel, *Night* (New York: Avon, 1969).

16. Ralph White, "Selective Inattention," *Psychology Today*, November 1971, pp. 47–50, 78–84.

17. For a penetrating analysis of the process involved in a number of disastrous political decisions, see Irving Janis' book, *Victims of Groupthink* (Boston: Houghton Mifflin, 1972).

18. "Pentagon Papers: The Secret War," *Time*, June 28, 1971, p. 12.

19. Jonathan Freedman and Scott Fraser, "Compliance Without Pressure: The Foot-in-the-Door Technique," *Journal of Personality and Social Psychology*, 4 (1966): 195–202.

20. Patricia Pliner, Heather Hart, Joanne Kohl, and Dory Saari, "Compliance Without Pressure: Some Further Data on the Foot-in-the-Door Technique," *Journal of Experimental Social Psychology*, 10 (1974): 17–22.

21. Robert Knox and James Inkster, "Postdecision Dissonance at Post Time," *Journal of Personality and Social Psychology*, 8 (1968): 319–323.

22. O. J. Frenkel and Anthony Doob, "Post-Decision Dissonance at the Polling Booth," *Canadian Journal of Behavioural Science*, 8 (1976): 347–350.

23. Robert Cialdini, John Cacioppo, Rodney Bassett, and John Miller, "Low-Ball Procedure for Producing Compliance: Commitment then Cost," *Journal of Personality and Social Psychology*, 36 (1978): 463–476.

24. *Ibid.*

25. Judson Mills, "Changes in Moral Attitudes Following Temptation, *Journal of Personality*, 26 (1958): 517–531.

26. Leon Festinger and J. Merrill Carlsmith, "Cognitive Consequences of Forced Compliance," *Journal of Abnormal and Social Psychology*, 58 (1959): 203–210.

27. Arthur Cohen, "An Experiment on Small Rewards for Discrepant Compliance and Attitude Change," in *Explorations in Cognitive Dissonance*, by J. W. Brehm and A. R. Cohen (New York: Wiley, 1962), pp. 73–78.

28. It should be mentioned, in passing, that the "saying-is-believing" phenomenon has produced some controversial data. The weight of the evidence tends to support the analysis presented in this text. For a more detailed discussion of this issue, read Elliot Aronson, "The Theory of Cognitive Dissonance: A Current Perspective," in *Advances in Experimental Social Psychology*," Vol. 4, ed. L. Berkowitz (New York: Academic Press, 1969), pp. 1–34.

29. Mills, *op. cit.*

30. Elliot Aronson, "Dissonance Theory: Progress and Problems," in *Theories of Cognitive Consistency: A Sourcebook*, ed. R. P. Abelson, E. Aronson, W. J. McGuire, T. M. Newcomb, M. J. Rosenberg, and P. H. Tannenbaum (Chicago: Rand McNally, 1968), pp. 5–27. Elliot Aronson, "The Theory of Cognitive Dissonance: A Current Perspective," in *Advances in Experimental Social Psychology*, Vol. 4, ed. L. Berkowitz (New York: Academic Press, 1969), pp. 1–34.

31. Elizabeth Nel, Robert Helmreich, and Elliot Aronson, "Opinion Change in the Advocate as a Function of the Persuasibility of His Audience: A Clarification of the Meaning of Dissonance," *Journal of Personality and Social Psychology*, 12 (1969): 117–124.

32. Michael Hoyt, Marc Henley, and Barry Collins, "Studies in Forced Compliance: Confluence of Choice and Consequence on Attitude Change," *Journal of Personality and Social Psychology*, 23 (1972): 204–210. Barry Schlenker and Patricia Schlenker, "Reactions Following Counterattitudinal Behavior Which Produces Positive Consequences," *Journal of Personality and Social Psychology*, 31 (1975): 962–971. Marc Riess and Barry Schlenker, "Attitude Change and Responsibility Avoidance as Modes of Dilemma Resolution in Forced-Compliance Situations," *Journal of Personality and Social Psychology*, 35 (1977): 21–30.

33. Robert Cialdini and David Schroeder, "Increasing Compliance by Legitimizing Paltry Contributions: When Even a Penny Helps," *Journal of Personality and Social Psychology*, 34 (1976): 599–604.

34. Jonathan Freedman, "Attitudinal Effects of Inadequate Justification," *Journal of Personality*, 31 (1963): 371–385.

35. Edward Deci, *Intrinsic Motivation* (New York: Plenum, 1975).

Edward Deci, "Effects of Externally Mediated Rewards on Intrinsic Motivation," *Journal of Personality and Social Psychology*, 18 (1971): 105–115. Edward L. Deci, John Nezlek, and Louise Sheinman, "Characteristics of the Rewarder and Intrinsic Motivation of the Rewardee," *Journal of Personality and Social Psychology*, 40 (1981): 1–10.

36. Mark R. Lepper and David Greene, "Turning Play into Work: Effects of Adult Surveillance and Extrinsic Rewards on Children's Intrinsic Motivation," *Journal of Personality and Social Psychology*, 31 (1975): 479–486.

37. Elliot Aronson and J. Merrill Carlsmith, "Effect of the Severity of Threat on the Devaluation of Forbidden Behavior," *Journal of Abnormal and Social Psychology*, 66 (1963): 584–588.

38. Jonathan Freedman, "Long-Term Behavioral Effects of Cognitive Dissonance," *Journal of Experimental Social Psychology*, 1 (1965): 145–155.

39. Robert Sears, John Whiting, Vincent Nowlis, and Pauline Sears, "Some Child-Rearing Antecedents of Aggression and Dependency in Young Children," *Genetic Psychology Monographs*, 47 (1953): 135–234.

40. Elliot Aronson and Judson Mills, "The Effect of Severity of Initiation on Liking for a Group," *Journal of Abnormal and Social Psychology*, 59 (1959): 177–181.

41. Harold Gerard and Grover Mathewson, "The Effects of Severity on Initiation on Liking for a Group: A Replication," *Journal of Experimental Social Psychology*, 2 (1966): 278–287.

42. Joel Cooper, "Reducing Fears and Increasing Assertiveness: The Role of Dissonance Reduction," *Journal of Experimental Social Psychology*, 16 (1980): 199–213.

43. James Michener, *Kent State: What Happened and Why* (New York: Random House, 1971).

44. *Ibid.*

45. Nikita Khrushchev, *Khrushchev Remembers*, tr. and ed. Strobe Talbot (Boston: Little, Brown, 1970).

46. Keith Davis and Edward E. Jones, "Changes in Interpersonal Perception as a Means of Reducing Cognitive Dissonance," *Journal of Abnormal and Social Psychology*, 61 (1960): 402–410.

47. David Glass, "Changes in Liking as a Means of Reducing

Cognitive Discrepancies Between Self-Esteem and Aggression," *Journal of Personality*, 32 (1964): 531–549.

48. Ellen Berscheid, David Boyce, and Elaine Walster (Hatfield), "Retaliation as a Means of Restoring Equity," *Journal of Personality and Social Psychology*, 10 (1968): 370–376.

49. Edward Jones and Richard Nisbett, *The Actor and The Observer: Divergent Perceptions of the Causes of Behavior* (New York: General Learning Press, 1971).

50. George Bernard Shaw, *Selected Prose*, ed. Diarmuid Russel (New York: Dodd, Mead, 1952).

51. Jack Brehm, "Increasing Cognitive Dissonance by a *Fait-Accompli*," *Journal of Abnormal and Social Psychology*, 58 (1959): 379–382.

52. John Darley and Ellen Berscheid, "Increased Liking as a Result of the Anticipation of Personal Contact," *Human Relations*, 20 (1967): 29–40.

53. Elliot Aronson and David Mettee, "Dishonest Behavior as a Function of Different Levels of Self-Esteem," *Journal of Personality and Social Psychology*, 9 (1968): 121–127.

54. Philip Zimbardo, *The Cognitive Control of Motivation* (Glencoe, Ill.: Scott, Foresman, 1969).

55. Jack Brehm, "Motivational Effects of Cognitive Dissonance," in *Nebraska Symposium on Motivation, 1962* (Lincoln: University of Nebraska Press, 1962), pp. 51–77.

56. Jack W. Brehm and Arthur R. Cohen, *Explorations in Cognitive Dissonance* (New York: Wiley, 1962).

57. Elliot Aronson, "The Cognitive and Behavioral Consequences of the Confirmation and Disconfirmation of Expectancies" (Harvard University, 1960, unpublished manuscript). Elliot Aronson and J. Merrill Carlsmith, "Performance Expectancy as a Determinant of Actual Performance," *Journal of Abnormal and Social Psychology*, 65 (1962): 178–182. Elliot Aronson and David R. Mettee, "Dishonest Behavior as a Function of Differential Levels of Induced Self-Esteem," *Journal of Personality and Social Psychology*, 9 (1968): 121–127. Elizabeth Nel, R. Helmreich, and Elliot Aronson, "Opinion Change in the Advocate as a Function of the Persuasibility of His Audience: A Clarification of the Meaning of Dissonance," *Journal of Person-*

ality and Social Psychology, 12 (1969): 117–124. Elliot Aronson, Thomas Chase, Robert Helmreich, and Ronald Ruhnke, "A Two-Factor Theory of Dissonance Reduction: The Effect of Feeling Stupid or Feeling 'Awful' on Opinion Change," *International Journal for Research and Communication*, 3 (1974): 59–74.

58. Milton J. Rosenberg, "When Dissonance Fails: On Eliminating Evaluation Apprehension from Attitude Measurement," *Journal of Personality and Social Psychology*, 1 (1965): 28–42.

59. Darwyn E. Linder, Joel Cooper, and Edward E. Jones, "Decision Freedom as a Determinant of the Role of Incentive Magnitude in Attitude Change," *Journal of Personality and Social Psychology*, 6 (1967): 245–254.

60. George Goethals, Joel Cooper, and Nancy Anahita, "Role of Foreseen, Foreseeable, and Unforeseeable Behavioral Consequences in the Arousal of Cognitive Dissonance," *Journal of Personality and Social Psychology*, 37 (1979): 1179–1185.

61. Daryl J. Bem, "Self-Perception: An Alternative Interpretation of Cognitive Dissonance Phenomena," *Psychological Review*, 74 (1967): 183–200.

62. Russell A. Jones, Darwyn E. Linder, Charles A Kiesler, Mark Zanna, and Jack W. Brehm, "Internal States or External Stimuli: Observers' Attitude Judgments and the Dissonance Theory-Self-Persuasion Controversy," *Journal of Experimental Social Psychology*, 4 (1968): 247–269. Jane A. Piliavin, I. M. Piliavin, E. P. Loewenton, C. McCauley, and P. Hammond, "On Observers' Reproduction of Dissonance Effects: The Right Answers for the Wrong Reasons?" *Journal of Personality and Social Psychology*, 13 (1969): 98–106.

63. Russell Fazio, Mark Zanna, and Joel Cooper, "Dissonance and Self-Perception: An Integrative View of Each Theory's Proper Domain of Application," *Journal of Experimental Social Psychology*, 13 (1977): 464–479. David Ronis and Anthony Greenwald, "Dissonance Theory Revised Again: Comment on the Paper by Fazio, Zanna, and Cooper," *Journal of Experimental Social Psychology*, 15 (1979): 62–69. Russell Fazio, Mark Zanna, and Joel Cooper, "On the Relationship of Data to Theory: A Reply to Ronis and Greenwald," *Journal of Experimental Social Psychology*, 15 (1979): 70–76.

64. Michael S. Pallak and Thane S. Pittman, "General Motiva-

tional Effects of Dissonance Arousal," *Journal of Personality and Social Psychology*, 21 (1972): 349–358.

65. Mark Zanna and Joel Cooper, "Dissonance and the Pill: An Attribution Approach to Studying the Arousal Properties of Dissonance," *Journal of Personality and Social Psychology*, 29 (1974): 703–709.

66. Charles Bond, "Dissonance and the Pill: An Interpersonal Simulation," *Personality and Social Psychology Bulletin*, 7 (1981): 398–403.

67. Mountain West Research, Inc., "Three Mile Island Telephone Survey," preliminary report on procedures and findings, report submitted to The U. S. Nuclear Regulatory Commission (NUREG CR-1093; 1979).

68. *Newsweek*, April 16, 1979, pp. 93, 35. CBS News-New York Times Poll, *The New York Times*, April 10, 1979, pp. 1, 16.

69. Danny Axsom and Joel Cooper, "Reducing Weight by Reducing Dissonance: The Role of Effort Justification in Inducing Weight Loss," in *Readings About the Social Animal*, ed. E. Aronson (San Francisco: Freeman, 1981), p. 181–196.

70. Lyndon B. Johnson, *The Vantage Point: Perspectives of the Presidency 1963–69* (New York: Holt, Rinehart and Winston, 1971).

Chapter 5. Human Aggression

1. Jean-Jacques Rousseau, *The Social Contract and Discourses* (New York: Dutton, 1930).

2. Sigmund Freud, *Beyond the Pleasure Principle* (London: Hogarth Press and Institute of Psycho-Analysis, 1948).

3. Sigmund Freud, "Why War?" (letter to Albert Einstein, 1932), in *Collected Papers*, Vol. 5, ed. Ernest Jones (New York: Basic Books, 1959), p. 282.

4. Anthony Storr, *Human Aggression* (New York: Bantam, 1970).

5. Zing Yang Kuo, "Genesis of the Cat's Response to the Rat," in *Instinct* (Princeton: Van Nostrand, 1961), p. 24.

6. Irenaus Eibl-Eibesfeldt, "Aggressive Behavior and Ritualized Fighting in Animals," in *Science and Psychoanalysis*, Vol. VI

(*Violence and War*), ed. J. H. Masserman (New York: Grune and Stratton, 1963).

7. John Paul Scott, *Aggression*, (Chicago: University of Chicago Press, 1958).
8. Konrad Lorenz, *On Aggression*, tr. Marjorie Wilson (New York: Harcourt, Brace and World, 1966).
9. Leonard Berkowitz, "The Frustration-Aggression Hypothesis Revisited," in *Roots of Aggression: A Re-examination of the Frustration-Aggression Hypothesis*, ed. L. Berkowitz (New York: Atherton, 1968).
10. John Nance, *The Gentle Tasaday: A Stone Age People in the Philippine Rain Forest* (New York: Harcourt Brace Jovanovich, 1975).
11. George T. Hunt, *The Wars of the Iroquois* (Madison: The University of Wisconsin Press, 1940).
12. Kirsti Lagerspetz, "Modification of Aggressiveness in Mice," in *Aggression in Behavior Change*, eds. S. Feshbach and A. Fraczek (New York: Praeger, 1979).
13. Konrad Lorenz, *On Aggression*, tr. Marjorie Wilson, (New York: Harcourt, Brace, and World, 1966).
14. Sherwood Washburn and David Hamburg, "The Implications of Primate Research," in *Primate Behavior: Field Studies of Monkeys and Apes*, ed. I. DeVore (New York: Holt, Rinehart and Winston), pp. 607–622.
15. Burney LeBoeuf, "Male-Male Competition and Reproductive Success in Elephant Seals," *American Zoologist*, 14 (1974): 163–176.
16. M. F. Ashley Montagu, *On Being Human* (New York: Hawthorne Books, 1950).
17. Peter Kropotkin, *Mutual Aid*, (New York: Doubleday, 1902).
18. Henry Nissen and Meredith P. Crawford, "Preliminary Study of Food-Sharing Behavior in Young Chimpanzees," *Journal of Comparative Psychology*, 22 (1936): 383–419.
19. *Time*, October 7, 1974.
20. Richard Leakey and Roger Lewin, *People of the Lake* (New York: Anchor Press/Doubleday, 1978).
21. Loren Eiseley, *The Immense Journey*, (New York: Random House, 1946), p. 140.

22. William Menninger, "Recreation and Mental Health," *Recreation*, 42 (1948): 340–346.

23. Leonard Berkowitz, *Control of Aggression* (unpublished, 1971).

24. Arthur Patterson, "Hostility Catharsis: A Naturalistic Quasi-Experiment," Paper presented at the annual convention of the American Psychological Association, New Orleans, September 1974.

25. Warren Johnson, "Guilt-Free Aggression for the Troubled Jock," *Psychology Today*, October 1970, pp. 70–73.

26. Gordon Russell, "Spectator Moods at an Aggressive Sports Event," *Journal of Social Psychology*, 3 (1981): 217–227.

27. Seymour Feshbach, "The Drive-Reducing Function of Fantasy Behavior," *Journal of Abnormal and Social Psychology*, 50 (1955): 3–11.

28. Jack Hokanson and Meredith Burgess, "The Effects of Three Types of Aggression on Vascular Process," *Journal of Abnormal and Social Psychology*, 64 (1962): 446–449.

29. Russell Geen and Michael Quanty, "The Catharsis of Aggression: An Evaluation of an Hypothesis," in *Advances in Experimental Social Psychology*, Vol. 10, ed. L. Berkowitz (New York: Academic Press, 1977), pp. 1–36.

30. Russell Geen, David Stonner, and G. Shope, "The Facilitation of Aggression by Aggression: A Study in Response Inhibition and Disinhibition," *Journal of Personality and Social Psychology*, 31 (1975): 721–726.

31. Ebbe Ebbesen, B. Duncan, and Vladimir Konecni, "Effects of Content of Verbal Aggression: A Field Experiment," *Journal of Experimental and Social Psychology*, 11 (1975): 192–204.

32. David Glass, "Changes in Liking as a Means of Reducing Cognitive Discrepancies Between Self-Esteem and Aggression," *Journal of Personality*, 32 (1964): 531–549. Keith E. Davis and Edward E. Jones, "Changes in Interpersonal Perception as a Means of Reducing Cognitive Dissonance," *Journal of Abnormal and Social Psychology*, 61 (1960): 402–410. See also Arnold H. Buss, "Physical Aggression in Relation to Different Frustrations," *Journal of Abnormal and Social Psychology*, 67 (1963): 1–7.

33. Michael Kahn, "The Physiology of Catharsis," *Journal of Per-*

sonality and Social Psychology, 3 (1966): 278–298. See also: Leonard Berkowitz, James Green, and Jacqueline Macaulay, "Hostility Catharsis as the Reduction of Emotional Tension," *Psychiatry*, 25 (1962): 23–31; and Richard DeCharms and Edward J. Wilkins, "Some Effects of Verbal Expression of Hostility," *Journal of Abnormal and Social Psychology*, 66 (1963): 462–470.

34. Anthony N. Doob and Larraine Wood, "Catharsis and Aggression: The Effects of Annoyance and Retaliation on Aggressive Behavior," *Journal of Personality and Social Psychology*, 22 (1972): 156–162.

35. Sigmund Freud, "Why War?" (letter to Albert Einstein, 1932), in *Collected Papers*, Vol. 5, ed. Ernest Jones (New York: Basic Books, 1959).

36. Dane Archer and Rosemary Gartner, "Violent Acts and Violent Times: A Comparative Approach to Postwar Homicide Rates," *American Sociological Review*, 41 (1976): 937–963.

37. Konrad Lorenz, *On Aggression*, tr. Marjorie Wilson (New York: Harcourt, Brace and World, 1966). William Menninger, "Recreation and Mental Health," *Recreation*, 42 (1948): 340–346.

38. Joseph Klapper, *The Effects of Mass Communication* (Glencoe, Ill.: Free Press, 1960).

39. Albert Bandura, Dorothea Ross, and Sheila Ross, "Transmission of Aggression Through Imitation of Aggressive Models," *Journal of Abnormal and Social Psychology*, 63 (1961): 575–582. Albert Bandura, Dorothea Ross, and Sheila Ross, "A Comparative Test of the Status Envy, Social Power, and Secondary Reinforcement Theories of Identificatory Learning," *Journal of Abnormal and Social Psychology*, 67 (1963): 527–534. Albert Bandura, Dorothea Ross, and Sheila Ross, "Vicarious Reinforcement and Initiative Learning," *Journal of Abnormal and Social Psychology*, 67 (1963): 601–607.

40. George Gerbner, Larry Gross, Nancy Signorielli, and Michael Morgan, "Television Violence, Victimization, and Power," *American Behavioral Scientist*, 23 (1980): 705–716.

41. Robert Liebert and Robert Baron, "Some Immediate Effects of Televised Violence on Children's Behavior," *Developmental Psychology*, 6 (1972): 469–475.

42. Ross Parke, Leonard Berkowitz, Jacques Leyens, Stephen West,

and Richard Sebastian, "Some Effects of Violent and Nonviolent Movies on the Behavior of Juvenile Delinquents," in *Advances in Experimental Social Psychology*, ed. L. Berkowitz (New York: Academic Press, 1977), pp. 135–172.

43. Leonard Eron and Rowell Huesmann, "Adolescent Aggression and Television," *Annals of the New York Academy of Sciences*, 347 (1980): 319–331.

44. National Institute of Mental Health, *Television and Behavior: Ten Years of Scientific Progress and Implications for the Eighties*, 1982.

45. Margaret Hanratty Thomas, Robert Horton, Elaine Lippincott, and Ronald Drabman, "Desensitization to Portrayals of Real-Life Aggression as a Function of Exposure to Television Violence," *Journal of Personality and Social Psychology*, 35 (1977): 450–458.

46. "Drop That Gun, Captain Video," *Newsweek*, March 10, 1975, pp. 81–82.

47. "The Violence Bag," *Newsweek*, December 13, 1971, p. 110.

48. Ed Diener and Darlene DeFour, "Does Television Violence Enhance Program Popularity?," *Journal of Personality and Social Psychology*, 36 (1978): 333–341.

49. Neil Malamuth, "Rape Fantasies as a Function of Exposure to Violent Sexual Stimuli," *Archives of Sexual Behavior*, 10 (1981): 33–47.

50. Neil Malamuth and James Check, "The Effects of Mass Media Exposure on Acceptance of Violence Against Women: A Field Experiment," *Journal of Research in Personality*, 15 (1981): 436–446.

51. Pamela Foa, "What's Wrong With Rape," in *Feminism and Philosophy*, eds. M. Vetterling-Broggin, F. Elliston, and J. English (Totowa, New Jersey: Littlefield Adams, 1978), p. 355.

52. Neil Malamuth, Scott Haber, and Seymour Feshbach, "Testing Hypotheses Regarding Rape: Exposure to Sexual Violence, Sex Differences, and the 'Normality' of Rapists," *Journal of Research in Personality*, 14 (1980): 121–137.

53. James Check and Neil Malamuth, "Can There Be Positive Effects of Participation in Pornography Experiments?" *Journal of Sex Research*, (1983) in press.

54. Roger Barker, Tamara Dembo, and Kurt Lewin, "Frustration and Regression: An Experiment with Young Children," *University of Iowa Studies in Child Welfare*, 18 (1941): 1–314.
55. Mary Harris, "Mediators Between Frustration and Aggression in a Field Experiment," *Journal of Experimental and Social Psychology*, 10 (1974): 561–571.
56. James Kulik and Roger Brown, "Frustration, Attribution of Blame, and Aggression," *Journal of Experimental and Social Psychology*, 15 (1979): 183–194.
57. Shabaz Mallick and Boyd McCandless, "A Study of Catharsis of Aggression," *Journal of Personality and Social Psychology*, 4 (1966): 591–596.
58. Leonard Berkowitz, "Some Aspects of Observed Aggression," *Journal of Personality and Social Psychology*, 2 (1965): 359–369.
59. Leonard Berkowitz and Russell Geen, "Film Violence and the Cue Properties of Available Targets," *Journal of Personality and Social Psychology*, 3 (1966): 525–530.
60. Leonard Berkowitz and Anthony LePage, "Weapons as Aggression-Eliciting Stimuli," *Journal of Personality and Social Psychology*, 7 (1967): 202–207.
61. Leonard Berkowitz, *Control of Aggression* (unpublished, 1971), p. 68.
62. Philip Zimbardo, "The Human Choice: Individuation, Reason, and Order Versus Deindividuation, Impulse, and Chaos," in *Nebraska Symposium on Motivation*, ed. W. Arnold and D. Levine, 17 (1969): 237–307.
63. Kenneth Clark, "The Pathos of Power: A Psychological Perspective," *American Psychologist*, 26 (1971): 1047–1057.
64. Aristotle, "Rhetoric," in *Aristotle, Rhetoric and Poetics*, tr. W. Rhys Roberts (New York: Modern Library, 1954), p. 22.
65. Robert Sears, Eleanor Maccoby, and Harry Levin, *Patterns of Child Rearing* (Evanston, Ill.: Row, Peterson, 1957). Diana Baumrind, "Effects of Authoritative Parental Control on Child Behavior," *Child Development*, 37 (1966): 887–907. Wesley Becker, "Consequences of Different Kinds of Parental Discipline," in *Review of Child Development Research*, Vol. 1, ed. M. L. Hoffman and L. W. Hoffman (New York: Russell Sage, 1964). David Owens and Murray Straus, "The Social Struc-

ture of Violence in Childhood and Approval of Violence As An Adult," *Aggressive Behavior* 1 (1975): 193–211.

66. Robert Hamblin, David Buckholt, Donald Bushell, Desmond Ellis, and Daniel Ferritor, "Changing the Game from 'Get the Teacher' to 'Learn'," *Trans-Action*, January 1969, pp. 20–31.

67. Craig Haney, "A Psychologist Looks at the Criminal Justice System," in *Challenges and Alternatives to the American Criminal Justice System*, ed. A. Calvin (Ann Arbor: University International Press, 1979), pp. 77–85.

68. Charles Eichmann, *The Impact of the Gideon Decision on Crime and Sentencing in Florida*, (Tallahassee: Division of Corrections Publications, 1966).

69. Craig Haney, Curtis Banks, and Philip Zimbardo, "Interpersonal Dynamics in a Simulated Prison," *International Journal of Criminology and Penology*, 1 (1973): 69–97.

70. Elliot Aronson and J. Merrill Carlsmith, "The Effect of Severity of Threat of the Devaluation of Forbidden Behavior," *Journal of Abnormal and Social Psychology*, 66 (1963): 584–588. Jonathan Freedman, "Long-Term Behavioral Effects of Cognitive Dissonance," *Journal of Experimental and Social Psychology*, 1 (1965): 145–155.

71. U. S. President's Commission on Law Enforcement and Administration of Justice, *The Challenge of Crime in a Free Society: A Report*. (Washington, D.C.: U. S. Government Printing Office, 1967).

72. Albert Bandura, Dorothea Ross, and Sheila Ross, "Imitation of Film-Mediated Aggressive Models," *Journal of Abnormal and Social Psychology*, 66 (1963): 3–11. Albert Bandura, Dorothea Ross, and Sheila Ross, "Vicarious Reinforcement and Imitative Learning," *Journal of Abnormal and Social Psychology*, 67 (1963): 601–607.

73. Paul Brown and Rogers Elliot, "Control of Aggression in a Nursery School Class," *Journal of Experimental Child Psychology* 2 (1965): 103–107.

74. Joel Davitz, "The Effects of Previous Training on Postfrustration Behavior," *Journal of Abnormal and Social Psychology*, 47 (1952): 309–315.

75. Robert A. Baron and C. Richard Kepner, "Model's Behavior

and Attraction Toward the Model as Determinants of Adult Aggressive Behavior," *Journal of Personality and Social Psychology*, 14 (1970): 335–344.

76. Robert A. Baron, "The Reduction of Human Aggression: A Field Study of the Influence of Incompatible Reactions," *Journal of Applied Social Psychology*, 6 (1976): 260–274.

77. Seymour Feshbach, "Dynamics and Morality of Violence and Aggression: Some Psychological Considerations," *American Psychologist*, 26 (1971): 281–292.

78. James Michener, *Kent State, What Happened and Why* (New York: Random House, 1971).

79. Norma Feshbach and Seymour Feshbach, "The Relationship Between Empathy and Aggression in Two Age Groups," *Developmental Psychology*, 1 (1969): 102–107.

80. Norma Feshbach, *Empathy Training: A Field Study in Affective Education*. Paper presented at the American Educational Research Association, Toronto, Ontario, Canada, March 1978. Norma Feshbach and Seymour Feshbach, *Empathy Training and the Regulation of Aggression: Potentialities and Limitations*. Paper presented at the Western Psychological Association convention, 1981.

Chapter 6. Prejudice

1. Alvin Poussaint, "A Negro Psychiatrist Explains the Negro Psyche," in *Confrontation* (New York: Random House, 1971), pp. 183–184.

2. Kenneth Clark and Mamie Clark, "Racial Identification and Preference in Negro Children," in *Readings in Social Psychology*, ed. T. M. Newcomb and E. L. Hartley (New York: Holt, 1947), pp. 169–178.

3. Philip Goldberg, "Are Women Prejudiced Against Women?" *Trans-Action*, April 1968, pp. 28–30.

4. Curtis Banks, "White Preference in Blacks: A Paradigm in Search of a Phenomenon," *Psychological Bulletin*, 83 (1976): 1179–1186. Colleen Ward, "Differential Evaluation of Male and Female Expertise: Prejudice Against Women?" *British Journal of Social and Clinical Psychology*, 18 (1979): 65–69. Colleen Ward,

"Prejudice Against Women: Who, When, and Why?" *Sex Roles*, 7 (1981): 163–171.

5. Bernice Neugarten, "Social Class and Friendship Among School Children," *American Journal of Sociology*, 51 (1946): 305–313.
6. Edward E. Jones and Keith E. Davis, "From Acts to Dispositions: The Attribution Process in Person Perception," in *Advances in Experimental Social Psychology*, ed. L. Berkowitz, Vol. 2 (New York: Academic Press, 1965). Harold H. Kelley, "The Processes of Causal Attribution," *American Psychologist*, 28 (1973): 107–128. Lee Ross, "The Intuitive Psychologist and his Shortcomings: Distortions in the Attribution Process," in *Advances in Experimental Social Psychology*, ed. L. Berkowitz, Vol. 10 (New York: Academic Press, 1977), pp. 173–220. Edward E. Jones, "The Rocky Road from Acts to Dispositions," *American Psychologist*, 34 (1979): 107–117.
7. Cookie Stephan, James Kennedy, and Elliot Aronson, "The Effects of Friendship and Outcome on Task Attribution," *Sociometry*, 40 (1977): 107–111. Cookie Stephan, Nan Presser, James Kennedy, and Elliot Aronson, "Attributions to Success and Failure after Cooperative or Competitive Interaction," *European Journal of Social Psychology*, 8 (1978): 269–274.
8. Thomas F. Pettigrew, "The Ultimate Attribution Error: Extending Allport's Cognitive Analysis of Prejudice," *Personality and Social Psychology Bulletin*, 5 (1979): 461–476.
9. *Ibid.*
10. Shirley Feldman-Summers and Sara B. Kiesler, "Those Who Are Number Two Try Harder: The Effect of Sex on Attributions of Causality," *Journal of Personality and Social Psychology*, 30 (1974): 80–85.
11. Kay Deaux and Tim Emswiller, "Explanations of Successful Performance on Sex-Linked Tasks: What Is Skill for Male is Luck for the Female," *Journal of Personality and Social Psychology*, 29 (1974): 80–85.
12. John G. Nicholls, "Causal Attributions and Other Achievement-Related Cognitions: Effects of Task Outcome, Attainment Value, and Sex," *Journal of Personality and Social Psychology*, 31 (1975): 379–389.
13. R. S. Weinberg, P. A. Richardson, and A. Jackson, "Effect of Situation Criticality on Tennis Performance of Males and Fe-

males," *Newsletter of the Society for the Advancement of Social Psychology*, 9 (1983): 8–9.

14. Kay Deaux and Janet Taynor, "Evaluation of Male and Female Ability: Bias Works Two Ways," *Psychological Reports*, 32 (1973): 261–262.
15. *Newsweek*, November 25, 1974, p. 39.
16. Meg Greenfield, "A Dirty Little Secret," *Newsweek*, May 30, 1983, p. 104.
17. Melvin Lerner, "Evaluation of Performance as a Function of Performer's Reward and Attractiveness," *Journal of Personality and Social Psychology*, 1 (1965): 355–360. Melvin Lerner, *The Justice Motive*, (New York: Plenum, 1980).
18. In Stephen Gould, *Ever Since Darwin: Reflections on Natural History* (New York: W. W. Norton, 1977), p. 243.
19. Karl Pearson and M. Moul, "The Problem of Alien Immigration into Great Britain, Illustrated by an Example of Russian and Polish Jewish Children," *Annals of Eugenics*, 1 (1925): 5–127.
20. Carl Word, Mark Zanna, and Joel Cooper, "The nonverbal mediation of self-fulfilling prophecies in interracial interaction," *Journal of Experimental Social Psychology*, 10 (1974): 109–120.
21. Irving Janis and Peter Field, "Sex Difference and Personality Factors Related to Persuasibility," in *Personality and Persuasibility*, ed. C. I. Hovland and I. L. Janis (New Haven: Yale University Press, 1959), pp. 55–68.
22. Frank Sistrunk and John McDavid, "Sex Variable in Conforming Behavior," *Journal of Personality and Social Psychology*, 17 (1971): 200–207.
23. Daryl Bem and Sandra Bem, "We're All Non-Conscious Sexists," *Psychology Today*, November (1970): 22–26, 115–116.
24. Lenore Weitzman, Deborah Eifler, Elizabeth Hokada, and Catherine Ross, "Sex Role Socialization in Picture Books for Preschool Children," *American Journal of Sociology*, 77 (1972): 1125–1150.
25. Ruth Hartley, "Children's Concepts of Male and Female Roles," *Merrill-Palmer Quarterly*, 6 (1960): 83–91.

26. Jean Lipman-Blumen, "How Ideology Shapes Women's Lives," *Scientific American*, 226 (1) (1972): 34–42.

27. Susan W. Gray, "Masculinity-Femininity in Relation to Anxiety and Social Acceptance," *Child Development*, 28 (1957): 203–214.

28. Inge K. Broverman, S. Vogel, D. Broverman, F. Clarkson and P. Rosenkrantz, "Sex-Role Stereotypes: A Current Appraisal," *Journal of Social Issues*, 28 (1972): 59–78.

29. Natalie Porter and Florence Geis, "Women and Nonverbal Leadership Cues: When Seeing Is Not Believing," in *Gender and Nonverbal Behavior*, eds. C. Mayo and N. Henley (New York: Springer-Verlag, 1981).

30. Sandra L. Bem, "Sex Role Adaptability: One Consequence of Psychological Androgyny," *Journal of Personality and Social Psychology*, 31 (1975): 634–643. Phyllis Chesler, *Women and Madness* (New York: Avon Books, 1972).

31. Matina S. Horner, "Femininity and Successful Achievement: A Basic Inconsistency," in *Feminine Personality and Conflict* ed. J. M. Bardwick et al. (Monterey, Calif.: Brooks/Cole, 1970). Matina S. Horner, "Toward an Understanding of Achievement-Related Conflicts in Women," *Journal of Social Issues*, 28 (1972): 157–175.

32. Frances Cherry and Kay Deaux, "Fear of Success versus Fear of Gender-Inconsistent Behavior: A Sex Similarity," Paper presented at the Midwestern Psychological Association convention, 1975.

33. John Dollard, *Class and Caste in a Southern Town* (New Haven: Yale University Press, 1937).

34. Bruno Bettelheim and Morris Janowitz, *Social Change and Prejudice, Including Dynamics of Prejudice* (New York: Free Press, 1964).

35. Melvin Tumin, Paul Barton, and Bernie Burrus, "Education, Prejudice, and Discrimination: A Study in Readiness for Desegregation," *American Sociological Review*, 23 (1958): 41–49.

36. Mitchel Levitas, *America In Crisis* (New York: Holt, Rinehart and Winston, 1969).

37. John Dollard, "Hostility and Fear in Social Life," *Social Forces*, 17 (1938): 15–26.

38. Edmund Roberts, quoted by Paul Jacobs and Saul Landau, *To Serve the Devil* Volume 2 (New York: Vintage Books, 1971), p. 71.

39. Charles Crocker, quoted by Paul Jacobs and Saul Landau, *To Serve the Devil* Volume 2 (New York: Vintage Books, 1971), p. 81.

40. Andrew Greeley and Paul Sheatsley, "The Acceptance of Desegregation Continues to Advance," *Scientific American*, 225 (6) (1971): 13–19. See also R. D. Vanneman and Thomas Pettigrew, "Race and Relative Deprivation in the Urban United States," *Race* 13 (1972): 461–486.

41. Muzafer Sherif, O. J. Harvey, B. Jack White, William Hood, and Carolyn Sherif, *Intergroup Conflict and Cooperation: The Robbers Cave Experiment* (Norman: University of Oklahoma Institute of Intergroup Relations, 1961).

42. Carl Hovland and Robert Sears, "Minor Studies of Aggression: Correlation of Lynchings with Economic Indices," *Journal of Psychology*, 9 (1940): 301–310.

43. Otto Klineberg, "Black and White in International Perspective," *American Psychologist*, 26 (1971): 119–128.

44. Albert Speer, *Inside the Third Reich: Memoirs*, tr. Richard Winston and Clara Winston (New York: Macmillan, 1970).

45. Neal Miller and Richard Bugelski, "Minor Studies in Aggression: The Influence of Frustrations Imposed by the In-Group on Attitudes Expressed by the Out-Group," *Journal of Psychology*, 25 (1948): 437–442.

46. Ronald Rogers and Steven Prentice-Dunn, "Deindividuation and Anger-Mediated Interracial Aggression: Unmasking Regressive Racism," *Journal of Personality and Social Psychology*, 41 (1981): 63–73.

47. Donald Weatherly, "Anti-Semitism and the Expression of Fantasy Aggression," *Journal of Abnormal and Social Psychology*, 62 (1961): 454–457.

48. Theodor Adorno, Else Frenkel-Brunswick, Daniel Levinson, and R. Nevitt Sanford, *The Authoritarian Personality* (New York: Harper, 1950).

49. Greeley and Sheatsley, *op. cit.*

50. Thomas Pettigrew, "Regional Differences in Anti-Negro Prej-

udice," *Journal of Abnormal and Social Psychology*, 59 (1959): 28–36.

51. Thomas Pettigrew, "Personality and Sociocultural Factors and Intergroup Attitudes: A Cross-National Comparison," *Journal of Conflict Resolution*, 2 (1958): 29–42.

52. Jeanne Watson, "Some Social and Psychological Situations Related to Change in Attitude," *Human Relations*, 3 (1950): 15–56.

53. Ian MacCrone, *Race Attitudes in South Africa* (London: Oxford University Press, 1937).

54. M. Venkatesan and J. Losco, "Women in Magazine Ads: 1959–1971," *Journal of Advertising Research*, 15 (1975): 49–54.

55. Richard Kolbe and Joseph LaVoie, "Sex-Role Stereotyping in Preschool Children's Picture Books," *Social Psychology Quarterly*, 44 (1981): 369–374.

56. Paul Lazarsfeld, ed. *Radio and the Printed Page* (New York: Duell, Sloan & Pearce, 1940).

57. Morton Deutsch and Mary Ellen Collins, *Interracial Housing: A Psychological Evaluation of a Social Experiment* (Minneapolis: University of Minnesota Press, 1951). See also Daniel Wilner, Rosabelle Walkley, and Stuart Cook, *Human Relations in Interracial Housing* (Minneapolis: University of Minnesota Press, 1955).

58. Jack Brehm, "Increasing Cognitive Dissonance by a *Fait-Accompli*," *Journal of Abnormal and Social Psychology*, 58 (1959): 379–382.

59. John Darley and Ellen Berscheid, "Increased Liking as a Result of the Anticipation of Personal Contact," *Human Relations*, 20 (1967): 29–40.

60. National Opinion Research Center, *General Social Surveys, 1972–1980: Cumulative Codebook* (Storrs, Connecticut: Roper Public Opinion Research Center, University of Connecticut, 1980).

61. Thomas Pettigrew, "Social Psychology and Desegregation Research," *American Psychologist*, 16 (1961): 105–112.

62. Kenneth Clark, "Desegregation: An Appraisal of the Evidence," *Journal of Social Issues*, 9 (1953): No. 4.

63. Samuel Stouffer, Edward Suchman, Leland DeVinney, Shir-

ley Star, and Robin Williams, Jr., "The American Soldier: Adjustment During Army Life," in *Studies in Social Psychology in WW II*, Vol. 1 (Princeton: Princeton University Press, 1949).

64. Bernard Kramer, *Residential Contact as a Determinant of Attitudes Toward Negroes* (Unpublished doctoral dissertation, Harvard University, 1951). Alvin Winder, "White Attitudes Towards Negro-White Interaction in an Area of Changing Racial Composition," *American Psychologist*, 7 (1952): 330–331.

65. Steven Asher and Vernon Allen, "Racial Preference and Social Comparison Processes," *Journal of Social Issues*, 25 (1969): 157–166. Walter Stephan and James Kennedy, "An Experimental Study of Inter-Ethnic Competition in Segregated Schools," *Journal of School Psychology*, 13 (1975): 234–247. Harold Gerard and Norman Miller, *School Desegregation* (New York: Plenum, 1976).

66. Walter G. Stephan, "School Desegregation: An Evaluation of Predictions Made in *Brown v. The Board of Education*," *Psychological Bulletin*, 85 (1978): 217–238.

67. Julius Lester, "Beep! Beep! Bang! Umgawa! Black Power!" in *Confrontation: Issues of the 70's*, ed. R. Kytle (New York: Random House, 1971), pp. 162–181.

68. Deutsch and Collins, *op. cit.*

69. Muzafer Sherif and Carolyn Sherif, *An Outline of Social Psychology* (New York: Harper & Bros., 1956). Sherif, Harvey, White, Hood, and Sherif, *op. cit.*

70. Morton Deutsch, "A Theory of Cooperation and Competition," *Human Relations*, 2 (1949): 129–152. Morton Deutsch, "An Experimental Study of the Effects of Cooperation and Competition upon Group Process," *Human Relations*, 2 (1949): 199–232.

71. Elliot Aronson, Cookie Stephan, Jev Sikes, Nancy Blaney, and Matt Snapp, *The Jigsaw Classroom* (Beverly Hills, Calif.: Sage Publications, 1978). Elliot Aronson and Neal Osherow, "Cooperation, Prosocial Behavior, and Academic Performance: Experiments in the Desegregated Classroom," in *Applied Social Psychology Annual*, Vol. 1, ed. L. Bickman (Beverly Hills, California: Sage, 1980), p. 163–196.

72. Walter Stephan, "An Experimental Study of Inter-Ethnic

Competition in Segregated Schools," *Journal of School Psychology*, 13 (1975): 234–247.

73. Robert Geffner, "The Effects of Interdependent Learning on Self-Esteem, Inter-Ethnic Relations, and Intra-Ethnic Attitudes of Elementary School Children: A Field Experiment" (Unpublished doctoral dissertation, University of California, Santa Cruz, 1978). Alex Gonzalez, "Classroom Cooperation and Ethnic Balance" (Unpublished doctoral dissertation, University of California, Santa Cruz, 1979).
74. William Lucker, David Rosenfield, Jev Sikes, and Elliot Aronson, "Performance in the Interdependent Classroom: A Field Study," *American Educational Research Journal*, 13 (1977): 115–123.
75. Diane Bridgeman, "Enhanced Role Taking through Cooperative Interdependence: A Field Study," *Child Development*, 52 (1981): 1231–1238.
76. Cookie Stephan, James Kennedy, and Elliot Aronson, "Attribution of Luck or Skill as a Function of Cooperating or Competing with a Friend or Acquaintance," *Sociometry*, 40 (1977): 107–111. Nan Presser, Cookie Stephan, James Kennedy, and Elliot Aronson, "Attributions to Success and Failure in Cooperative, Competitive, and Interdependent Interaction," *European Journal of Social Psychology*, 8 (1978): 269–274. Cookie Stephan, Mary Burnham, and Elliot Aronson, "Attributions for Success and Failure after Cooperation, Competition, or Team Competition," *European Journal of Social Psychology*, 9 (1979): 109–114.
77. Alex Gonzalez, "Classroom Cooperation and Ethnic Balance" (Unpublished doctoral dissertation, University of California, Santa Cruz, 1979).
78. Thomas Pettigrew, "Social Psychology and Desegregation Research," *American Psychologist*, 15 (1961): 61–71.

Chapter 7. Attraction: Why People Like Each Other

1. Charles Darwin, *The Expression of Emotions in Man and Animals* (New York: Appleton, 1910).
2. Dale Carnegie, *How to Win Friends and Influence People* (New York: Simon & Schuster, 1937).

3. H. H. Remmers and D. H. Radler, "Teenage Attitudes," *Scientific American*, 198 (6) (1958): 25–29.

4. Thomas Lemann and Richard Solomon, "Group Characteristics as Revealed in Sociometric Patterns and Personality Ratings," *Sociometry*, 15 (1952): 7–90.

5. George Homans, *Social Behavior: Its Elementary Forms* (New York: Harcourt, Brace and World, 1961).

6. Elaine Walster (Hatfield), Vera Aronson, Darcy Abrahams, and Leon Rottman, "Importance of Physical Attractiveness in Dating Behavior," *Journal of Personality and Social Psychology*, 5 (1966): 508–516.

7. Donn Byrne, "Attitudes and Attraction," in *Advances in Experimental Social Psychology*, Vol. 4, ed. L. Berkowitz (New York: Academic Press, 1969).

8. Muzafer Sherif, "Experiments in Group Conflict," *Scientific American*, 195 (1956): 53–58.

9. Elliot Aronson, Cookie Stephan, Jev Sikes, Nancy Blaney, and Matthew Snapp, *The Jigsaw Classroom* (Beverly Hills: Sage Publications, 1978). Elliot Aronson and Neal Osherow, "Cooperation, Prosocial Behavior, and Academic Performance: Experiments in the Desegregated Classroom," in *Applied Social Psychology Annual*, Volume 1, ed. L. Bickman (Beverly Hills, California: Sage, 1980), p. 163–196.

10. Elliot Aronson and Judson Mills, "The Effect of Severity of Initiation on Liking for a Group," *Journal of Abnormal and Social Psychology*, 59 (1959): 177–181.

11. Elliot Aronson and Darwyn Linder, "Gain and Loss of Esteem as Determinants of Interpersonal Attractiveness," *Journal of Experimental Social Psychology*, 1 (1965): 156–171. Elliot Aronson and Phillip Worchel, "Similarity versus Liking as Determinants of Interpersonal Attractiveness," *Psychonomic Science*, 5 (1966): 157–158. Harold Sigall and Elliot Aronson, "Liking for an Evaluator as a Function of Her Physical Attractiveness and Nature of the Evaluations," *Journal of Experimental Social Psychology*, 5 (1969): 93–100.

12. Theresa Amabile, "Brilliant but Cruel: Perceptions of Negative Evaluators," *Journal of Experimental Social Psychology*, 19 (1983): 146–156.

13. Morton Deutsch and Leonard Solomon, "Reactions to Evalu-

ations by Others as Influenced by Self-Evaluations," *Sociometry*, 22 (1959): 93–112.

14. Edward E. Jones, *Ingratiation* (New York: Appleton-Century-Crofts, 1964).

15. Helen Hall Jennings, *Leadership and Isolation* (2nd ed.; New York: Longman, Green, 1959).

16. Bernice Lott and Albert Lott, "The Formation of Positive Attitudes Toward Group Members," *Journal of Abnormal and Social Psychology*, 61 (1960): 297–300.

17. Jack Brehm and Ann Cole, "Effect of a Favor Which Reduces Freedom," *Journal of Personality and Social Psychology*, 3 (1966): 420–426.

18. Leo Tolstoy, *War and Peace* (New York: Simon and Schuster, 1942).

19. J. Bigelow, ed., *The Autobiography of Benjamin Franklin* (New York: G. P. Putnam's Sons, 1916), pp. 216–217.

20. Jon Jecker and David Landy, "Liking a Person as a Function of Doing Him a Favor," *Human Relations*, 22 (1969): 371–378.

21. Melvin Lerner and Carolyn Simmons, "Observer's Reaction to the 'Innocent Victim': Compassion or Rejection?" *Journal of Personality and Social Psychology*, 4 (1966): 203–210.

22. Albert J. Lott, Bernice E. Lott, Thomas Reed, and Terry Crow, "Personality-Trait Descriptions of Differentially Liked Persons," *Journal of Personality and Social Psychology*, 16 (1960): 284–290.

23. Robert Bales, "Task Roles and Social Roles in Problem Solving Groups," in *Readings in Social Psychology*, ed. E. E. Maccoby, T. M. Newcomb, and E. L. Hartley (3rd ed.; New York: Holt, 1958), pp. 437–447. Robert Bales and Philip Slater, "Role Differentiation in Small Decision-Making Groups," in *The Family, Socialization, and Interaction Process*, ed. T. Parsons and R. F. Bales (Glencoe, Ill.: Free Press, 1955).

24. Elliot Aronson, Ben Willerman, Joanne Floyd, "The Effect of a Pratfall on Increasing Interpersonal Attractiveness," *Psychonomic Science*, 4 (1966): 227–228.

25. Kay Deaux, "To Err is Humanizing: But Sex Makes a Difference," *Representative Research in Social Psychology*, 3 (1972): 20–28.

26. Elliot Aronson, Robert Helmreich, and James LeFan, "To Err Is Humanizing—Sometimes: Effects of Self-Esteem, Competence, and a Pratfall on Interpersonal Attraction," *Journal of Personality and Social Psychology*, 16 (1970): 259–264.

27. Abraham Tesser and Michael Brodie, "A Note on the Evaluation of a 'Computer Date,' " *Psychonomic Science*, 23 (1971): 300.

28. Walster, Aronson, Abrahams, and Rottman, *op. cit.*

29. Gregory White, "Physical Attractiveness and Courtship Progress," *Journal of Personality and Social Psychology*, 39 (1980): 660–668.

30. Karen Dion, Ellen Berscheid, and Elaine Walster (Hatfield), "What Is Beautiful Is Good," *Journal of Personality and Social Psychology*, 24 (1972): 285–290.

31. A. S. Tan, "TV Beauty Ads and Role Expectations of Adolescent Female Viewers," *Journalism Quarterly*, 56 (1979): 283–288.

32. Karen Dion and Ellen Berscheid, "Physical Attractiveness and Sociometric Choice in Nursery School Children" (mimeographed research report, 1971).

33. Karen Dion, "Physical Attractiveness and Evaluations of Children's Transgressions," *Journal of Personality and Social Psychology*, 24 (1972): 207–213. Similar findings were reported recently by Berkowitz and Frodi. Leonard Berkowitz and Ann Frodi, "Reactions to a Child's Mistakes as Affected by Her/His Looks and Speech," *Social Psychology Quarterly*, (1982), in press.

34. Thomas Baglan, "Effects of Interpersonal Attraction and Type of Behavior on Attributions," *Psychological Reports*, 48 (1981): 299–304.

35. Harold Sigall and Elliot Aronson, "Liking for an Evaluator as a Function of Her Physical Attractiveness and Nature of the Evaluations," *Journal of Experimental and Social Psychology*, 5 (1969): 93–100.

36. Harold Sigall and Nancy Ostrove, "Beautiful But Dangerous: Effects of Offender Attractiveness and Nature of the Crime on Juridic Judgment," *Journal of Personality and Social Psychology*, 31 (1975): 410–414.

37. Harold Sigall and David Landy, "Radiating Beauty: Effects of Having a Physically Attractive Partner on Person Perception," *Journal of Personality and Social Psychology*, 28 (1973): 218–224.

38. Mark Snyder, Elizabeth Decker Tanke, and Ellen Berscheid, "Social Perception and Interpersonal Behavior: On the Self-Fulfilling Nature of Social Stereotypes," *Journal of Personality and Social Psychology*, 35 (1977): 656–666.

39. Byrne, *op. cit.*

40. Harold Sigall, "The Effects of Competence and Consensual Validation on a Communicator's Liking for the Audience," *Journal of Personality and Social Psychology*, 16 (1970): 251–258.

41. Gary Marks, Norman Miller, and Geoffrey Maruyama, "Effect of Targets' Physical Attractiveness on Assumptions of Similarity," *Journal of Personality and Social Psychology*, 41 (1981): 198–206. Donald Granberg and Michael King, "Cross-Lagged Panel Analysis of the Relation between Attraction and Perceived Similarity," *Journal of Experimental Social Psychology*, 16 (1980): 573–581.

42. Paul Secord and Carl Beckman, "Interpersonal Congruency, Perceived Similarity, and Friendship," *Sociometry*, 27 (1964): 115–127.

43. Elaine Walster (Hatfield), "The Effect of Self-Esteem of Romantic Liking," *Journal of Experimental and Social Psychology*, 1 (1965): 184–197.

44. Sara B. Kiesler and Roberta L. Baral, "The Search for a Romantic Partner: The Effects of Self-Esteem and Physical Attractiveness on Romantic Behavior," in *Personality and Social Behavior*, ed. Kenneth J. Gergen and David Marlowe (Reading, Mass.: Addison-Wesley, 1970).

45. Joel Grube, Randall Kleinhesselink, and Kathleen Kearney, "Male Self-Acceptance and Attraction Toward Women," *Personality and Social Psychology Bulletin*, 8 (1982): 107–112.

46. Gary Van Gorp, John Stempfle, and David Olson, "Dating Attitudes, Expectations, and Physical Attractiveness" (unpublished paper), reported in Zick Rubin, *Liking and Loving: An Invitation to Social Psychology* (New York: Holt, Rinehart and Winston, 1973), p. 68.

47. Edward E. Jones, Linda Bell, and Elliot Aronson, "The Reciprocation of Attraction from Similar and Dissimilar Others: A Study in Person Perception and Evaluation," in *Experimental Social Psychology* (New York: Holt, Rinehart and Winston, 1971), pp. 142–183.

48. Robert Winch, *Mate Selection: A Study of Complementary Needs* (New York: Harper & Row, 1958).

49. Ellen Berscheid, "Interpersonal Attraction," in *Handbook of Social Psychology*, eds. G. Lindzey and E. Aronson (3rd ed.; Reading, Massachusetts: Addison-Wesley, 1984), in press. Ellen Berscheid and Elaine Walster (Hatfield), *Interpersonal Attraction* (Reading, Massachusetts: Addison-Wesley, 1973). Denise Kandel, "Similarity in Real-Life Adolescent Friendship Pairs," *Journal of Personality and Social Psychology*, 36 (1978): 306–312. D. K. B. Nias, "Marital Choice: Matching or Complementation?" in *Love and Attraction*, eds. M. Cook and G. Wilson (Oxford: Pergamon, 1979). D. Fishbein and M. H. Thelen, *Husband-Wife Similarity and Marital Satisfaction: A Different Approach.* Paper presented at the Midwestern Psychological Association convention, 1981.

50. Elliot Aronson and Darwyn Linder, "Gain and Loss of Esteem as Determinants of Interpersonal Attractiveness," *Journal of Experimental and Social Psychology*, 1 (1965): 156–171. See also: Harold Gerard and Charles W. Greenbaum, "Attitudes Toward an Agent of Uncertainty Reduction," *Journal of Personality*, 30 (1962): 485–495; David Mettee, Shelley E. Taylor, and H. Friedman, "Affect Conversion and the Gain-Loss Like Effect," *Sociometry*, 36 (1973): 505–519; Elliot Aronson and David R. Mettee, "Affective Reactions to Appraisal from Others," in *Foundations of Interpersonal Attraction* (New York: Academic Press, 1974); Gerald L. Clore, Nancy H. Wiggins, and Stuart Itkin, "Gain and Loss in Attraction: Attributions from Nonverbal Behavior," *Journal of Personality and Social Psychology*, 31 (1975): 706–712.

51. *Ibid.*

52. Benedictus de Spinoza, "The Ethics," in *Spinoza's Ethics and 'De Intellectus Emendatione,'* tr. Andrew Boyle (New York: Dutton, 1910).

53. David R. Mettee, Shelley E. Taylor, and H. Friedman, "Affect Conversion and the Gain-Loss Like Effect," *Sociometry*, 36 (1973): 505–519.

54. David R. Mettee and Elliot Aronson, "Affective Reactions to Appraisal from Others," *Foundations of Interpersonal Attraction* (New York: Academic Press, 1974).

55. O. J. Harvey, "Personality Factors in Resolution of Conceptual Incongruities," *Sociometry*, 25 (1962): 336–352.
56. Harold Stevenson, Rachael Keen, and Robert Knights, "Parents and Strangers as Reinforcing Agents for Children's Performance," *Journal of Abnormal and Social Psychology*, 67 (1963): 183–185.
57. Joanne Floyd, Effects of Amount of Reward and Friendship Status of the Other on the Frequency of Sharing in Children (Unpublished doctoral dissertation, University of Minnesota, 1964).
58. Marylyn Rands, George Levinger, and Glenn Mellinger, "Patterns of Conflict Resolution and Marital Satisfaction," *Journal of Family Issues*, 2 (1981): 297–321.
59. Vincent P. Skotko, "The Relation between Interpersonal Attraction and Measures of Self-Disclosure," *Journal of Social Psychology*, 112 (1980): 311–312. Richard Archer and Joseph Burleson, "The Effects of Timing of Self-Disclosure on Attraction and Reciprocity," *Journal of Personality and Social Psychology*, 38 (1980): 120–130. Dalmas Taylor, Robert Gould, and Paul Brounstein, "Effects of Personalistic Self-Disclosure," *Personality and Social Psychology Bulletin*, 7 (1981): 487–492.

Chapter 8. Interpersonal Communication and Sensitivity

1. Carl Rogers, "Interpersonal Relationships: Year 2000," *Journal of Applied Behavioral Science*, 4 (1968): 265–280.
2. Quoted in E. Hoover, "The Great Group Binge," *West Magazine, Los Angeles Times*, January 8, 1967, pp. 8–13.
3. Sigmund Koch, "Psychology Cannot Be a Coherent Science," *Psychology Today*, September 1969, p. 68.
4. Michael Kahn, *Sensitivity Training at Kresge College* (unpublished, 1971).
5. Carl Rogers, "The Group Comes of Age," *Psychology Today*, December 1969, p. 58.
6. Nancy E. Adler and Daniel Goleman, "Goal Setting, T-Group Participation, and Self-Rated Change: An Experimental Study," *Journal of Applied Behavioral Science*, 11 (1975): 197–209.

7. Matthew Miles, "Changes During and Following Laboratory Training: A Clinical Experimental Study," *Journal of Applied Behavior Science*, 1 (1965): 215–242. Douglas Bunker, "Individual Applications of Laboratory Training," *Journal of Applied Behavior Science*, 1 (1965): 131–148. I. M. Valiquet, *Contribution to the Evaluation of a Management Development Program* (unpublished master's thesis, Massachusetts Institute of Technology, 1964).

8. Marvin Dunnette and John Campbell, "Effectiveness of T-Group Experiences in Managerial Training and Development," *Psychological Bulletin*, 70 (1968): 73–104.

9. Jerry Shapiro and Robert Ross, "Sensitivity Training for Staff in an Institution for Adolescent Offenders: A Preliminary Investigation," *American Journal of Corrections*, (1970): 14–19.

10. Jerry Shapiro and Robert Ross, "Sensitivity Training in an Institution for Adolescents," *Journal of Applied Behavior Science*, 7 (1971): 710–723.

11. Irwin Rubin, "The Reduction of Prejudice Through Laboratory Training," *Journal of Applied Behavior Science*, 3 (1967): 29–50.

12. Michael Jay Diamond and Jerry Shapiro, "Changes in Locus of Control as a Function of Encounter Group Experiences: A Study and Replication," *Journal of Abnormal Psychology*, 82 (1973): 514–518.

13. Charles Tart, "Increases in Hypnotizability Resulting from a Prolonged Program for Enhancing Personal Growth," *Journal of Abnormal Psychology*, 75 (1970): 260–266. Jerrold Shapiro and Michael Diamond, "Increases in Hypnotizability as a Function of Encounter Group Training: Some Confirming Evidence," *Journal of Abnormal Psychology*, 79 (1972): 112–115.

14. Marvin D. Dunnette, "People Feeling: Joy, More Joy, and the 'Slough of Despond'," *Journal of Applied Behavior Science*, 5 (1969): 25–44.

15. *Ibid.*

16. Ralph Cranshaw, "How Sensitive is Sensitivity Training?" *American Journal of Psychiatry*, 126 (1969): 868–873.

17. James Cadden, Frederic Flach, Sara Blakeslee, and Randolph Charton, "Growth in Medical Students Through Group Process," *American Journal of Psychiatry*, 126 (1969): 862–868.

18. Charles Seashore, "What is Sensitivity Training?" *NTL Institute News and Reports*, April 1968.

19. Dianna Hartley, Howard Roback, and Stephen Abramowitz, "Deterioration Effects in Encounter Groups," *American Psychologist*, 31 (1976): 247–255. Cary Cooper, "How Psychologically Dangerous are T-groups and Encounter Groups?" *Human Relations*, 28 (1975): 249–260. Cary Cooper, "Adverse and Growthful Effects of Experiential Learning Groups. The Role of the Trainer, Participant, and Group Characteristics," *Human Relations*, 30 (1977): 1103–1129.

20. C. Cooper, *op cit*.

21. Kahn, *op. cit*.

22. Morton Lieberman, Irvin Yalom, and Matthew B. Miles, *Encounter Groups: First Facts* (New York: Basic Books, 1973). See also Will Schutz, "Not Encounter and Certainly Not Facts," *Journal of Humanistic Psychology*, 15 (1975): 7–18.

23. Michael Jay Diamond and W. Charles Lobitz, "When Familiarity Breeds Respect: The Effects of an Experimental Depolarization Program on Police and Student Attitudes Toward Each Other," *Journal of Social Issues*, 29 (1973): 95–109.

Chapter 9. Social Psychology as a Science

1. Elliot Aronson and Judson Mills, "The Effect of Severity of Initiation on Liking for a Group," *Journal of Abnormal and Social Psychology*, 59 (1959): 177–181.

2. Robert Liebert and Robert Baron, "Some Immediate Effects of Televised Violence on Children's Behavior," *Developmental Psychology*, 6 (1972): 469–475.

3. Elliot Aronson and J. Merrill Carlsmith, "Experimentation in Social Psychology," in *Handbook of Social Psychology*, Vol. 2, ed. G. Lindzey and E. Aronson (2nd ed.; Reading, Mass.: Addison-Wesley, 1969), pp. 1–79.

4. Stanley Milgram, "Behavioral Study of Obedience," *Journal of Abnormal and Social Psychology*, 67 (1963): 371–378.

5. Elliot Aronson, Harold Sigall, and Thomas Van Hoose, "The Cooperative Subject: Myth or Reality?" *Journal of Experimental and Social Psychology*, 6 (1970): 1–10.

6. Solomon Asch, "Effects of Group Pressure Upon the Modification and Distortion of Judgment," in *Groups, Leadership, and Men*, ed. M. H. Kuetzkow (Pittsburgh: Carnegie, 1951), pp. 117–190. Solomon Asch, "Studies of Independence and Conformity: A Minority of One Against a Unanimous Majority," *Psychological Monographs*, 70 (1956): No. 9, Whole No. 416.
7. Leonard Bickman and M. Zarantonello, "The Effects of Deception and Level of Obedience on Subjects' Ratings of the Milgram Study," *Personality and Social Psychology Bulletin*, 4 (1978): 81–85.
8. Elliot Aronson, "Avoidance of Inter-Subject Communication," *Psychological Reports*, 19 (1966): 238.

Name Index

Subject Index